MW01089836

Turn-of-the-Century Decorative Millwork

Doors, Windows, Stained Glass, etc.

Wholesale Sash, Door and
Blind Manufacturers' Association

DOVER PUBLICATIONS, INC.
Mineola, New York

Copyright

Copyright © 1996 by Dover Publications, Inc.
All rights reserved under Pan American and International Copyright Conventions.

Published in Canada by General Publishing Company, Ltd., 30 Lesmill Road, Don Mills, Toronto, Ontario.
Published in the United Kingdom by Constable and Company, Ltd., 3 The Lanchesters, 162–164 Fulham Palace Road, London W6 9ER.

Bibliographical Note

This Dover edition, first published in 1996, is an unabridged, slightly corrected republication of the *Universal Design Book,* published in Chicago by Shattock & McKay, 1902. The illustrations originally in color on pages 33, 34, 35, 36, 76, 77, 78, 79, 229, 230, 231 and 232 are reproduced in black and white in the present edition.

Library of Congress Cataloging-in-Publication Data

Turn-of-the-century decorative millwork : doors, windows, stained glass, etc. / Wholesale Sash, Door and Blind Manufacturers' Association.
    p.   cm.
    Originally published: Universal design book. Chicago : Shattock & McKay, 1902.
    Includes index.
    ISBN 0-486-29280-0 (pbk.)
    1. Finish carpentry—Charts, diagrams, etc. 2. Architecture, Victorian—United States. I. Wholesale Sash, Door and Blind Manufacturers' Association of the Northwest. II. Universal design book.
TH5605.T87   1996
747'.3—dc20
                           96-27382
                                CIP

Manufactured in the United States of America
Dover Publications, Inc., 31 East 2nd Street, Mineola, N.Y. 11501

UNIVERSAL
DESIGN BOOK

CONTAINING

OFFICIAL PRICE LISTS.

ILLUSTRATING

MOULDINGS,
BALUSTERS, STAIR WORK,
CORNER BLOCKS,
BRACKETS,
HEAD BLOCKS, SPINDLES,
BASE BLOCKS,
COLUMNS, FRAMES,
MANTELS,
INTERIOR FINISH,

SASH, DOORS, BLINDS,

MILL WORK
OF EVERY DESCRIPTION,
LEADED
ART GLASS,
WHEEL CUT GLASS,
WINDOW GLASS,
VENETIAN BLINDS,
SLIDING BLINDS,
GRILLES.

Adopted by the Wholesale Sash, Door and Blind Manufacturers' Association of the Northwest, January 20th, 1902.

CHICAGO :
SHATTOCK & McKAY, PUBLISHERS,
180-182 MONROE STREET.

[ORIGINAL TITLE PAGE]

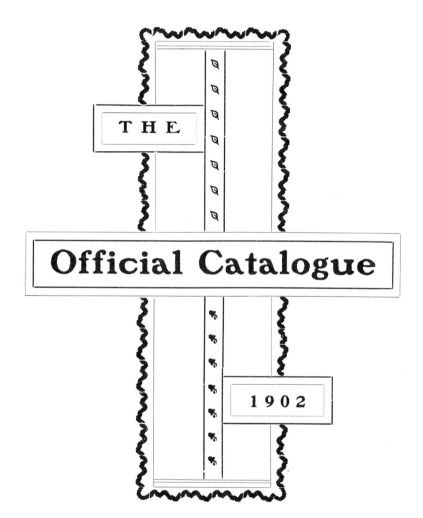

THE

Official Catalogue

1902

INDEX

▼ ▼ ▼ ▼ ▼

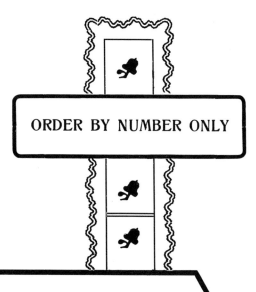

ORDER BY NUMBER ONLY

On all orders sent us where patterns or designs are specified by number, we will understand that the number is taken from this book, if it appears therein, unless the order specifies that the number is taken from some other book. When ordering from other book than ours, do not fail to specify from whose catalogue the numbers are taken and also the date of issue of the book.

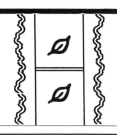

DO NOT CUT THIS BOOK

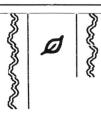

TO THE TRADE

AFTER examining this, our new catalogue, we are confident you will agree with us that it is the most complete book of its kind ever issued. No effort has been spared by us to make it attractive, comprehensive and best adapted to the convenience and requirements of the trade.

We wish to call particular attention to the many new designs and ideas contained therein, and at the same time to emphasize the fact that our facilities for furnishing all kinds of mill work are unsurpassed.

We solicit your orders and will endeavor to handle them in a manner that will be satisfactory to you.

Write us for any desired information and we will be pleased to be of service to you.

DIRECTIONS FOR ORDERING.

Valuable time will be saved us in serving our patrons by their close observance of the following directions:

Unless otherwise specified, or covered by standing instructions to the contrary, we will understand all orders as calling for **REGULAR WESTERN STYLES OF GOODS,** as described in this Catalogue.

The universal rule in ordering mill work is to give the width first and then the height.

WINDOWS AND SASH.

A—The term Sash indicates a single piece.

B—The term Window means two pieces, an upper and a lower Sash, made with either plain or check rail.

C—In ordering regular sizes of Sash or Windows, give size of glass and number of lights and thickness; if a Window, whether check or plain rail; state whether open or glazed, and if glazed, whether with single or double strength glass.

D—In ordering odd sizes, give the size of opening to be filled and describe as above.

E—When measurements are given in inches, it usually indicates the glass size, and we will so understand it; when given in feet and inches the outside measure or opening is understood.

F—In ordering Segment or Circle-head Sash and Windows, give the number of style desired (see page 10) and the radius of Circle or Segment. If no number or proper description is given in ordering, we will substitute for Circle Head Style No. 2, and for Segment Head Style No. 4, using our regular radius, which is the width of the Sash for Segment Heads and one-half the width of Sash for Circle Heads.

DOORS.

G—In ordering always give width, height, thickness, number of panels and quality. If full instructions are not given, to save time in shipment, we assume that our Standard Door, 1⅜ inch, Four Panel O. G. No. 1 quality is desired, and will fill order accordingly.

H—If other than Four Panel O. G. Doors are required, for panel Doors give number and arrangement of

panels and style of Sticking; for Sash Doors give number of style desired; indicate whether open or glazed, and if glazed, style of glazing.

I—When Moulded Doors are required state whether flush or raised mould is desired, and if to be moulded on one or two sides.

BLINDS.

In Ordering, Specify Whether Outside (O. S.) or Inside (I. S.) Blinds are Wanted.

J—OUTSIDE BLINDS. In ordering Outside Blinds, if regular, give size of glass and number of lights in window for which they are intended, and size of opening to be filled, if odd; give thickness and state if rolling slats (R. S.), stationary slats (S. S.), or half rolling and half stationary slats (½ R. S., ½ S. S.) are required. If other than these styles are required, order must so state.

K—The regular opening for Outside Blinds is one (1) inch longer than Check Rail Windows of corresponding glass size. Where Blinds of extra length for brick buildings are desired, order must so state, and Blinds will then be made two (2) inches longer than sash opening.

L—Our Standard Blinds are 1⅛ inch thick, full rolling slats made for regular openings, as above described. When not otherwise specified we assume this to be the style desired, and fill orders accordingly.

M—INSIDE BLINDS. In ordering it is best to give exact outside measure of opening to be filled. Give thickness, number of folds and state if all panels, all slats or half panel and half slats, giving sketch of any unusual arrangement of panels.

N—If Blinds are to be cut, state how many times and give distance from top of window to center of meeting rail.

O—If Blinds are to fold into pockets, give size of pockets.

P—State quality, whether No. 1, for paint or oil finish.

Q—When description of window only is given, as in ordering O. S. Blinds, we furnish our standard measurement of Inside Blinds, which is the same as the check rail window opening, 1⅛ inch thick, four fold where practicable, made to cut once at check rail.

MOULDINGS.

R—In ordering, give numbers as shown in this catalogue and name kind of wood. If other styles than are shown herein are required, furnish detail or sketch with correct measurements.

S—Unless otherwise instructed, we will fill orders with our Standard White Pine Mouldings, No. 1 Paint Quality, in miscellaneous long lengths, 10, 12, 14 and 16 feet long.

FRAMES.

T—In ordering, state whether for Outside or Inside Frames.

U—For Window Frames give size, thickness and full description of window, stating whether for frame, brick or veneer buildings. If for frame or brick veneer building, give width of studding. If for brick building give thickness of wall. State if frames are desired with or without pulleys.

V—For Outside Door Frames give size and thickness of Door, and state whether frames are required with stops or with rabbeted jambs, and if sill is to be Pine or Oak. If for frame building give width of studding; if for brick building, give thickness of wall.

W—For Inside Door Frames give size and thickness of Door and width and thickness of jambs; state whether stops or rabbeted jambs are required, and advise if thresholds are desired.

Official Grades of Sash, Doors and Blinds.

*Adopted by the Wholesale Sash, Door and Blind Manufacturers'
Association of the Northwest.*

DOORS.

AAA. Oil Finish Doors.—Material for
AAA. Oil Finish Doors must be Clear, no
white sap admitted. Workmanship must be
good.

AA. Oil Finish Doors.—Material for AA.
Oil Finish Doors must be Clear, with the exception that white sap will be admitted, not
to exceed twenty-five (25) per cent of the
face of any one piece. Workmanship must
be good.

A. Doors.—Material in A. Doors must
be Clear, with the exception that water stains
and small pin knots not exceeding one-fourth
(¼) inch in diameter may be admitted. No
piece to contain more than two (2) such defects and no door more than five (5) such
defects on each side; white sap not consid-
ered a defect. Workmanship must be good.

B. Doors.—Material in B. Doors may contain knots not to exceed one (1) inch in diameter, and blue sap showing on both sides not
to exceed fifty (50) per cent in any one piece
of the door and gum spots showing on one
(1) side of a piece only and other slight
defects, shall not exceed ten (10) in number
on each side and each white pine stile, bottom
and lock rail must contain at least one (1)
and not to exceed three (3) such defects;
plugs admitted and not regarded as a defect.
Slight defects in workmanship admitted.

C. Doors.—Material in C. Doors may
contain all stained sap and small worm holes
and fine shake; also knots not exceeding one
and three-fourths (1¾) inches in diameter.
Twenty (20) defects may be allowed on each
side, also slight defects in workmanship.

Each piece of white Pine in a No. C Door
must contain a defect. Not more than six
(6) defects allowed in any one piece.

D. Doors.—D Doors are regarded as a cull
door and must contain large coarse knots and
may contain rot, worm holes, shake and other
serious defects.

A Standard Door may be through tennon,
blind tennon or dowelled.

WINDOWS.

Check Rail Windows may contain two (2)
knots three-eighths (⅜) inch in diameter or
one red knot five-eighths (⅝) inch in diameter in each piece of a window. White sap
and not over thirty-three and one-third
(33 1-3) per cent blue sap may be admitted
in any one window. Workmanship must be
good.

Plain Rail Windows and Sash may contain
blue sap and small knots.

BLINDS.

No. 1. Outside Blinds must be made of
Clear lumber, except that small, sound pin
knots, water stain and white sap may be admitted. Workmanship must be good.

WOODS ADMISSIBLE.

Woods other than Michigan, Wisconsin and
Minnesota White Pine admitted in Doors,
Blinds and Windows, except in Oil Finish
Goods.

CIRCLE and SEGMENT TOP WINDOWS.

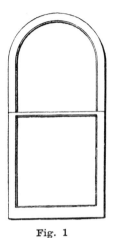

Fig. 1

Circle inside and outside.

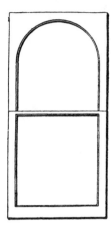

Fig. 2

Circle outside, Square
inside.

In ordering Segment or Circle-head Sash and Windows, give the number of style desired and the radius of Circle or Segment. If no number or proper description is given in ordering, we will substitute for Circle Head Style No. 2, and for Segment Head Style No. 4, using our regular radius, which is the width of the Sash for Segment Heads and one-half the width of Sash for Circle Heads.

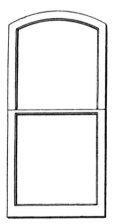

Fig. 3

Segment inside and
outside.

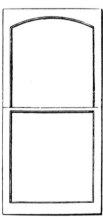

Fig. 4

Segment outside, Square
inside.

Windows made in the above styles can be filled with any number of lights desired.

PLAIN RAIL WINDOWS.

Twelve Lights, 1⅛-in. Thick.

Size of Glass.			Price, Open.	Price, Glazed.	Size of Opening.				Weight, Open.	Weight, Glazed.
7	x	9	$0.75	$2.15	2	1 x 3	5 ½		5	13
8	x	10	.80	2.40	2	4 x 3	9¼		6	14
		12	.88	2.70		4	6		8	18
		14	.97	3.25		5	2		8	19
		16	1.07	3.75		5	10		9	20
9	x	12	.96	2.95	2	7 x 4	6		9	20
		13	1.00	3.30		4	10		9	21
		14	1.05	3.50		5	2		9	22
		15	1.10	3.75		5	6		9	24
		16	1.16	3.95		5	10		9	26
		18	1.26	4.70		6	6		10	28
10	x	12	1.02	3.25	2	10 x 4	6		9	21
		14	1.11	3.70		5	2		9	23
		15	1.16	4.15		5	6		10	24
		16	1.20	4.20		5	10		10	26
		18	1.30	4.90		6	6		10	29
		20	1.42	5.65		7	2		11	31
12	x	14	1.23	4.80	3	4 x 5	2		10	25
		16	1.33	5.35		5	10		10	28
		18	1.42	5.80		6	6		10	31

PLAIN RAIL WINDOWS.

Eight Lights, 1⅛-in. Thick.

Size of Glass.			Price, Open.	Price, Glazed.	Size of Opening.				Weight, Open.	Weight, Glazed.
8	x	10	$0.69	$1.85	1	8½ x 3	9¼		5	10
		12	.76	2.20		4	6		5	12
		14	.85	2.50		5	2		7	14
		16	.95	2.75		5	10		8	19
9	x	12	.78	2.20	1	10½ x 4	6		6	14
		14	.87	2.50		5	2		7	17
		16	.97	3.05		5	10		9	20
10	x	12	.82	2.40	2	0½ x 4	6		8	15
		14	.90	2.70		5	2		8	18
		16	1.00	2.95		5	10		9	20
		18	1.10	3.70		6	6		10	23
12	x	14	.95	3.10	2	4½ x 5	2		9	19
		16	1.06	3.45		5	10		11	22
		18	1.15	4.05		6	6		12	25

1⅜-inch Plain Rail Windows, same price as 1⅜-inch Check Rail Windows. Sizes not listed, extra price.

For sash extras see pages 42 and 43.

CHECK RAIL WINDOWS.

Twelve Lights.   1⅜ in. thick.

Size of Glass.			Price Open.	Price Glazed.	Size of Opening.				Weight Open.	Weight Glazed.
8	x	10	$ .93	$2.55	2	4½ x 3	10		8	19
		12	1.03	3.00			4	6	8	20
		14	1.13	3.55			5	2	9	22
9	x	12	1.12	3.15	2	7½ x 4	6		10	22
		13	1.17	3.50			4	10	10	24
		14	1.22	3.55			5	2	11	24
		15	1.28	3.95			5	6	11	25
		16	1.34	4.35			5	10	11	27
10	x	12	1.19	3.45	2	10½ x 4	6		11	23
		14	1.29	3.90			5	2	12	26
		15	1.35	4.40			5	6	12	27
		16	1.40	4.45			5	10	13	29
		18	1.51	5.15			6	6	13	32
		20	1.65	5.95			7	2	14	34
12	x	14	1.44	4.85	3	4½ x 5	2		14	28
		16	1.55	5.35			5	10	14	30
		18	1.66	5.85			6	6	14	32
		20	1.80	6.75			7	2	14	36

CHECK RAIL WINDOWS.

Eight Lights.   1⅜ in. thick.

Size of Glass.			Price Open.	Price Glazed.	Size of Opening.				Weight Open.	Weigh. Glazed.
9	x	12	$ .91	$2.50	1	11 x 4	6		8	17
		14	1.01	2.80	1	11 x 5	2		9	18
		16	1.13	3.30	1	11 x 5	10		9	19
10	x	12	.95	2.55	2	1 x 4	6		9	18
		14	1.05	2.85	2	1 x 5	2		11	19
		16	1.17	3.25	2	1 x 5	10		12	22
		18	1.28	4.05	2	1 x 6	6		13	24
		20	1.41	4.45	2	1 x 7	2		13	26
12	x	14	1.11	3.30	2	5 x 5	2		11	23
		16	1.23	3.65	2	5 x 5	10		12	24
		18	1.34	4.10	2	5 x 6	6		13	27
		20	1.48	5.00	2	5 x 7	2		14	30
14	x	16	1.32	4.45	2	9 x 5	10		13	28
		18	1.43	4.80	2	9 x 6	6		14	31
		20	1.57	5.30	2	9 x 7	2		15	35
		22	1.83	6.40	2	9 x 7	10		16	37
		24	2.10	7.05	2	9 x 8	6		17	40

For prices on Segment and Circle Tops and other extras see list of sash extras on pages 42-43.

All Check Rail Windows plowed and bored.

CHECK RAIL WINDOWS.
Four Lights. 1⅜ in. Thick.

Size of Glass.	Price Open.	Price Glazed, S. S.	Price Glazed, D. S.	Size of Opening.	Weight Open.	Weight Gl. S. S.	Weight Gl. D. S.
10 x 20	$0.80	$2.20	------------	2 1 x 3 10	6	19	------------
22	.86	2.50	------------	4 2	6	19	------------
24	.90	2.55	------------	4 6	7	21	------------
26	.95	2.75	------------	4 10	7	21	------------
28	1.00	2.95	------------	5 2	8	22	------------
30	1.06	3.30	------------	5 6	8	22	------------
32	1.12	3.55	------------	5 10	9	23	------------
34	1.19	4.10	------------	6 2	9	24	------------
36	1.23	4.30	------------	6 6	9	25	------------
12 x 20	.86	2.50	------------	2 5 x 3 10	6	19	------------
22	.92	2.85	------------	4 2	6	19	------------
24	.96	2.95	------------	4 6	7	21	------------
26	1.01	3.15	------------	4 10	7	21	------------
28	1.06	3.30	------------	5 2	9	22	------------
30	1.12	3.65	------------	5 6	10	24	------------
32	1.18	3.85	------------	5 10	12	25	------------
34	1.25	4.35	------------	6 2	12	26	------------
36	1.29	4.40	------------	6 6	12	27	------------
38	1.38	4.85	------------	6 10	13	28	------------
40	1.43	5.15	------------	7 2	13	30	------------
42	1.53	5.50	------------	7 6	14	31	------------
44	1.69	6.20	------------	7 10	14	32	------------
46	1.82	6.50	------------	8 2	15	33	------------
48	1.96	6.60	------------	8 6	15	35	------------
14 x 24	1.04	3.40	------------	2 9 x 4 6	11	23	------------
26	1.09	3.80	------------	4 10	11	23	------------
28	1.14	3.90	------------	5 2	12	24	------------
30	1.20	4.25	------------	5 6	12	26	------------
32	1.26	4.50	$6.25	5 10	12	28	31
34	1.33	4.95	6.90	6 2	13	28	31
36	1.37	5.00	7.00	6 6	13	30	33
38	1.46	5.40	7.55	6 10	13	30	33
40	1.51	5.50	7.65	7 2	14	31	34
42	1.61	6.65	8.80	7 6	14	32	35
44	1.77	7 00	9.00	7 10	15	33	36
46	1.90	7.45	9.80	8 2	15	34	37
48	2.04	8.15	10.45	8 6	16	36	39
15 x 24	1.10	4.00	5.10	2 11 x 4 6	11	24	27
26	1.15	4.30	5.70	4 10	11	24	27
28	1.20	4.45	6.20	5 2	12	25	28
30	1.26	4.65	6.50	5 6	12	27	30
32	1.31	4.95	6 90	5 10	12	29	32
34	1.38	5.50	7.35	6 2	13	29	32
36	1.42	5.60	7.90	6 6	13	31	33
38	1.51	6.00	8.05	6 10	13	31	33
40	1.56	6.60	8.70	7 2	14	32	35
42	1.66	7.15	9.45	7 6	14	33	36
44	1.82	7.35	9.65	7 10	15	34	37
46	1.95	8.50	11.10	8 2	15	35	39
48	2.09	8.70	11.25	8 6	16	37	40

Open Windows made for glass 11 inches wide, same price as 12-inch. Open Windows made for glass 13 or 13½ inches wide, same price as 14-inch. All Check Rail Windows plowed and bored. Window glazed double strength, weighs 3 pounds more than same size glazed single strength. Windows with 14-inch glass, open, weigh 1½ pounds more than same height in 12-inch glass. For Windows prepared for oil finish, add 20 per cent to the open list. For Windows 1¾ inches thick, add 50 per cent to list of 1⅜-inch open Windows. When ordering Windows, always say if wanted glazed or open. Sizes not listed, extra price.

CHECK RAIL WINDOWS.

Two Lights, 1⅜ in. thick.

Size of Glass.	Price Open.	Price Glazed, S. S.	Price Glazed, D. S.	Size of Opening.	Weight Open.	Weight Gl. S. S.	Weight Gl. D. S.
16 x 24	$ .83	$2.25	$2.95	1 8⅛ x 4 6	5	19	21
26	.88	2.65	3.50	4 10	5	19	21
28	.93	2.70	3.55	5 2	7	21	23
30	.99	2.80	3.80	5 6	8	22	24
32	1.04	3.00	4.00	5 10	9	23	25
34	1.11	3.40	4.65	6 2	10	24	26
36	1.15	3.50	4.70	6 6	10	24	26
18 x 24	.83	2.45	3.30	1 10⅛ x 4 6	6	20	22
26	.88	2.70	3.65	4 10	6	20	22
28	.93	2.85	3.85	5 2	8	22	24
30	.99	2.90	3.95	5 6	9	24	27
32	1.04	3.10	4.20	5 10	9	24	27
34	1.11	3.65	4.90	6 2	10	25	28
36	1.15	3.85	5.25	6 6	10	25	28
38	1.23	4.25	5.40	6 10	11	26	29
40	1.28	4.55	5.80	7 2	11	26	29
20 x 24	.83	2.65	3.40	2 0⅛ x 4 6	7	21	23
26	.88	2.80	3.65	4 10	7	21	23
28	.93	2.95	3.85	5 2	8	22	25
30	.99	3.15	4.15	5 6	8	22	25
32	1.04	3.45	4.55	5 10	9	23	26
34	1.11	3.80	4.95	6 2	9	24	27
36	1.15	4.00	5.15	6 6	10	25	28
38	1.23	4.50	5.75	6 10	11	26	30
40	1.28	4.65	6.00	7 2	11	26	30
22 x 24	.86	2.75	3.60	2 2⅛ x 4 6	7	22	26
26	.91	2.95	3.85	4 10	7	22	26
28	.96	3 15	4.10	5 2	8	23	27
30	1.02	3.40	4.50	5 6	8	23	27
32	1.07	3.70	4.90	5 10	10	24	28
34	1.14	4 20	5.40	6 2	10	25	29
36	1.18	4.50	6.10	6 6	10	25	29
38	1.26	4.80	6.25	6 10	11	26	30
40	1.31	5.60	7.20	7 2	11	26	30
42	1.41	5.70	7.30	7 6	11	28	32
44	1.56	6.40	8.25	7 10	12	30	34
46	1.69	6.55	8.40	8 2	12	31	35
48	1.83	6.75	8.60	8 6	13	33	38
24 x 24	.89	3.05	4.05	2 4⅛ x 4 6	8	23	26
26	.94	3.10	4.10	4 10	8	23	26
28	.99	3.40	4.45	5 2	9	24	27
30	1.05	3.60	4.85	5 6	10	24	27
32	1.10	3.85	5.00	5 10	12	25	28
34	1.17	4.25	5.55	6 2	12	25	28
36	1.21	4.35	5.60	6 6	12	27	30
38	1.29	5.30	6.85	6 10	12	28	31
40	1.34	5.35	6.90	7 2	13	29	33

For sash extras see pages 42-43.

(*Continued on next page.*)

CHECK RAIL WINDOWS.

(*Continued.*)

Two Lights, 1⅜ in. thick.

Size of Glass.	Price, Open.	Price Glazed, S. S.	Price Glazed, D. S.	Size of Opening.	Weight, Open.	Weight, Gl. S. S.	Weight, Gl. D. S.
24 x 42	$1.44	$6.25	$8.10	2 4⅛ x 7 6	13	29	33
44	1.59	6.45	8.30	7 10	14	30	34
46	1.72	6.60	8.45	8 2	14	30	34
48	1.86	8.20	10.25	8 6	15	31	35
26 x 26	.98	3.65	4.80	2 6⅛ x 4 10	10	23	26
28	1.03	4.05	5.25	5 2	11	24	27
30	1.09	4.20	5.45	5 6	12	25	28
32	1.14	4.25	5.55	5 10	12	26	30
34	1.21	4.95	6.40	6 2	13	27	31
36	1.25	5.00	6.45	6 6	13	28	32
38	1.33	5.60	7.30	6 10	13	28	32
40	1.38	5.70	7.35	7 2	14	30	34
42	1.48	6.30	8.15	7 6	14	30	34
44	1.63	7.15	9.30	7 10	15	32	36
46	1.76	8.05	10.15	8 2	15	32	36
48	1.90	8.25	10.35	8 6	16	34	39
28 x 28	1.07	4.15	5.45	2 8⅛ x 5 2	11	26	30
30	1.13	4.25	5.55	5 6	12	27	31
32	1.18	4.95	6.40	5 10	12	28	32
34	1.25	5.25	6.80	6 2	12	28	32
36	1.29	5.50	7.20	6 6	13	30	34
38	1.37	5.60	7.30	6 10	14	30	34
40	1.42	5.70	7.35	7 2	15	32	36
42	1.52	7.05	9.15	7 6	15	32	37
44	1.67	7.95	10.00	7 10	16	34	38
46	1.80	8.15	10.20	8 2	16	35	39
48	1.94	9.40	11.90	8 6	17	36	40
30 x 32	1.23	5.00	6.45	2 10⅛ x 5 10	13	28	33
34	1.30	5.50	7.20	6 2	13	28	33
36	1.34	5.60	7.30	6 6	14	29	34
38	1.42	5.65	8.05	6 10	14	29	34
40	1.47	6.65	8.70	7 2	15	30	35
42	1.57	7.50	9.45	7 6	15	30	35
44	1.72	7.65	9.65	7 10	16	31	36
46	1.85	8.85	11.25	8 2	16	31	36
48	1.99	9.00	11.40	8 6	17	32	28
50	2.14	9.20	11.60	8 10	18	34	40

For windows 1¾ thick, add 50 per cent to list of 1⅜-inch open windows.

For windows prepared for oil finish, add 20 per cent to the open list.

For windows glazed with AA. Glass, add 10 per cent to 1⅜-inch glazed list.

For additional sash extras, see pages 42 and 43.

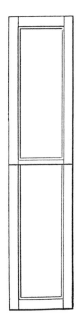

PANTRY CHECK RAIL WINDOWS.

Two Lights, 1⅜ Inch Thick.

One Light Wide.

Size of Glass.	Price, Open.	Price, Glazed.	Size of Opening.	Weight Open.	Weight Glazed.
12 x 24	$0.73	$2.15	1 4⅛ x 4 6	6	13
26	.78	2.55	4 10	6	13
28	.83	2.60	5 2	7	14
30	.89	2.70	5 6	7	14
32	.94	2.90	5 10	8	15
34	1.01	3.30	6 2	8	15
36	1.05	3.40	6 6	8	15
14 x 24	.76	2.20	1 6⅛ x 4 6	9	16
26	.81	2.60	4 10	9	16
28	.86	2.65	5 2	10	17
30	.92	2.75	5 6	10	17
32	.97	2.95	5 10	11	19
34	1.04	3.35	6 2	11	19
36	1.08	3.45	6 6	12	21

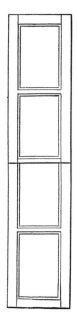

PANTRY CHECK RAIL WINDOWS.

Four Lights, 1⅜ Inch Thick.

One Light Wide.

Size of Glass.	Price, Open.	Price, Glazed.	Size of Opening.	Weight Open.	Weight Glazed.
9 x 12	$0.72	$1.90	1 1⅛ x 4 6	5	15
14	.82	2.05	5 2	5	16
16	.93	2.40	5 10	6	17
12 x 14	.85	2.60	1 4⅛ x 5 2	7	17
16	.96	2.90	5 10	8	18
18	1.07	3.40	6 6	9	20

All Check Rail Windows plowed and bored.

Sizes not listed, extra price.

 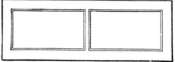

TRANSOMS.

One and two lights. 1⅜ in. thick.

Size of Opening.	Price, Open	Price, Glazed, Two Light.	Price, Glazed, One Light.	One Light, Glazed, Double Strength.	Weight, Glazed, S. S.	Weight, Glazed, D. S.
2 6 x 1 0	$0.47	$1.15	$1.30		6	
1 2	.47	1.20	1.35		6	
1 4	.50	1.35	1.50		6	
2 8 x 1 0	.50	1.20	1.35		6	
1 2	.50	1.30	1.45		6	
1 4	.53	1.45	1.55		6½	
1 6	.57	1.70	1.85		6½	
2 10 x 1 2	.51	1.35	1.50		6½	
1 4	.57	1.70	1.85		6½	
1 6	.60	1.90	2.05		7	
1 8	.64	2.10	2.25		7	
3 0 x 1 2	.57	1.50	1.65		6½	
1 4	.60	1.75	1.90		7	
1 6	.64	2.05	2.20		7½	
1 8	.71	2.35	2.50		8	
3 6 x 1 8	.79	2.60	2.90	$3.75	9	10
1 10	.79	2.95	3.25	4.10	9	10
2 0	.86	3.25	3.55	4.55	9½	10½
4 0 x 1 4	.93	2.40	2.70	3.55	9	10
1 6	.93	2.70	3.00	3.95	9	10
1 8	1.00	3.20	3.45	4.65	10	11
1 10	1.00	3.75	4.05	5.35	10	11
2 0	1.07	4.15	4.45	6.00	11	12
4 6 x 1 6	1.07	3.35	3.70	4.95	10	11
1 8	1.07	3.70	4.05	5.50	11	12
1 10	1.15	4.10	4.45	6.00	11	12
2 0	1.15	4.60	4.95	6.70	12	13
5 0 x 1 6	1.15	3.40		6.15	11	12½
1 8	1.15	3.90		6.70	11	12½
1 10	1.22	4.30		7.35	12	13½
2 0	1.22	4.60		8.55	12	13½
2 2	1.29	4.95		8.60	13	14½
5 6 x 1 6	1.29	4.05		7.55	11	12½
1 8	1.29	4.40		7.55	11	12½
1 10	1.36	4.75		8.70	12	13½
2 0	1.36	5.45		8.70	13	14½
2 2	1.43	5.95		10.15	13	14½
2 4	1.43	6.20		10.85	14	15½
2 6	1.50	6.85		13.20	15	16½
6 0 x 1 8	1.43	4.80		7.70	12	13½
1 10	1.50	5.25		9.20	14	16
2 0	1.50	5.60		10.95	15	17
2 2	1.57	6.35		11.00	16	18
2 4	1.57	6.90		13.50	17	19
2 6	1.65	8.35		13.55	18	20
2 8	1.72	8.40		15.75	19	23
2 10	1.86	9.55		15.90	20	24

For prices on Segment and Circle Tops and other Extras, see list of Sash extras on pages 42, 43.
For Transoms 1¾ in. thick, add 50 per cent to 1⅜ in. open.
For special designs of transoms see page 31.

CELLAR SASH.

 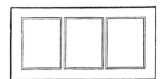

Two Lights.

Size of Glass.	Thickness.	Price Open.	Price Single Glazed.	Price Double Glazed.	Size of Opening.	Weight Open.	Weight Glazed.
10 x 12	1⅜	$0.43	$1.05	$1.85	2 1 x 16	4	6
14	"	.43	1.15	2.05	18	4	6
16	"	.50	1.35	2.40	20	4	6
18	"	.57	1.55	2.70	22	5	8
12 x 12	"	.50	1.35	2.20	2 5 x 16	5	8
14	"	.50	1.40	2.45	18	5	8
16	"	.57	1.65	2.85	20	5	8
18	"	.57	1.70	3.05	22	6	9
20	"	.65	2.00	3.45	24	6	9
14 x 16	"	.65	1.90	3.30	2 9 x 20	5	8
18	"	.65	2.05	3.55	22	5	8
20	"	.72	2.25	3.90	24	6	11
22	"	.72	2.50	4.40	26	6	11
24	"	.79	2.70	4 80	28	6	12

Three Lights.

Size of Glass.	Thickness.	Price Open.	Price Single Glazed.	Price Double Glazed.	Size of Opening.	Weight Open.	Weight Glazed.
7 x 9	1⅛	$0.43	$0.95	$1.55	2 1 x 13	4	6
8 x 10	"	.43	1.05	1.85	2 4 x 14	4	6
9 x 12	"	.50	1.35	2.35	2 7 x 16	4	7
13	"	.50	1.40	2.45	17	4	7
14	"	.50	1.50	2.60	18	5	8
10 x 12	"	.50	1.40	2 45	2 10 x 16	5	8
14	"	.57	1.65	2.85	18	5	8
16	"	.57	1.85	3.25	20	5	8
12 x 12	"	.57	1.70	3.00	3 4 x 16	6	9
14	"	.65	2.00	3.45	18	6	10
16	"	.65	2.20	3.90	20	6	10

For Three Light Cellar Sash made 1⅜ inch thick add 10 cents to list.
Sizes not listed, extra price.

BARN SASH.

Four Light.

Size of Glass.	Thickness.	Price Open.	Price Glazed.	Weight Open.	Weight Glazed.
8 x 10	1⅛	$0.43	$1.15	3	6
9 x 12	"	.50	1.45	5	9
14	"	.50	1.60	5	10
10 x 12	"	.50	1.60	5	9
14	"	.57	1.80	5	10

STALL SASH.

One Light.

Size of Glass.	Thickness.	Price Open.	Price Glazed.	Weight Open.	Weight Glazed.
8 x 10	1⅛	$0.35	$0.70	2	4
10 x 12	"	.43	.85	2	4
14	"	.50	1.00	3	6
12 x 16	"	.57	1.20	3	6

HOT BED SASH.

Made for 6 or 7 inch glass.

Size of Opening.	Thickness.	Price Open.	Price Glazed.	Weight Open.	Weight Glazed.
3 0 x 6 0	1⅜	$2.30	$6.10	15	29
3 0 x 6 0	1¾	3.45	7.50	22	36

Sizes not listed, extra price.

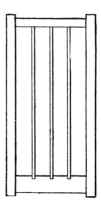

15 and 18 LIGHT WINDOWS.

No. 52. For 15-light windows, add to list of 12-light, one-quarter.
No. 53. For 18-light windows, add to list of 12-light, one-half.

GLAZED STORM SASH.

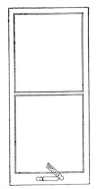

Two-Light Storm Sash.
Bottom rail ventilator open.

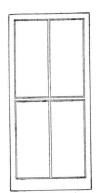

Four-Light Storm Sash.

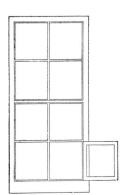

Eight-Light Storm Sash.
Swing light ventilator.

Twelve-Light Storm Sash.
Double ventilator.

STORM SASH.

1⅛ inch Storm Sash, same price as 1⅜ inch Check Rail Window, same opening.
1⅜ inch Storm Sash, add 15 per cent to 1⅜ inch Check Rail open list.
For Ventilators in top or bottom rail. add 10 cents net each.
For Swing Light, add 40 cents net.

PLEASE NOTICE.

Our regular Storm Sash are made with 2¼ inch stiles.   3 inch stiles, when so specified, will be furnished without extra charge.   We can make one or more Ventilators in bottom rail of each sash as per cuts above.

IF VENTILATORS ARE WANTED, ORDER MUST SO STATE.
PLACE YOUR ORDER FOR STORM SASH EARLY.

WEATHER STRIPS.

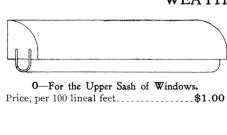

0—For the Upper Sash of Windows.
Price, per 100 lineal feet_____**$1.00**

3—For the Center of Double Doors.
Price, per 100 lineal feet_____**$1.60**

1—For the Lower Sash of Windows.
Price, per 100 lineal feet_____**$1.00**

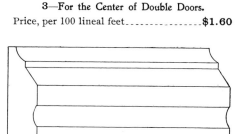

4—For Bottom of Light Doors.
Price, per 100 lineal feet_____**$1.75**

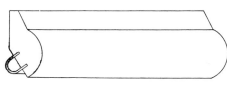

1½—For Sides and Tops of Doors.
Price, per 100 lineal feet_____**$1.45**

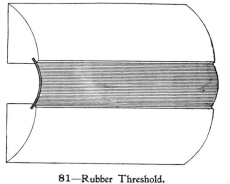

81—Rubber Threshold.
Made in lengths of 3 ft., 3 ft. 6 in., 4 ft. and 5 ft.
3 feet, $1.00 each; 3 feet 6 inches, $1.20 each;
4 feet, $1.30 each; 5 feet, $1.60 each.

2—For the Center of Windows.
Price, per 100 lineal feet_____**$1.45**

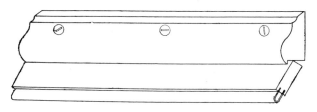

80—Spring Door Bottom.
Two sizes, 2 feet 8 inches and 3 feet.   Price per dozen_____**$6.50**

COTTAGE FRONT CHECK RAIL WINDOWS.

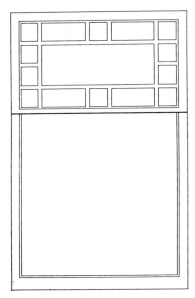

67   68

Made in two pieces, to open.

List Price. **67** 1⅜ Inches Thick.

Size of Opening.	Bottom Light.	Top Light.	Price, Open.	Price, Glazed, D. S., 5 inch Border Lights, Colored.	Weight, Open.	Weight, Glazed.
3 8 x 5 2	40 x 42	40 x 14	$3.17	$11.90	12	44
4 0 x 5 6	44 x 44	44 x 16	3.43	13.75	15	52
4 4 x 5 10	48 x 46	48 x 18	3.73	17.85	16	60
4 6 x 6 2	50 x 48	50 x 20	3.80	20.30	17	65
4 8 x 6 6	52 x 50	52 x 22	4.04	22.30	18	70
5 0 x 7 2	56 x 56	56 x 24	4.37	30.45	22	85

List Price. **68** 1⅜ Inches Thick.

Size of Opening.	Bottom Light.	Top Light.	Price, Open.	Price, Glazed, D. S.,	Weight, Open.	Weight, Glazed.
3 8 x 5 2	40 x 42	40 x 14	$1.67	$11.00	12	44
4 0 x 5 6	44 x 44	44 x 16	1.93	13.10	15	52
4 4 x 5 10	48 x 46	48 x 18	2.23	17.25	16	60
4 6 x 6 2	50 x 48	50 x 20	2.30	19.90	17	65
4 8 x 6 6	52 x 50	52 x 22	2.54	22.50	18	70
5 0 x 7 2	56 x 56	56 x 24	2.87	30.80	22	85

For 1¾ inches thick, add 50 per cent to price of Open Sash.

Sash extras, pages 42 and 43.

For cottage front windows with leaded glass top lights in colors, see pages 33 to 36.

COTTAGE FRONT SINGLE SASH.

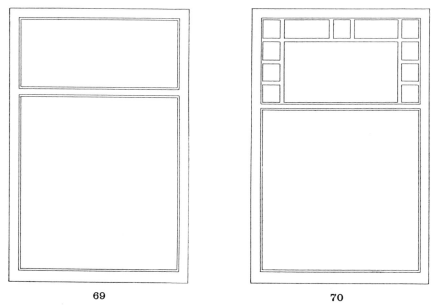

69   70

Made in one piece, to set stationary.

List Price. **69** 1⅜ Inches Thick.

Size of Opening.			Bottom Light.	Top Light.	Price, Open.	Price, Glazed, D. S.	Weight, Open.	Weight, Glazed.
3	8 x 5	2	40 x 42	40 x 14	$1.92	$11.35	12	44
4	0 x 5	6	44 x 44	44 x 16	2.22	13.45	15	52
4	4 x 5	10	48 x 46	48 x 18	2.56	17.60	16	60
4	6 x 6	2	50 x 48	50 x 20	2.65	20.30	17	65
4	8 x 6	6	52 x 50	52 x 22	2.92	22.90	18	70
5	0 x 7	2	56 x 56	56 x 24	3.30	31.20	22	85

List Price. **70** 1⅜ Inches Thick.

Size of Opening.			Bottom Light.	Top Light.	Price, Open.	Price, Glazed, D. S. 5 inch Border. Lights, Colored.	Weight, Open.	Weight, Glazed.
3	8 x 5	2	40 x 42	40 x 14	$3.12	$12 10	12	44
4	0 x 5	6	44 x 44	44 x 16	3.42	13.90	15	52
4	4 x 5	10	48 x 46	48 x 18	3.76	18.00	16	60
4	6 x 6	2	50 x 48	50 x 20	3.85	20.45	17	65
4	8 x 6	6	52 x 50	52 x 22	4.12	22.45	18	70
5	0 x 7	2	56 x 56	56 x 24	4.50	30.60	22	85

For 1¾ inches thick, add 50 per cent to price of open sash.

For cottage front windows with leaded glass top lights in colors, see pages 33 to 36.

Sash extras, pages 42 and 43.

COTTAGE FRONT SASH and TRANSOMS.

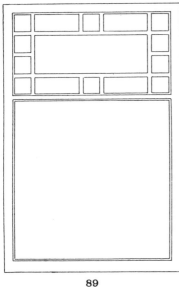

89

Made in one piece, to set stationary.

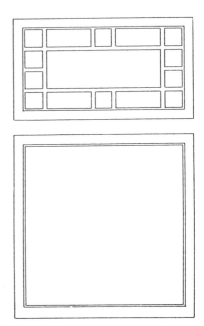

90

List Price. **89** 1⅜ Inches Thick.

Size of Opening.	Bottom Light.	Top Light.	Price, Open.	Price, Glazed, D. S., 5 inch Border Lights, Colored.	Weight, Open.	Weight, Glazed.
3 8 x 5 2	40 x 42	40 x 14	$3.42	$12.10	12	44
4 0 x 5 6	44 x 44	44 x 16	3.72	13.90	15	52
4 4 x 5 10	48 x 46	48 x 18	4.06	18.00	16	60
4 6 x 6 2	50 x 48	50 x 20	4.15	20.45	17	65
4 8 x 6 6	52 x 50	52 x 22	4.42	22.45	18	70
5 0 x 7 2	56 x 56	56 x 24	4.80	30.60	22	85

List Price. **90** 1⅜ Inches Thick.

Sizes of Openings.		Sizes of Glass.		Price, Open.	Price, Glazed, D. S., 5 inch Border Lights, Colored.	Weight, Open.	Weight Glazed.
Lower Sash.	Transom.	Lower Sash.	Transom.				
3 8 x 3 8	3 8 x 16	40 x 39	40 x 12	$3.76	$10.40	12	44
4 0 x 3 10	4 0 x 18	44 x 41	44 x 14	4.00	13.85	15	52
4 4 x 4 0	4 4 x 20	48 x 43	48 x 16	4.24	17.85	16	60
4 6 x 4 2	4 6 x 22	50 x 45	50 x 18	4.38	20.45	17	65
4 8 x 4 4	4 8 x 24	52 x 47	52 x 20	4.45	21.25	18	70
5 0 x 4 6	5 0 x 26	56 x 49	56 x 22	4.69	25.10	22	85

For 1¾ inches thick, add 50 per cent to price of Open Sash.
For cottage front windows with leaded glass top lights in colors, see pages 33 to 36.
Sash extras, pages 42 and 43.

COTTAGE FRONT SASH and TRANSOMS.

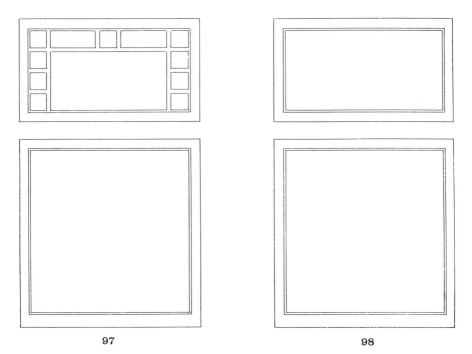

97   98

List Price. 97 1⅜ Inches Thick.

Sizes of Openings.		Sizes of Glass.		Price, Open.	Price, Glazed, D. S., 5 inch Border Lights, Colored.	Weight Open.	Weight Glazed.
Lower Sash.	Transom.	Lower Sash.	Transom.				
3 8 x 3 8	3 8 x 16	40 x 39	40 x 12	$3.40	$10.20	12	44
4 0 x 3 10	4 0 x 18	44 x 41	44 x 14	3.70	13.60	15	52
4 4 x 4 0	4 4 x 20	48 x 43	48 x 16	3.94	17.55	16	60
4 6 x 4 2	4 6 x 22	50 x 45	50 x 18	4.08	20.20	17	65
4 8 x 4 4	4 8 x 24	52 x 47	52 x 20	4.15	21.00	18	70
5 0 x 4 6	5 0 x 26	56 x 49	56 x 22	4.39	24.90	22	85

List Price. 98 1⅜ Inches Thick.

Sizes of Openings.		Sizes of Glass.		Price, Open.	Price, Glazed, D. S.	Weight Open.	Weight Glazed.
Lower Sash.	Transom.	Lower Sash.	Transom.				
3 8 x 3 8	3 8 x 16	40 x 39	40 x 12	$2.20	$9.60	12	44
4 0 x 3 10	4 0 x 18	44 x 41	44 x 14	2.50	13.10	15	52
4 4 x 4 0	4 4 x 20	48 x 43	48 x 16	2.74	17.55	16	60
4 6 x 4 2	4 6 x 22	50 x 45	50 x 18	2.88	19.75	17	65
4 8 x 4 4	4 8 x 24	52 x 47	52 x 20	2.95	21.25	18	70
5 0 x 4 6	5 0 x 26	56 x 49	56 x 22	3.19	25.10	22	85

For 1¾ inches thick, add 50 per cent to price of Open Sash.
For cottage front windows with leaded glass top lights in colors, see pages 33 to 36.
Sash extras, pages 42 and 43.

COTTAGE FRONT CHECK RAIL WINDOWS.

 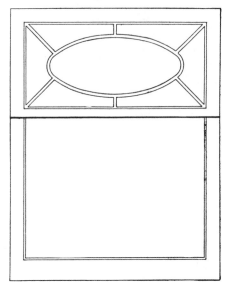

130   131

Made in two pieces, to open.

List price 1⅜ in. thick.

130

Size of Opening.	Bottom Light. Inches.	Top Light. Inches.	Open.	Glazed D. S. with Colored Margin Lights.	Add if 1¾ inches thick.	Weight Open lbs.	Weight Glazed lbs.
3 8 x 5 2	40 x 42	40 x 14	$ 2.57	$11.95	$1.29	12	44
4 0 x 5 6	44 x 44	44 x 16	2.83	14.05	1.42	14	52
4 4 x 5 10	48 x 46	48 x 18	3.13	18.20	1.57	16	59
4 6 x 6 2	50 x 48	50 x 20	3.20	20.85	1.60	17	65
4 8 x 6 6	52 x 50	52 x 22	3.44	23.55	1.72	18	69
5 0 x 7 2	56 x 56	56 x 24	3.77	31.80	1.89	22	85

List price 1⅜ in. thick.

131

Size of Opening.	Bottom Light. Inches.	Top Light. Inches.	Open.	Glazed D. S.	Add if 1¾ inches thick.	Weight Open lbs.	Weight Glazed. lbs.
3 8 x 5 2	40 x 42	40 x 14	$6.37	$17.70	$3.19	12	44
4 0 x 5 6	44 x 44	44 x 16	6.63	20.40	3.32	14	52
4 4 x 5 10	48 x 46	48 x 18	6.93	25.50	3.47	16	59
4 6 x 6 2	50 x 48	50 x 20	7.04	28.60	3.52	17	65
4 8 x 6 6	52 x 50	52 x 22	7.24	32.30	3.62	18	69
5 0 x 7 2	56 x 56	56 x 24	7.57	41.65	3.79	22	58

For cottage front windows with leaded glass top lights in colors, see pages 33 to 36.

COTTAGE FRONT CHECK RAIL WINDOWS.

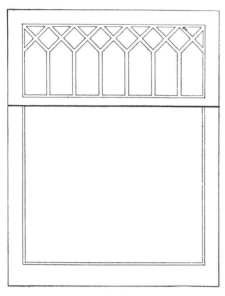

132

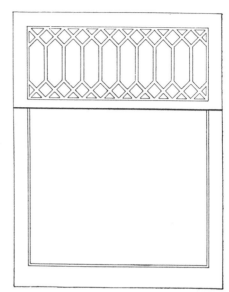

133

Made in two pieces, to open.

List price. 1⅜ in. thick.

132

Size of Opening.	Bottom Light. Inches.	Top Light. Inches.	Open.	Glazed, D. S.	Add if 1¾ in. thick.	Weight, Open	Weight. Glazed.
3 8 x 5 2	40 x 42	40 x 14	$6.07	$16.50	$3.04	12	44
4 0 x 5 6	44 x 44	44 x 16	6.33	18.65	3.17	15	52
4 4 x 5 10	48 x 46	48 x 18	6.63	22.80	3.32	16	60
4 6 x 6 2	50 x 48	50 x 20	6.70	26.80	3.35	17	65
4 8 x 6 6	52 x 50	52 x 22	6.94	29.45	3.47	18	70
5 0 x 7 2	56 x 56	56 x 24	7.27	37.75	3.64	22	85

List price. 1⅜ in. thick.

133

Size of Opening.	Bottom Light. Inches.	Top Light. Inches.	Open.	Glazed, D. S.	Add if 1¾ in. thick.	Weight, Open	Weight Glazed.
3 8 x 5 2	40 x 42	40 x 14	$12.07	$24.30	$6.04	12	44
4 0 x 5 6	44 x 44	44 x 16	12.33	26.45	6.17	15	52
4 4 x 5 10	48 x 46	48 x 18	12.63	30.60	6.32	16	60
4 6 x 6 2	50 x 48	50 x 20	12.70	33.25	6.35	17	65
4 8 x 6 6	52 x 50	52 x 22	12.94	35.90	6.47	18	75
5 0 x 7 2	56 x 56	56 x 24	13.27	44.20	6.64	22	85

For cottage front windows with leaded glass top lights in colors, see pages 33 to 36.

QUEEN ANNE WINDOWS.

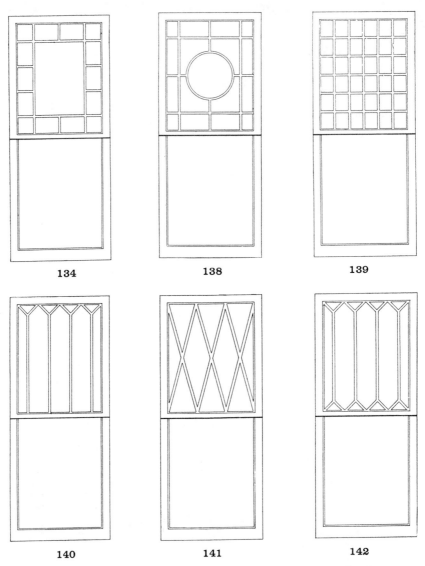

134   138   139

140   141   142

134. 1⅜ inch, add $1.40 to list price of two-light window, same size, open or glazed.
138.   "   "   5.20   "   "   "   "   "   "
139.   "   "   3.60   "   "   "   "   "   "
140. For 1⅜ inch Windows with glass not wider than 20 inches, add $1.80 to list price of two-light windows of same size. For 1⅜ inch Windows with glass wider than 20 inches, add 40 cents to list price for each additional 4 inches or fraction thereof in width.
141. For 1⅜ inch Windows with glass not wider than 20 inches, add $2.00 to list price of two-light windows of same size. For 1⅜ inch windows with glass wider than 20 inches, add 60 cents to list price for each additional 6 inches or fraction thereof in width.
142. For 1⅜ inch Windows with glass not wider than 20 inches, add $2.60 to list price of two-light windows of same size. For 1⅜ inch windows with glass wider than 20 inches, add 60 cents to list price for each additional 4 inches or fraction thereof in width.
   For windows 1¾ in. thick add 50 per cent to the list of 1⅜ in. open windows.
   Prices of above are for margin lights, glazed, plain or colored, as desired.

QUEEN ANNE WINDOWS.

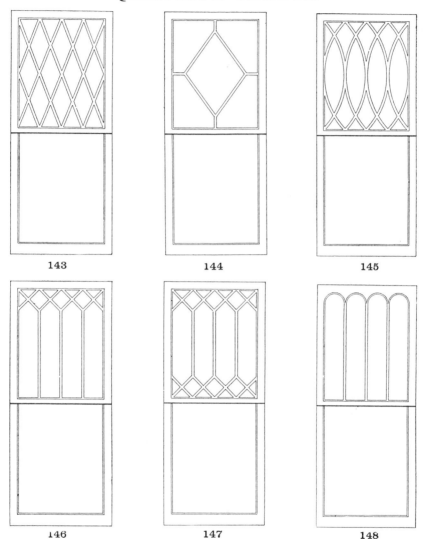

The above cuts all show check rail windows in two pieces and not single sash in one piece.

143. For 1⅜ inch Windows, with glass not wider than 20 inches, add $4.40 to list price of two-light windows of same size.   For 1⅜ inch Windows, with glass wider than 20 inches, add $1.00 to list price for each additional 4 inches or fraction thereof in width.

144. For 1⅜ inch Windows, add $1.45 to list of two-light windows same size.

145. For 1⅜ inch Windows, with glass not wider than 24 inches, add $14.00 to list price of two-light windows of same size.   For 1⅜ inch Windows, with glass wider than 24 inches, add $3.50 to list price for each additional 6 inches or fraction thereof in width.

146. For 1⅜ inch Windows, with glass not wider than 20 inches, add $2.60 to list price of two-light windows of same size.   For 1⅜ inch Windows, with glass wider than 20 inches, add 60 cents to above list price for each additional 4 inches or fraction thereof in width.

147. For 1⅜ inch Windows, with glass not wider than 20 inches, add $4.40 to list price of two-light windows of same size.   For 1⅜ inch Windows, with glass wider than 20 inches, add $1.00 to list price for each additional 4 inches or fraction thereof in width.

148. For 1⅜ inch Windows, with glass not wider than 20 inches, add $2 55 to list price of two-light windows of same size.   For 1⅜ inch Windows, with glass wider than 20 inches, add 65 cents to above list price for each additional 4 inches or fraction thereof in width.

For windows 1¾ in. think add 50 per cent to the list of 1⅜ in. open windows.
Above windows are glazed plain glass.

149

QUEEN ANNE SASH.

GLAZED PLAIN GLASS.

149

For 1⅜ inch thick add $1.35 to half the list price of a two-light window, glazed with D. S. glass, of similar size.

150

150

For 1⅜ inch thick add $1.55 to half the list price of a two-light window, glazed with D. S. glass, of similar size.

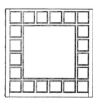

151

151

For 1⅜ inch thick add $2.15 to half the list price of a two-light window, glazed with D. S. glass, of similar size.

152

152

For 1⅜ inch thick add $6.20 to half the list price of a two-light window, glazed with D. S. glass, of similar size.

153

153

For 1⅜ inch thick add $4.35 to half the list price of a two-light window, glazed with D. S. glass, of similar size.

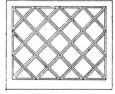

154

154

For 1⅜ inch thick add $6.35 to half the list price of a two-light window, glazed with D. S. glass, of similar size; or add $6.20 to the list price of a one-light transom, glazed with D. S. glass, of similar size.

For sash 1¼ inch thick add 50 per cent to the list of 1⅜ open sash.

If above sash are glazed with white chipped or colored glass (any color except ruby) add 70 cents per square foot of glass measure to prices named above.

QUEEN ANNE TRANSOMS.

GLAZED PLAIN GLASS.

155

For 1⅜ inch thick, add $7.20 to list price of 1⅜ inch 1-light transom glazed with D. S. glass of same size.

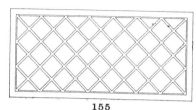

155

156

For 1⅜ inch thick, add $5.00 to list price of 1⅜ inch 1-light transom glazed with D. S. glass of same size.

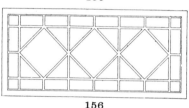

156

157

For 1⅜ inch thick, add $3.10 to list price of 1⅜·inch 1-light transom glazed with D. S. glass of same size.

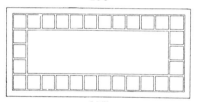

157

158

For 1⅜ inch thick, not more than 3 feet 4 inches wide, add $5.00 to list price of 1⅜ inch 1-light transom of same size.

For transoms over 3 feet 4 inches wide, add 60 cents to above list for every additional 4 inches or fraction thereof in width.

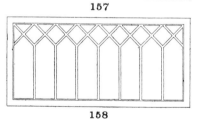

158

159

For 1⅜ inch thick, not more than 3 feet 4 inches wide, add $9.40 to list price of 1⅜ inch 1-light transom of same size.

For transoms over 3 feet 4 inches wide, add $1.00 to above list for every additional 4 inches or fraction thereof in width.

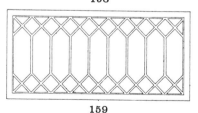

159

160

For 1⅜ inch thick, add 90 cents to list price of 1-light transom glazed with D. S. glass of same size.

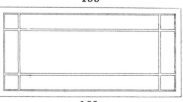

160

If above sash are glazed with white chipped or colored glass (any color except ruby) add 70 cents per square foot glass measure to prices named above.

TRANSOMS.

SEGMENT, CIRCLE TOP and GOTHIC
GLAZED PLAIN GLASS.

161

162

ADD TO LIST

For Segment Head Transoms, 161 and 162, 1⅜ inches
thick, 3 feet 4 inches in width and under _____ $0.85
For Segment Head Transoms, 161 and 162, 1¾ inches
thick, 3 feet 4 inches in width and under _____ 1.30
For Segment Head Transoms, 161 and 162, 1⅜ inches
thick, over 3 feet 4 inches in width _____ 1.45
For Segment Head Transoms, 161 and 162, 1¾ inches
thick, over 3 feet 4 inches in width _____ 2.15

163

164

ADD TO LIST

For Half Circle and Gothic Head Transoms, 163 and 164,
1⅜ inches thick, 3 feet 4 inches in width and under $1.75
For Half Circle and Gothic Head Transoms, 163 and 164,
1¾ inches thick, 3 feet 4 inches in width and under 2.60
For Half Circle and Gothic Head Transoms, 163 and 164,
1⅜ inches thick, over 3 feet 4 inches in width _____ 2.85
For Half Circle and Gothic Head Transoms, 163 and 164,
1¾ inches thick, over 3 feet 4 inches in width _____ 4.30

165

To List Price
of Square Top

For Transoms 165, 1⅜ in. thick, not over 3 ft. 4 in. in width, add $2.50
" 1⅜ in. " over 3 ft. 4 in. " " 3.60
" 1¾ in. " not over 3 ft. 4 in. " " 3.75
" 1¾ in. " over 3 ft. 4 in. " " 5.40

166

To List Price
of Square Top

For Transoms 166, 1⅜ in. thick, not over 3 ft. 4 in. in width, add $4.70
" 1⅜ in. " over 3 ft. 4 in. " " 6.90
" 1¾ in. " not over 3 ft. 4 in. " " 7.00
" 1¾ in. " over 3 ft. 4 in. " " 10.40

167

To List Price
of Square Top

For Transoms 167, 1⅜ in. thick, not over 3 ft. 4 in. in width, add $3.50
" 1⅜ in. " over 3 ft. 4 in. " " 5.70
" 1¾ in. " not over 3 ft. 4 in. " " 5.20
" 1¾ in. " over 3 ft. 4 in. " " 8.60

FRONT WINDOW with LEADED GLASS TOP.

Design A.

See preceding pages for ordinary sizes.   Write us for prices, specifying size wanted.
Made in two pieces.

LANDSCAPE WINDOW with LEADED GLASS TOP SASH.

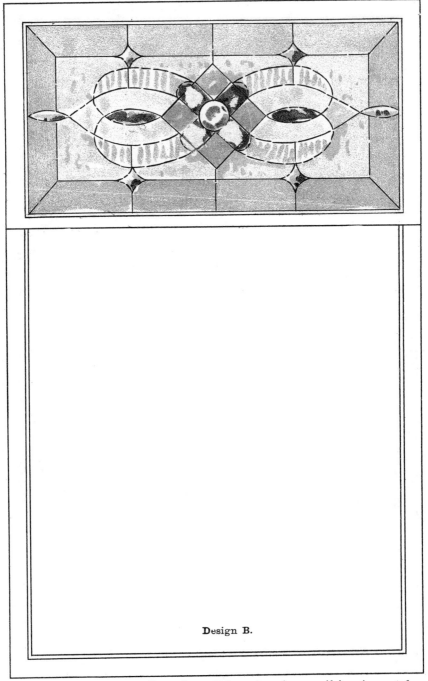

Design B.

See preceding pages for ordinary sizes.   Write us for prices, specifying size wanted.

LANDSCAPE SASH with LEADED GLASS in TOP LIGHT.

Design C.

See preceding pages for ordinary sizes. Write us for prices, specifying size wanted.
Made in one piece.

LANDSCAPE SASH with LEADED GLASS in TOP LIGHT.

Design D.

See preceding pages for ordinary sizes.   Write us for prices, specifying size wanted.

TRIPLE FRONT WINDOWS.

167 A   167 B

167 C

167 D

Send for prices, giving outside measures and thickness of each check rail window, single sash and transoms; and when ordering also give width of mullions, thickness of transom bar in frame, and if circular or segment top, the radius.

CHURCH WINDOWS.

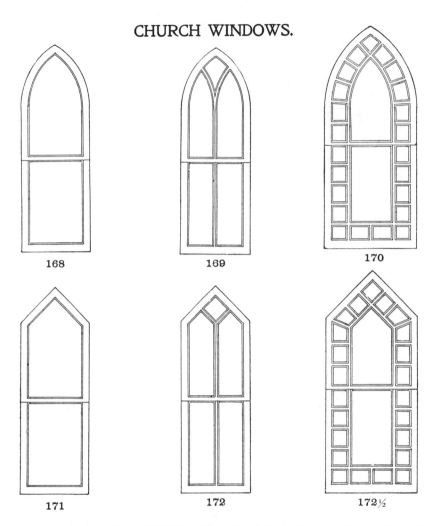

No. 168.   For 1⅜ inch windows add $1.75 to list price of 1⅜ inch square top windows of same width and height.

No. 169.   For 1⅜ inch windows add $3.50 to list price of 1⅜ inch square top windows of same width and height.

No. 170.   For 1⅜ inch windows add $5.90 to list price of 1⅜ inch square top windows of same width and height.

No. 171.   For 1⅜ inch windows add $1.75 to list price of 1⅜ inch square top windows of same width and height.

No. 172.   For 1⅜ inch windows add $3.50 to list price of 1⅜ inch square top windows of same width and height.

No. 172½. For 1⅜ inch windows add $5.90 to list price of 1⅜ inch square top windows of same width and height.

For 1¾ inch windows like above add 50 per cent to above prices.

If above windows are glazed with enamel, white chipped or colored cathedral glass, add 70 cents per square foot to list price of same windows glazed with plain glass.

CIRCLE-FACE WINDOWS.

We can furnish Circle-face Windows or Sash, glazed or open, at lowest prices. Send for estimates giving full information as to size, thickness and radius of circle.

When ordering, give radius measured to outside of top sash, and say whether frames are made with square jambs like detail A, or radiating jambs like detail B.

If made like detail B give distance measured straight across between jambs from outside edges of the top sash.

DETAIL A.

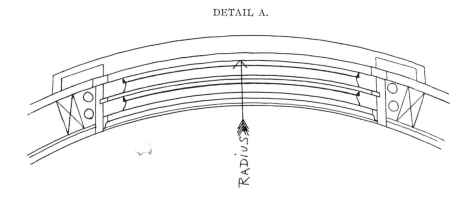

DETAIL B.

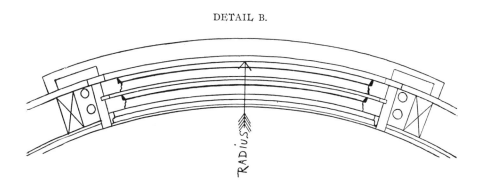

GABLE FRAMES and SASH.

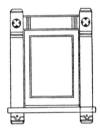

Sash No. 173½
Frame No. 3047

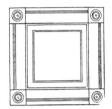

Sash No. 174
Frame No. 304

Sash No. 175
Frame No. 3049

Sash No. 176
Frame No. 3050

Sash No. 177
Frame No. 3051

Sash No. 178
Frame No. 3053

List Price, Sash 1⅜ Inches Thick and Frame.

SASH No.	Size of Opening.	Price Open.	Price Glazed.	FRAME No.	4 Inch Studing. Price.
173½	2 0 x 2 5	$0 57	$2.10	3047	$1.90
174	2 0 x 2 5	.57	2.10	3048	1.60
175	2 0 x 2 0	4.85	6.15	3049	2.65
176	2 0 x 2 5	2.72	4.25	3050	2.40
177	2 0 x 2 0	6.25	7.80	3051	2.65
178	2 0 x 2 5	1.42	2.95	3053	2.65

GABLE FRAMES and SASH.

Sash No. 161
Frame No. 3184

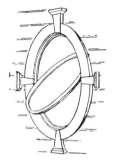

Sash No. 162
Frame No. 3183

Sash No. 163
Frame No. 3182

Sash No. 164
Frame No. 3181

Sash No. 165
Frame No. 3180

Sash No. 166
Frame No. 3179

List Prices, Sash 1⅜ Inches Thick and Frame.

SASH No.	Size of Opening.				Price Open.	Price Glazed.	FRAME No.	4 Inch Studing. Price.
161	1	8	x 2	8	$4.95	$7.20	3184	$6.40
162	1	8	x 2	8	8.30	10.55	3183	3.75
163	2	0	x 2	0	11.25	13.80	3182	3.45
164	2	0	x 2	2	3.70	5.50	3181	4.90
165	1	8	x 2	8	3.65	5.90	3180	2.65
166	2	0	x 1	2	6.50	7.75	3179	4.10

SASH EXTRAS.

Irregular and Intermediate Sizes same as next larger listed size.
All items are list unless specified net.

ADD TO
LIST

No. 1. For segment head windows and transoms, Fig. 3 and 4, 1⅜ inches thick, 3 feet 4 inches in width and under \$0.85

No. 2. For the same, 1¾ inches thick.. 1.30

No. 3. For segment head windows and transoms, Fig. 3 and 4, 1⅜ inches thick, over 3 feet 4 inches in width. 1.45

No. 4. For the same, 1¾ inches thick.. 2.15

No. 5. For half circle head, inside and outside, Fig. 1, 1⅜ inches thick, 3 feet 4 inches wide and under...... 1.75

No. 6. For the same, 1¾ inches thick.. 2.60

No. 7. For half circle head, inside and outside, Fig. 1, 1⅜ inches thick, over 3 feet 4 inches in width.......... 2.85

No. 8. For the same, 1¾ inches thick.. 4.30

No. 9. For half circle head, circle outside and square inside, windows, Fig 2, 1⅜ inches thick, 3 feet 4 inches in width and under........ 2.15

No. 10. For the same, 1¾ inches thick. 3.25

No. 11. For half circle head, circle outside and square inside, windows, Fig. 2, 1⅜ inches thick, over 3 feet 4 inches in width, panel corners.... 4.00

No. 12. For the same, 1¾ inches thick. 6.00

No. 13. For gothic head windows No. 168, 1⅜ inches thick, 3 feet 4 inches in width and under 1.75

No. 14. For the same, 1¾ inches thick. 2.60

No. 15. For gothic head windows, No. 168, 1⅜ inches thick, over 3 feet 4 inches in width 2.85

No. 16. For the same, 1¾ inches thick. 4.30

No. 17. For gothic head windows, No. 169, 1⅜ inches thick, 3 feet 4 inches in width and under 3.50

No. 18. For the same, 1¾ inches thick. 5.25

No. 19. For gothic head windows, No. 169, 1⅜ inches thick, over 3 feet 4 inches in width 5.75

ADD TO
LIST

No. 20. For the same, 1¾ inches thick. 8.60

No. 21. For peak head windows, No. 172, 1⅜ inches thick, 3 feet 4 inches in width and under 3.50

No. 22. For the same, 1¾ inches thick. 5.25

No. 23. For peak head windows, No. 172, 1⅜ inches thick, over 3 feet 4 inches in width 5.75

No. 24. For the same, 1¾ inches thick. 8.60

No. 25. For windows, sash or transoms, 1¾ inches thick, add 50 per cent to 1⅜-inch open list.

No. 26. For windows, sash or transoms, made 2¼ inches thick, add 100 per cent to 1¾-inch list.

No. 27. For 1⅛-inch two and four-light check rail windows, same price as 1⅜-inch check rail open list.

No. 28. For 1⅛-inch two and four light windows, plain rail, deduct 10 per cent from 1⅜-inch check rail open list.

No. 29. For 1⅜-inch plain rail windows, same price as 1⅜-inch check rail windows.

No. 30. For open windows made for glass 11 inches wide, same price as 12-inch.

No. 31. For open windows made for glass 13 or 13½ inches wide, same price as 14-inch.

No. 32. For bottom rails wider than 3⅜ inches and not over 4½ inches, add 15 cents to open list.

No. 33. For stiles wider than 2¼ inches, for each ¼-inch or fraction thereof add 5 per cent to list of open sash.

No. 34. For 1½-inch check rails for 1⅜-inch check windows, add 20 cents to list.

No. 35. For 1¾-inch check rails for 1¾-inch check windows, add 30 cents to list.

No. 36. For open windows, two lights, wider than 30-inch glass, add for every 4 inches or fraction thereof 20 cents list for 1⅜-inch, and 30 cents for 1¾-inch.

SASH EXTRAS—*Continued.*

No. 37. For open windows, four lights, wider than 15-inch glass, add for every four inches or fraction thereof 20 cents list for 1⅜-inch, and 30 cents for 1¾-inch.

No. 38. For open windows, eight lights, wider than 2-9 opening, add for every 4 inches or fraction thereof 20 cents list for 1⅜-inch, and 30 cents for 1¾-inch.

No. 39. For open windows, twelve lights, wider than 3-4½ opening, add for every 4 inches or fraction thereof 20 cents list for 1⅜-inch, and 30 cents for 1¾-inch.

No. 40. For open windows longer than listed lengths, add for every 4 inches or fraction thereof 20 cents for 1⅜-inch, and 30 cents for 1¾-inch.

No. 41. For open transoms and cellar sash larger than listed sizes, add 3 cents list for 1⅜-inch, and 4½ cents list for 1¾-inch, for every inch additional in either height or width.

No. 42. For 1⅜ inch single sash, open, 2, 4, 8 or 12 lights, of same sizes as windows for glass of same sizes, add to price of windows 15 cents list.

No. 43. For 1⅜ inch single sash, open, 1, 2, 4 and 6 lights, add to price of half window for glass of same sizes 15 cents list.

No. 44. For 1⅜-inch windows, sash or transoms prepared for oil finish, add 20 per cent to open list.

No. 45. For O G lugs on 1⅜-inch windows, add 15 cents to list for each sash with lugs.

No. 46. For 1⅜-inch open square marginal lights, up to 6 inches square, add for each light 10 cents list.

No. 47. For 1⅜-inch windows and sash made with numerous square, small lights, larger than 6 inches square, add 8 cents list per light.

No. 48. For 1⅜ open marginal light windows, with segment, half circle, or gothic head, add twice amount shown by the rules for similar heads, and 10 cents for each marginal light.

No. 49. For 1⅜ sash made with diamond or irregular shaped lights, add 20 cents list per light.

No. 50. For circle sash add to list for two half circles and the list of a sash of the same size.

No. 51. For oriel or cottage windows charge same price as windows same height, with extra addition for extra width.

15 and 18-LIGHT WINDOWS.

No. 52. For 15-light windows, add to list of 12-light, one-quarter.

No. 53. For 18-light windows, add to list of 12-light, one-half.

STORM SASH.

No. 54. 1⅛-inch storm sash, same price as 1⅜-inch check rail windows, same opening.

No. 55. 1⅜-inch storm sash, add 15 per cent to 1⅜-inch check rail open list.

No. 56. For ventilators in top or bottom rail, add 10 cents net.

No. 57. For swing light, add 40 cents net.

FRONT SASH, OPEN.

No. 58. Regular stiles and rails, 1⅜ inches thick, per lineal foot around opening, 10 cents list per lineal foot; 1¾ inches, 15 cents list.

No. 59. For bead stop, add 3 cents per lineal foot list.

STORE SASH.

No. 60. 3½-inch stiles, 4½-inch bottom rail, per lineal foot, 1⅜ inches, 20 cents 1¾ inches, 30 cents list.

No. 61. For price on paneling, see under store doors.

OUTSIDE BLINDS.

TWELVE-LIGHTED WINDOWS.

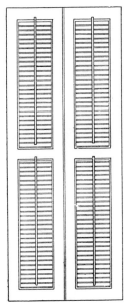

Rolling Slats.

Size of Glass.	Price, Rolling Slats.	Price, Stationary or Half Stationary Slats.		Size of Opening.			Weight.	
	1⅛ thick.	1⅛ thick.	1⅜ thick.				1⅛ in.	1⅜ in.
8x10	$1.30	$1.50	$1.75	2	4½ x 3	11	14	18
12	1.50	1.70	2.00		4	7	16	20
14	1.65	1.85	2.20		5	3	18	22
9x12	1.65	1.85	2·20	2	7½ x 4	7	18	22
13	1.75	1.95	2.30		4	11	19	24
14	1.80	2.00	2.35		5	3	20	25
15	1.95	2.15	2.55		5	7	21	25
16	2.00	2.20	2.60		5	11	23	29
10x12	1.75	1.95	2.30	2	10½ x 4	7	20	25
14	1.85	2.05	2.40		5	3	22	27
15	2.00	2.20	2.60		5	7	23	29
16	2.10	2.30	2.70		5	11	25	31
18	2.35	2.55	3.00		6	7	27	34
20	2.60	2.80	3.30		7	3	30	37

For 12 inch Twelve-Light Blinds, add 15 per cent. to list price of 10 inch.

For 1⅜ inch Rolling Slat Blinds, deduct 15 cents from list price of 1⅜ inch Stationary Slat.

Segment Head Blinds, add $1.75 per pair.   Half Circle Head Blinds, add $3.50 per pair.

Size of Blinds measure same as Check Rail Windows, with the addition of 1 inch to bottom rail for sub-sill frame, which can be cut off if necessary.

For Mullion Blinds taking same height and nearest width, add 10 per cent to list.

Sizes not listed, extra price.

EIGHT-LIGHTED WINDOWS.

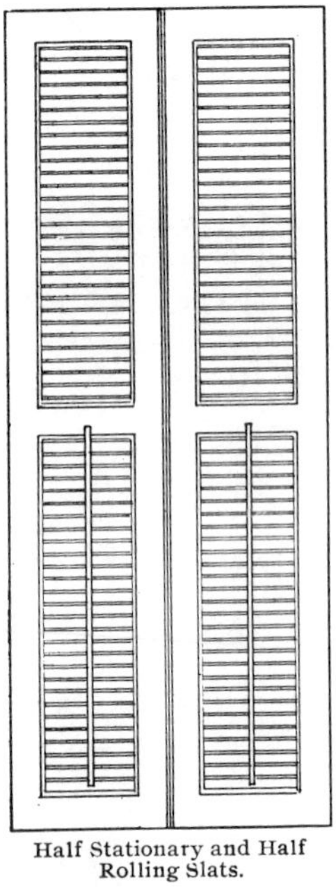

Size of Glass.	Price, Rolling Slats.	Price, Stationary or Half Stationary Slats.		Size of Opening.			Weight.	
	1⅛ thick.	1⅛ thick.	1⅜ thick.				1⅛ in.	1⅜ in.
9x12	$1.50	$1.70	$2.00	1	11 x 4	7	15	19
14	1.65	1.85	2.20		5	3	16	20
16	1.85	2.05	2.40		5	11	18	22
10x12	1.50	1.70	2.00	2	1 x 4	7	16	20
14	1 65	1.85	2.20		5	3	18	22
16	1.85	2.05	2.40		5	11	20	25
18	2.10	2.30	2.70		6	7	22	27
20	2.30	2.50	2.95		7	3	23	29
12x14	1.65	1.85	2.20	2	5 x 5	3	20	25
16	1.85	2.05	2.40		5	11	23	29
18	2.10	2.30	2.70		6	7	24	30
20	2.30	2.50	2.95		7	3	26	32

For 1⅜ inch Rolling Slat Blinds, deduct 15 cents from the list of 1⅜ inch Stationary Slat Blinds.

☞ Our Regular Stock Rolling Slat Blinds are made with O. G. Stiles. We make Square Stiles on Rolling Slat Blinds only on special orders. Stationary and Half Stationary Slat Blinds are made with Square Stiles.

For Blind Extras see page 47.

Half Stationary and Half Rolling Slats.

OUTSIDE BLINDS.

FOUR-LIGHTED WINDOWS.

Size of Glass.	Price Rolling Slats. 1⅛ thick	Price Stationary or Half Stationary Slats. 1⅛ thick	1⅜ thick	Size of Opening.				Weight. 1⅛ in.	1⅜ in.
12 x 20	$1.30	$1.50	$1.75	2	5 x 3	11		14	18
22	1.35	1.55	1.80		4	3		15	19
24	1.50	1.70	2.00		4	7		16	20
26	1.60	1.80	2.10		4	11		17	21
28	1.65	1.85	2 20		5	3		18	23
30	1.80	2.00	2.35		5	7		19	24
32	1.85	2.05	2.40		5	11		20	25
34	2.00	2.20	2.60		6	3		22	28
36	2.10	2.30	2.70		6	7		23	29
38	2.25	2.45	2.90		6	11		24	30
40	2.30	2.50	2.95		7	3		25	31
14 x 24	1.65	1.85	2.20	2	9 x 4	7		20	25
26	1.75	1.95	2.30		4	11		20	25
28	1.80	2.00	2.35		5	3		22	27
30	1.95	2.15	2.55		5	7		23	29
32	2.00	2.20	2.60		5	11		24	30
34	2.25	2.45	2.90		6	3		26	32
36	2.30	2.50	2.95		6	7		27	34
38	2.45	2.65	3.15		6	11		28	35
40	2.50	2.70	3.20		7	3		30	37
42	2.65	2.85	3.40		7	7		32	40
44	2.80	3.00	3.55		7	11		33	41
46	2.95	3.15	3.75		8	3		34	42
48	3.00	3.20	3.80		8	7		36	4 5

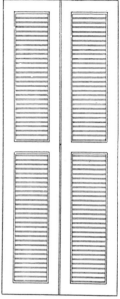

Stationary Slats.

For 15 in. glass add 10 per cent to list price of 14 in. Blinds for Two-Lighted Windows, with glass, 20, 22 or 24 in. wide, same price as Blinds for Four-Lighted Windows with 12 in. glass, same height. Blinds for Two-Lighted Windows, with glass, 26 or 28 inches wide, same price as Blinds for Four-Lighted Windows with 14 in. glass, same height. Blinds for Two-Lighted Windows, with glass, 30 in. wide, same price as Blinds for Four-Lighted Windows, with 15 in. glass, same height. Blinds for 34 in. glass and longer made three panels, unless otherwise ordered.

BLINDS FOR TWO-LIGHTED PANTRY WINDOWS.—(1⅛ inches thick.)

Size of Glass.	Price Single Blind.	Size of Opening.			Weight	Size of Glass.	Price Single Blind.	Size of Opening.			Weight
12 x 24	$1.00	1	4⅛ x 4	7	8	14 x 24	$1.10	1	6⅛ x 4	7	9
26	1.10	1	4⅛ x 4	11	9	26	1.15		4	11	10
28	1.10	1	4⅛ x 5	3	10	28	1.25		5	3	11
30	1.15	1	4⅛ x 5	7	10	30	1.30		5	7	12
32	1.25	1	4⅛ x 5	11	11	32	1.30		5	11	13
34	1.35	1	4⅛ x 6	3	12	34	1.45		6	3	14
36	1.45	1	4⅛ x 6	7	13	36	1.50		6	7	14
						40	1.65		7	3	16

BLINDS FOR FOUR-LIGHTED PANTRY WINDOWS.—(1⅛ inches thick.)

Size of Glass.	Price Single Blind	Size of Opening.			Weight	Size of Glass	Price Single Blind	Size of Opening.			Weight
8 x 10	$0.95	1	0⅛ x 3	11	7	10 x 12	$1.00	1	2⅛ x 4	7	8
9 x 12	1.00	1	1⅛ x 4	7	8	14	1.10		5	3	10
14	1.10	1	1⅛ x 5	3	9	16	1.25		5	11	11
16	1.25	1	1⅛ x 5	11	10	18	1.45		6	7	13
18	1.45	1	1⅛ x 6	7	11						

For 12 and 14 inch, see Two-Light List above, same height.
Sizes not listed, extra price.
For Blind Extras, see page 47.

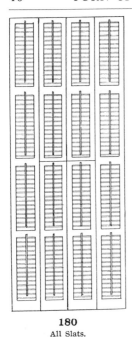

180
All Slats.

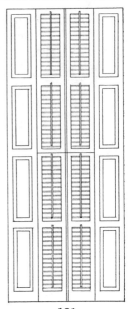

181
½ Panels, ½ Slats.

INSIDE BLINDS.

DIRECTIONS FOR ORDERING.

First—In all cases give the exact outside measure of Blinds wanted.

Second—Give the number of folds.

Third—State if Blinds are to be all slats, or half panels and half slats.

Fourth—State distance from top of window to center of meeting rail of sash, or where Blinds are to be cut.

Fifth—Give thickness of Blinds.

Sixth—If Blinds fold in pockets, give size of pockets.

Seventh—State if Blinds are to be painted or finished in oil.

Eighth—If for oil finish, extra price.

PRICES.

1⅛ inches O. G. Stiles and Rails, Bevel Panel or Rolling Slats, measuring height of window, per foot:

Two-fold, up to and including 2 feet wide _____ $0.75
Three-fold, up to and including 2 feet 11 inches wide _____ .95
Four-fold, up to and including 2 feet 11 inches wide _____ 1.15
Four-fold, over 2 feet 11 inches wide and under 4 feet _____ 1.30
Six-fold, over 2 feet 11 inches wide and under 4 feet _____ 1.75

The above prices are for White Pine.

If hardwood, such as Cherry, Ash, Maple, or Black Walnut are wanted, we charge extra price.

We make Inside Blinds that are not excelled, either in workmanship or style, in any market.

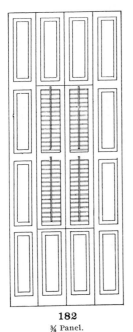

182
¾ Panel.

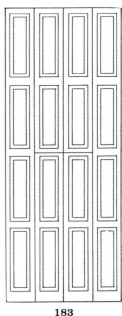

183
All Panel.

BLIND EXTRAS.

Irregular and Intermediate Sizes same as next larger listed size.
All items are list unless specified net.

No. 1. Window and door blinds wider than listed sizes, add 15 per cent for every 4 inches or fraction thereof.

No. 2. Window blinds longer than listed sizes, for every 2 inches, 1⅛-inch, add 20 cents; 1⅜-inch, add 25 cents.

No. 3. For 15-inch glass add 10 per cent to list price of 14-inch.

No. 4. Blinds for two-lighted windows, with glass 20, 22 or 24 inches wide, same price as blinds for four-lighted windows with 12-inch glass, same height.

No. 5. Blinds for two-lighted windows with glass 26 or 28 inches wide, same price as blinds for four-lighted windows with 14-inch glass, same height.

No. 6. Blinds for two-lighted windows, with glass 30 inches wide, same price as blinds for four lighted windows with 15-inch glass, same height.

No. 7. Blinds for 34-inch glass and longer made in three panels, unless otherwise ordered.

No. 8. For 1⅜-inch rolling slat blinds deduct 15 cents from the list of 1⅜-inch stationary slat blinds.

No. 9. Our regular stock rolling slat blinds are made with O G stiles.

No. 10. We make square stiles on rolling slat blinds only on special orders.

No. 11. Stationary and half stationary blinds are made with square stiles.

No. 12. Mullion blinds, add to price of pairs, same description, 10 per cent.

No. 13. For segment heads add $1.75. For half circle heads add $3.50. For circle corner heads add $3.50. For elliptic heads add $3.50. For gothic heads add $3.50.

No. 14 Solid mould panel shutters, add 25 per cent to list of stationary slat blinds, same thickness

No. 15. For solid mould panel shutters, add 25 per cent to list of stationary slat blinds of same thickness.

No. 16. For shutters, bead and butt outside, solid mould one side, add to list of stationary slat blinds of same size, 45 per cent.

No. 17. For stiles over 1¾ inches wide add 20 cents list per pair for every half inch.

No. 18. In ordering, state if blinds are to be a pair or single piece, to each opening.

No. 19. All door blinds are made in pairs and rabbeted, same as window blinds, unless otherwise ordered.

No. 20. Door blinds made in one piece 10 per cent extra.

INSIDE SLIDING BLINDS.

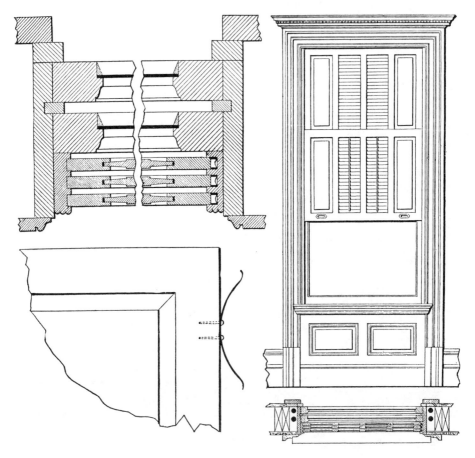

Above section shows that no special frame is required to use our sliding blinds. The guideway is fastened on pulley stile, acting as a stop for the sash,

These sliding blinds are made ½-inch in thickness, and though constructed of light material possess great strength and lasting qualities.

Can be closed with the window raised and cannot blow open or rattle, thus giving the best medium of ventilation.

They do not interfere with curtains or window ornaments, and admit light and air from any part of the window.

These blinds are specially made to order in the white or finished complete; either varnished in the natural colors of the different woods or stained and varnished, or wood filled and cabinet or rubbed finish. All trimmings and hardware we furnish, which is included in the price of blinds given on page 49.

LIST PRICE INSIDE SLIDING BLINDS.

Per lineal foot in height, including Guideways and all necessary Hardware.

WOOD AND FINISH

White Pine, Poplar, Cypress, Basswood, Spruce and Yellow Pine.	2 DIV. Under 24 in.	3 DIV. 24 to 32 in.	4 DIV. 32 to 40 in.	5 DIV. 40 to 48 in.	6 DIV. 48 to 60 in.
In White (no finish)	$0.65	$0.75	$0.85	$1.00	$1.15
Varnish Finish (2 coat)	.75	.90	1.05	1.20	1.40
Varnish Finish (3 coat)	.80	.95	1.15	1.30	1.55
Oil Rubbed Cabinet Finish	.85	1.05	1.20	1.40	1.65

Plain Oak, Common Ash, Red Gum (Hazel), Maple and Chestnut.					
In White (no finish)	.75	.85	1.00	1.10	1.25
Varnish Finish (3 coat)	.90	1.05	1.25	1.50	1.75
Oil Rubbed Cabinet Finish	1.00	1.20	1.40	1.60	1.85

Quartered Oak, Butternut, Quartered Sycamore, California Red Wood and White Ash.					
In White (no finish)	.85	.95	1.10	1.25	1.40
Varnish Finish (3 coat)	1.00	1.15	1.35	1.60	1.85
Oil Rubbed Cabinet Finish	1.10	1.30	1.50	1.75	2.00

Black Walnut, Cherry, Curly Birch and Bird's Eye Maple.					
In White (no finish)	1.00	1.10	1.30	1.60	1.90
Varnish Finish (3 coat)	1.15	1.30	1.55	1.85	2.15
Oil Rubbed Cabinet Finish	1.25	1.45	1.65	2.00	2.40

Mahogany.					
In White (no finish)	1.10	1.25	1.45	1.80	2.10
Varnish Finish (3 coat)	1.25	1.50	1.75	2.10	2.45
Oil Rubbed Cabinet Finish	1.35	1.65	1.90	2.30	2.70

For combination of woods average the prices of the several woods.

Convex Blinds _____$4.00 per window extra.
Gothic, Segment, Oval or Circle Tops_____ 2.00 "   "   "
Extra Heavy Lifts, Bronze or Old Copper (put on with screws)_____10 cents each.
Drop Pulls, Bronze or Old Copper_____15 "   "
Concealed Metal Operator, per division_____12 "   "

PLEASE NOTE—That above list prices include all necessary Hardware or Trimming, and in comparing cost with folding blinds or other makes of sliding blinds, this should be taken into consideration. **Above prices subject to discount.**

Will make net estimates on weighted blinds or on special designs from architects' details.

DIRECTIONS FOR ORDERING.

Give the exact measurement of the opening which the blinds are to fill. Where guideways take the place of stops, state distance from face of casing to inner face of lower sash. If windows are circle head or segment inside, send exact pattern or give radius. Full information for adjusting these blinds accompany each order.

VENETIAN BLINDS.

Above cut shows the blinds as used in a Double or Mullion Window.

In the left hand window the blind is partly raised, the slats being arranged to exclude the light.   In the right hand window the blind is lowered, with upper slats arranged to admit light, and the lower ones to exclude it.   In the blind each slat is independent in its action, consequently any number of slats can be closed or left open at will and in any desired part of the blind.   The control of light and air is therefore practically absolute in these blinds.

Give opening size wanted filled.

LIST PRICES VENETIAN BLINDS.

CLASSIFICATION OF WOODS.	Price per square foot.	
	2⅜ inch Slats.	2 inch Slats.
Spruce, Whitewood, Linden and Yellow Pine, finished natural, stained to imitate Hardwoods, or painted in dark colors	$0.19	$0.21
Painted in light colors or tints	.21	.23
Painted in enamels	.24	.26
Enameled, rubbed between coats	.38	.40
White Pine, Cypress, Hazel, Plain Oak, Ash, Elm, Chestnut and ordinary Maple,	.21	.23
Plain Birch and Butternut	.22	.24
Quartered Oak and Quartered Sycamore	.24	.26
Cherry, Black Walnut, California Redwood and White Ash	.30	.32
Red Mahogany, Curly Birch, Bird's Eye and White Maple	.38	.40

With the exception of Painted and Enameled work, the above prices are in Varnish Finish. Add to above list for ordinary Rubbed Finish 3 cents per square foot.

No Blind figured to contain less than 15 square feet.

Above prices subject to discount.

Our Venetian Blinds do not require any special frame, are easily applied, and are the most simply constructed on the market. Venetian Blinds do not interfere with curtains or draperies, and are becoming more popular every year.

DOOR BLINDS and SWING WATER CLOSET DOORS.

DOOR BLINDS.

Only carried in stock in pairs.

SIZE.					Thickness.	Price.
2	6	x	6	6	1⅛	$3.15
2	8	x	6	8	"	3.30
2	10	x	6	10	"	3.50
3	0	x	7	0	"	3.65

1⅜ inches thick, add to list price of 1⅛ inches, 20 per cent.

In ordering, state if Blinds are to be a pair or single piece, to each opening.

All Door Blinds are made in pairs and rabbeted, same as Window Blinds, unless otherwise ordered.

Sizes not listed, extra price.

Door Blinds made rolling slats unless otherwise ordered. If made stationary slats, extra price.

SWING WATER CLOSET DOORS.

184

184 B

185

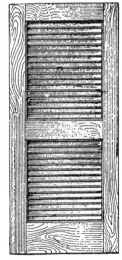

186

LL DOORS shown in succeeding pages are made of well seasoned lumber, mortised together throughout, and none but good material used. All doors, except odd work, are made one inch longer, and ⅜ inch wider than size given on list.

All 1⅛ doors are made with 3-inch stiles unless otherwise specified.

All quotations on doors are for regular stock sizes which are :

2 feet 6 inches x 6 feet 6 inches.

2 "   8 "   x 6 "   8   "

2 "   8 "   x 6 " 10   "

2 "   8 "   x 7 "

2 " 10 "   x 6 " 10   "

2 " 10 "   x 7 "

3 "   x 7 "

EXTRAS.

2 feet 8 inches x 7 feet 6 inches _____ ⎫ Add 50c per dozen to price
2 feet 10 inches x 7 feet 6 inches _____ ⎭ of stock sizes.

2 feet 8 inches x 8 feet _____ ⎫ Add $1.00 per dozen to
2 feet 10 inches x 8 feet _____ ⎭ price of stock sizes.

For doors over 8 feet add $1.50 per dozen to price of stock sizes.

For 1⅛ doors add 40c per dozen.

For odd sized doors add 25c each to price of regular stock sizes.

For painted doors add 25c per dozen.

For hardwood doors add $3.00 per dozen.

For 4 panel doors add 15c per dozen.

Our doors are not liable to warp, as our stiles are all paired.

SCREEN DOORS.

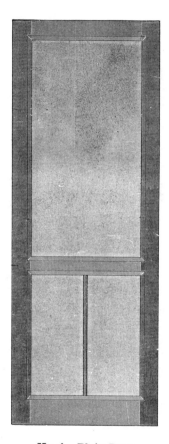

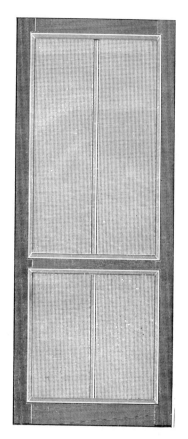

No. 4. Plain Door.
⅞x 3 inch stile.
Per dozen_____⅞, $8.20; 1⅛, $8.87
Finished with walnut stain.

No. 3½.
Made with stiles 1⅛x3 in. and painted green.
Price for stock sizes, per dozen_____
_____⅞, $8.87; 1⅛, $9.07

SUBJECT TO DISCOUNT.

SCREEN DOORS.

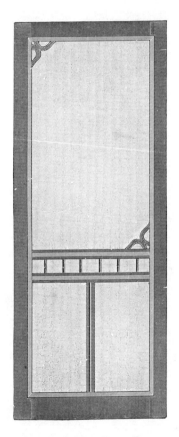

No. 5. Fancy.

Finished with one coat of varnish.
Made with 4 in. stiles.

Price for stock sizes_____$10.00

No. 20.

Finished with one coat of varnish.
Made with 4 in. stiles.

Price for stock sizes_____$10.33

SUBJECT TO DISCOUNT.

SCREEN DOORS.

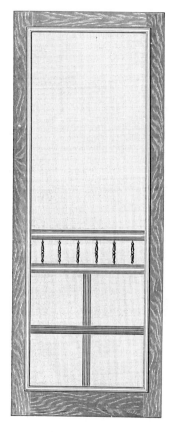

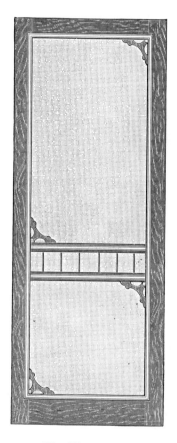

No. 14. Fancy.

Finished in two coats of varnish.
Made with 4 in. stile.

Price for stock sizes_____$12.67

No. 17. Fancy.

Finished with mahogany stain and varnished.
Made with 4 in. stile.

Price for stock sizes_____$12.67

SUBJECT TO DISCOUNT.

SCREEN DOORS.

No. 10. Fancy.

Finished with two coats of varnish.
Made with 4 in. stile.

Price for stock sizes_____$12.67

No. 15. Fancy.

Finished with two coats of varnish.
Made with 4 in. stile.

Price for stock sizes_____$13.00

SUBJECT TO DISCOUNT.

SCREEN DOORS.

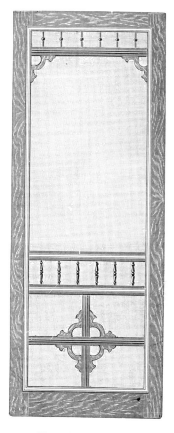

No. 9. Fancy.

Finished with two coats of varnish.
⅞ doors are made with 4 in. stile.
1⅛ doors are made with 3 in. stile.

Price for stock sizes_____$14.67

No. 19. Fancy.

Finished with two coats of varnish.
⅞ doors have 4 in. stile.
1⅛ doors have 3 in. stile.

Price for stock sizes_____$14.67

SUBJECT TO DISCOUNT.

SECTIONS OF STICKING.

For Solid Moulded Doors.

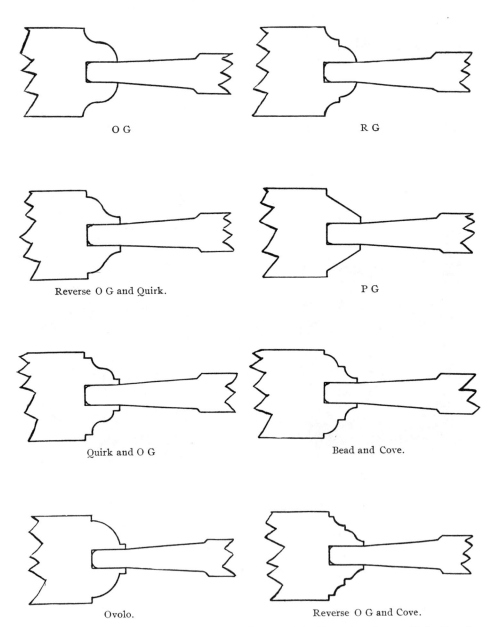

O G

R G

Reverse O G and Quirk.

P G

Quirk and O G

Bead and Cove.

Ovolo.

Reverse O G and Cove.

Our standard sticking for white pine doors is the O G, and unless otherwise specified, all orders are entered accordingly.

SECTION OF MOULDED DOORS.

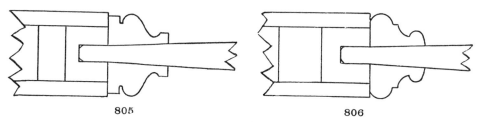

805   806

Showing styles of flush mouldings.

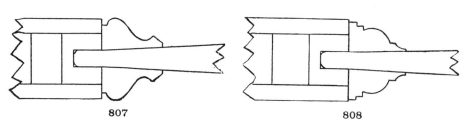

807   808

Showing styles of flush mouldings.

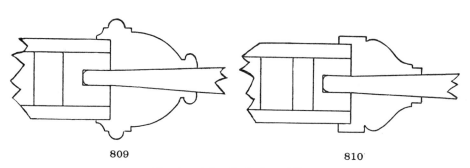

809   810

Showing styles of raised mouldings.

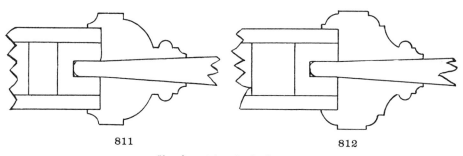

811   812

Showing styles of raised mouldings.

In ordering, give style of moulding required, referring to numbers on this page.

SECTIONS OF DOOR AND WINDOW FRAMES.

STANDARD FRAMES FOR FRAME BUILDING.

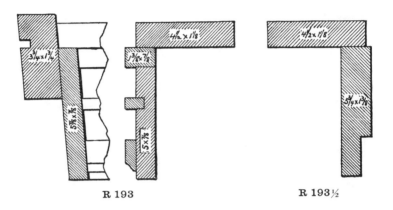

R 193   R 193½

STANDARD FRAMES FOR BRICK BUILDING.

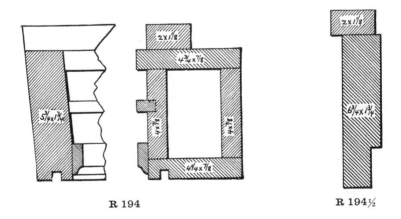

R 194   R 194½

Write for prices, giving sizes and width of jambs.

200—O. G. FOUR-PANEL DOORS.

RAISED PANELS BOTH SIDES.

SIZE.	Thickness, Inches.	Price A Quality.	Price B Quality.	Price C Quality	SIZE.	Thickness, Inches.	Price A Quality.	Price B Quality.	Price C Quality.
2 0 x 6 0	1⅛	$2.80	$2.65	$1.95	2 4 x 7 0	1⅜	$4.75	$4.25	
2 6 x 6 0	"	3.30	3.15		2 6 x 7 0	"	4.80	4.30	
2 8 x 6 0	"	3.55	3.40		2 8 x 7 0	"	4.95	4.40	
3 0 x 6 0	"	3.75	3.55		2 10 x 7 0	"	5.15	4.55	
2 4 x 6 4	"	3.15	3.00		3 0 x 7 0	"	5.25	4.60	$3.15
2 0 x 6 6	"	3.00	2.85		2 6 x 7 6	"	5.60	5.05	
2 6 x 6 6	"	3.30	3.15	2.10	2 8 x 7 6	"	5.75	5.15	
2 6 x 6 8	"	3.50	3.30		2 10 x 7 6	"	5.90	5.25	
2 8 x 6 8	"	3.50	3.30	2.30	3 0 x 7 6	"	6.05	5.35	
2 10 x 6 10	"	4.15	3.95	2.65	2 6 x 8 0	"	6.55	5.95	
3 0 x 7 0	"	4.65	4.45	3.10	2 8 x 8 0	"	6.70	6.05	
2 0 x 6 0	1⅜	3.25	2.80		3 0 x 8 0	"	7.00	6.25	
2 6 x 6 0	"	3.80	3.30		3 0 x 8 6	"	8.15	7.35	
2 8 x 6 0	"	4.00	3.45		3 0 x 9 0	"	9.50	8.65	
3 0 x 6 0	"	4.30	3.65		2 6 x 6 6	1¾	6.35	5.50	
2 4 x 6 4	"	3.65	3.15		2 8 x 6 8	"	6.70	5.75	
2 6 x 6 4	"	3.80	3.30		2 10 x 6 10	"	7.95	6.85	
2 0 x 6 6	"	3.45	3.00		2 6 x 7 0	"	8.00	7.20	
2 4 x 6 6	"	3.80	3.30		2 8 x 7 0	"	8.25	7.35	
2 6 x 6 6	"	3.80	3.30	2.15	2 10 x 7 0	"	8.60	7.60	
2 8 x 6 6	"	4.00	3.45		3 0 x 7 0	"	8.75	7.70	
2 10 x 6 6	"	4.60	4.00		2 6 x 7 6	"	9.35	8.45	
3 0 x 6 6	"	4.70	4.05		2 8 x 7 6	"	9.60	8.60	
2 0 x 6 8	"	3.60	3.15		2 10 x 7 6	"	9.85	8.75	
2 4 x 6 8	"	3.90	3.40		3 0 x 7 6	"	10.10	8.95	
2 6 x 6 8	"	4.00	3.45		2 6 x 8 0	"	10.95	9.95	
2 8 x 6 8	"	4.00	3.45	2.40	2 8 x 8 0	"	11.20	10.10	
3 0 x 6 8	"	5.15	4.50		3 0 x 8 0	"	11.70	10.45	
2 6 x 6 10	"	4.45	3.95		3 0 x 8 6	"	13.60	12.25	
2 8 x 6 10	"	4.60	4.05		3 0 x 9 0	"	15.85	14.45	
2 10 x 6 10	"	4.75	4.15	2.75					

O. G. FOUR-PANEL INCH DOORS.

RAISED PANELS ONE SIDE.

SIZE.	Thickness, Inches.	Price A Quality.	Price B Quality.
2 0 x 6 0	1	$2.05	$1.90
2 4 x 6 4	"	2.30	2.15
2 0 x 6 6	"	2.15	2.05
2 6 x 6 6	"	2.30	2.15
2 8 x 6 8	"	2.60	2.45

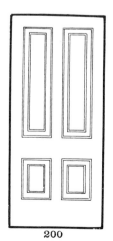

200

Inch Doors finish up about 1⅜ inch thick and have Bevel Raised Panels one side.

For Doors prepared for Oil Finish, hand-smoothed, add $2.60 to list.

For Stock Doors selected for Oil Finish, machine-smoothed, add 50 cents to list.

Sizes not listed, extra price.

For Door Extras see pages 72–73.

O G 5-PANEL DOORS.

201

Size of Opening.				A Quality, 1⅜ in. thick.	B Quality 1⅜ in. thick.	A Quality, 1¾ in. thick.	B Quality 1¾ in. thick.
2	6 x 6	6		$4.00	$3.50	$6.55	$5.70
2	6 x 6	8		4.20	3.65	6.90	5.95
2	8 x 6	8		4.20	3.65	6.90	5.95
2	6 x 6	10		4.65	4.15	7.65	6.80
2	8 x 6	10		4.80	4.25	7.90	6.95
2	10 x 6	10		4.95	4.35	8.15	7.05
2	6 x 7	0		5.00	4.50	8.20	7.40
2	8 x 7	0		5.15	4.60	8.45	7.55
2	10 x 7	0		5.35	4.75	8 80	7.80
3	0 x 7	0		5.45	4.80	8.95	7.90
2	6 x 7	6		5.80	5.25	9.55	8.65
2	8 x 7	6		5.95	5.35	9.80	8.80
2	10 x 7	6		6.10	5.45	10.05	8.95
3	0 x 7	6		6.25	5.55	10.30	9.15
3	0 x 8	0		7.20	6.45	11.90	10.65
3	0 x 8	6		8.35	7.55	13.80	12.45
3	0 x 9	0		9.70	8.85	16.05	14.65

O G 5-CROSS PANEL DOORS.

202½

Size of Opening				A Quality 1⅜ in. thick	B Quality 1⅜ in. thick	A Quality 1¾ in. thick	B Quality 1¾ in. thick
2	6 x 6	6		$4.20	$3.70	$6.75	$5.90
2	6 x 6	8		4.40	3.85	------	------
2	8 x 6	8		4·40	3.85	7.10	6.15
2	6 x 6	10		4.85	4.35	------	------
2	8 x 6	10		5.00	4.45	------	------
2	10 x 6	10		5.15	4.55	8.35	7.25
2	6 x 7	0		5.20	4.70	8.40	7.60
2	8 x 7	0		5.35	4.80	8.65	7.75
2	10 x 7	0		5.55	4.95	9.00	8.00
3	0 x 7	0		5.65	5.00	9.15	8.10
2	6 x 7	6		6.00	5.45	9.75	8.85
2	8 x 7	6		6.15	5.55	10.00	9.00
2	10 x 7	6		6.30	5.65	10.25	9.15
3	0 x 7	6		6.45	5.75	10.50	9.35
3	0 x 8	0		7.40	6.65	12.10	10.85
3	0 x 8	6		8.55	7.75	14.00	12.65
3	0 x 9	0		9.90	9.05	16.25	14 85

For doors made with three cross panels and two perpendicular panels same as five cross panel doors.

For door extras see pages 72 and 73.

Sizes not listed extra price.

BEAD and COVE 5-PANEL DOORS.

202

Size of Opening				A Quality 1⅜ in. Thick	B Quality 1⅜ in. Thick.	A Quality 1¾ in. Thick.	B Quality 1¾ in. thick.
2	6	x	6	6	$4.15	$3.65	$6.70	$5.85
2	6	x	6	8	4.35	3.80	7.05	6.10
2	8	x	6	8	4.35	3.80	7.05	6.10
2	6	x	6	10	4.80	4.30	7.80	6.95
2	8	x	6	10	4.95	4.40	8.05	7.10
2	10	x	6	10	5.10	4.50	8.30	7.20
2	6	x	7	0	5.15	4.65	8.35	7.55
2	8	x	7	0	5.30	4.75	8.60	7.70
2	10	x	7	0	5.50	4.90	8.95	7.95
3	0	x	7	0	5.60	4.95	9.10	8.05
2	6	x	7	6	5.95	5.40	9.70	8.80
2	8	x	7	6	6.10	5.50	9.95	8.95
2	10	x	7	6	6.25	5.60	10.20	9.10
3	0	x	7	6	6.40	5.70	10.45	9.30
3	0	x	8	0	7.35	6.60	12.05	10.80
3	0	x	8	6	8.50	7.70	13.95	12.60
3	0	x	9	0	9.85	9.00	16.20	14.80

BEAD and COVE 5-CROSS PANEL DOORS.

202½

Size of Opening.				A Quality, 1⅜ inches thick.	B Quality, 1⅜ inches thick.	A Quality, 1¾ inches thick.	B Quality, 1¾ inches thick.
2	6	x	6	6	$4.35	$3.85	$6.90	$6.05
2	6	x	6	8	4.55	4.00	------	------
2	8	x	6	8	4.55	4.00	7.25	6.30
2	6	x	6	10	5.00	4.50	------	------
2	8	x	6	10	5.15	4.60	------	------
2	10	x	6	10	5.30	4.70	8.50	7.40
2	6	x	7	0	5.35	4.85	8.55	7.75
2	8	x	7	0	5.50	4.95	8.80	7.90
2	10	x	7	0	5.70	5.10	9.15	8.15
3	0	x	7	0	5.80	5.15	9.30	8.25
2	6	x	7	6	6.15	5.60	9.90	9.00
2	8	x	7	6	6.30	5.70	10.15	9.15
2	10	x	7	6	6.45	5.80	10.40	9.30
3	0	x	7	6	6.60	5.90	10.65	9.50
3	0	x	8	0	7.55	6.80	12.25	11.00
3	0	x	8	6	8.70	7.90	14.15	12.80
3	0	x	9	0	10.05	9.20	16.40	15.00

For doors made with three cross panels and two perpendicular panels same as five cross panel doors.

For door extras see pages 72 and 73.

Sizes not listed, extra price.

4-PANEL MOULDED DOORS.

Flush or Sunk Moulding.

203

Size of Opening.	Moulded One Side. 1⅜ in. Thick.	Moulded Two Sides. 1⅜ in. Thick.	Moulded One Side, 1¾ in. Thick.	Moulded Two Sides, 1¾ in. Thick.
2 6 x 6 6	$4.50	$4.95	$7.20	$7.70
2 6 x 6 8	4.75	5.20	7.60	8.15
2 8 x 6 8	4.75	5.20	7.60	8.15
2 10 x 6 10	5.55	6.05	8.90	9.50
2 6 x 7 0	5.65	6.20	9.05	9.70
2 8 x 7 0	5.80	6.35	9.30	9.95
2 10 x 7 0	6.00	6.55	9.65	10.30
3 0 x 7 0	6.10	6.65	9.80	10.45
2 6 x 7 6	6.55	7.15	10.50	11.20
2 8 x 7 6	6.70	7.30	10.75	11.45
2 10 x 7 6	6.85	7.45	11.00	11.70
3 0 x 7 6	7.00	7.60	11.25	11.95
3 0 x 8 0	8.05	8.70	12.95	13.70
3 0 x 8 6	9.30	10.00	15.00	15.85

4-PANEL MOULDED DOORS.

Raised Moulding.

204

Size of Opening.	Moulded One Side. 1⅜ in. Thick.	Moulded Two Sides. 1⅜ in. Thick.	Moulded One Side 1¾ in. Thick.	Moulded Two Sides. 1¾ in. Thick.
2 6 x 6 6	$5.20	$6.10	$8.05	$9.05
2 6 x 6 8	5.50	6.40	8.50	9.60
2 8 x 6 8	5.50	6.40	8.50	9.60
2 10 x 6 10	6.35	7.35	9.85	11.05
2 6 x 7 0	6.50	7.60	10.10	11.40
2 8 x 7 0	6.65	7.75	10.35	11.65
2 10 x 7 0	6.85	7.95	10.70	12.00
3 0 x 7 0	6.95	8.05	10.85	12.15
2 6 x 7 6	7.50	8.70	11.65	13.05
2 8 x 7 6	7.65	8.85	11.90	13.30
2 10 x 7 6	7.80	9.00	12.15	13.55
3 0 x 7 6	7.95	9.15	12.40	13.80
3 0 x 8 0	9.10	10.40	14.20	15.70
3 0 x 8 6	10.45	11.85	16.40	18.10

Sizes not listed, extra price.
For Door Extras, see pages 72, 73.

O G SASH DOORS.

Raised Panels, Two Sides.

210 and 211. List Prices, 1⅜ Inches Thick.

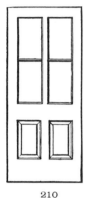

Size of Opening.	210 Open.	210 Glazed.	211 Open.	211 Glazed.
2 6 x 6 6	$4.15	$5.55	$4.15	$5.75
2 8 x 6 8	4.35	6.00	4.35	6.20
2 10 x 6 10	5.10	7.00	5.10	7.20
2 6 x 7 0	5.15	6.70	5.15	7.00
3 0 x 7 0	5.60	7.85	5.60	8.20
3 0 x 7 6	6.40	9.10	6.40	9.90
3 0 x 8 0	7.35	10.35	7.35	12.10

Sash Doors, 1½ inch thick, same price as 1⅜ inch.

For price of 1¾ inch O G Sash Doors, add the difference between 1⅜ and 1¾ inch O G Four-Panel Doors, same size, see table on page 74.

Sizes not listed, extra price.

210   211

212 and 213. Raised Panels, Two Sides.

List Prices, 1⅜ Inches Thick.

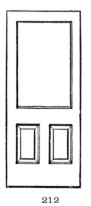

Size of Opening.	212 Open.	212 Gl. D. S.	213 Open.	213 Glazed.
2 6 x 6 6	$4.15	$6.75	$4.90	$6.35
2 8 x 6 8	4.35	7.50	5.10	6.70
2 10 x 6 10	5.10	8.70	5.85	7.70
2 6 x 7 0	5.15	8.75	5.90	7.85
3 0 x 7 0	5.60	10.25	6.35	8.60
3 0 x 7 6	6.40	11.95	7.15	10.05
3 0 x 8 0	7.35	13.00	8.10	12.00

For price of 1¾ inch O G Sash Doors, add the difference between 1⅜ and 1¾ inch O G Four-Panel Doors, same size, see table on page 74.

Sizes not listed, extra price.

212   213

Prices of O G Sash Doors do not include beads for glass; for prices of such, see Door Extras, pages 72-73, notes 19 and 20.

O G SASH DOORS.

Raised Panels, Two Sides.

212½ and 214. List Prices, 1⅜ Inches Thick.

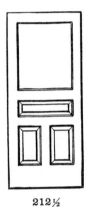

SIZE.			212½ Open.	212½ Gl. D. S.	214 Open.	214 Glazed.
2	6 x 6	6	$4.35	$6.65	$4.55	$6.85
2	8 x 6	8	4.55	7.15	4.75	7.35
2	10 x 6	10	5.30	8.45	5.50	8.65
2	6 x 7	0	5.35	7.95	5.55	8.15
3	0 x 7	0	5.80	9.40	6.00	9.60
3	0 x 7	6	6.60	11.20	6.80	11.40
3	0 x 8	0	7.55	13.10	7.75	13.30

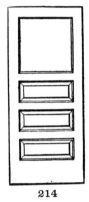

For 1¾ price add difference between 1⅜ and 1¾ Four-Panel O G Door, same size, see page 60.

212½

214

215 and 215½. Raised Panel, Two Sides.

List Price, 1⅜ Inches Thick.

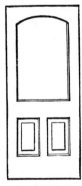

SIZE.			215 Open.	215 Gl. D. S.	215½ Open.	215½ Gl. D. S.
2	6 x 6	6	$4.90	$7.50	$4.90	$7.50
2	8 x 6	8	5.10	8.25	5.10	8.25
2	10 x 6	10	5.85	9.45	5.85	9.45
2	6 x 7	0	5.90	9.50	5.90	9.50
3	0 x 7	0	6.35	11.00	6.35	11.00
3	0 x 7	6	7.15	12.70	7.15	12.70
3	0 x 8	0	8.10	13.75	8.10	13.75

215

215½

For price of 1¾ inch O. G. Sash Doors, add the difference between 1⅜ and 1¾ inch O. G. Four-Panel Doors, same size, see table on page 74.

Sizes not listed, extra price.

FRONT DOORS.

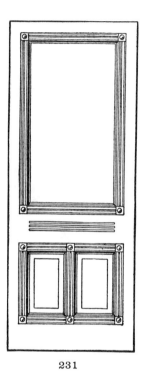

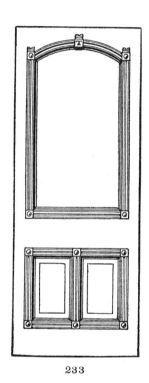

231   233

List Price 1⅜ Inches Thick.

Size of Opening.				231		233	
				Open	Glazed D. S.	Open.	Glazed D. S.
2	8 x 6	8		$ 6.30	$ 9.45	$ 7.30	$10.45
2	10 x 6	10		7.05	10.65	8.05	11.65
2	8 x 7	0		7.35	10.95	8.35	11.95
3	0 x 7	0		7.75	12.40	8.75	13.40
3	0 x 7	6		8.80	14.35	9.80	15.35
3	0 x 8	0		10.00	15.65	11.00	16.65

For prices of 1¾-inch doors add to above list the difference between 1⅜ and 1¾-inch four-panel O G Doors, same size, see table on page 74.

Sizes not listed, extra price.

FRONT DOORS.

307

298

List Price, 1⅜ Inches Thick.

Size of Opening.				307		298	
				Open.	Glazed, D. S.	Open.	Glazed, D. S.
2	8 x 6	8		$5.15	$8.30	$5.45	$7.30
2	10 x 6	10		5.90	9.50	6.20	8.55
2	8 x 7	0		6.10	9.70	6.40	8.70
3	0 x 7	0		6.40	10.60	6.70	9.25
3	0 x 7	6		--------	--------	7.50	11.10
3	0 x 8	0		--------	--------	8.45	12.65

For price of 1¾ inch doors, add to above list the difference between 1⅜ and 1¾ inch four-panel O. G. Doors, same size, see table on page 74.

Sizes not listed, extra price.

FRONT DOORS.

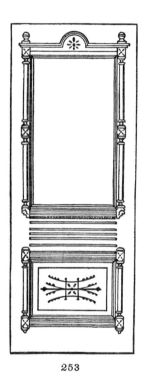

253

406

List Price, 1⅜ Inches Thick.

Size of Opening.					253		406	
					Open.	Glazed, D. S.	Open.	Glazed, D. S.
2	8	x	6	8	$9.15	$13.15	$5.25	$9.20
2	10	x	6	10	9.86	14.45	5.95	10.45
3	0	x	7	0	10.35	14.95	6.35	10.95

For price of door No. 406, 1¾ thick, add to above list the difference between 1⅜ and 1¾ inch 4 panel O G doors, same size; and for door No. 253, 1¾ thick, add the difference between four panel O G Doors, same size, see table on page 74.

DOOR EXTRAS.

Irregular and Intermediate Sizes same as next larger listed size.
All items are list unless specified net.

No. 1. For doors over three feet in width up to 3 feet 6 inches, add 20 per cent to list of 3-foot door, same height.

No. 2. For doors over 3 feet 6 inches in width, and not wider than 4 feet, add 50 per cent to list of 3-foot door, same height.

No. 3. For doors over 4 feet in width, and not wider than 5 feet, same as two 3-foot doors, same height.

No. 4. For doors over 5 feet in width, and not exceeding 5 feet 6 inches wide, add 15 per cent to the sum of the list of two 3-foot doors, same height.

No. 5. For doors over 5 feet 6 inches in width, and not exceeding 6 feet wide, add 25 per cent to the sum of the list of two 3-foot doors, same height.

No. 6. For doors over 6 feet in width, and not exceeding 6 feet 6 inches wide, add 20 per cent to the list on a 6-foot door, as made by rule 5.

No. 7. For doors over 6 feet 6 inches wide, and not exceeding 7 feet in width, add 30 per cent to the list on a 6-foot door, as made by rule 5.

No. 8. For doors 1⅞ inches thick, add 40 per cent to 1¾-inch list.

No. 9. For doors 2¼ inches thick, add 60 per cent to 1¾-inch list.

No. 10. For AAA, doors free from sap, machine smoothed for oil finish, add $2.00 to list. For hand smoothing doors for oil finish, add 60 cents additional.

No. 11. For AA, selected stock doors, machine smoothed for oil finish, add 50 cents to list.

No. 12. For doors, 1⅜, with segment panels, O G, add $2.00 to list; 1¾, $3.00.

No. 13. For 1⅜-inch doors, circle top, elliptic, gothic or peak head, either single or in pairs, add $2.90 each door list. For 1¾-inch doors add $4.35 each door list.

No. 14. For double astragal for sliding doors, add 50 cents net.

No. 15. For single astragal for folding doors, add 25 cents net.

No. 16. For rabbeting stock door on solid, per pair, add 30 cents net.

No. 17. For astragal joint on solid for doors in pairs with one stile for each door extra width, add 50 cents net per pair.

No. 18. For rabbeting and beading, folding doors, made extra width for rabbeting add per pair 50 cents net.

No. 19. For beads around glass, on one-light square-top sash doors, add 10 cents net This does not include regular listed cottage doors.

No. 20. For beads around glass, on two or more light square-head sash doors, add for each light 7 cents net.

No. 21. For banding sliding doors, per pair, add $2.90 list.

No. 22. For ovolo or P G five-panel doors, use bead and cove five-panel list.

No. 23. Bevel panels for doors are standard.

No. 24. Doors over 3 feet up to 3 feet 6 inches, may be made 3 panels wide.

No. 25. Doors over 3 feet 6 inches up to 4 feet, may be made 3 or 4 panels wide.

No. 26. Doors over 4 feet up to 5 feet, may be made 4 panels wide.

DOOR EXTRAS—*Continued.*

No. 27. Doors over 5 feet up to 7 feet, may be made 5 or 6 panels wide.

No. 28. Additional panels 20 cents each list.

No. 29. Horizontal panels, or part horizontal (more than one) and part vertical, add 40 cents list.

No. 30. Doors over 9 feet long and not exceeding 10 feet, add 10 per cent to the difference in the list between 8-foot and 9-foot listed doors.

No. 31. For wide doors made with less panels than specified in Nos. 24, 25, 26, 27, extra price.

No. 32. Flush moulded panels (door No. 203), for extra panels over four, for panel and moulding one side, 1⅜-inch doors, add 40 cents list.

No. 33. For extra panel and flush moulding two sides, 1⅜-inch doors, add 55 cents list.

No. 34. For extra panel and flush moulding one side, 1¾-inch doors, add 45 cents list.

No. 35. For extra panel and flush moulding two sides, 1¾-inch doors, add 60 cents list.

No. 36. For doors P G, ovolo, cove and bead, or bead and cove sticking four-panel, add 15 cents list to four-panel O G doors.

No. 37. Solid mould sticking on back side of cottage front doors is standard.

No. 38. For price of machine chamfered doors No. 207, use list as shown under flush moulded door No. 203.

No. 39. For price of raised moulded doors add 100 per cent to difference between O G and flush moulded doors of same size.

No. 40. Doors, sizes not listed, will take price of next larger size.

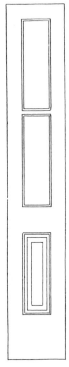

SIDE LIGHTS FOR DOORS.

WITH MOULDED PANEL BELOW.

Width and Height.				Thickness.	Price per Pair, Unglazed.	Price per Pair, Glazed.
12	x	6	6	1⅜	$3.65	$4.80
12	x	6	8	"	3.75	4.90
12	x	6	10	"	3.85	5.15
12	x	7	0	"	3.95	5.25
12	x	7	6	"	4.15	5.85
14	x	6	6	"	3.80	5.20
14	x	6	8	"	3.90	5.30
14	x	6	10	"	4.00	5.55
14	x	7	0	"	4.10	5.65
14	x	7	6	"	4.30	6.20
14	x	8	0	"	4.60	6.70

For 1¾-inch thick, add 50 per cent.
Prices are for either two or three lights in each sash.
10-inch same price as 12-inch.   Subject to door discount.
State in ordering whether two or three lights are wanted.
For O G deduct 70 cents per pair from above list.

197   198

1¾-INCH DOOR TABLE.

Differences to add for list price between 1⅜ and 1¾ inch Four-Panel Doors.

SIZE.				O G Doors A Quality.	O G Doors B Quality
2	6	x	6	6	$2.55	$2.20
2	8	x	6	8	2.70	2.30
2	10	x	6	10	3.20	2.70
2	8	x	7	0	3.30	2.95
2	10	x	7	0	3.45	3.05
3	0	x	7	0	3.50	3.10
2	8	x	7	6	3.85	3.45
2	10	x	7	6	3.95	3.50
3	0	x	7	6	4.05	3.60
3	0	x	8	0	4.70	4.20
3	0	x	8	6	5.45	4.90

FANCY PAINTED COTTAGE DOORS.

A 1

A 2
Glazed Plain.

A 3
Glazed Sand Blast.

A 4
Glazed Sand Blast.

These Doors always in stock and can be shipped promptly, but in the following sizes only :
2-6 x 6-6, 1⅜.　　2-8 x 6-8, 1⅜.　　2-10 x 6-10, 1⅜　　2-8 x 7-0, 1⅜.　　3-0 x 7-0, 1⅜.
For net prices see our Discount Sheet.

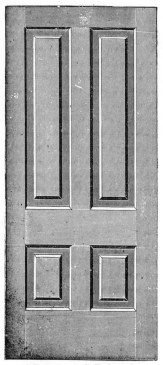

4-Panel, O G Painted.

PAINTED DOORS.

Our Painted Doors are well manufactured, shellaced and painted two coats of light colored paint.

They are good sellers and it will pay you to carry them in stock.

All of our Painted Doors are carefully crated before shipping to avoid damage in transit.

We manufacture these doors in the following sizes, which we always have on hand ready for prompt shipment:

FOUR-PANEL PAINTED DOORS.

2-6x6-6, 1⅛.
2-8x6-8, 1⅛.
2-6x6-6, 1⅜.
2-8x6-8, 1⅜.

PAINTED SASH DOORS.

2-6x6-6, 1⅜.
2-8x6-8, 1⅜.

For Prices on Painted Doors, see our price folder.

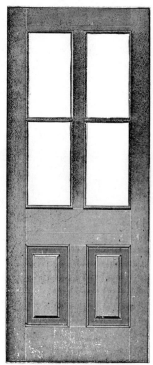

210.   Painted.

PAINTED DOORS.

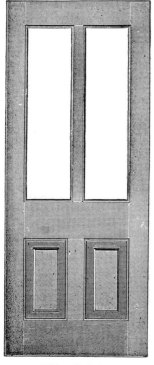

211. Painted.

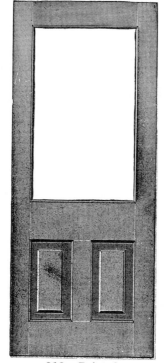

212. Painted.

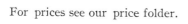

For prices see our price folder.

213. Painted.

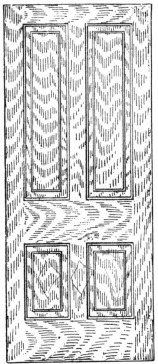

4-Panel, O G Grained.

OAK GRAINED DOORS.

Our Oak Grained Doors are un-excelled. They are painted two coats, best lead and oil paint, and are carefully oil finished.

Doors finished by our process have all the appearance of the genuine oak, at a much lower cost.

For prices on Grained Doors see our Discount Sheet.

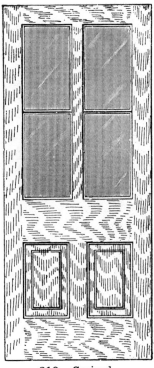

210. Grained.

211 Grained.

OAK
GRAINED
DOORS

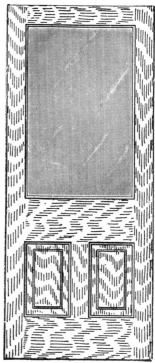

212 Grained.

We carry in stock the following:

FOUR-PANEL
GRAINED DOORS.

2-6x6-6, 1⅛.
2-8x6-8, 1⅛.
2-6x6-6, 1⅜.
2-8x6-8, 1⅜.

GRAINED
SASH DOORS.

2-6x6-6, 1⅜.
2-8x6-8, 1⅜.

213 Grained.

These Doors are carefully crated to avoid damage in shipment . . . .

CHINA CLOSETS.

1313   1314

In writing for price give opening to fill and depth of shelves. Also state if open or glazed doors.

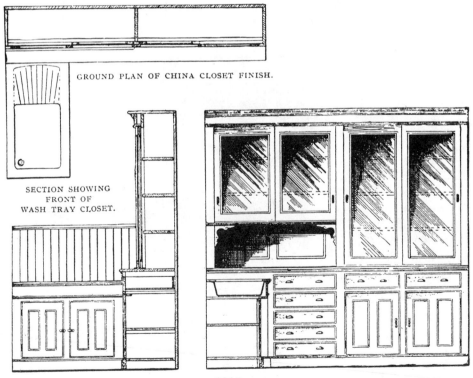

GROUND PLAN OF CHINA CLOSET FINISH.

SECTION SHOWING
FRONT OF
WASH TRAY CLOSET.

1315

In asking price give size of opening to fill, depth of shelves, style of glazing and kind of wood. We make cases of drawers and wardrobes of all kinds. Write for estimates.

CUPBOARD DOORS and SASH.

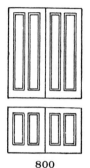

Usual sizes made and prices per square foot given below.

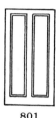

800
Full Set.

801

CUPBOARD PANEL DOORS.

802
For tops.

Usual sizes made, two panels each:

1-4x4-0	1-6x4-0	1-8x4-0
1-4x4-6	1-6x4-6	1-8x4-6
1-4x4-8	1-6x4-8	1-8x4-8
1-4x5-0	1-6x5-0	1-8x5-0

803
For bottoms.

1-4x2-0	1-6x2-0	1-8x2-0
1-4x2-6	1-6x2-6	1-8x2-6
1-4x2-8	1-6x2-8	1-8x2-8
1-4x3-0	1-6x3-0	1-8x3-0

PRICE, No. 1 QUALITY.

⅞ inch thick _____ per square ft., $0.19   1⅛ inch thick _____ per square ft., $0.27
For No. 2 quality deduct 5 per cent from above.

CUPBOARD SASH.

Usual sizes made, two light each:

1-4x4-0	1-6x4-0	1-8x4-0
1-4x4-6	1-6x4-6	1-8x4-6
1-4x4-8	1-6x4-8	1-8x4-8
1-4x5-0	1-6x5-0	1-8x5-0
1-4x5-6	1-6x5-6	1-8x5-6

804

PRICE, OPEN—UNGLAZED.

⅞ inch thick _____ per square ft., $0.14   1⅛ inch thick _____ per square ft., $0.19

For Glazed Cupboard Sash we add proportionate (according to size of glass), as per glazed window list.

Door discount applies to Cupboard Panel Doors.

Open Sash discount applies to Cupboard Sash.

INTERIOR DOORS and FINISH.

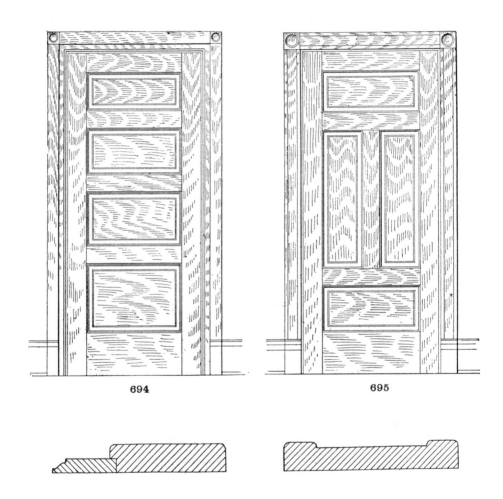

694   695

WRITE FOR PRICES.

INTERIOR DOORS and FINISH.

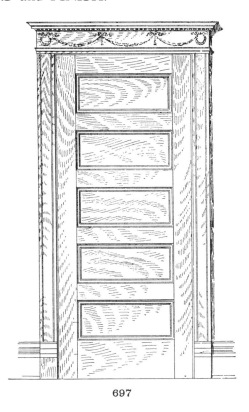

696

697

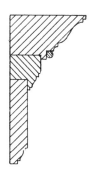

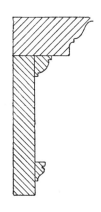

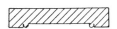

WRITE FOR PRICES.

INTERIOR DOORS and FINISH.

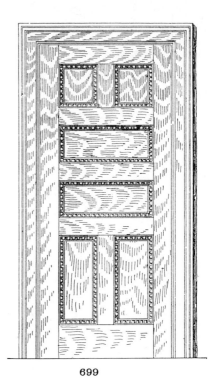

698

699

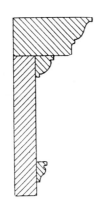

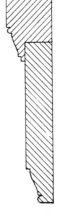

WRITE FOR PRICES.

INSIDE DOORS.

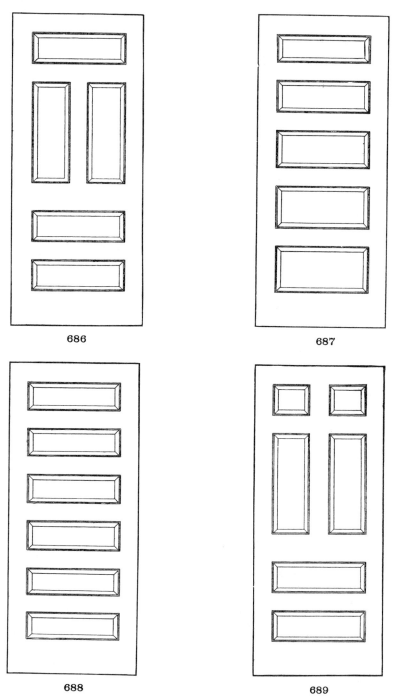

686   687

688   689

Doors of above styles we make to order either solid hardwood or veneered.

INSIDE DOORS.

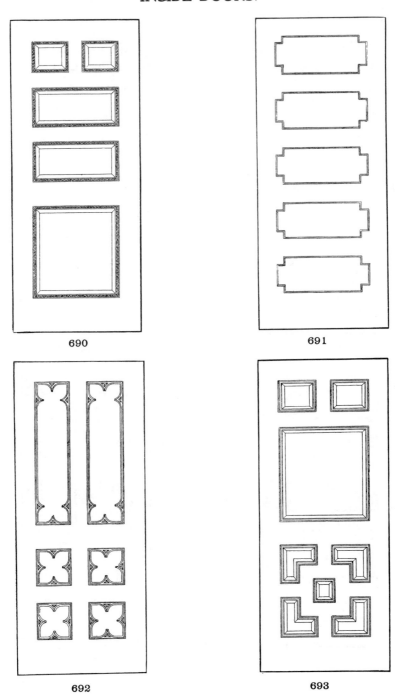

690

691

692

693

Our veneered doors are made from selected stock, chosen for its beauty of grain and uniformity of color.

INSIDE DOORS.

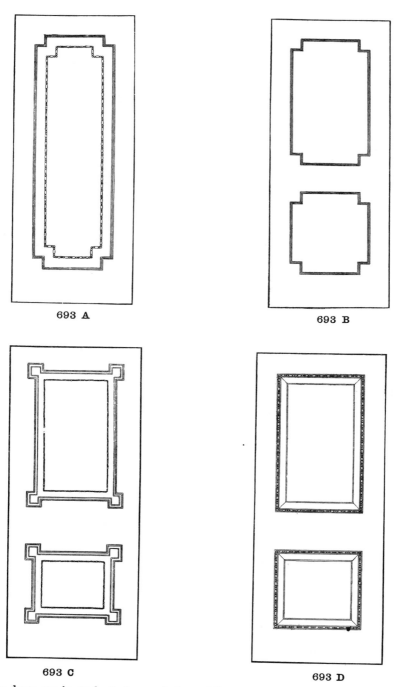

693 A   693 B

693 C   693 D

These doors can be made flush or raised moulding or solid stuck. See pages 60 and 61 for sections.

INSIDE DOORS.

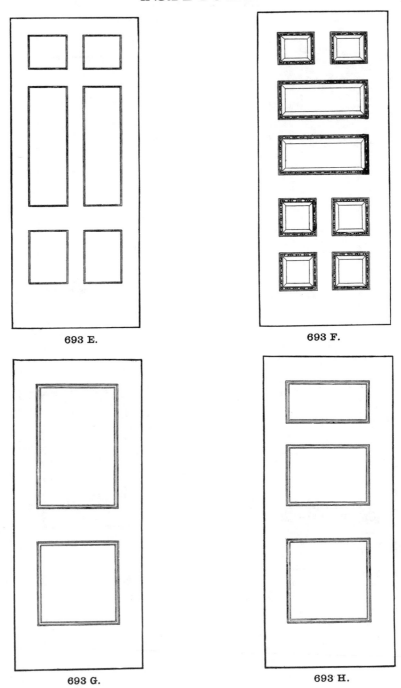

693 E.   693 F.

693 G.   693 H.

We make these Doors to order, Veneered in any of the Cabinet Woods, or if desired, in solid White Pine or Hardwood.

For finish, style and reliable qualities, our work cannot be excelled.

SPECIAL FRONT DOORS.

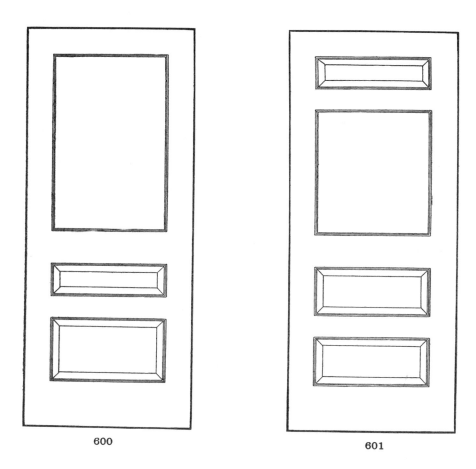

600   601

These special doors we make to order in any size. Made in white or yellow Pine or any of the hardwoods. We are prepared to glaze these doors with sand blast, polished bevel plate, or leaded art glass of handsome design.

Nothing made superior to the quality of our work.

SPECIAL FRONT DOORS.

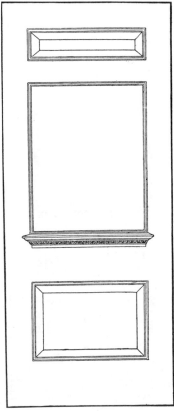

602   603

These special doors we make to order in any size.   Made in white or yellow Pine or any of the hardwoods.   We are prepared to glaze these doors with sand blast, polished bevel plate, or leaded art glass of handsome design.

Nothing made superior to the quality of our work.

SPECIAL FRONT DOORS.

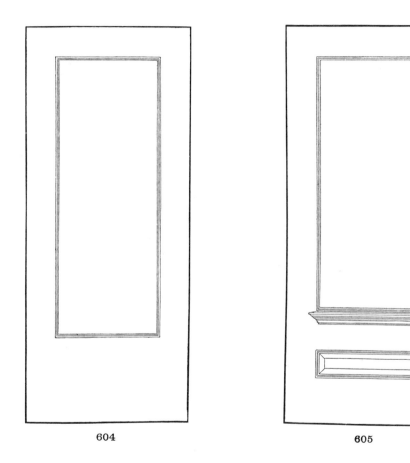

604   605

Built to order either solid or veneered in hardwood. Can also be made in white or yellow Pine and Cypress.

We build them right, using only first class material and work out all details with exactness, the carvings executed in the highest style of art.

Our veneered doors are made from selected stock, chosen for its beauty of grain and uniformity of color.

For finish, style and enduring quality, we guarantee them equal to any made.

SPECIAL FRONT DOORS.

606

607

These special doors we make to order in any size.   Made in white or yellow Pine or any of the hardwoods.   We are prepared to glaze these doors with sand blast, polished bevel plate, or leaded art glass of handsome design.

Nothing made superior to the quality of our work.

SPECIAL FRONT DOORS.

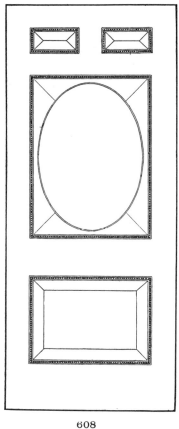

608

609

Built to order either solid or veneered in hardwood. Can also be made in white or yellow Pine and Cypress.

We build them right, using only first class material and work out all details with exactness, the carvings executed in the highest style of art.

Our veneered doors are made from selected stock, chosen for its beauty of grain and uniformity of color.

For finish, style, and enduring quality, we guarantee them equal to any made.

SPECIAL FRONT DOORS.

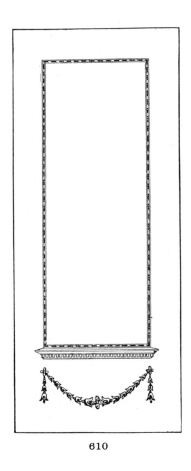

610

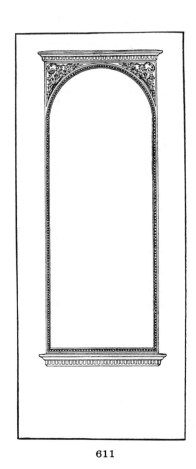

611

These special doors we make to order in any size. Made in white or yellow Pine or any of the hardwoods. We are prepared to glaze these doors with sand blast, polished bevel plate, or leaded art glass of handsome design.

Nothing made superior to the quality of our work.

SPECIAL FRONT DOORS.

612   613

Built to order either solid or veneered in hardwood. Can also be made in white or yellow Pine and Cypress.

We build them right, using only first class material and work out all details with exactness, the carvings executed in the highest style of art.

Our veneered doors are made from selected stock, chosen for its beauty of grain and uniformity of color.

For finish, style and enduring quality, we guarantee them equal to any made.

SPECIAL FRONT DOORS.

614

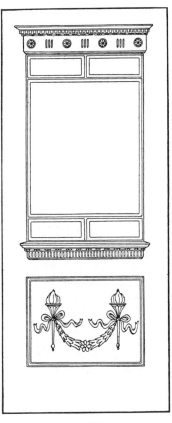

615

These special doors we make to order in any size.   Made in white or yellow Pine or any of the hardwoods.   We are prepared to glaze these doors with sand blast, polished bevel plate, or leaded art glass of handsome design.

Nothing made superior to the quality of our work.

SPECIAL FRONT DOORS.

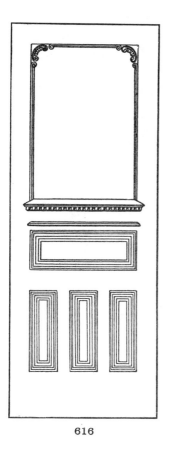

616

617

Built to order either solid or veneered in hardwood. Can also be made in white or yellow Pine and Cypress.

We build them right, using only first class material and work out all details with exactness, the carvings executed in the highest style of art.

Our veneered doors are made from selected stock, chosen for its beauty of grain and uniformity of color.

For finish, style and enduring quality, we guarantee them equal to any made.

SPECIAL FRONT DOORS.

618   619

These special doors we make to order in any size. Made in white or yellow Pine or any of the hardwoods. We are prepared to glaze these doors with sand blast, polished bevel plate, or leaded art glass of handsome design.

Nothing made superior to the quality of our work.

SPECIAL FRONT DOORS.

702

703

Bead and Cove Sticking.

SIZE.			PRICES OF 702.		PRICES OF 703.		Add for 1¾ inches Thick.
			Open.	Glazed. D. S.	Open.	Glazed, D. S.	
2	8 x 6	8	1⅜	$5.00	$6.90	$4.95	$6.85	$2.70
2	10 x 6	10	"	5.75	7.85	5.70	7.80	3.20
2	8 x 7	0	"	5.95	8.05	5.90	8.00	3.30
3	0 x 7	0	"	6.25	8.80	6.20	8.75	3.50
3	0 x 7	6	"	7.05	10.20	7.00	10.15	4.05

If wanted veneered in any of the hardwoods consult our discount sheet for prices.

SPECIAL FRONT DOORS.

704

705

Bead and Cove Sticking.

SIZE				PRICES OF 704.		PRICES OF 705.		Add for 1¾ inches Thick.
				Open.	Glazed, D. S.	Open.	Glazed, D. S.	
2	8 x 6	8	1⅜	$4.90	$7.00	$5.20	$7.30	$2.70
2	10 x 6	10	"	5.65	8.20	5.95	8.50	3.20
2	8 x 7	0	"	5.85	8.20	6.15	8.50	3.30
3	0 x 7	0	"	6.15	9.30	6.45	9.60	3.50
3	0 x 7	6	"	6.95	10.55	7.25	10.85	4.05

If wanted veneered in any of the hardwoods consult our discount sheet for prices.

SPECIAL FRONT DOORS.

706

707

Bead and Cove Sticking.

SIZE.		PRICES OF 706.		PRICES OF 707.		Add for 1¾ inches Thick.
		Open.	Glazed, D. S.	Open.	Glazed, D. S.	
2 8 x 6 8	1⅜	$4.75	$7.30	$5.50	$8.05	$2.70
2 10 x 6 10	"	5.50	8.65	6.25	9.40	3.20
2 8 x 7 0	"	5.70	8.85	6.45	9.60	3.30
3 0 x 7 0	"	6.00	9.60	6.75	10.35	3.50
3 0 x 7 6	"	6.80	11.45	7.55	12.20	4.05

If wanted veneered in any of the hardwoods consult our discount sheet for prices.

SPECIAL FRONT DOORS.

708

709

Bead and Cove Sticking.

SIZE.		PRICES OF 708.		PRICES OF 709.		Add for 1¾ inches Thick.
		Open.	Glazed, D. S.	Open.	Glazed, D. S.	
2 8 x 6 8	1⅜	$5.60	$7.95	$5.80	$7.70	$2.70
2 10 x 6 10	''	6.35	9.50	6.55	8.65	3.20
2 8 x 7 0	''	6.55	9.15	6.75	8.85	3.30
3 0 x 7 0	''	6.85	10.45	7.05	9.60	3.50
3 0 x 7 6	''	7.65	11.85	7.85	11.00	4.05

If wanted veneered in any of the hardwoods consult our discount sheet for prices.

SPECIAL FRONT DOORS.

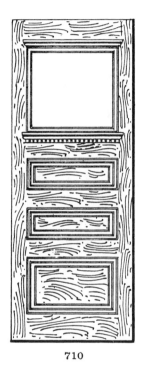

710

711

Bead and Cove Sticking.

SIZE.			PRICES OF 710.		PRICES OF 711.		Add for 1¾ inches Thick.
			Open.	Glazed, D. S.	Open.	Glazed, D. S.	
2	8 x 6	8	1⅜	$5.80	$7.70	$6.10	$8.00	$2.70
2	10 x 6	10	"	6.55	8.65	6.85	8.95	3.20
2	8 x 7	0	"	6.75	8.85	7.05	9.15	3.30
3	0 x 7	0	"	7.05	9.60	7.35	9.90	3.50
3	0 x 7	6	"	7.85	11.00	8.15	11.30	4.05

If wanted veneered in any of the hardwoods consult our discount sheet for prices.

SPECIAL FRONT DOORS.

FLUSH MOULDED ONE SIDE.

712

713

SIZE.				PRICES OF 712.		PRICE OF 713.	Add for 1¾ inches Thick.
				Open.	Glazed, D. S.		
2	8 x 6	8	1⅜	$12.00	$13.90	$11.00	$2.70
2	10 x 6	10	"	12.75	14.85	11.75	3.20
2	8 x 7	0	"	12.95	15.05	11.95	3.30
3	0 x 7	0	"	13.25	15.80	12.25	3 50
3	0 x 7	6	"	14.05	17.20	13.05	4.05

If wanted veneered in any of the hardwoods consult our discount sheet for prices.

SPECIAL FRONT DOORS.

FLUSH MOULDED ONE SIDE.

714

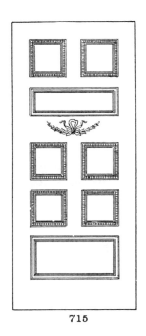

715

SIZE.				PRICES OF 714.	PRICES OF 715.	Add for 1¾ inches Thick.
2	8 x 6	8	1⅜	$11.00	$11.00	$2.70
2	10 x 6	10	"	11.75	11.75	3.20
2	8 x 7	0	"	11.95	11.95	3.30
3	0 x 7	0	"	12.25	12.25	3.50
3	0 x 7	6	"	13.05	13.05	4.05

If wanted veneered in any of the hardwoods consult our discount sheet for prices.

SPECIAL FRONT DOORS.

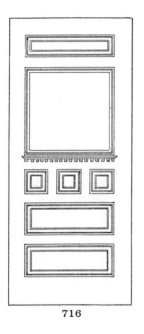

716

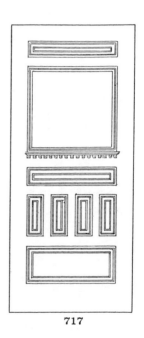

717

Bead and Cove Sticking.

SIZE.				PRICES OF 716.		PRICES OF 717.		Add for 1¾ inches Thick.
				Open.	Glazed, D. S.	Open.	Glazed, D. S.	
2	8 x 6	8	1⅜	$5.70	$7.60	$5.80	$7.70	$2.70
2	10 x 6	10	"	6.45	8.55	6.55	8.65	3.20
2	8 x 7	0	"	6.65	8.75	6.75	8.85	3.30
3	0 x 7	0	"	6.95	9.50	7.05	9.60	3.50
3	0 x 7	6	"	7.75	10.90	7.85	11.00	4.05

If wanted veneered in any of the hardwoods consult our discount sheet for prices.

FRONT and VESTIBULE DOORS.

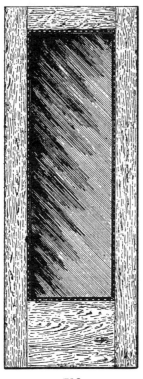

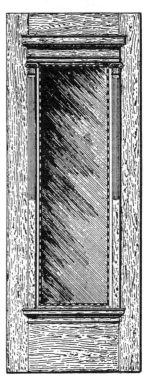

718 719

SIZE.			PRICES OF 718.		PRICES OF 719.		Add for 1¾ inches Thick.
			Open.	Glazed.	Open.	Glazed.	
2 8 x 6 8	1⅜		$6.00	Prices Furnished on Application	$13.00	Prices Furnished on Application	$2.70
2 10 x 6 10	"		6.85		13.85		3.20
2 8 x 7 0	"		7.15		14.15		3.30
3 0 x 7 0	"		7.55		14.55		3.50
3 0 x 7 6	"		8.55		15.55		4.05

In writing for glazed prices on these doors state with what kind of glass they are to be glazed.

If wanted veneered in any of the hardwoods consult our discount sheet for prices.

FRONT and VESTIBULE DOORS.

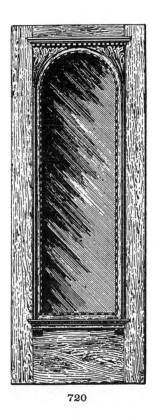

720

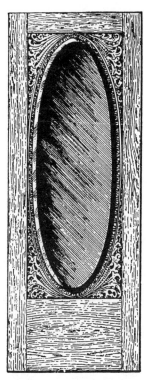

721

SIZE.			PRICES OF 720.		PRICES OF 721.		Add for 1¾ inches Thick.
			Open	Glazed.	Open.	Glazed.	
2	8 x 6	8	1⅜	$17.50	Prices Furnished on Application	$23.25	Prices Furnished on Application	$2.70
2	10 x 6	10	"	18.35		24.20		3.20
2	8 x 7	0	"	18.65		24.60		3.30
3	0 x 7	0	"	19.05		24.90		3.50
3	0 x 7	6	"	20.05		26.05		4.05

In writing for glazed prices on these doors state with what kind of glass they are to be glazed.

If wanted veneered in any of the hardwoods consult our discount sheet for prices.

FRONT and VESTIBULE DOORS.

722

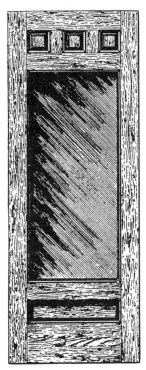

723

SIZE.				PRICES OF 722.		PRICES OF 723.		Add for 1¾ inches Thick.
				Open.	Glazed.	Open.	Glazed.	
2	8 x 6	8	1⅜	$7.15	Prices Furnished on Application	$5.15	Prices Furnished on Application	$2.70
2	10 x 6	10	"	7.90		5.90		3.20
2	8 x 7	0	"	8.10		6.10		3.30
3	0 x 7	0	"	8.40		6.40		3.50
3	0 x 7	6	"	9 20		7.20		4.05

In writing for glazed prices on these doors state with what kind of glass they are to be glazed.

If wanted veneered in any of the hardwoods consult our discount sheet for prices.

FRONT and VESTIBULE DOORS.

724

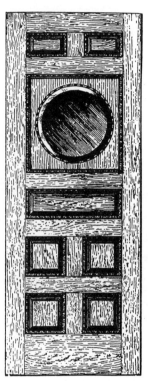

725

SIZE.			PRICES OF 724.		PRICES OF 725.		Add for 1¾ inches Thick.
			Open.	Glazed.	Open.	Glazed.	
2	8 x 6	8 1⅜	$13.00	Prices Furnished on Application	$12.00	Prices Furnished on Application	$2.70
2	10 x 6	10 "	13.75		12.75		3.20
2	8 x 7	0 "	13.95		12.95		3.30
3	0 x 7	0 "	14.25		13.25		3.50
3	0 x 7	6 "	15.05		14.05		4.05

In writing for glazed prices on these doors, state with what kind of glass they are to be glazed.

If wanted veneered in any of the hardwoods consult our discount sheet for prices.

FRONT and VESTIBULE DOORS.

726

727

SIZE.		PRICES OF 726.		PRICES OF 727.		Add for 1¾ inches Thick.
		Open.	Glazed.	Open.	Glazed.	
2 8 x 6 8	1⅜	$12.00	Prices Furnished on Application	$16.00	Prices Furnished on Application	$2.70
2 10 x 6 10	"	12.75		16.75		3.20
2 8 x 7 0	"	12.95		16.95		3.30
3 0 x 7 0	"	13.25		17.25		3.50
3 0 x 7 6	"	14.05		18.05		4.05

In writing for glazed prices on these doors, state with what kind of glass they are to be glazed.

We are prepared to furnish these handsome front doors or any modification of them in pine or any of the hardwoods, both solid and veneered. Specify style of glazing wanted.

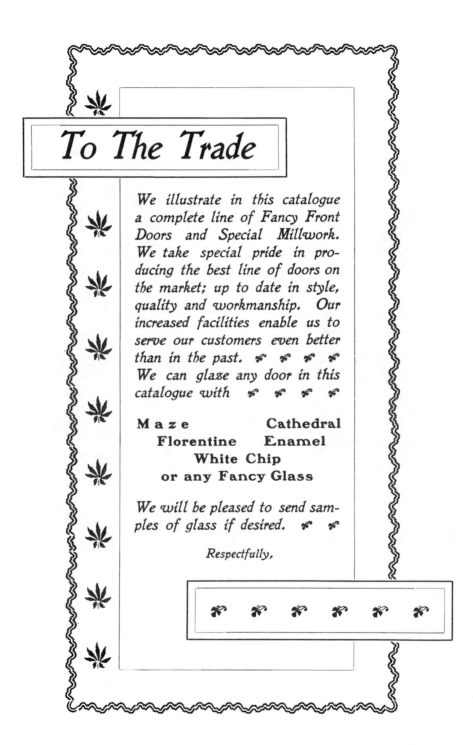

To The Trade

We illustrate in this catalogue a complete line of Fancy Front Doors and Special Millwork. We take special pride in producing the best line of doors on the market; up to date in style, quality and workmanship. Our increased facilities enable us to serve our customers even better than in the past. ❦ ❦ ❦ ❦
We can glaze any door in this catalogue with ❦ ❦ ❦ ❦

Maze   **Cathedral**
Florentine   **Enamel**
White Chip
or any Fancy Glass

We will be pleased to send samples of glass if desired. ❦ ❦

Respectfully,

OUR SPECIAL COTTAGE DOORS.

Monarch A   Monarch B

2-6 x 6-6, 1⅜ and 2-8 x 6-8, 1⅜, Fancy Doors.   Write for prices.

OUR SPECIAL COTTAGE DOORS.

Monarch E   Venus

2-6 x 6-6, 1⅜ and 2-8 x 6-8, 1⅜, Fancy Doors.   Write for prices.

OUR SPECIAL COTTAGE DOORS.

Vixen   Carnival

2-6 x 6-6, 1⅜ and 2-8 x 6-8, 1⅜, Fancy Doors.   Write for prices.

OUR SPECIAL COTTAGE DOORS.

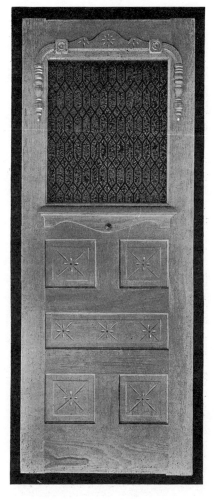

Moonstone   Imp

2-6 x 6-6, 1⅜ and 2-8 x 6-8, 1⅜, Fancy Doors.   Write for prices.

OUR SPECIAL COTTAGE DOORS.

Best   Ruby

2-6 x 6-6, 1⅜ and 2-8 x 6-8, 1⅜, Fancy Doors.   Write for prices.

OUR SPECIAL COTTAGE DOORS.

Extra   Better

2-6 x 6-6, 1⅜ and 2-8 x 6-8, 1⅜, Fancy Doors.   Write for prices.

OUR SPECIAL COTTAGE DOORS.

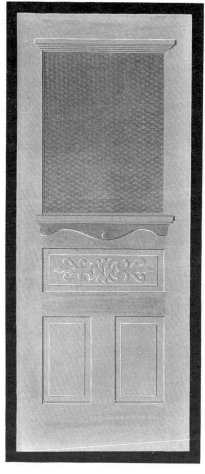

Good

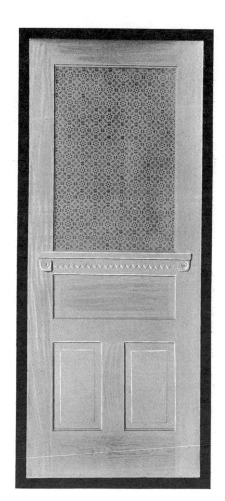

Diamond

2-6 x 6-6, 1⅜ and 2-8 x 6-8, 1⅜, Fancy Doors.   Write for prices.

OUR SPECIAL COTTAGE DOORS.

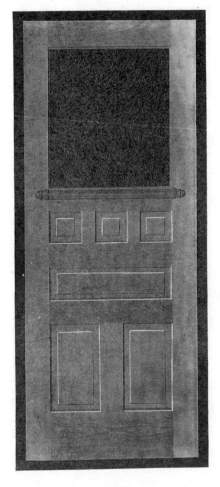

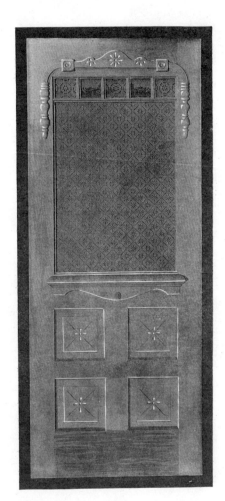

Pearl   Opal

2-6 x 6-6, 1⅜ and 2-8 x 6-8, 1⅜, Fancy Doors.   Write for prices.

OUR SPECIAL COTTAGE DOORS.

United A

United B

2-6 x 6-6, 1⅜ and 2-8 x 6-8, 1⅜, Fancy Doors.   Write for prices.

OUR SPECIAL COTTAGE DOORS.

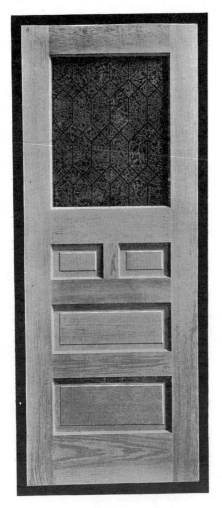

United D   United E

2-6 x 6-6, 1⅜ and 2-8 x 6-8, 1⅜, Fancy Doors.   Write for prices.

OUR SPECIAL COTTAGE DOORS.

United **F**   United **G**

2-6 x 6 6, 1⅜ and 2-8 x 6-8, 1⅜, Fancy Doors.   Write for prices.

OUR SPECIAL COTTAGE DOORS.

United **H**   **Winner**

2-6 x 6-6, 1⅜ and 2-8 x 6-8, 1⅜, Fancy Doors.   Write for prices.

Mill Work

We give special attention to orders for this class of work. Our new mill is equipped with the latest improved machinery and appliances and we are prepared to execute all orders for turned work, carving, stair work and fine interior finish, promptly and at prices that will be satisfactory to our customers

STORE DOORS.

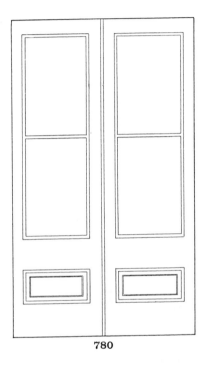

780

Moulded panels outside, O G finish inside.

Size of Opening.	1⅜ Thick.		1¾ Thick.	
	Per Pair Open.	Per Pair Glazed D. S.	Per Pair Open.	Per Pair Glazed D. S.
5 0 x 7 0	$10.75	$18.20	$17.15	$24.60
7 6	12.20	21.35	19.70	28.85
8 0	13.60	23.00	22.40	31.80
8 6	16.25	26.70	26.55	37.00
6 0 x 7 6	13.55	26.15	21.65	34.25
8 0	14.80	27.40	24.20	36.80
8 6	16.45	30.85	27.35	41.75
9 0	17.75	32.15	30.45	44.85

For doors 2¼ inches thick, add 60 per cent to 1¾ list.

Above doors are not made for shutters.   For door extras see pages 72-73.

See page 7 in ordering.

SPECIAL STORE DOORS.

783

Size of Opening.	1⅜ Thick.		1¾ Thick.	
	Per Pair Open.	Per Pair Glazed D. S.	Per Pair Open.	Per Pair Glazed D. S.
5 0 x 7 0	$11.25	$18.70	$17.65	$25.10
7 6	12.70	21.85	20.20	29.35
8 0	14.10	23.50	22.90	32.30
8 6	16.75	27.20	27.05	37.50
6 0 x 7 6	14.05	26.65	22.15	34.75
8 0	15.30	27.90	24.70	37.30
8 6	16.95	31.35	27.85	42.25
9 0	18.25	32.65	30.95	45.35

For door extras see pages 72-73.

For doors 2¼ inches thick, add 60 per cent to 1¾ list.

See page 7 in ordering.

SPECIAL STORE DOORS.

783½

Size of Opening.			1¾ Thick.	
			Per Pair Open.	Per Pair Glazed D. S.
5	0 x 7	0	$27.00	$42.50
	7	6	28.35	46.95
	8	0	30.10	49.50
	8	6	33.90	61.10
6	0 x 7	6	30.10	54.40
	8	0	31.85	58.85
	8	6	33.90	76.20
	9	0	36.30	84.60

For doors 2¼ inches thick, add 60 per cent to 1¾ list.

For door extras see pages 72-73.

See page 7 in ordering.

SPECIAL STORE DOORS.

785

Size of Opening.				1¾ Thick.	
				Per Pair Open.	Per Pair Glazed D. S.
5	0 x 7	0		$30.00	$45.50
		7	6	31.35	49.95
		8	0	33.10	52.50
		8	6	36.90	64.10
6	0 x 7	6		33.10	57.40
		8	0	34.65	61.85
		8	6	36.90	79.20
		9	0	39.30	87.60

For doors 2¼ inches thick, add 60 per cent to 1¾ list.

For door extras see pages 72-73.

See page 7 in ordering.

STORE FRONTS.

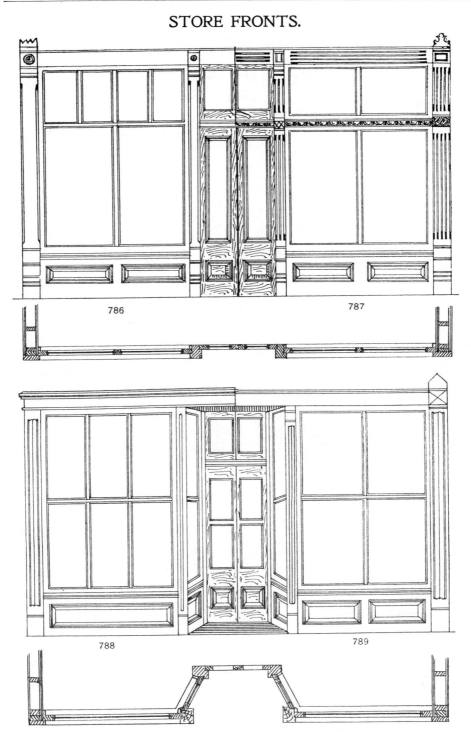

Give width inside the building and height of ceiling.

WRITE FOR PRICES.

STORE FRONTS.

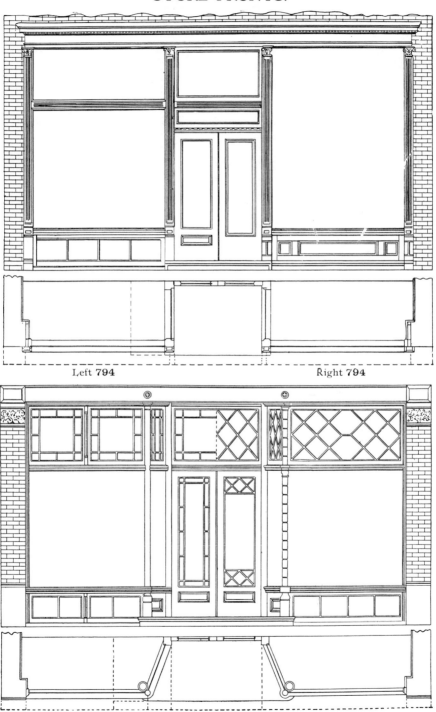

Left **794**   Right **794**

Left **795**   Right **795**
Give width inside the building and height of ceiling.
WRITE FOR PRICES.

STORE FRONTS,

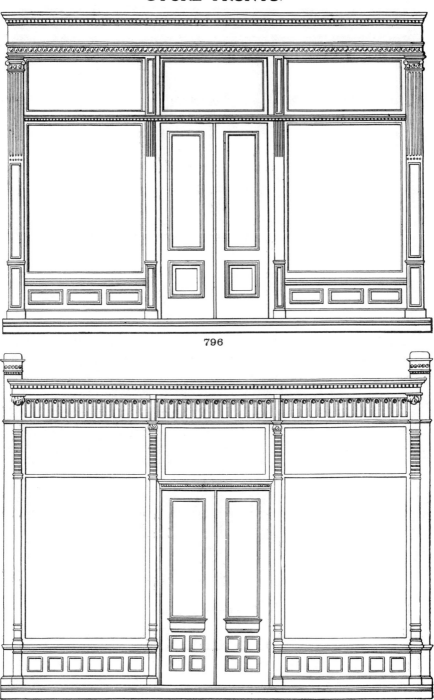

796

797

Give width inside the building and height of ceiling.

WRITE FOR PRICES.

STORE FRONTS.

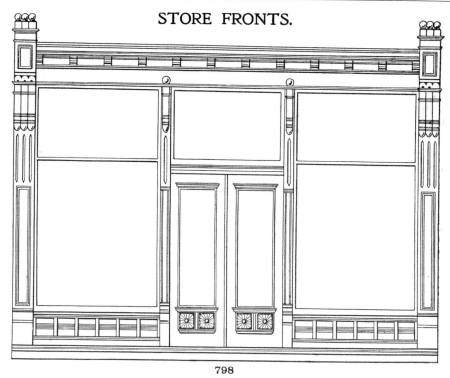

798

799

Give width inside the building and height of ceiling.

WRITE FOR PRICES.

SINK and TABLE LEGS.

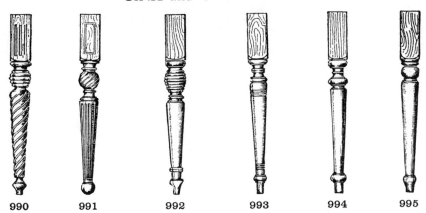

990   991   992   993   994   995

Table and Sink legs usually made 1¾, 2¼ and 3¾ inches square.   Write for prices, giving size kind of wood and quantity.

BASE ANGLE BEADS.

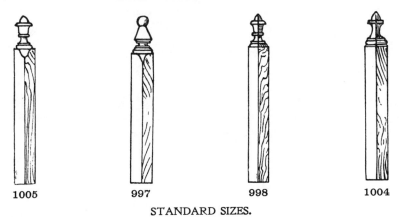

1005   997   998   1004

STANDARD SIZES.

1⅜ x 1⅜ inches, 12 and 14 inches long.

CORNER BEADS.

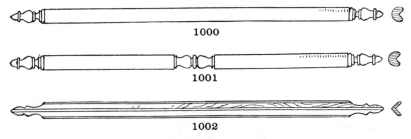

1000

1001

1002

STANDARD SIZES.

1⅛ x 1⅛ inches, 4 feet long.   1⅜ x 1⅜ inches, 4 feet long.
1¾ x 1¾ inches, 4 feet long.

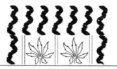

Building Papers

We handle a full line of Building Papers, including the following :

RED ROSIN SIZED SHEATHING,

      "   "   "

      "   "   "

PLAIN BOARD,   **CEDAR CARPET LINING,**

TARRED BOARD,   **DARK CORRUGATED CARPET**

TARRED FELT,   **LINING,**

INODOROUS BOARD,   **DEADENING FELT, Etc., Etc.**

For Prices see our Discount Sheets.

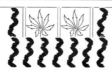

STOCK CORNER BLOCKS.
1⅛ inches thick.

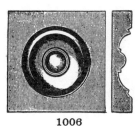

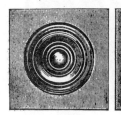

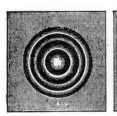

1006	1007	1008
$5.00 per 100.	$6.00 per 100.	$5.50 per 100.

STOCK HEAD BLOCKS.
1⅛ inches thick.

1009	1010	1011
$10.00 per 100.	$18.00 per 100.	$16.00 per 100.

STOCK BASE BLOCKS.
1⅜ inches thick.

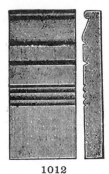

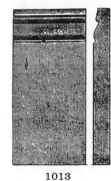

1012	1013	1014
$11.00 per 100.	$9.00 per 100.	$10.00 per 100.

Above prices are for Blocks not over 5⅝ inches wide. Always specify width of casing when ordering.

CORNER BLOCKS.

1⅛ inches thick.

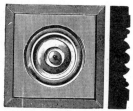

1015
$7.00 per 100.

1016
$7.80 per 100.

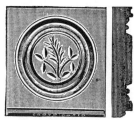

1017
$9.00 per 100.

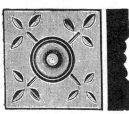

1018
$7.80 per 100.

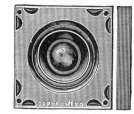

1019
$9.60 per 100.

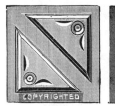

1020
$14.40 per 100.

1021
$8.40 per 100.

1022
$6.60 per 100.

1023
$6.60 per 100.

1024
$9.60 per 100.

1025
$7.20 per 100.

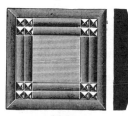

1026
$10.80 per 100.

1027
$24.00 per 100.

1027½
$6.60 per 100.

1029
$22.00 per 100.

HEAD BLOCKS.

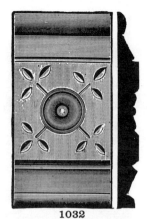

1030
1⅛x5⅝x11. $14.40 per 100.

1031
1⅛x5⅝x11. $16.80 per 100.

1032
1⅛x5⅝x11. $13.20 per 100.

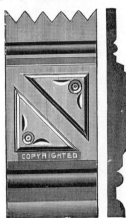

1033
1⅛x5⅝x12. $26.40 per 100.

1034
1⅛x5⅝x11. $15.60 per 100.

1035
1⅛x5⅝x12. $24.00 per 100.

1036
1⅛x5⅝x11. $15.60 per 100.

1037
1⅜x5⅝x11. $40.00 per 100.

1037½
1⅜x5⅝x12. $13.20 per 100.

The lengths of Head Blocks above given are for Blocks 5⅝ inches wide. For Blocks 5 inches wide the length will be ½ inch less than for Blocks 5½ inches wide. For Blocks 4½ inches wide the length will be 1 inch less than for Blocks 5½ inches wide. For Blocks 4 inches wide the length will be 1½ inches less than for Blocks 5½ inches wide.
Head Blocks made to suit casings. Always specify width when ordering.

BASE BLOCKS.

1039
1⅜x5⅝x12___$21.60 per 100

1040
1⅜x5⅝x11___$16.80 per 100

1041
1⅜x5⅝x10___$16.80 per 100

1042
1⅜x5⅝x10___$16.80 per 100

1043
1⅜x5⅝x11___$16.80 per 100

1044
1⅜x5⅝x11___$16.80 per 100

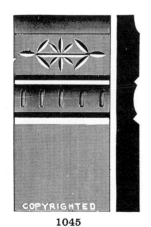

1045
1⅜x5⅝x11___$16.80 per 100

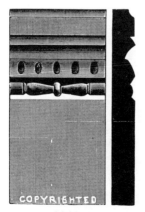

1046
1⅛x5⅝x10___$16.80 per 100

1047
1⅜x5⅝x12___$24.00 per 100

Base Blocks made to suit casings. Always specify width when ordering.

PRICES on CORNER and PLINTH BLOCKS.

ADOPTED BY

Wholesale Sash, Door and Blind Manufacturers' Association

OF THE NORTHWEST.

EFFECTIVE SEPTEMBER 5th 1901.

No.		Price.
1006		$ 5.00
1007		6.00
1008		5.50
1009		10.00
1010		18.00
1011		16.00
1012		11.00
1013		9.00
1014		10.00
1015		7.00
1016		7.80
1017		9.00
1018		7.80
1019		9.60
1020		14.40
1021		8.40
1022		6.60
1023		6.60
1024		9.60
1025		7.20
1026		10.80
1027		24.00
1028		24.00
1029		22.00
1030		14.40
1031		16.80
1032		13.20
1033		26.40
1034		15.60
1035		24.00
1036		15.60
1037		40.00
1038		45.00
1039		21.60
1040		16.80
1041		16.80
1042		16.80
1043		16.80
1044		16.80
1045		16.80
1046		16.80
1047		24.00
2706	4½ to 6 in. x 1⅛	5.00
2707	“ “ “	5.00
2708	“ “ “	5.50
2709	“ “ “	5.50
2710	“ “ “	5.00
2711	“ “ “	5.00
2712	“ “ “	5.00
2713	“ “ “	5.50
2714	“ “ “	5.50
2715	“ “ “	5.00
2716	“ “ “	6.00
2717	“ “ “	5.00
2718	“ “ “	6.00
2719	“ “ “	5.00
2720	“ “ “	5.50
2721	“ “ “	6.00
2722	“ “ “	6.00
2723	“ “ “	5.50
2724	“ “ “	12.00
2725	“ “ “	12.00
2726	“ “ “	8.40
2727	“ “ “	8.40
2728	“ “ “	24.00
2729	“ “ “	24.00
2730	“ “ “	8.40
2731	“ “ “	7.80
2732	“ “ “	6.60
2733	“ “ “	24.00
2734	“ “ “	24.00
2735	“ “ “	6.60
2736	“ “ “	7.80
2737	“ “ “	7.80
2738	“ “ “	6.60
2739	4½ to 6 in. x 1⅛	$ 7.80
2740	“ “ “	5.50
2741	“ “ “	30.00
2742	“ “ “	10.20
2743	“ “ “	7.00
2744	“ “ “	132.00
2745	“ “ “	7.80
2747	“ “ “	30.00
2748	“ “ “	21.60
2749	“ “ “	5.00
2750	“ “ “	5.50
2751	“ “ “	6.00
2752	4½ to 5¾ in. sq. x 1⅛	18.00
2752	6 6¾ “ x 1⅛	21.60
2752	5 5¾ “ x 1⅜	21.60
2752	6 6¾ “ x 1⅜	24.00
2754	1⅝ x 8 in	32.00
2755	2¾ x 4½ in	36.00
2755	3⅛ x 2½ in	26.00
2759	5 to 6 in. sq. x 1⅛	30.00
2759	6 to 6¾ “ x 1⅜	36.00
2759	7 to 8½ “ x 1⅜	42.00
2759	6 to 6¾ “ x 1¾	42.00
2759	7 to 8¼ “ x 1¾	45.60
2760	4 in. diameter	36.00
2761	3¾ in. sq	48.00
2761	4¾ “	68.00
2762	2¾ x 6 in	56.00
2762	3¾ x 8 in	80.00
2763	1 in. diameter	7.00
2763	1¼ “ “	8.00
2763	1½ “ “	9.00
2763	1¾ “ “	10.00
2763	2 “ “	12.00
2763	2¼ “ “	14.00
2763	2½ “ “	16.00
2763	2¾ “ “	18.00
2763	3¼ “ “	20.00
2764	1 “ “	8.00
2764	1¼ “ “	10.00
2764	1½ “ “	12.00
2764	1¾ “ “	13.00
2764	2 “ “	14.00
2765	2⅜ in. sq	16.00
2766	1⅞ “	13.00
2767	1¾ in. diameter	10.00
2768	1⅞ in sq	13.00
2768	2⅜ “	16.00
2768	3¼ “	32.00
2769	1¾ “	12.00
2770	1¾ in. diameter	10.00
2770	2½ “ “	18.00
2771	1⅛ “ “	8.00
2771	1⅜ “ “	9.00
2771	1⅝ “ “	10.00
2771	2⅞ “ ”	14 00
2772	4½ to 6 in. sq. x 1⅛	5.50
2773	4½ to 6 “ x 1⅛	7.00
2776	4½ to 6 “ x 1⅜	10.80
2777	4½ to 6 “ x 1⅜	18.00
2778	4½ to 6 “ x 1⅛	12.00
2779	4½ to 6 “ x 1⅛	24.00
2780	4½ to 6 “ x 1⅛	5.00
2787	5 to 6 “ x 1⅛	22.00
2788	5 to 6 “ x 1⅛	30.00
2790	5 to 6 “ x 1⅛	12.00
2791	5 to 6 “ x 1⅛	12.00
2792	5 to 6 “ x 1⅛	8.40
2793	5 to 6 “ x 1⅛	8.40
2794	5 to 6 “ x 1⅛	7.80
2795	5 to 6 “ x 1⅛	9.00
2796	5 to 6 “ x 1⅛	7.20
2800	5½ x 8 x 1⅛	9.00
2801	5½ x 7 x 1⅛	9.60
2802	5½ x 10 x 1⅛	10.00
2803	5½ x 10 x 1⅛	$18.00
2804	5½ x 10 x 1⅛	10.00
2805	5½ x 10 x 1⅛	12.00
2806	5½ x 11 x 1⅛	18.00
2807	5½ x 11 x 1⅛	19.20
2808	5½ x 10 x 1⅛	14.40
2809	5½ x 10 x 1⅛	10.00
2810	5½ x 10 x 1⅛	10.00
2811	5½ x 12 x 1⅛	14.00
2812	5½ x 12 x 1⅛	16.00
2813	5½ x 12 x 1⅛	14.00
2814	5½ x 11 x 1⅛	15.60
2815	5½ x 11 x 1⅛	13.20
2816	5½ x 11 x 1⅛	13.20
2817	5½ x 10 x 1⅛	14.40
2818	5½ x 10 x 1⅛	13.20
2819	5½ x 12 x 1⅛	14.40
2820	5½ x 12 x 1⅛	18.00
2821	5½ x 9½ x 1⅛	14.40
2822	5½ x 10 x 1⅛	36.00
2823	5½ x 10 x 1⅛	20.40
2824	5½ x 10 x 1⅛	14.40
2825	5½ x 11 x 1⅛	144.00
2826	5½ x 10 x 1⅛	14.40
2827	5½ x 10½ x 1⅛	11.00
2828	5½ x 10 x 1⅛	13.20
2829	5½ x 10½ x 1⅛	36.00
2830	5½ x 11 x 1⅛	24.00
2831	5½ x 10½ x 1⅛	14.00
2832	5 in. to 5¾ x 9 x 1⅜	48.00
2832	6 in. to 6¾ x 10 x 1⅜	54.00
2833	5 in. to 5¾ x 13 x 1⅜	60.00
2833	6 in. to 6¾ x 13 x 1⅜	72.00
2833	7 in. to 8 x 13 x 1⅜	90.00
2834	5½ x 12½ x 1⅜	72.00
2835	5½ x 11½ x 1⅛	15.60
2836	5½ x 12 x 1⅛	28.80
2837	5½ x 12 x 1⅛	60.00
2838	5½ x 10 x 1⅛	10.00
2839	5½ x 12½ x 1⅜	30.00
2844	5½ x 12 x 1⅛	66.00
2853	5½ x 11 x 1⅛	10.00
2855	5½ x 11 x 1⅜	60.00
2856	5½ x 10 x 1⅛	18.00
2900	5½ x 10 x 1⅜	11.00
2901	5½ x 9 x 1⅜	9.00
2902	5½ x 9 x 1⅜	9.00
2903	5½ x 8 x 1⅜	9.00
2904	5½ x 10 x 1⅜	11.00
2905	5½ x 10 x 1⅜	9.00
2906	5½ x 10 x 1⅜	11.00
2907	5½ x 10 x 1⅜	10.00
2908	5½ x 10 x 1⅜	10.00
2909	5½ x 12 x 1⅜	14.40
2910	5½ x 10 x 1⅜	10.00
2911	5½ x 10 x 1⅜	10.00
2912	5½ x 10 x 1⅜	10.00
2913	5½ x 10 x 1⅜	11.00
2914	5½ x 12 x 1⅜	24.00
2915	5½ x 11 x 1⅜	11.00
2916	5½ x 11 x 1⅜	11.00
2917	5½ x 11 x 1⅜	13.00
2918	5½ x 12 x 1⅜	13.00
2929	5½ x 12 x 1⅜	13.00
2935	5½ x 10 x 1⅜	9.00
2936	5½ x 12 x 1⅜	24.00
2937	5½ x 10 x 1⅜	9.00
2938	5½ x 10 x 1⅜	10.00
2940	5½ x 11 x 1⅜	9.50
2941	5½ x 10 x 1⅜	9.00
2942	5½ x 11 x 1⅜	9.00
2944	5½ x 11 x 1⅜	9.00
2949	5½ x 10 x 1⅜	9.00
2950	5½ x 12 x 1⅜	9.50

We can
furnish
anything
in

Stair Work

as promptly
and as
cheaply
as any
house in
the
business

We can
supply it
in any wood
that is to
be found
in the
market

STAIR GROUND PLANS.

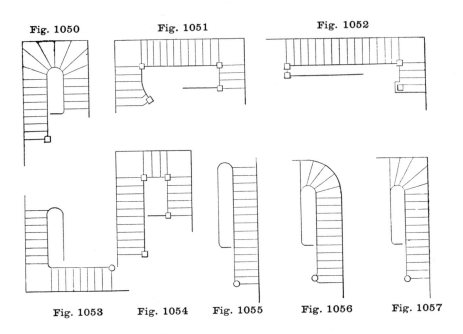

Fig. 1050   Fig. 1051   Fig. 1052

Fig. 1053   Fig. 1054   Fig. 1055   Fig. 1056   Fig. 1057

DIRECTIONS NECESSARY FOR ORDERING STAIRS and STAIR RAILING.

When a flight of stairs is wanted, we should know the height of story from floor to floor, width of joists in second story, width and run of stairs, the size of cylinder, style of base used in the hall, with rough sketch showing about the shape of stairs wanted.

For STAIR RAILING—Straight Flight.

We require the width of rise and step as sawed out on string board, the number of risers, the size of cylinder from face to face of string or face board, which way it turns at head of stairs, and the number of feet of straight rail required at landing. Unless we receive plan showing otherwise, we always suppose the top riser for a straight flight of stairs to be placed at the edge or spring of cylinder.

For CIRCULAR or WINDING STAIRS.

We should have an exact plan of stairs as built, giving the width of rise and step, the location of risers in cylinder, etc.; and, when there are straight steps below or above the cylinder, always give the distance from the first square riser to the edge or spring line of cylinder, on the face of string or face board. *Always write your address in full on the plans.*

STAIR RAILS.

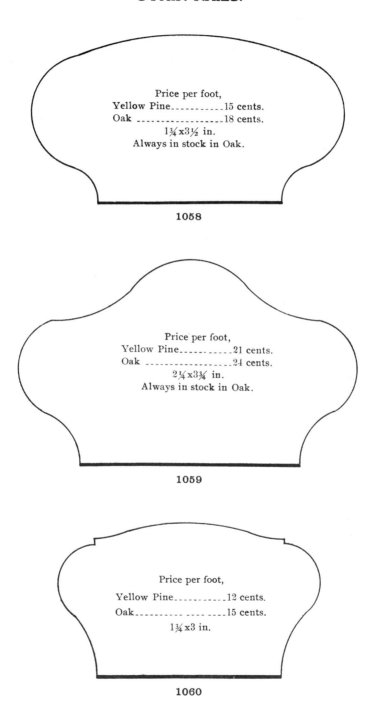

Price per foot,
Yellow Pine_____15 cents.
Oak _____18 cents.
1¾x3½ in.
Always in stock in Oak.

1058

Price per foot,
Yellow Pine_____21 cents.
Oak _____24 cents.
2¼x3¾ in.
Always in stock in Oak.

1059

Price per foot,
Yellow Pine_____12 cents.
Oak_____ ____ ____15 cents.
1¾x3 in.

1060

STAIR RAILS.

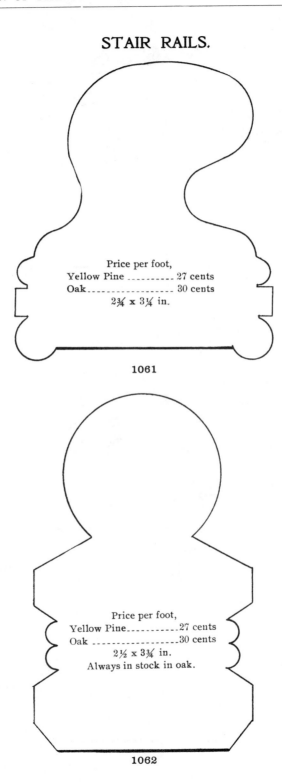

Price per foot,
Yellow Pine _____ 27 cents
Oak _____ 30 cents
2¾ x 3¼ in.

1061

Price per foot,
Yellow Pine _____ 27 cents
Oak _____ 30 cents
2½ x 3¾ in.
Always in stock in oak.

1062

STAIR RAILS.

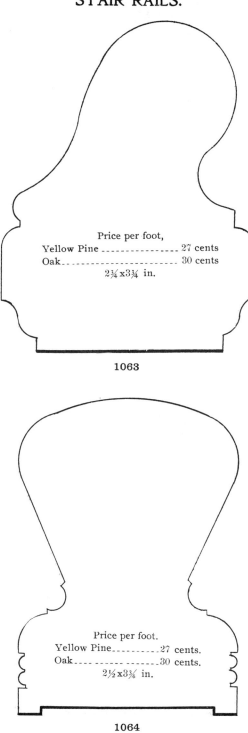

Price per foot,
Yellow Pine _____ 27 cents
Oak _____ 30 cents
2¾ x 3¾ in.

1063

Price per foot.
Yellow Pine _____ 27 cents.
Oak _____ 30 cents.
2½ x 3¾ in.

1064

STAIR RAILS.

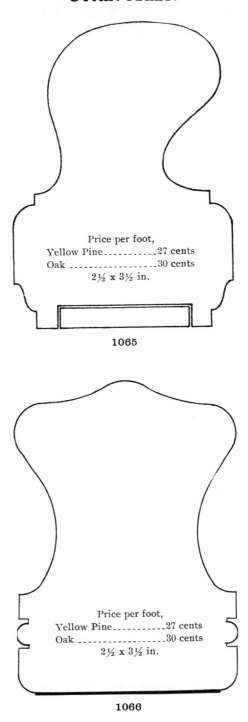

Price per foot,
Yellow Pine............27 cents
Oak ....30 cents
2½ x 3½ in.

1065

Price per foot,
Yellow Pine............27 cents
Oak ....30 cents
2½ x 3½ in.

1066

STAIR RAILS.

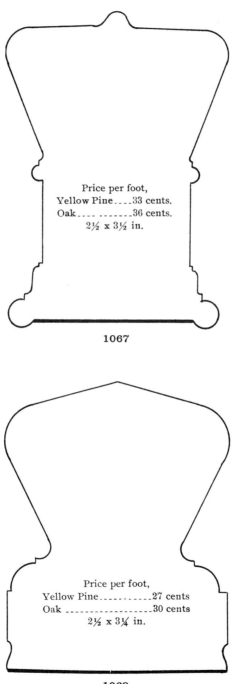

Price per foot,
Yellow Pine____33 cents.
Oak____ _____36 cents.
2½ x 3½ in.

1067

Price per foot,
Yellow Pine_____27 cents
Oak _____30 cents
2½ x 3¼ in.

1068

PRICES OF STAIR BALUSTERS AND NEWELS.

1¾ to ¾ and ⅞ as shown on page 149.

No.	Yellow Pine	Oak	No.	Yellow Pine	Oak
900	$0.18	$0.21	914	$0.21	$0.24
901	.18	.21	915	.27	.30
902	.24	.20	916	.21	.24
903	.18	.21	917	.21	.24
904	.18	.21	918	.40	.42
905	.18	.21	919	.40	.42
906	.21	.24	920	.33	.36
907	.24	.27	921	.33	.36
908	.15	.18	922	.42	.45
909	.42	.45	923	.39	.42
910	.42	.45	924	.39	.42
911	1.75	1.88	925	1.17	1.20
912	.27	.30	926	1.17	1.20
913	2.10	2.25			

STAIR STARTING NEWELS.

6 inch shaft as shown on pages 150-151.

No.	Yellow Pine	Oak	No.	Yellow Pine	Oak
927	$7.13	$7.50	942	$15.30	$15.40
928	7.13	7.50	943	15.40	15.75
929	9.00	9.75	944	16.50	17.00
930	10.50	10.90	945	12.00	12.40
933	6.00	6.40	946	16.50	17.00
934	12.00	12.40	947	12.75	13.15
935	7.13	7.50	948	15.00	15.75
939	10.50	10.90	949	15.00	15.75
940	15.00	15.40	950	19.50	20.00
941	18.40	18.75			

ANGLE AND LANDING POSTS.

5 inch shaft as shown on page 150.

No.	Yellow Pine	Oak	No.	Yellow Pine	Oak
931	$4.50	$4.90	937	$5.25	$5.65
932	9.00	9.40	938	7.50	.90
936	9.75	10.05			

Above prices are for Plain Red Oak.   For other woods write for price.

STAIR BALUSTERS.

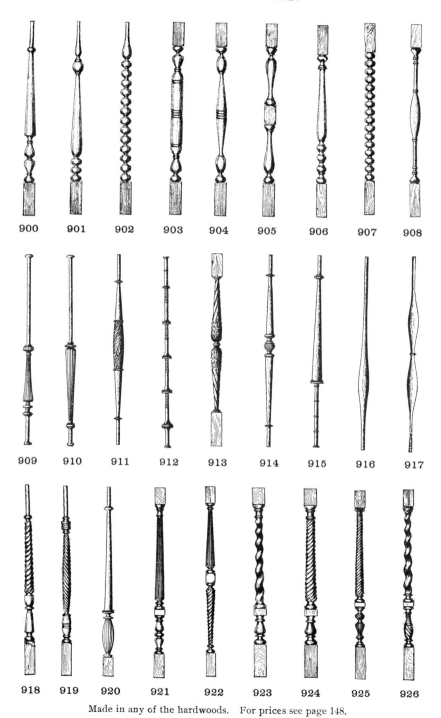

Made in any of the hardwoods.   For prices see page 148.

MAIN, ANGLE and LANDING NEWELS.

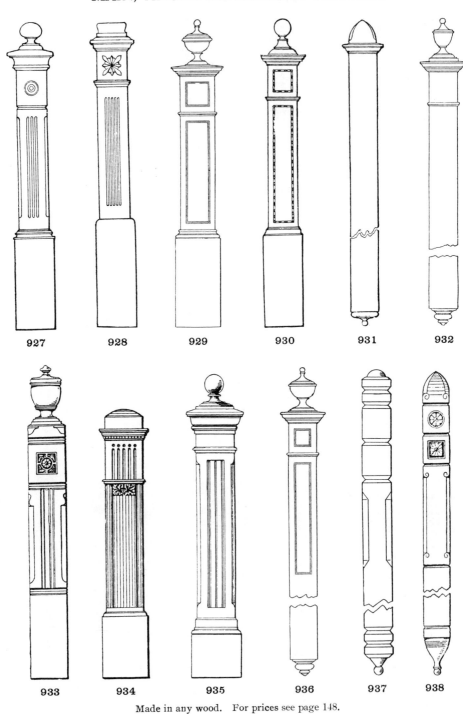

927   928   929   930   931   932

933   934   935   936   937   938

Made in any wood.   For prices see page 148.

MAIN STAIR NEWELS.

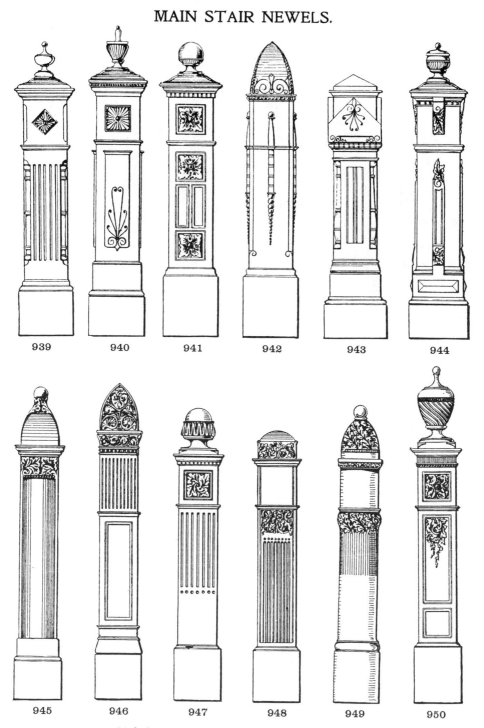

939   940   941   942   943   944

945   946   947   948   949   950

Made in any kind of wood.   For prices see page 148.

STAIR ELEVATIONS.

1139   1140

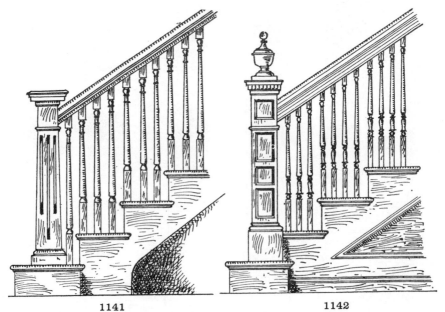

1141   1142

Before asking prices or ordering stairways read carefully page 142.

WRITE FOR PRICES.

STAIR ELEVATIONS.

1143

1144

1145

1146

Before asking prices or ordering stairways read carefully page 142.

WRITE FOR PRICES.

STAIR ELEVATIONS.

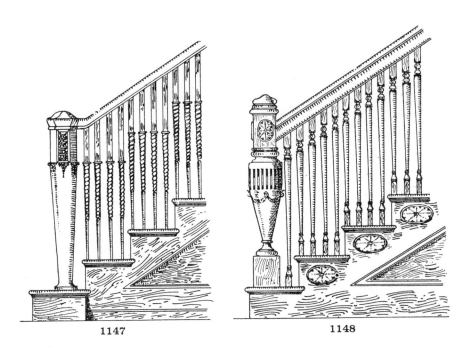

1147   1148

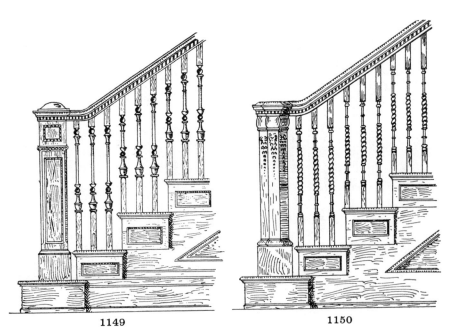

1149   1150

Before asking prices or ordering stairways read carefully page 142.

WRITE FOR PRICES.

STAIR ELEVATIONS.

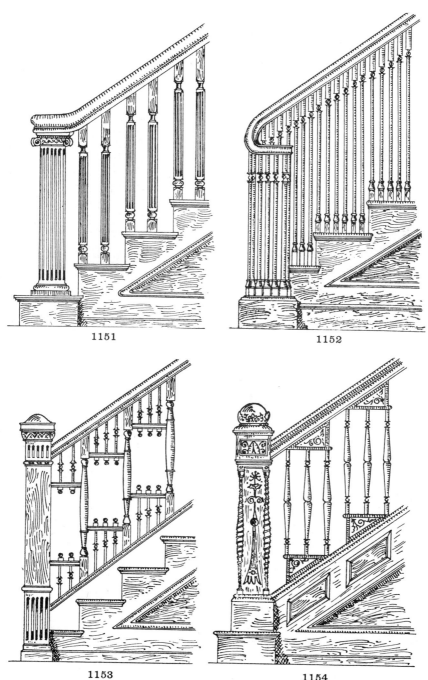

1151

1152

1153

1154

Before asking prices or ordering stairways read carefully page 142.

WRITE FOR PRICES.

STAIR ELEVATIONS.

1186

1187

1188

1189

Before asking prices or ordering stairways read carefully page 142.

WRITE FOR PRICES.

STAIR ELEVATIONS.

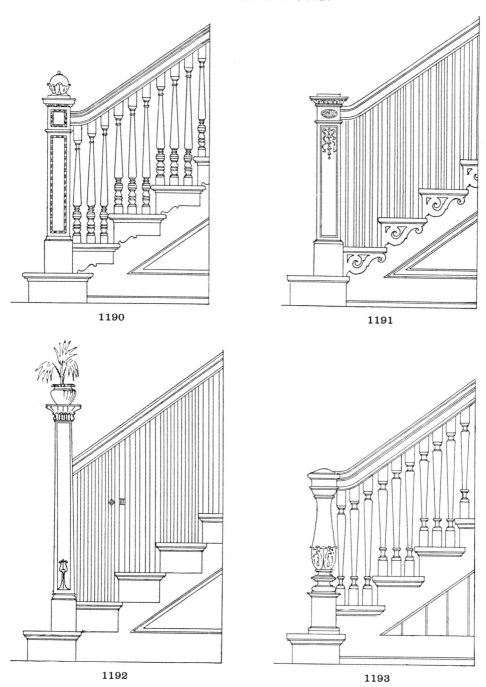

1190

1191

1192

1193

Before asking prices or ordering stairways read carefully page 142.

WRITE FOR PRICES.

STAIR ELEVATIONS.

1194

1195

1196

1197

Before asking prices or ordering stairways read carefully page 142.

WRITE FOR PRICES.

STAIR ELEVATIONS.

1198

1199

Before asking prices or ordering stairways read carefully page 142.

WRITE FOR PRICES.

STAIR INTERIORS.

1155

Before asking prices or ordering stairways read carefully page 142.

STAIR INTERIORS.

1156

STAIR INTERIORS.

1158

Before asking prices or ordering stairways read carefully page 142.

STAIR INTERIORS.

1157

Before asking prices or ordering stairways read carefully page 142.

STAIR BRACKETS.

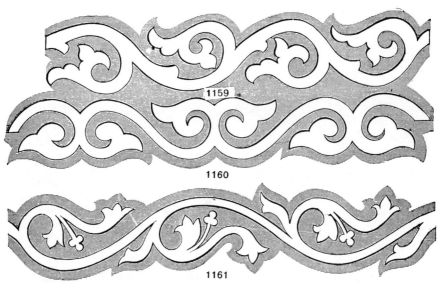

Level Brackets for Stairs, 4 inches wide, ¼ inch thick.   Price per foot, Yellow Pine, 6 cents; Oak, 8 cents.

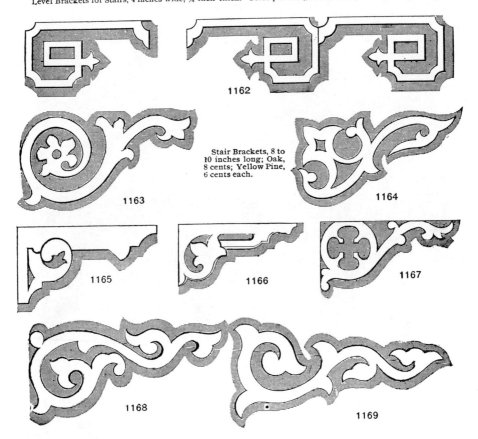

Stair Brackets, 8 to 10 inches long; Oak, 8 cents; Yellow Pine, 6 cents each.

PANELED WAINSCOTING—with Cap and Base
Three feet, six inches high over all.

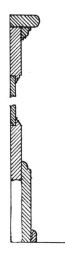
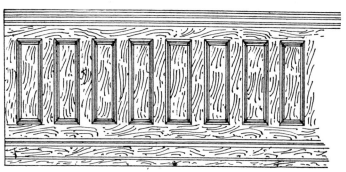

1180

Plain Sawed Oak _____per running foot, $1.50
Quarter   "   _____   "   "   1.75

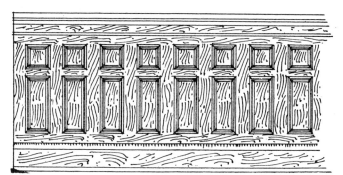

1181

Plain Sawed Oak _____per running foot, $2.00
Quarter   "   _____   "   "   2.25

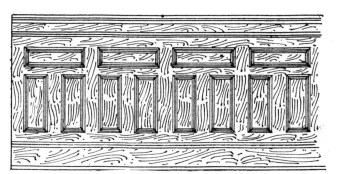

1182

Plain Sawed Oak _____per running foot, $2.00
Quarter   "   _____   "   "   2.25

TURNED ROSETTES.

WHITE PINE.

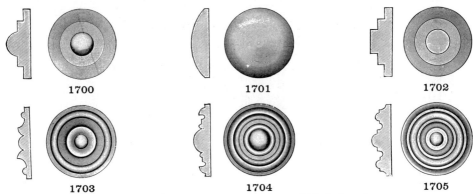

Write for prices, giving size, quantity, and kind of wood.

TURNED DOWELS, BALLS AND DROPS.

IN SOFT WOODS.

Dowels, ½ inch diameter, for 1¾ inch balls, per 100 lineal feet_____$0.90
  "   ⅜ inch diameter, for 1⅜ inch balls,   "   "   " _____ .90

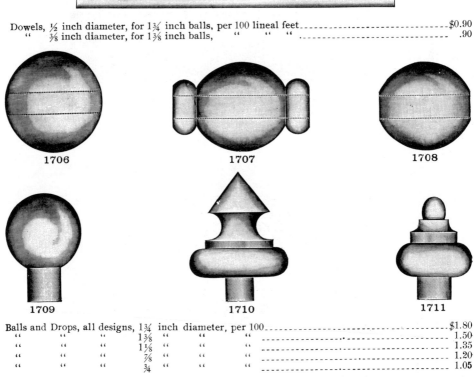

Balls and Drops, all designs, 1¾ inch diameter, per 100_____$1.80
  "   "   "   1⅜ "   "   " _____ 1.50
  "   "   "   1⅛ "   "   " _____ 1.35
  "   "   "   ⅞   "   "   " _____ 1.20
  "   "   "   ¾   "   "   " _____ 1.05

If balls are cross-bored, add 25 cents per 100 net extra.   Above prices for Pine or Poplar.   Write for prices in hardwood.

VERGE BOARDS.

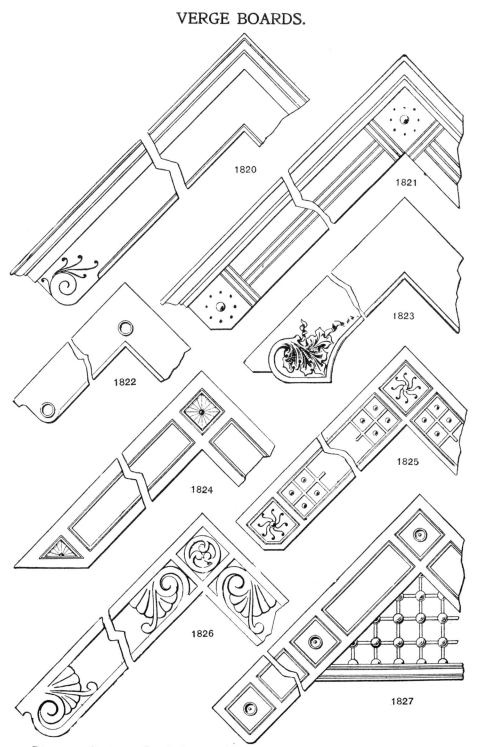

Prices on application.   Give thickness, width of board, length of rafter and pitch of roof.

ADJUSTABLE GABLE ORNAMENTS.

Can be Fitted to any Pitch of Roof.

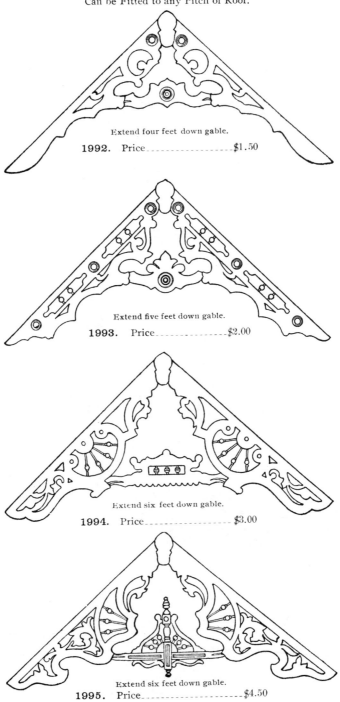

Extend four feet down gable.

1992. Price................$1.50

Extend five feet down gable.

1993. Price.............$2.00

Extend six feet down gable.

1994. Price................$3.00

Extend six feet down gable.

1995. Price..................$4.50

Can be Fitted to Either Old or New Houses.

GABLE ORNAMENTS.

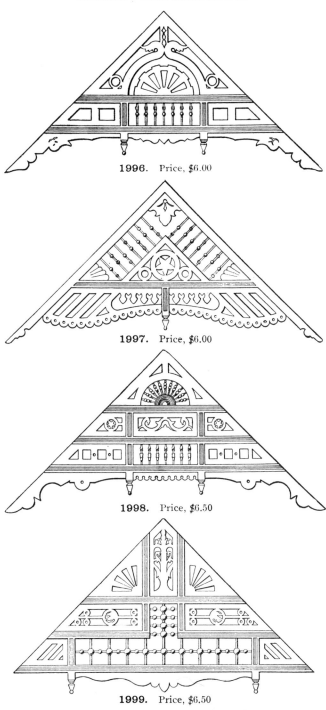

1996. Price, $6.00

1997. Price, $6.00

1998. Price, $6.50

1999. Price, $6.50

We make these ornaments to fit any size or pitch. Unless otherwise ordered, we make them six feet across at base.

GABLE ORNAMENTS, CRESTINGS and FINIALS.

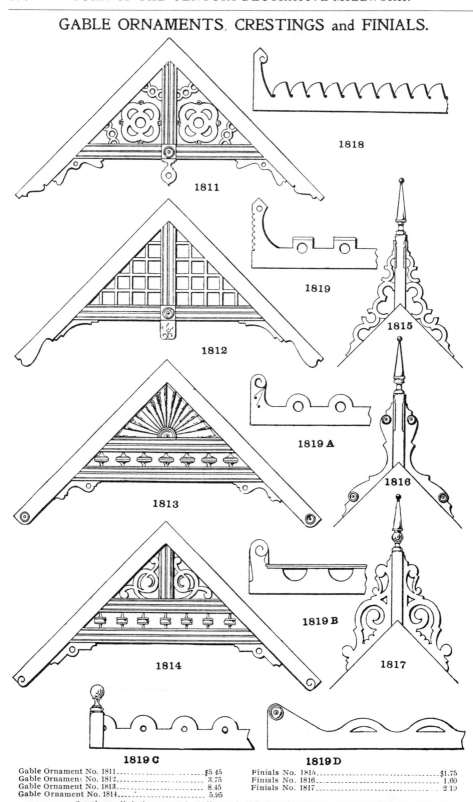

1818

1811

1819

1812

1815

1819 A

1813

1816

1819 B

1814

1817

1819 C

1819 D

Gable Ornament No. 1811....................$5 45
Gable Ornament No. 1812.................... 3.75
Gable Ornament No. 1813.................... 8.45
Gable Ornament No. 1814.................... 5.95

Finials No. 1815..........................$1.75
Finials No. 1816.......................... 1.60
Finials No. 1817.......................... 2 10

Crestings, all designs, ⅞x6, including ends 10 inches high, 12 cents per lineal foot.

PORCH RAILS.

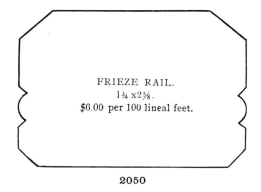

FRIEZE RAIL.
1¾ x2⅝.
$6.00 per 100 lineal feet.

2050

TOP OR HAND RAIL.
1¾ x3.
$6.75 per 100 lineal feet.

2051

BOTTOM OR FOOT RAIL.
1¾ x3.
$6.75 per 100 lineal feet.

2052

PORCH RAILS.

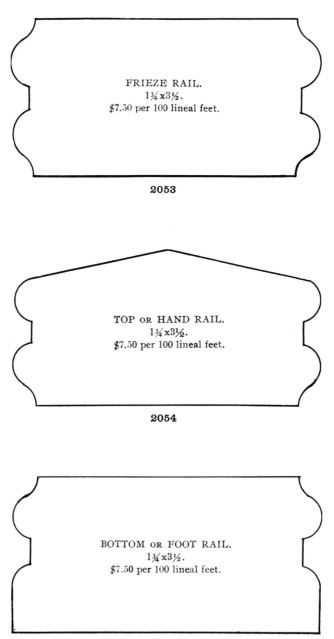

FRIEZE RAIL.
1¾ x 3½.
$7.50 per 100 lineal feet.

2053

TOP OR HAND RAIL.
1¾ x 3½.
$7.50 per 100 lineal feet.

2054

BOTTOM OR FOOT RAIL.
1¾ x 3½.
$7.50 per 100 lineal feet.

2055

PORCH RAILS and BALUSTER STOCK.

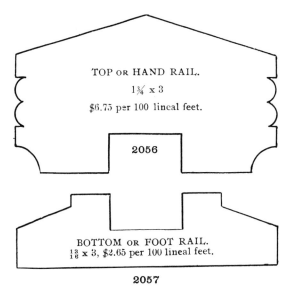

TOP or HAND RAIL.

$1\frac{3}{4}$ x 3

$6.75 per 100 lineal feet.

2056

BOTTOM or FOOT RAIL.
$1\frac{3}{16}$ x 3, $2.65 per 100 lineal feet.

2057

BALUSTER
STOCK.
$1\frac{3}{4}$ x $1\frac{3}{4}$.
$3.55 per 100
lineal feet.

2058

BALUSTER
STOCK.
$1\frac{3}{8}$ x $1\frac{3}{8}$.
$1.95 per 100
lineal feet.

2059

BALUSTER STOCK.
$1\frac{3}{4}$ x $1\frac{3}{4}$
$3.55 per 100 lineal feet.

2060

BALUSTER STOCK
$1\frac{3}{8}$ x $1\frac{3}{8}$
$1.95 per 100 lineal ft.

2061

BRACKETS.

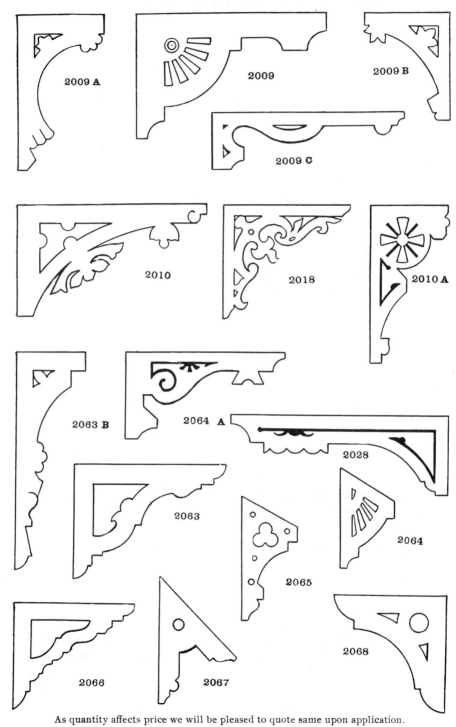

As quantity affects price we will be pleased to quote same upon application.

BRACKETS.

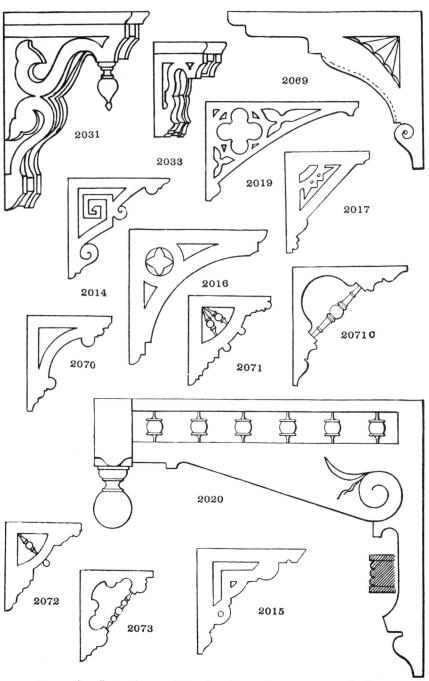

2069

2031

2033

2019

2017

2014

2016

2071C

2070

2071

2020

2072

2073

2015

As quantity affects price we will be pleased to quote same upon application.

BRACKETS.

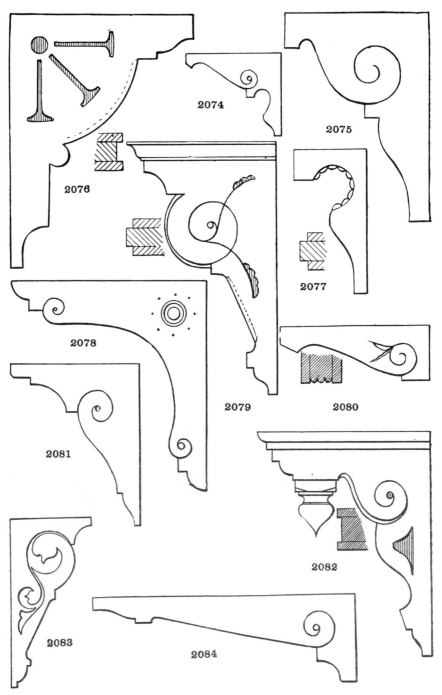

As quantity affects price we will be pleased to quote same upon application.

BRACKETS.

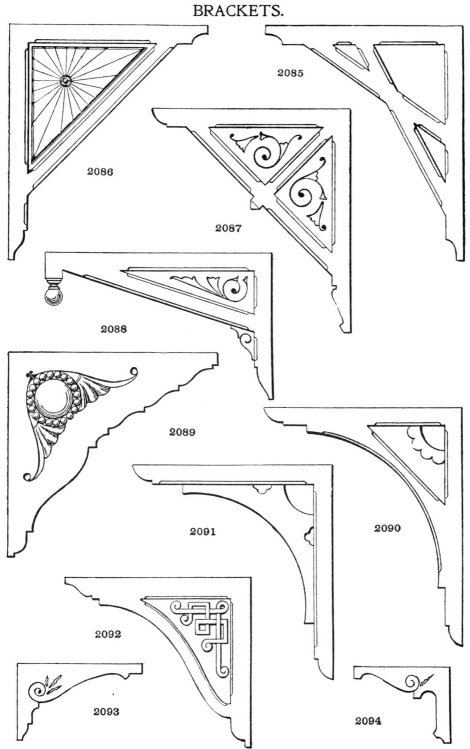

As quantity affects price we will be pleased to quote same upon application.

WHITE PINE STOCK BRACKETS.

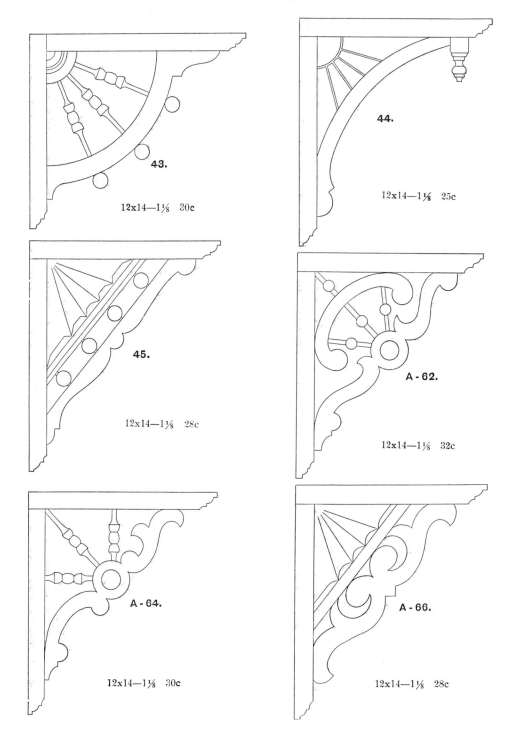

43.

12x14—1⅛ 30c

44.

12x14—1⅛ 25c

45.

12x14—1⅛ 28c

A - 62.

12x14—1⅛ 32c

A - 64.

12x14—1⅛ 30c

A - 66.

12x14—1⅛ 28c

BRACKETS.

THESE DESIGNS ALWAYS IN STOCK—OTHER PATTERNS MADE TO ORDER.

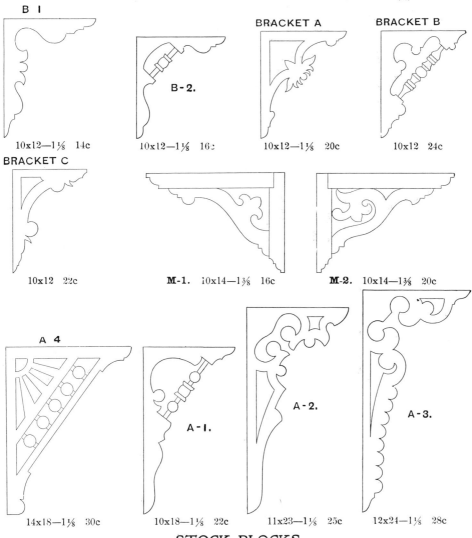

B I

10x12—1⅛ 14c

B-2.

10x12—1⅛ 16c

BRACKET A

10x12—1⅛ 20c

BRACKET B

10x12 24c

BRACKET C

10x12 22c

M-1. 10x14—1⅜ 16c

M-2. 10x14—1⅜ 20c

A 4

14x18—1⅛ 30c

A-1.

10x18—1⅛ 22c

A-2.

11x23—1⅛ 25c

A-3.

12x24—1⅛ 28c

STOCK BLOCKS.

FOR PRICES ON BLOCKS SEE REGULAR LISTS AND DISCOUNTS.

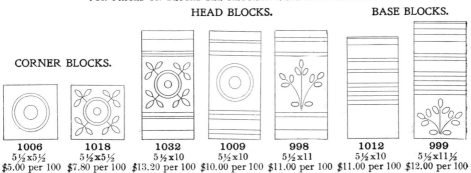

HEAD BLOCKS.

BASE BLOCKS.

CORNER BLOCKS.

1006	1018	1032	1009	998	1012	999
5½x5½	5½x5½	5½x10	5½x10	5½x11	5½x10	5½x11½
$5.00 per 100	$7.80 per 100	$13.20 per 100	$10.00 per 100	$11.00 per 100	$11.00 per 100	$12.00 per 100

PORCH BALUSTERS.

HEAVY TURNED BALUSTERS.

| 2100 | 2102 | 2103 | 2104 | 2105 | 2106 |

Size 20 to 24 x 2¾ inches, 24c each.

SAWED BALUSTERS.

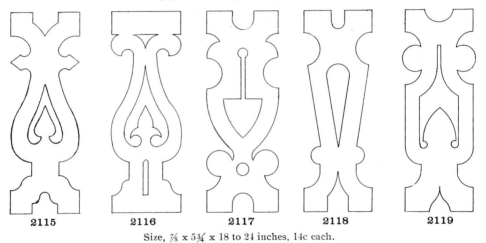

| 2115 | 2116 | 2117 | 2118 | 2119 |

Size, ⅞ x 5¾ x 18 to 24 inches, 14c each.

ORDINARY TURNED BALUSTERS.

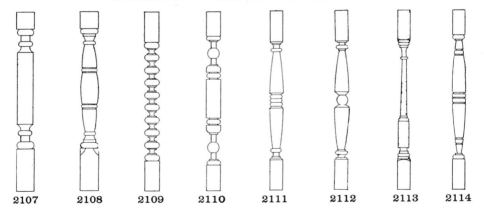

| 2107 | 2108 | 2109 | 2110 | 2111 | 2112 | 2113 | 2114 |

Size, 1¾ x 20 or 24 inches, 15c each.

PORCH SPINDLES.

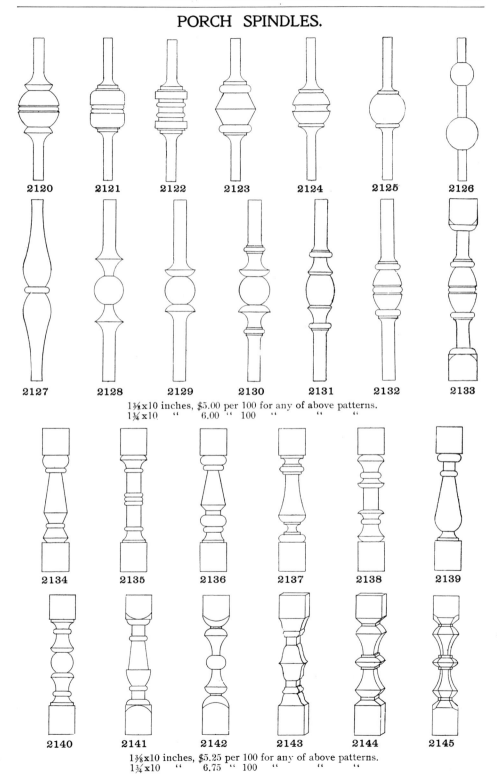

2120   2121   2122   2123   2124   2125   2126

2127   2128   2129   2130   2131   2132   2133

1⅜x10 inches, $5.00 per 100 for any of above patterns.
1¾x10   "   6.00 " 100   "   "   "

2134   2135   2136   2137   2138   2139

2140   2141   2142   2143   2144   2145

1⅜x10 inches, $5.25 per 100 for any of above patterns.
1¾x10   "   6.75 " 100   "   "   "

STOCK COLUMNS, SPINDLES, BALUSTERS and NEWELS.

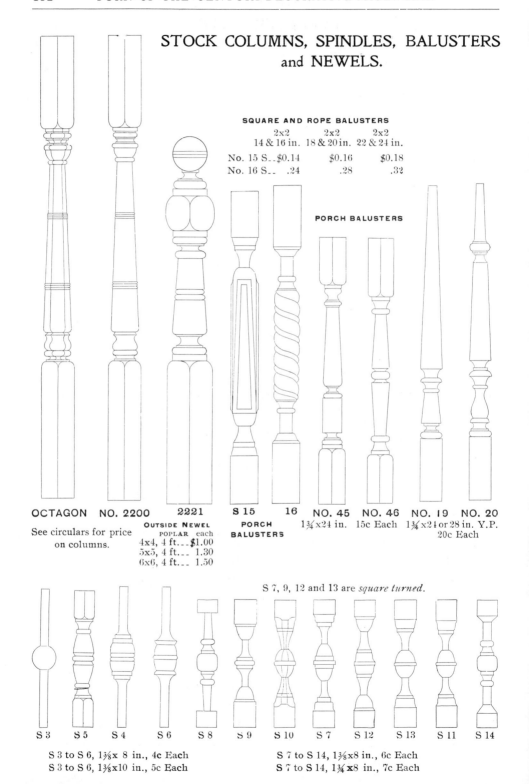

SQUARE AND ROPE BALUSTERS

	2x2 14 & 16 in.	2x2 18 & 20 in.	2x2 22 & 24 in.
No. 15 S__	$0.14	$0.16	$0.18
No. 16 S__	.24	.28	.32

PORCH BALUSTERS

OCTAGON   NO. 2200   2221

See circulars for price on columns.

OUTSIDE NEWEL
POPLAR   each
4x4, 4 ft.__$1.00
5x5, 4 ft.__ 1.30
6x6, 4 ft.__ 1.50

S 15   16
PORCH BALUSTERS

NO. 45   NO. 46
1¾x24 in.   15c Each

NO. 19   NO. 20
1¾x24 or 28 in. Y.P.
20c Each

S 7, 9, 12 and 13 are *square turned.*

S 3   S 5   S 4   S 6   S 8   S 9   S 10   S 7   S 12   S 13   S 11   S 14

S 3 to S 6, 1⅜x 8 in., 4c Each
S 3 to S 6, 1⅜x10 in., 5c Each

S 7 to S 14, 1⅜x8 in., 6c Each
S 7 to S 14, 1¾x8 in., 7c Each

PORCH COLUMNS.

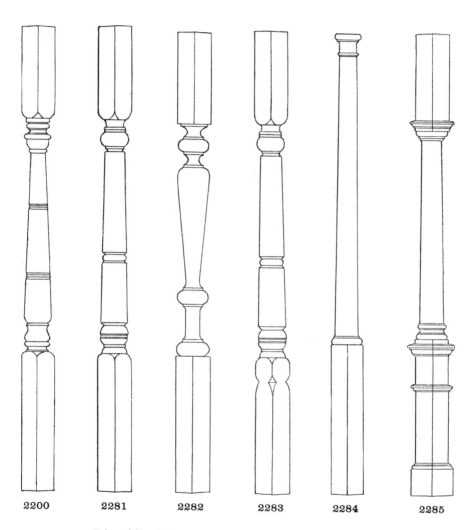

| 2200 | 2281 | 2282 | 2283 | 2284 | 2285 |

Price of No. 2200.   Price of No. 2285.

4x4. 8 ft., $0.90   5x5, 8 ft., $1.45   6x6. 8 ft., $1.90   5x5, 8 ft., $2.00   6x6, 8 ft., $2.40
4x4, 9 ft., 1.00   5x5, 9 ft., 1.60   6x6, 9 ft., 2.20   5x5, 9 ft., 2.15   6x6, 9 ft., 2.60
4x4, 10 ft., 1.10   5x5, 10 ft., 1.75   6x6, 10 ft., 2.40   5x5, 10 ft., 2.35   6x6, 10 ft., 2.75

For columns No. 2281, 2282 and 2283, add 10 cents net to price of No. 2200. For column No. 2284, add 20 cents net to price of No. 2200. Made of No. 1 Poplar, nice stock and smooth workmanship.

PORCH COLUMNS.

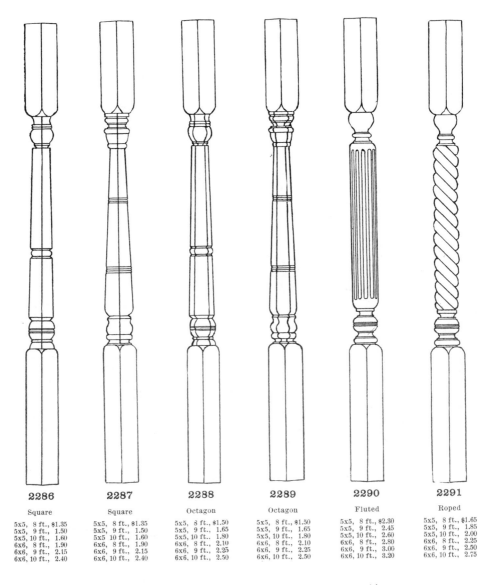

2286	2287	2288	2289	2290	2291
Square	Square	Octagon	Octagon	Fluted	Roped
5x5, 8 ft., $1.35	5x5, 8 ft., $1.35	5x5, 8 ft., $1.50	5x5, 8 ft., $1.50	5x5, 8 ft., $2.30	5x5, 8 ft., $1.65
5x5, 9 ft., 1.50	5x5, 9 ft., 1.50	5x5, 9 ft., 1.65	5x5, 9 ft., 1.65	5x5, 9 ft., 2.45	5x5, 9 ft., 1.85
5x5, 10 ft., 1.60	5x5 10 ft., 1.60	5x5, 10 ft., 1.80	5x5, 10 ft., 1.80	5x5, 10 ft., 2.60	5x5, 10 ft., 2.00
6x6, 8 ft., 1.90	6x6, 8 ft., 1.90	6x6, 8 ft., 2.10	6x6, 8 ft., 2.10	6x6, 8 ft., 2.80	6x6, 8 ft., 2.25
6x6, 9 ft., 2.15	6x6, 9 ft., 2.15	6x6, 9 ft., 2.25	6x6, 9 ft., 2.25	6x6, 9 ft., 3.00	6x6, 9 ft., 2.50
6x6, 10 ft., 2.40	6x6, 10 ft., 2.40	6x6, 10 ft., 2.50	6x6, 10 ft., 2.50	6x6, 10 ft., 3.20	6x6, 10 ft., 2.75

Made of No. 1 Poplar, nice stock and smooth workmanship.

PORCH COLUMNS and NEWELS.

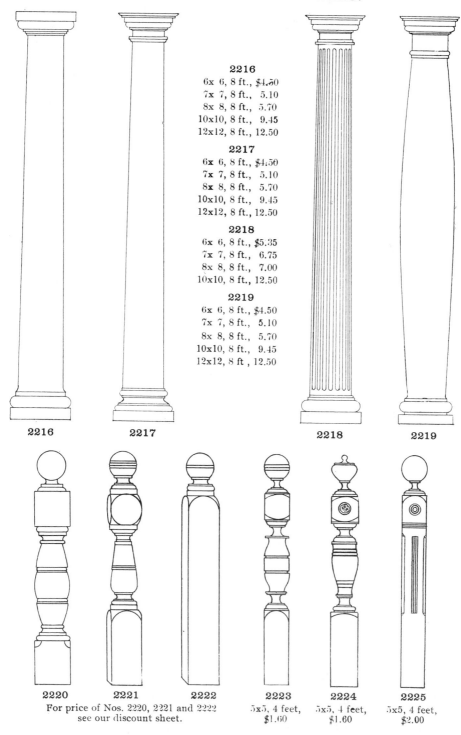

2216
6x 6, 8 ft., $4.50
7x 7, 8 ft., 5.10
8x 8, 8 ft., 5.70
10x10, 8 ft., 9.45
12x12, 8 ft., 12.50

2217
6x 6, 8 ft., $4.50
7x 7, 8 ft., 5.10
8x 8, 8 ft., 5.70
10x10, 8 ft., 9.45
12x12, 8 ft., 12.50

2218
6x 6, 8 ft., $5.35
7x 7, 8 ft., 6.75
8x 8, 8 ft., 7.00
10x10, 8 ft., 12.50

2219
6x 6, 8 ft., $4.50
7x 7, 8 ft., 5.10
8x 8, 8 ft., 5.70
10x10, 8 ft., 9.45
12x12, 8 ft , 12.50

2216   2217   2218   2219

2220   2221   2222   2223   2224   2225

For price of Nos. 2220, 2221 and 2222
see our discount sheet.

5x5, 4 feet,
$1.60

5x5, 4 feet,
$1.60

5x5, 4 feet,
$2.00

PORCH COLUMNS and NEWELS.

A2238
7¾ in. shaft, 8 ft. long
$7.50

B2238
7¾ in. shaft, 8 ft. long
$11.65

2240
7¾ in. shaft, 8 ft. long
$10.50

2239
7¾ in. shaft, 8 ft. long
$14.25

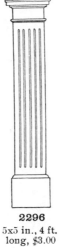

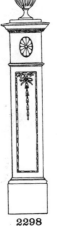

2294
5x5 in., 4 ft.
long, $1.50

2295
5x5 in., 4 ft.
long, $2.65

2296
5x5 in., 4 ft.
long, $3.00

2297
5x5 in., 4 ft.
long, $3.75

2298
5x5 in., 4 ft.
long, $6.00

2299
5x5 in., 4 ft.
long, $6.40

TWIN COLUMNS on PEDESTALS.

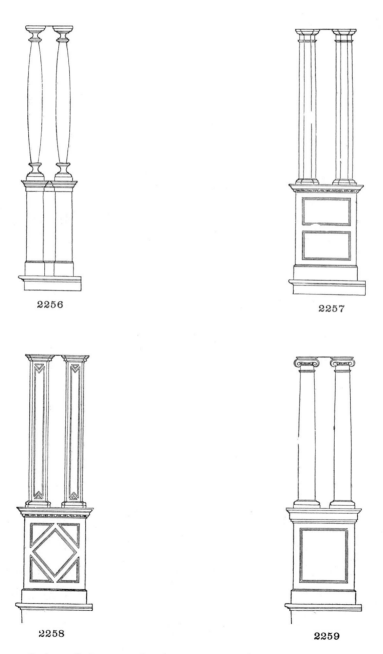

Designs offering suggestions for Porch Columns resting on Pedestals.

PORCH DESIGNS.

Design O 1.   Design O 2.   Design O 3.

Design O 4.   Design O 5.   Design O 6.

Made from stock patterns of Columns, Newels, Balusters, Rails, Spindles and Brackets shown on preceding pages.

PORCH DESIGNS.

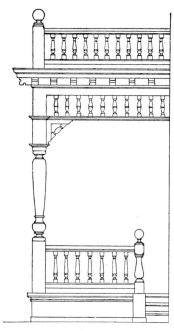

Design A.

Design B.

Design C.

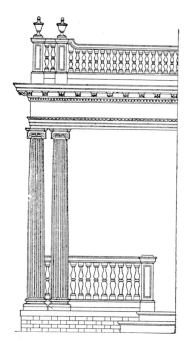

Design D.

WRITE FOR PRICES

PORCH DESIGNS

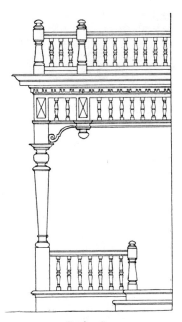

Design I.

Design J.

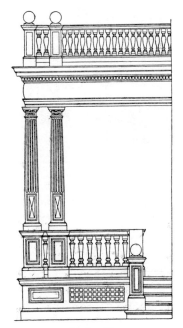

Design K.

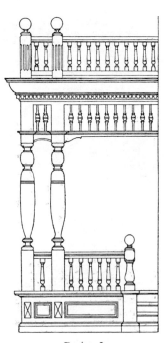

Design I.

WRITE FOR PRICES.

PORCH DESIGNS.

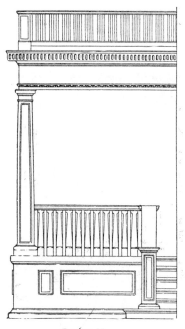

Design N.

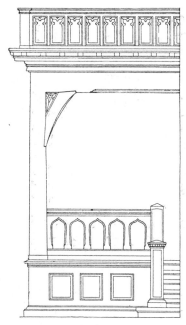

Design O.

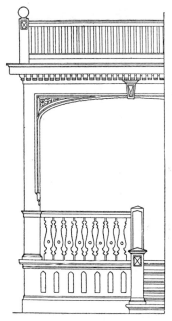

Design P

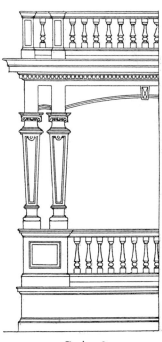

Design Q.

WRITE FOR PRICES.

PORCH VIEWS.

2266.   Write for prices.   Send ground plan with size of porch and number and location of columns, and show space left open for entrance.

PORCH VIEWS.

2267 Write for prices. Send ground plan with size of porch and number and location of columns, and show space left open for entrance.

PORCH VIEWS.

2268.   Write for prices.   Send ground plan with size of porch and number and location of columns, and show space left open for entrance.

PORCH VIEWS.

2269. Write for prices. Send ground plan with size of porch and number and location of columns and show space left open for entrance.

PORCH VIEWS.

2270. Write for prices.   Send ground plan with size of porch and number and location of columns, and show space left open for entrance.

PORCH VIEWS.

2271. Write for prices. Send ground plan with size of porch and number and location of columns, and show space left open for entrance.

PORCH VIEWS.

2272.   Write for prices.   Send ground plan with size of porch and number and location of columns, and show space left open for entrance.

PORCH VIEWS.

2273. Write for prices. Send ground plan with size of porch and number and location of columns, and show space left open for entrance.

CHURCH WINDOWS.

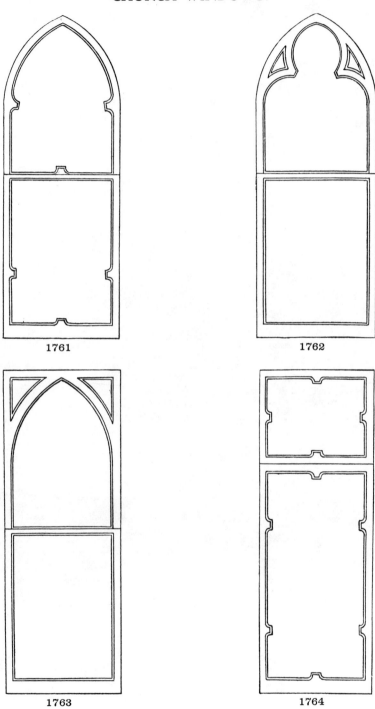

1761

1762

1763

1764

WRITE FOR PRICES.

CHURCH DOORS.

1765

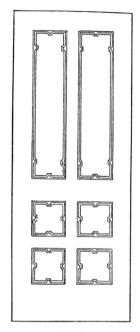

1766

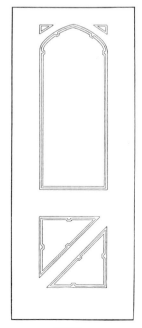

1767

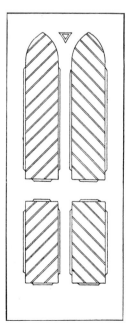

1768

WRITE FOR PRICES.

MULLION CHURCH WINDOWS.

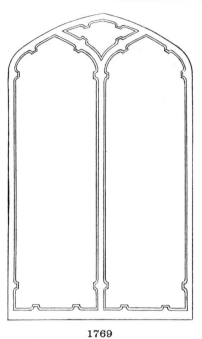

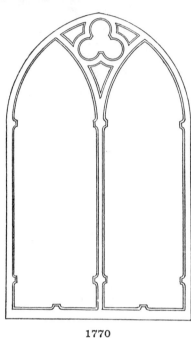

1769

1770

CHURCH DOORS.

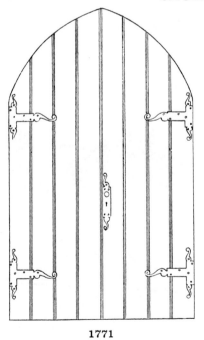

1771

1772

WRITE FOR PRICES.

ALTAR RAIL.

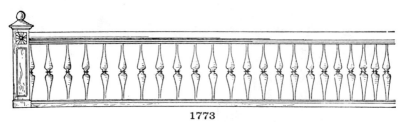

1773

Price per lineal foot of Rail and Balusters__$0.75   Posts, each_____$3.75

1774

Price per lineal foot of Rail and Balusters_$1.20   Posts, each_____$4.00

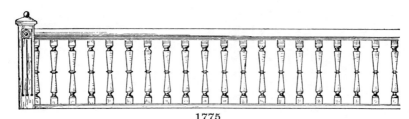

1775

Price per lineal foot of Rail and Balusters__$0.60   Posts, each_____$3.50

1776

Price per lineal foot of Rail and Balusters_$1.50   Posts, each _____$4.00

Price is based on Oak or woods of equal value, not filled or varnished. Usual height of rail, 24 inches. For pine or poplar for paint work, deduct 10 per cent. For circle or segment shaped railing, write for prices.

CHURCH PULPITS.

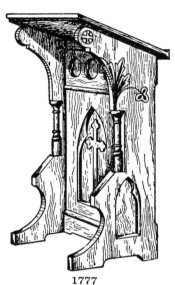

1777
Price, $20.75
Usual size made: Top, 20x24 inches. Height, 42 inches.

1788
Price, $22.50
Usual size made; 24x36 inches. Bible top, 18x22 inches. Height to top of bible top, 42 inches.

1789
Price, $24.00
Usual size made; 22x32 inches. Bible top, 18x22 inches. Height to top of bible top, 42 inches.

1790
Price, $26.25
Usual size made; 24x36 inches. Bible top, 18x22 inches. Height to top of bible top, 42 inches.

Above prices are based on Oak or woods of equal value. If made of Poplar or Pine for paint work, deduct 10 per cent. If finished in oil and varnish, add 20 per cent.

PEW ENDS FOR CHURCHES.

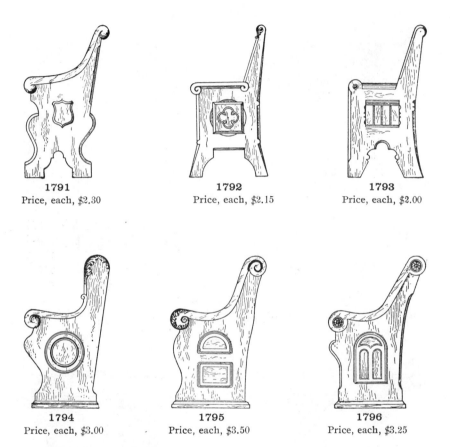

1791
Price, each, $2.30

1792
Price, each, $2.15

1793
Price, each, $2.00

1794
Price, each, $3.00

1795
Price, each, $3.50

1796
Price, each, $3.25

The above prices are based on oak or woods of equal value.   Plowed out inside ready to receive seats and backs.   For pew ends made of poplar for paint work, deduct 10 per cent.

CUTS OF PEW BODIES.

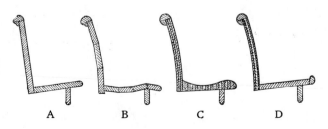

A   B   C   D

The above cuts show the different styles of pew bodies we manufacture.   Style "A" is the most reasonable in price and the style in most common use.

CHURCH SEATS.

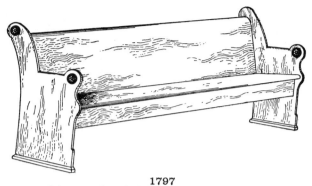

1797
Price complete, including pew ends, as shown.

8 foot seats, not filled or varnished, per lineal foot_____$1.75
10 "   "   "   "   "   "   "   _____ 1.15
12 "   "   "   "   "   "   "   _____ 1.00

1798
Price complete including pew ends, as shown.

8 foot seats, not filled or varnished, per lineal foot_____$1.50
10 "   "   "   "   "   "   "   _____ 1.35
12 "   "   "   "   "   "   "   _____ 1.25

1799
Price complete including pew ends, as shown.

8 foot seats, not filled or varnished, per lineal foot_____$1.80
10 "   "   "   "   "   "   "   _____ 1.65
12 "   "   "   "   "   "   "   _____ 1.50

The usual size of church seats made, is: Back, 18 inches high; seat, 14 inches wide; height of seat, 16½ inches. Pew ends, 1¼ inch thick. Above prices are based on oak or woods of equal value. For church seats made of pine or poplar, for paint work, deduct 10 per cent from above prices. If finished in oil and varnished, add 20 per cent. Above prices are for style "A" back and seat, as shown on page 206.

WINDOW FRAMES for FRAME BUILDINGS.

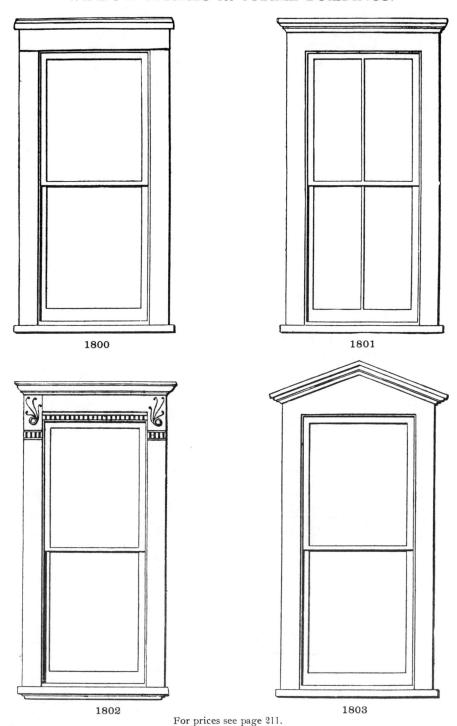

1800

1801

1802

1803

For prices see page 211.

WINDOW FRAMES for FRAME BUILDINGS.

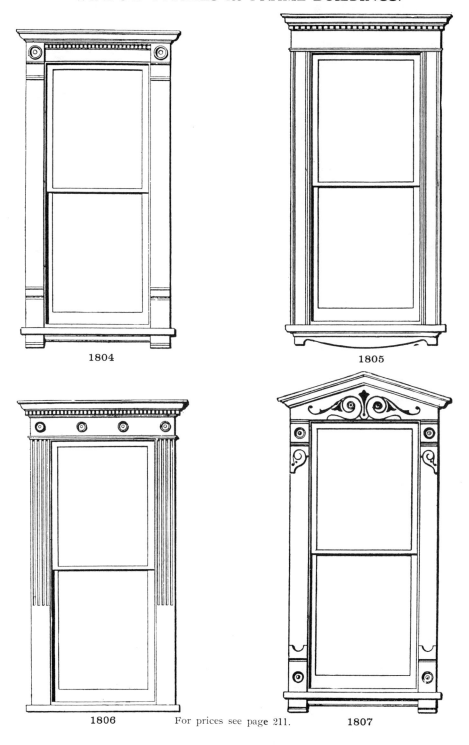

1804

1805

1806

For prices see page 211.

1807

GOTHIC WINDOW FRAMES.

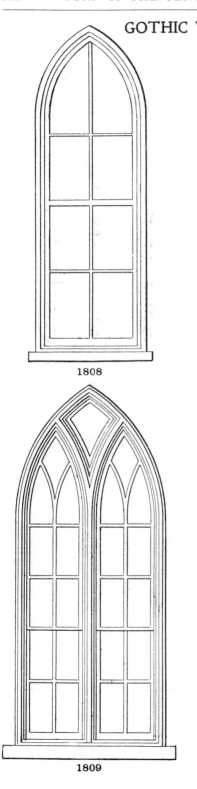

1808

1809

1810

When ordering Gothic Windows, Doors or Frames, give radius and size of opening.

Write for prices on above frames, giving sizes, width of jambs and full information.

PRICE LIST of WINDOW and DOOR FRAMES.

FRAMES for WOOD BUILDINGS.

Window Frames, 4 inch Studding, ordinary sizes up to 2 lt. 30 x 40.

No.				Knock Down	Put Together
1800.	Plain Drip Cap, with pulleys			$2.05	$2.35
1801.	Crown Mould Cap,	"		2.45	2.70
1802.	Fancy Cap,	"		3.70	4.30
1803.	"	"		2.70	3.00
1804.	"	"		3.70	4.30
1805.	"	"		4.40	4.95
1806.	"	"		4.80	5.20
1807.	"	"		5.00	5.55

OUTSIDE DOOR FRAMES.

Ordinary Sizes.

1⅜ inch Rabbeted Jambs for 4 inch Studding.

No.		Knock Down	Put Together
1800.	Plain Drip Cap	$2.55	$2.70
1801.	Crown Mould Cap	2.95	3.20
1802.	Fancy Cap	4 20	4.70
1803.	"	3.25	3.65
1804.	"	4.20	4.70
1805.	"	4.95	5.30
1806.	"	5.30	6.80
1807.	"	5.55	6.00

OUTSIDE DOOR FRAMES for TRANSOM.

Ordinary Sizes.

1⅜ inch Rabbeted Jambs, for 4 inch Studding, 1800, 1801 _____ add 50c.
1⅜ " " " 4 " " 1802, 1803, 1804, 1805, 1806, 1807 _____ " $1.05

FRAMES for BRICK BUILDINGS.

	Knock Down	Put Together
Box Window Frames, with pulleys, ordinary sizes up to 2 lt., 30 x 40	$2.70	$2.95
Outside Door Frames, 1¾ inch Jamb Rabbeted for 13 inch wall, ordinary sizes	2.55	2.70
" " " " " " transom	3.05	3.30

INSIDE DOOR FRAMES, Knock Down.

Ordinary sizes, ⅞ x 5¾ inch Jamb, White Pine					$0.95
" " " " " Yellow Pine					.80
" " " " " Cypress					.95
" " " " " Plain Red Oak					1.25
" " " " " for Transom, with 1¾ inch Transom Bar, White Pine					1.30
" " " " " " " " " " " Yellow "					1.00
" " " " " " " " " " " Cypress					1.30
" " " " " " " " " " " Plain Red Oak					1.75
Ordinary sizes, 1⅛ x 5¾ inch Jamb, White Pine					1.05
" " " " " Yellow "					.95
" " " " " Cypress					1.05
" " " " " Plain Red Oak					1.45
" " " " " for Transom, with 1¾ inch Transom Bar, White Pine					1.55
" " " " " " " " " " " Yellow "					1.20
" " " " " " " " " " " Cypress					1.55
" " " " " " " " " " " Plain Red Oak					2.95

GABLE SASH FRAMES for FRAME BUILDINGS.

No.									
3047.	For 2 0 x 2-5 Sash for 4 inch Studding, put together								$1.90
3048.	" " " " " " "								1.55
3050.	" " " " " " "								2.40
3053.	" " " " " " "								2.65
3049.	For Sash, 2 ft. diam. circle outside, square inside, for 4 inch Studding, put together								2.65
3051.	" " " " " " " " "								2.65

No Window or Door Stops included with price of frames. Prices of frames subject to discount.

TURNED BEADS.

White or Yellow Pine, Oak, Birch, or woods of equal value.

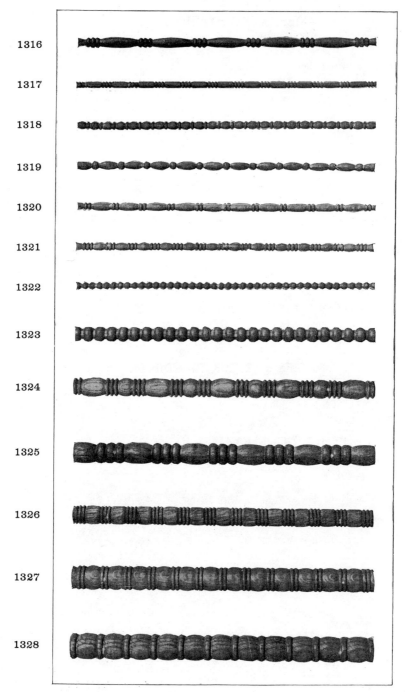

Furnished any diameter up to 2 inches—specify diameter when ordering.   Price up to and including ⅞ inch diam.
Full Round, $4.50 per 100 lineal feet. Add for quartering, $1.20 per 100 lineal feet. Add for halving, 60c per 100 lineal feet.
For over ⅞ inch diameter send for prices, stating quantity wanted. For large quantity will make special prices.

TURNED BEADS.

White or Yellow Pine, Oak, Birch, or woods of equal value.

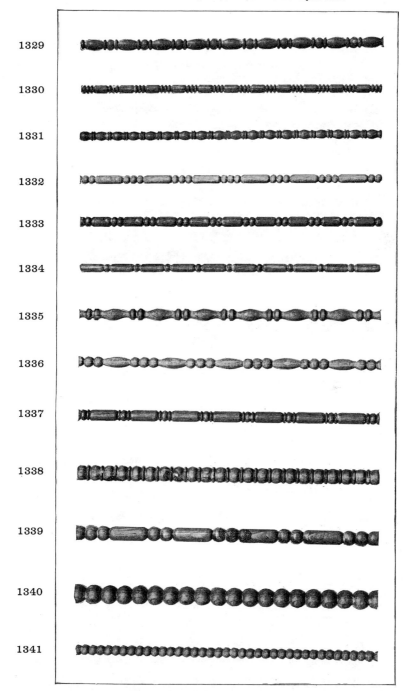

1329

1330

1331

1332

1333

1334

1335

1336

1337

1338

1339

1340

1341

Furnished any diameter up to 2 inches—specify diameter when ordering. Price up to and including ⅞ inch. diam.
Full Round, $4.50 per 100 lineal feet. Add for quartering, $1.20 per 100 lineal feet. Add for halving, 60c per 100 lineal feet.
For over ⅞ inch diameter send for prices, stating quantity wanted.   For large quantity will make special prices.

EMBOSSED PICTURE MOULDINGS.

White or Yellow Pine, Oak, Birch, or woods of equal value.

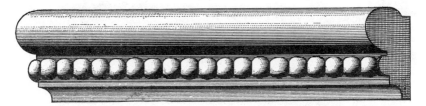

1342 Two-thirds size, ⅞x1½, $4.00 per 100 lineal feet.

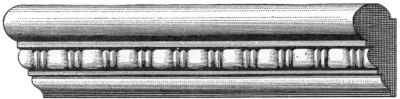

1343 Two-thirds size, ⅞x1½, $4.00 per 100 lineal feet.

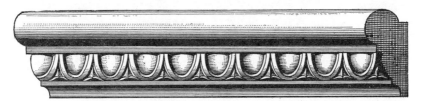

1344 Two-thirds size, ⅞x1½, $4.00 per 100 lineal feet.

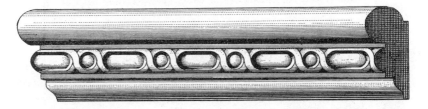

1345 Two-thirds size, ⅞x1½, $4.00 per 100 lineal feet.

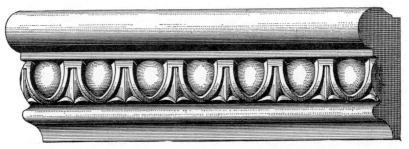

1346 Two-thirds size, ⅞x2¼, $4.50 per 100 lineal feet.

EMBOSSED MOULDINGS.

White or Yellow Pine, Oak, Birch, or woods of equal value.

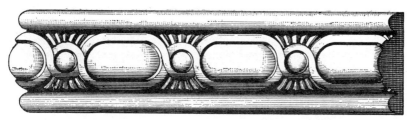

1359. Two-thirds size, ⅜x1⅝, $3.25 per 100 lineal feet.

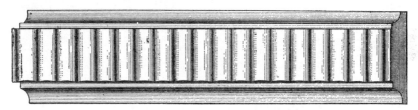

1360. Two-thirds size, ⅜x1½, $3.25 per 100 lineal feet.

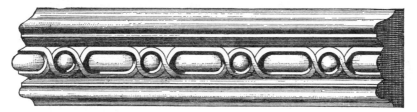

1361. Two-thirds size, ½x1¾, $4.00 per 100 lineal feet.

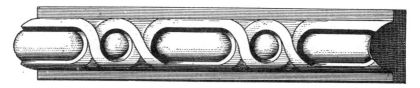

1362. Full size, ½x¾, $2.50 per 100 lineal feet.

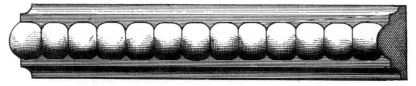

1363. Full size, ⅜x⅞, $2.25 per 100 lineal feet.

EMBOSSED MOULDINGS.

White or Yellow Pine, Oak, Birch, or woods of equal value.

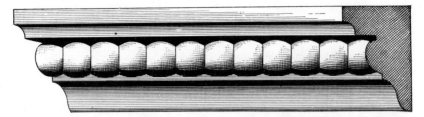

1354.   Full size, ¾ x 1⅛, $3.25 per 100 lineal feet.

1355.   Two-thirds size, ¾ x 1½, $3.50 per 100 lineal feet.

1356.   Full size, ½ x 1¼, $3.25 per 100 lineal feet.

1357.   Two-thirds size, ⅝ x 2½, $4.50 per 100 lineal feet.

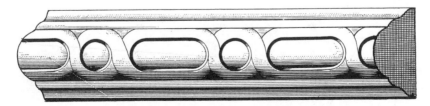

1358.   Full size, ½ x 1, $2.75 per 100 lineal feet.

EMBOSSED MOULDINGS.

White or Yellow Pine, Oak, Birch, or woods of equal value.

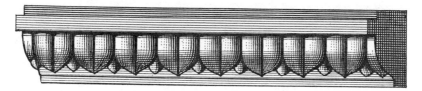

1359½. Size, ½x⅞ inches. Price, $2.50 per 100 lineal feet.

1360½. Size, ⅜x½ inch. Price, $2.25 per 100 lineal feet.

1361½. Size, 1⅜x1⅜ inches. Price, $2.75 per 100 lineal feet.

1362½. Size, ⅜x¾ inches. Price, $2.75 per 100 lineal feet.

1363½. Size, ⁵⁄₁₆x⅝ inches. Price, $2.50 per 100 lineal feet.

EMBOSSED MOULDINGS.

White or Yellow Pine, Oak, Birch, or woods of equal value.

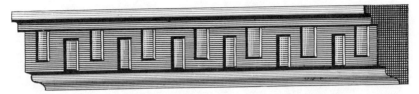

1364.   Size, $\frac{1}{2}$x$\frac{7}{8}$ inches, $2.50 per 100 lineal feet.

1365.   Size, $\frac{5}{16}$x$\frac{7}{8}$ inches, $2.50 per 100 lineal feet.

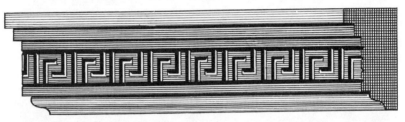

1366.   Size, $\frac{5}{8}$x1$\frac{1}{8}$ inches, $3.00 per 100 lineal feet.

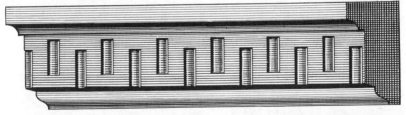

1367.   Size, $\frac{5}{8}$x1$\frac{1}{8}$ inches, $3.00 per 100 lineal feet.

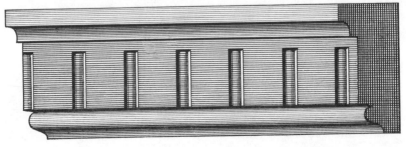

1368.   Size, $\frac{3}{4}$x1$\frac{1}{2}$ inches, $3.50 per 100 lineal feet.

EMBOSSED MOULDINGS.

White or Yellow Pine, Oak, Birch, or woods of equal value.

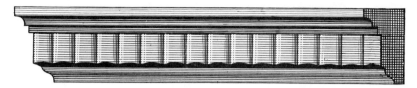

1369. Size, ½ x ⅞ inches, $2.50 per 100 lineal feet.

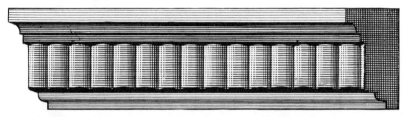

1370. Size, ⅝ x 1⅛ inches, $3.00 per 100 lineal feet.

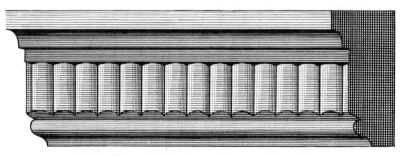

1371. Size, ¾ x 1½ inches, $3.50 per 100 lineal feet.

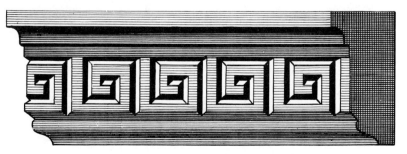

1372. Size, ¾ x 1½ inches, $3.50 per 100 lineal feet.

EMBOSSED MOULDINGS.

White or Yellow Pine, Oak, Birch, or woods of equal value.

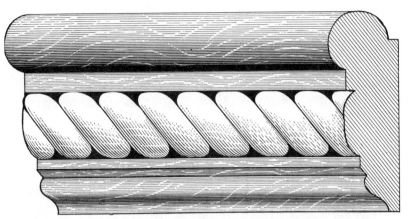

1374.   Size, ⅞x2¼ inches, $4.50 per 100 lineal feet.

1375.   Size, ⅞x2 inches, $4.00 per 100 lineal feet.

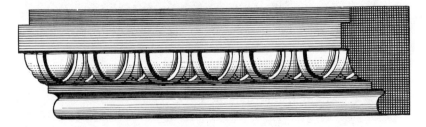

1376.   Size, ¾x1¼ inches, $3.00 per 100 lineal feet.

1378.   Size, $\frac{5}{16}$x½ inches, $2.50 per 100 lineal feet.

EMBOSSED MOULDINGS.

White or Yellow Pine, Oak, Birch or woods of equal value.

1379. Size, $\frac{5}{16}$x$1\frac{3}{16}$ inches, $2.25 per 100 lineal feet.

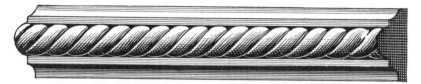

1380. Size, $\frac{3}{8}$x$\frac{7}{8}$ inches, $2.50 per 100 lineal feet.

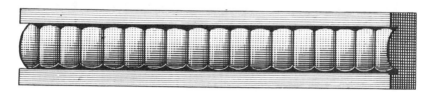

1381. Size, $\frac{3}{8}$x$\frac{7}{8}$ inches, $2.25 per 100 lineal feet.

1382. Size, $\frac{5}{16}$x$1\frac{1}{8}$ inches, $2.75 per 100 lineal feet.

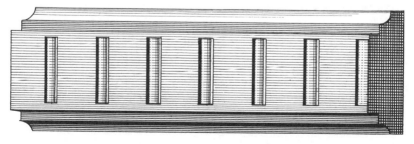

1383. Size, $\frac{3}{8}$x$1\frac{1}{2}$ inches, $3.25 per 100 lineal feet.

EMBOSSED MOULDINGS.

White or Yellow Pine, Oak, Birch, or woods of equal value.

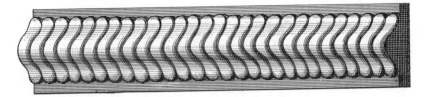

1384   Size, $\frac{5}{16}$ x $\frac{7}{8}$ inches, $2.50 per 100 lineal feet.

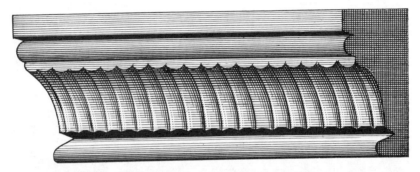

1385   Size, $\frac{3}{4}$ x $1\frac{5}{8}$ inches, $3.75 per 100 lineal feet.

1386½   Size, ½ x $1\frac{1}{2}$ inches, $3.25 per 100 lineal feet.

1387½   Size, $\frac{3}{4}$ x $1\frac{5}{8}$ inches, $3.75 per 100 lineal feet.

EMBOSSED MOULDINGS.

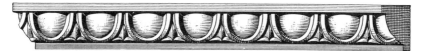

1349.   Full size, 3/8 x 1/2, $2.25 per 100 lineal feet.

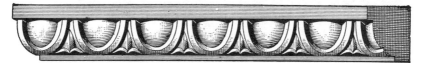

1350.   Full size, 3/8 x 5/8, $2.25 per 100 lineal feet.

1351.   Full size, 1/2 x 1 1/16, $2.50 per 100 lineal feet.

1352.   Full size, 5/8 x 3/4, $2.50 per 100 lineal feet.

1388.   Size, 7/8 x 3 inches.   Price, $5.00 per 100 lineal feet.
1389.   Size, 7/8 x 2 1/2 inches.   Price, $4.50 per 100 lineal feet.
1390.   Size, 3/4 x 2 inches.   Price, $4.00 per 100 lineal feet.

EMBOSSED MOULDINGS.

White or Yellow Pine, Oak, Birch, or woods of equal value.

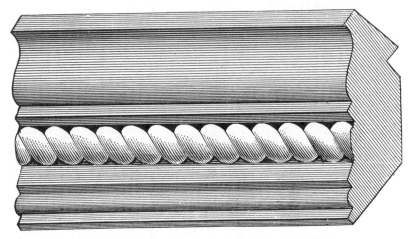

1391½   Size, ⅞x2½ inches, $4.50 per 100 lineal feet.

1392½   Size, ⅞x2½ inches, $4.50 per 100 lineal feet.

1393½   Size, ½x1⅜ inches, $2.50 per 100 lineal feet.

PICKETS, FENCE POSTS and FENCE POST CAPS.

PICKETS,

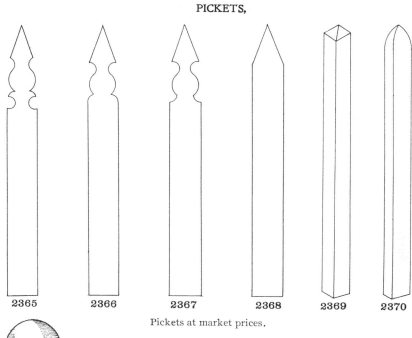

| 2365 | 2366 | 2367 | 2368 | 2369 | 2370 |

Pickets at market prices.

FENCE POSTS and FENCE POST CAPS.

2371
Cedar Fence Post.
6 inches by 8 feet___$1.40

2372
6 inch_____40c

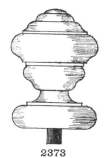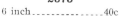

2373
6 inch_____40c

2374
6 inch_____40c

2375
6 inch_____40c

DIMENSION SHINGLES.

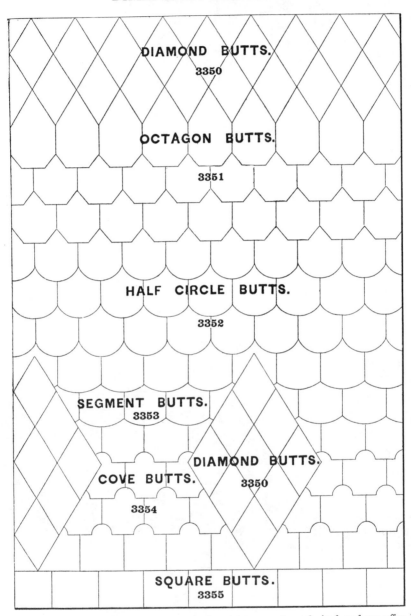

DIAMOND BUTTS.
3350

OCTAGON BUTTS.
3351

HALF CIRCLE BUTTS.
3352

SEGMENT BUTTS.
3353

COVE BUTTS.
3354

DIAMOND BUTTS.
3350

SQUARE BUTTS.
3355

We are prepared to furnish Ornamental Shingles, cut to any shape desired, and can offer inducements in prices. Write for quotations.

SHINGLES REQUIRED IN A ROOF.

To the square foot it takes 9 if exposed 4 inches; 8 if exposed 4½ inches; and 7⅕ if exposed 5 inches to the weather.

Find the number of shingles required to cover a roof 38 feet long and the rafters on each side 14 feet. Shingles exposed 4½ inches.

Ans. 28x38=1064 (sq. ft.)x8=8512 shingles.

PATENT ROTARY FASTENERS.

FOR STORM SASH and
WINDOW SCREENS.

Don't fasten your Storm Sash and Window Screens to your windows with screws or buttons from the outside in the old way. Avoid all this trouble and dangerous climbing by using the "ROTARY" fastener which can be applied and operated from the inside of a room with the least possible trouble.

Figure 1 shows the "Rotary" fastener as applied to an ordinary window with one set (four fasteners) to a window. The two upper fasteners are shown in their locked position, while the two lower ones appear with the slots in position to enter the cam flange over the pins in the window frame and the handles for drawing the sash inward until the pins engage with the flange on the fastener.

Figures 2 and 3 give the same illustrations enlarged to about one-half full size.

The "Rotary" is highly approved by architects, contractors, dealers and users.

It is the best device of its kind yet invented, because: It is the cheapest. It is the simplest. It is the most practical. It is the strongest and most durable. It is easily applied to either new or old sash. It can be applied to storm sash whether fitted between the hanging stile or put on the outside of the casing. It has no screws or fixtures to get lost; consequently always ready for use. It has no equal. You cannot afford to be without them.

Figure 1.

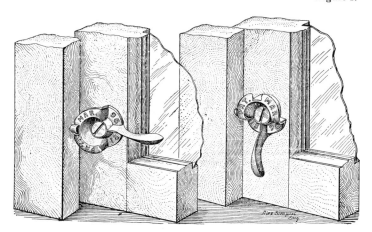

Figure 2.   Figure 3.

For prices see our Discount Sheet.

ROTARY FASTENERS.

Packed 6 sets in a box, with screws and pins, complete.

WOOD CARPET and PARQUET FLOORING

IS NOT, as many people suppose, a temporary floor covering to be laid down and taken up at pleasure, but is a permanent new floor on top of the old one, and is carefully fitted into all the offsets and runs around all the projections of the room and is firmly nailed down with small brads; and when finished has the effect of a thick European floor. We make it, however, in the same elaborate and beautiful designs, by the process of gluing the wood on cloth instead of to another piece of wood an inch or so thick, and we make it at a much less cost, as we utilize the floor already down, and thus occupy but five-sixteenths of an inch, instead of one inch or more (as with thick parquet).

Where disappointments have arisen from any kind of hardwood floors, it has invariably been from not understanding the proper treatment, or in expecting too much of them. The treatment of floors should be the same as the European.

The common remark "that a bare floor is so cheerless" comes wholly from the impression given by an ordinary pine floor, with its unsightly cracks, and from not having seen the effect of a well-laid Parquet Floor, in combination with the furniture and other articles, in keeping with the character of the room in which it is laid.

WOOD CARPET and PARQUETRY Is made in the uniform thickness of five-sixteenths of an inch. The woods used are all kiln dried and prepared so as to prevent shrinkage. Care must be taken to preserve them from dampness until the floor is laid and finished. The straight carpeting, 36 and 28 inches wide, rolls up like an oilcloth, and is thus readily shipped. The borders and strips are twelve feet long, and the Parquet Flooring comes in sheets 2x6 feet, and make a solid package for shipping.

RUGS Are being extensively used, on account of their healthfulness and convenience in keeping the room clean and free from dust. They are generally used on the middle part of the room, leaving a margin of about two feet around sides of the room for furniture to stand on. The floor upon which they lie should be a good one, with some degree of ornamentation, and free from joints and cracks. The dust on the floor is easily removed with a damp cloth or brush, and the rug can be rolled up at pleasure, and be taken out to be freed from dust. Rugs are now made to order at a very moderate cost, and of any desired shape and size.

ESTIMATES Free of charge for floors or borders, with full instructions and working drawing, will be cheerfully given to parties sending us a sketch of the ground plan, with measurements of the space desired to be covered. State what class of room it is for, also if a cheap or ornamented floor is desired. Our floors vary from $1.25 to $18.00 per yard. It is better to say how expensive a floor is desired, and the design will be made in accordance.

PARQUET BORDERS.

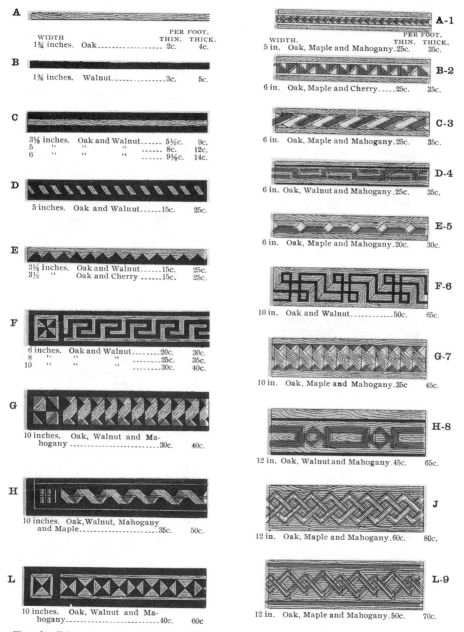

A
PER FOOT.
WIDTH   THIN.   THICK.
1¾ inches.   Oak _____ 2c.   4c.

B
1⅜ inches.   Walnut _____3c.   5c.

C
3½ inches.   Oak and Walnut _____ 5½c.   9c.
5   "   "   "   _____ 8c.   12c.
6   "   "   "   _____ 9½c.   14c.

D
5 inches.   Oak and Walnut _____15c.   25c.

E
3½ inches.   Oak and Walnut _____15c.   25c.
3½   "   Oak and Cherry _____15c.   25c.

F
6 inches.   Oak and Walnut _____20c.   30c.
8   "   "   "   ____25c.   35c.
10   "   "   "   ____30c.   40c.

G
10 inches.   Oak, Walnut and Mahogany _____30c.   40c.

H
10 inches.   Oak, Walnut, Mahogany
and Maple_____35c.   50c.

L
10 inches.   Oak, Walnut and Ma-
hogany_____40c.   60c

A-1
PER FOOT.
WIDTH.   THIN.   THICK.
5 in.   Oak, Maple and Mahogany_25c.   35c.

B-2
6 in.   Oak, Maple and Cherry_____25c.   35c.

C-3
6 in.   Oak, Maple and Mahogany_25c.   35c.

D-4
6 in.   Oak, Walnut and Mahogany_25c.   35c.

E-5
6 in.   Oak, Maple and Mahogany_20c.   30c.

F-6
10 in.   Oak and Walnut_____50c.   65c.

G-7
10 in.   Oak, Maple and Mahogany_35c   45c.

H-8
12 in.   Oak, Walnut and Mahogany_45c.   65c.

J
12 in.   Oak, Maple and Mahogany_60c.   80c.

L-9
12 in.   Oak, Maple and Mahogany_50c.   70c.

We make all Parquets and Borders in two thicknesses; ⁵⁄₁₆ inch, which we call thin goods, and ⅜ inch, which
we call thick goods.

PARQUET CENTERS and WOOD CARPETS.

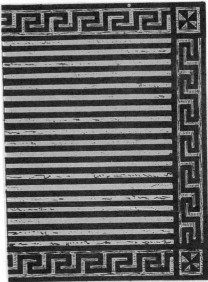

M   PARQUET CENTERS.   **R**

For price of Borders see preceding page.
Price of Centers, strips in 12 foot lengths, not glued on canvas per square yard, $1.00.
Parquet designs in rich cabinet woods, made to order for floors, wainscot, center pieces, borders, etc., at from 30 cents
    to $1.50 per square foot.
        Inform us as to your requirements and we will submit special designs in natural color of wood.

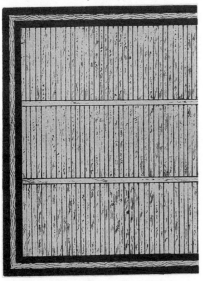
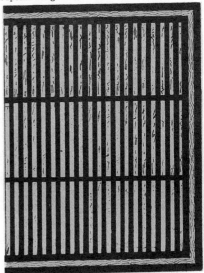

S   **T**

WOOD CARPET.—Standard Goods.

36 inches wide $\frac{5}{16}$ inches thick all oak or maple	per yard	$1.25
28 " " " "	"	1.15
36 " " " " oak and walnut or cherry, or gum and maple	"	1.50
28 " " " " " " " " " " "	"	1.25

The straight carpeting, 36 and 28 inches wide, rolls up like an oilcloth, and is thus readily shipped.

PARQUET CENTERS and BORDERS.

N

MAHOGANY and OAK.

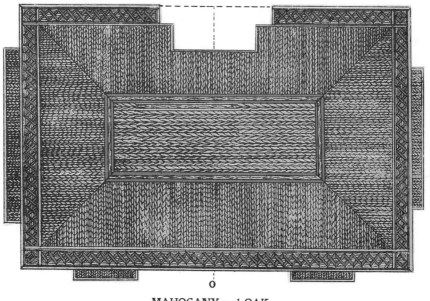

O

MAHOGANY and OAK.

Write for prices, giving ground plan and dimensions of room.

PARQUET CENTERS.

P
ALL OAK.
Thin, 25 cents per square foot.
Thick, 40 "   "   "   "   "

X
OAK and WALNUT.
Thin, 35 cents per square foot.
Thick, 50 "   "   "   "   "

Y
OAK and CHERRY.
Thin, 35 cents per square foot.
Thick, 50 "   "   "   "   "

Z
OAK and CHERRY.
Thin, 35 cents per square foot.
Thick, 50 "   "   "   "   "

SPECIAL FINISH for CASED OPENING.

522

This opening can also be filled with any of the grilles shown on pages 240 to 251.

CAPITALS.

FOR INTERIOR OR EXTERIOR USE.

523   524   525

526   527   528

Designs of caps that can be used in connection with above columns.   Write for prices.

WINDOW and DOOR CAPS.

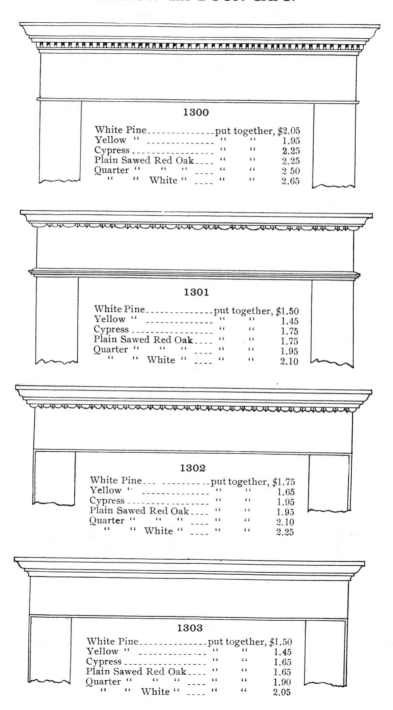

1300

White Pine_____put together, $2.05
Yellow " _____ "   "   1.95
Cypress_____ "   "   2.25
Plain Sawed Red Oak____ "   "   2.25
Quarter "   "   " ____ "   "   2 50
   "   " White " ____ "   "   2.65

1301

White Pine_____put together, $1.50
Yellow " _____ "   "   1.45
Cypress_____ "   "   1.75
Plain Sawed Red Oak____ "   "   1.75
Quarter "   "   " ____ "   "   1.95
   "   " White " ____ "   "   2.10

1302

White Pine___ _____put together, $1.75
Yellow " _____ "   "   1.65
Cypress_____ "   "   1.95
Plain Sawed Red Oak____ "   "   1.95
Quarter "   "   " ____ "   "   2.10
   "   " White " ____ "   "   2.25

1303

White Pine_____put together, $1.50
Yellow " _____ "   "   1.45
Cypress_____ "   "   1.65
Plain Sawed Red Oak____ "   "   1.65
Quarter "   "   " ____ "   "   1.90
   "   " White " ____ "   "   2.05

All above prices are for Caps of ordinary widths, 3 feet and under.

WINDOW and DOOR CAPS with COMPOSITION ORNAMENTS.

1304

White Pine	put together	$3.55
Yellow "	"	"	3.45
Cypress	"	"	3.75
Plain Sawed Red Oak	"	"	3.75
Quarter Sawed Red Oak	"	"	4.00
" White "	"	"	4.15

1305

White Pine	put together,	$6.75
Yellow "	"	"	6.70
Cypress	"	"	7.00
Plain Sawed Red Oak	"	"	7.00
Quarter " " "	"	"	7.20
" " White "	"	"	7.35

Prices of above include the Capitals and Ornamentation at top of side Casings.

1306

White Pine	put together,	$3.25
Yellow "	"	"	3.15
Cypress	"	"	3.45
Plain Sawed Red Oak	"	"	3.45
Quarter Sawed Red Oak	"	"	3.60
" White "	"	"	3.75

1307

White Pine	put together,	$2.25
Yellow "	"	"	2.40
Cypress	"	"	2.50
Plain Sawed Red Oak	"	"	2.50
Quarter Sawed Red Oak	"	"	2.85
" White "	"	"	3.00

All above prices are for **C**aps of ordinary widths, 3 feet and under.

WOOD CARVINGS.

1308   Price, $2.25

1309   Price, $2.25

1310   Price, $2.25

1311   Price, $2.25

1312   Price, $2.25

1312½   Price, $2.25

White or Yellow Pine, Oak, Birch, or woods of equal value.
Sizes, 4 inches by 37½ inches to 4 inches by 43½ inches.

RAISED WOOD CARVINGS.

Made ¼ inch thick unless otherwise ordered.

No. 142.
5x24, 90c.   5x30, $1.13.   5x36, $1.35

No. 143.
4½x18, 38c.   4½x24, 53c.

No. 144.
5x30, 98c.   5x36, $1.13.

No. 145.
3½x18, 24c.   3½x28, 30c.

No. 146.
3½x18, 27c.   3½x24, 35c.

No. 147.   3x11, 18c.

No. 148.   2x10, 15c.

RAISED WOOD CARVINGS.

Made ¼ inch thick unless otherwise ordered.

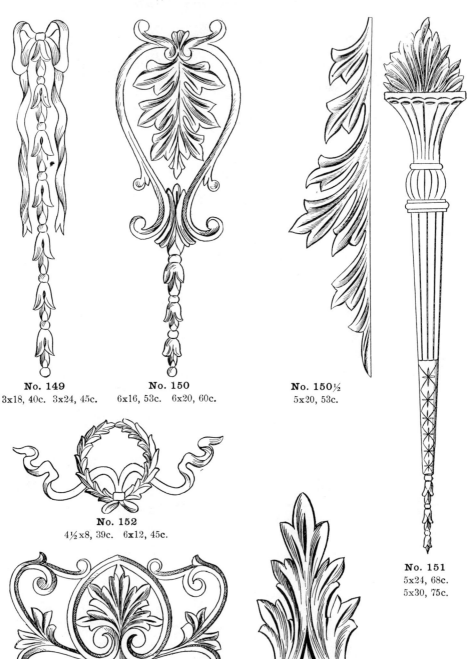

No. 149
3x18, 40c. 3x24, 45c.

No. 150
6x16, 53c. 6x20, 60c.

No. 150½
5x20, 53c.

No. 152
4½x8, 39c. 6x12, 45c.

No. 151
5x24, 68c.
5x30, 75c.

No. 153
5x11, 45c. 5x14, 53c.

No. 154
4x6, 21c. 4x10, 24c.

RAISED WOOD CARVINGS.

Made ¼ inch thick unless otherwise ordered.

No. 155
2¾x12 inches. Price, 24c.
2¾x16 " " 30c.

No. 156
4x6½ inches. Price, 18c.

No. 157
3½x7 inches. Price, 18c.

No. 158
3x5 inches. Price, 12c.
4x7 " " 15c.

No. 159
4x4 inches. Price, 9c.

No. 160
8x8 inches. Price, 38c.
6x6 " " 30c.

No. 161
5x5 inches. Price, 23c.

INSIDE GRILLES.

529.   Price, $2.00 per square foot.

528.   Price, $2.00 per square foot.

522.   Price, $2.25 per square foot.

588.   Price, $2.00 per square foot.

INSIDE GRILLES.

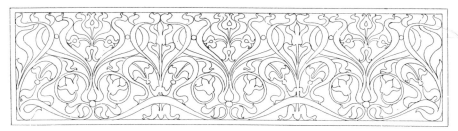

593.　Price, $2.25 per square foot.

524.　Price, $2.50 per square foot.

508.　Price, $1.80 per square foot.

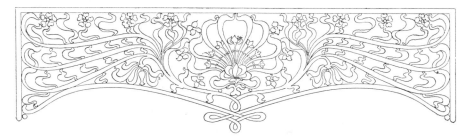

594.　Price, $2.25 per square foot.

INSIDE GRILLES.

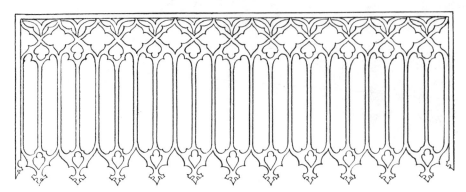

518   Price, $1.70 per square foot.

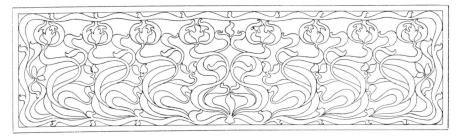

595.   Price, $2.25 per square foot

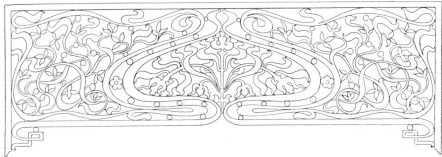

592.   Price, $2.25 per square foot.

506.   Price, $1.80 per square foot.

INSIDE GRILLES.

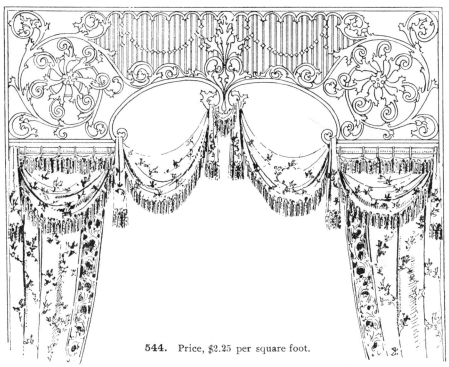

544. Price, $2.25 per square foot.

543. Price $2.00 per square foot.

INSIDE GRILLES.

512.   Price, $2.00 per square foot.

513.   Price, $1.80 per square foot.

523.   Price, $2.00 per square foot.

500.   Price, $2.50 per square foot.

INSIDE GRILLES.

559. $2.00 per square foot.

545. $1.80 per square foot.

INSIDE GRILLES.

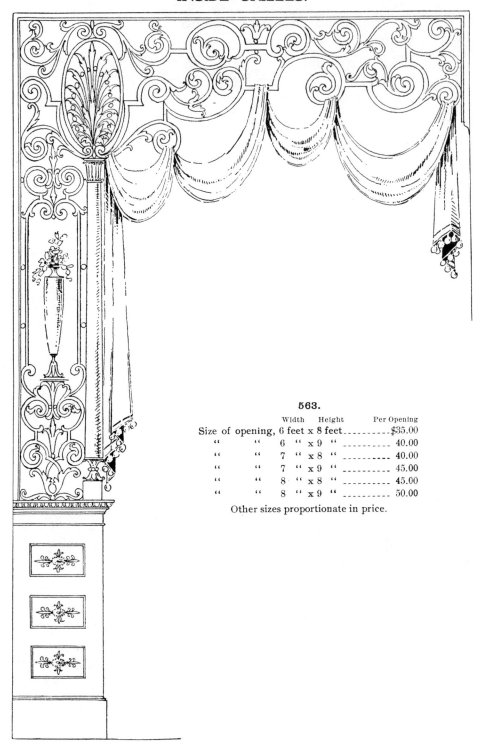

563.

		Width	Height	Per Opening
Size of opening,		6 feet	x 8 feet	$35.00
"	"	6 "	x 9 "	40.00
"	"	7 "	x 8 "	40.00
"	"	7 "	x 9 "	45.00
"	"	8 "	x 8 "	45.00
"	"	8 "	x 9 "	50.00

Other sizes proportionate in price.

INSIDE GRILLES.

562

		Width	Height		Per Grille
Size of opening,		6 feet	x 8 feet	----------------------	$33.00
"	"	6 "	x 9 "	----------------------	38.00
"	"	7 "	x 8 "	----------------------	38.00
"	"	7 "	x 9 "	----------------------	43.00
"	"	8 "	x 8 "	----------------------	43.00
"	"	8 "	x 9 "	----------------------	45.00

Other sizes proportionate in price.

Above prices are for Grilles "in the white." If finished in oil and varnish add to above prices 20%.
Made of White or Yellow Pine, Cypress, Oak, Ash, Birch, Maple or woods of equal value.

INSIDE GRILLES.

564

For opening, 7 feet x 8 feet_____$70.00
    "   7 "   x 9 " _____ 76.00
    "   8 "   x 8 " _____ 82.00

For opening, 8 feet x 9 feet_____$88.00
    "   9 "   x 9 " _____ 94.00

Above prices are for Grilles "in the white."   If finished in oil and varnish add to above prices 20%.
Made of White or Yellow Pine, Cypress, Oak, Ash, Birch, Maple or woods of equal value.

INSIDE GRILLES.

582

For opening 6 feet x 8 feet_____$45.00
"   7 "   x 8 " _____ 50.00
"   7 "   x 9 " _____ 55.00
"   8 "   x 8 " _____ 55.00
"   8 "   x 9 " _____ 60.00

Above prices are for Grilles "in the white."   If finished in oil and varnish add to above prices 20%.
Made of White or Yellow Pine, Cypress, Oak, Ash, Birch, Maple or woods of equal value.

INSIDE GRILLES.

577

For opening 6 feet x 8 feet_____$45.00
  " 7 " x 8 " _____ 50.00
  " 7 " x 9 " _____ 55.00
  " 8 " x 8 " _____ 55.00
  " 8 " x 9 " _____ 60.00

Above prices are for Grilles "in the white."   If finished in oil and varnish add to above prices 20%.
Made of White or Yellow Pine, Cypress, Oak, Ash, Birch, Maple or woods of equal value.

INSIDE GRILLES.

560

For opening, 6 feet x 8 feet_____$55.00
"   7 " x 8 " _____ 60.00
"   7 " x 9 " _____ 65.00
"   8 " x 8 " _____ 65.00
"   8 " x 9 " _____ 70.00

Above prices are for Grilles "in the white." If finished in oil and varnish add to above prices 20%.
Made in White or Yellow Pine, Cypress, Oak, Ash, Birch, Maple or woods of equal value.

HARDWOOD MANTELS,
GRATES,
ANDIRONS and FIRE SETS.

O N the following pages you will find our Special Designs of Mantels, made in Oak, natural or antique finish; Red Birch, finished natural or imitation Cherry or Mahogany. Mantels made in Curly Birch, Birdseye Maple or Enamel finish will have to be made specially, and prices will be furnished on application.

List prices are for Mantels complete without fire, brick, which can be bought from your local dealer, thereby saving freight. Tile can be had in any shade or tint. Would suggest that you leave selection of tile with us.

A Mantel boxed for shipment weighs about 300 pounds.

In ordering, give width of chimney breast, and kind of wood and finish wanted.

WOOD MANTELS.

1240.

1240A.

In ordering give length and height of shelf and size of fire opening.
Made of pine, yellow pine or cypress, or any of the hardwoods.

WRITE FOR PRICES.

WOOD MANTELS.

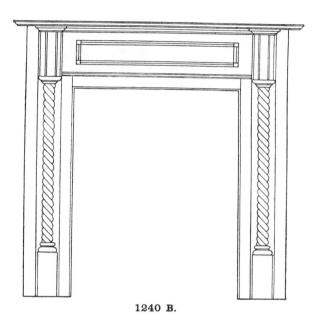

1240 B.

1241.

In ordering give length and height of shelf and size of fire opening.
Made of pine, yellow pine or cypress, or any of the hardwoods.

WRITE FOR PRICES.

HARDWOOD MANTELS.

1694

An Admirable Design for Parlor, Library or Dining Room.

A very tall mantel, yet extremely well proportioned and very graceful. Veneered columns, beautifully figured from base to capitals, and supporting handsome cornice and shelf; elegantly hand-carved out of the solid wood. Has extra large mirror, which produces a very pleasing effect. Made of the finest selected quarter-sawed oak or red birch; piano polish finish; height, 94 inches; width, 60 inches; tile opening, 42x42 inches; first quality French bevel plate mirror, 30x40 inches; columns, 4½ inches.

Mantel only, without trimmings.____$141.50   Mantel, with outfit "A"_____$171.50
Mantel, with outfit "B"_____ 182.50   Mantel, with outfit "C"_____ 178.50
Mantel, with outfit "D"_____$196.50

For full description of outfits, see pages 279 and 280. In ordering, please specify which outfit is wanted with mantel. If mantel is wanted with outfit different from those priced above, write for price on same.

PRICES SUBJECT TO DISCOUNT.

HARDWOOD MANTELS.

1580½

This is an Appropriate Mantel for Parlor or any Room.

A choice design that appeals to the best taste. Elaborate hand-carved renaissance capitals and other artistic carvings; swelled shelf and very heavy cornice. A fine illustration of the skill and experience of our designers.

Made of the choicest quarter-sawed oak or birch; finish, piano polish; height, 7 feet 8 inches; width, 5 feet; tile opening, 42x42 inches; heavy veneered columns, 4½ inches.

Mantel only, without trimmings____$117.50   Mantel, with outfit "A"_____$147.50
Mantel, with outfit "B"_____ 158.50   Mantel, with outfit "C"_____ 154.50
Mantel, with outfit "D"_____$173.50

For full description of outfits, see pages 279 and 280. In ordering, please specify which outfit is wanted with mantel. If mantel is wanted with outfit different from those priced above, write for price on same.

PRICES SUBJECT TO DISCOUNT.

HARDWOOD MANTELS.

1691

Suitable for any Room in the House.

A mantel with good proportions; and stands without a rival in either design or price. Genuine hand-carved upper and lower capitals; heavy veneered columns supporting shelf and cornice; columns stand out from the mantel; heavy shelf; very fine dental work. Notice height of mantel. Fine enough for any residence in which it may be placed.

Made of finest selected quarter-sawed oak or red birch; piano polish finish; height, 93 inches; width, 60 inches; tile opening, 42x39 inches; first quality French bevel plate mirror, 24x40 inches; columns, 4½ inches.

Mantel only, without trimmings____$ 95.00	Mantel, with outfit "A"_____$125.00
Mantel, with outfit "B"_____ 136.00	Mantel, with outfit "C"_____ 132.00
Mantel, with outfit "D"_____$150.00	

For full description of outfits, see pages 279 and 280. In ordering please specify which outfit is wanted with mantel. If mantel is wanted with outfit different from those priced above, write for price on same.

PRICES SUBJECT TO DISCOUNT.

HARDWOOD MANTELS.

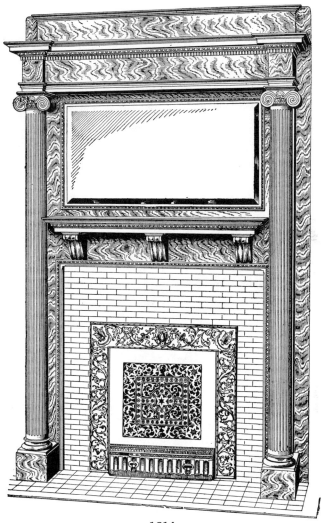

1614

A Highly Classic Design.

In which is embodied the finest FEATURES OF ARCHITECTURE according to the ancient orders. We call special attention to every feature in detail.   Is exceptionally handsome in golden oak finish.

Made of finest selected quarter-sawed oak or birch ; finish, piano polish ; height 7 feet, 9 inches ; width 5 feet ; tile opening, 42x42 inches ; best quality French bevel plate mirror 20x40 inches ; columns, 5 inches.

Mantel only, without trimmings____$ 86.50	Mantel, with outfit "A"_____$116.50
Mantel, with outfit "B"_____ 127.50	Mantel, with outfit "C"_____ 123.50
Mantel, with outfit "D"_____$141.50	

For full description of outfits, see pages 279 and 280.   In ordering please specify which outfit is wanted with mantel. If mantel is wanted with outfit different from those priced above, write for price on same.

PRICES SUBJECT TO DISCOUNT.

HARDWOOD MANTELS.

1704

Suited for Parlor, Sitting Room or any Room.

A new design of excellent proportions throughout. Has very handsome cornice and shelf and other nice features.

Made of finest selected quarter-sawed oak or birch; piano polish finish; heavy veneered columns; height, 88 inches; width, 60 inches; tile opening, 42x39 inches; first quality French bevel plate mirror 18x40 inches; columns, 4¼ inches.

Mantel only, without trimmings____$ 79.50   Mantel, with outfit "A"_____$109.50
Mantel, with outfit "B"_____ 120.50   Mantel, with outfit "C"_____ 116.50
Mantel, with outfit "D"_____$134.00

For full description of outfits, see pages 279 and 280. In ordering please specify which outfit is wanted with mantel. If mantel is wanted with outfit different from those priced above, write for price on same.

PRICES SUBJECT TO DISCOUNT.

HARDWOOD MANTELS.

1647

An Entirely New Design for Parlor, Library or any Room.

A very artistic design, of which imitations have been attempted, with poor success. Shelf supported by nicely shaped hand carved brackets; cornice resting on six handsomely carved columns, which stand out in semi-circle; cornice and shelf swelled; swelled sides, which are handsomely veneered. This mantel is one of the most exquisite designs that has ever been made.

Made of the finest selected quarter-sawed oak or red birch; finished piano polish; height, 7 feet, 4 inches; width, 5 feet; tile opening, 42x39 inches; finest quality French bevel plate mirror, 20x42 inches.

Mantel only, without trimmings____$ 95.00	Mantel, with outfit "A"_____$124.75
Mantel, with outfit "B" _____ 135.75	Mantel, with outfit "C"_____ 131.75
	Mantel, with outfit "D"_____$149.75	

For full description of outfits, see pages 279 and 280. In ordering please specify which outfit is wanted with mantel. If mantel is wanted with outfit different from those priced above, write for prices on same.

PRICES SUBJECT TO DISCOUNT.

HARDWOOD MANTELS.

1706

A New and Appropriate Design for Any Room in the House.

And will appeal to an artistic eye at first glance. Handsome shaped mirror in direct harmony with shaped top; graceful veneered columns with hand-carved caps arranged for reception of ornaments.

Made of finest selected quarter-sawed oak or birch; finish, piano polish; height, 84 inches; width, 60 inches; tile opening, 42x39 inches; first quality French beveled mirror 18x36 inches.

Mantel only, without trimmings.....$ 65.00	Mantel, with outfit "A"...........$ 95.00
Mantel, with outfit "B"............ 106.00	Mantel, with outfit "C"...........$102.00
	Mantel, with outfit "D"..................$120.00	

For full description of outfits, see pages 279 and 280. In ordering, please specify which outfit is wanted with mantel. If mantel is wanted with outfit different from those priced above, write for price on same.

PRICES SUBJECT TO DISCOUNT.

HARDWOOD MANTELS.

1682

A Very Handsome, Classic Design for Parlor, Library or Hall.

Beautifully veneered columns, rich, embellished with hand-carved caps; heavy shelf and very handsome cornice, showing artistic mouldings and dentals in handsome relief.

Made in finest selected quarter-sawed oak or birch; piano polish finish; height, 7 feet; width, 5 feet; tile opening, 42x39 inches; best quality French plate mirror, 18x36 inches.

Mantel only, without trimmings......$58.50   Mantel, with outfit "A".............$88.50
Mantel, with outfit "B".............. 99.50   Mantel, with outfit "C".............. 95.50
Mantel, with outfit "D".................$114.00

For full description of outfits, see pages 279 and 280. In ordering, please specify which outfit is wanted with mantel. If mantel is wanted with outfit different from those priced above, write for price on same.

PRICES SUBJECT TO DISCOUNT.

HARDWOOD MANTELS.

1720½

This is an Appropriate Mantel for Parlor or any Room.

Large mirror, nicely set off with handsome carving; beautifully figured veneered columns with hand carved capitals. An especially pretty effect is also obtained by the massive square base blocks.

The wood in this mantel is selected with greatest care to obtain rich grain effects. Can be had in quarter-sawed oak or birch; height, 84 inches; width, 60 inches; tile opening, 42x39 inches; heavy French beveled mirror plate, 18x36 inches; columns, **3½** inches.

Mantel only, without trimmings_____$46.00	Mantel, with outfit "A"_____$76.00
Mantel, with outfit "B"_____ 87.50	Mantel, with outfit "C"_____ 83.00
Mantel, with outfit "D"_____ $101.50.	

For full description of outfits, see pages 279 and 280. In ordering please specify which outfit is wanted with mantel. If mantel is wanted with outfit different from those priced above, write for price on same.

PRICES SUBJECT TO DISCOUNT.

HARDWOOD MANTELS.

1719

A Beautiful and Imposing Design.

Faultless in appearance and perfect in construction; heavy veneered columns supporting rich and heavy cornice; large handsome mirror.

Made of finest selected quarter-sawed oak or red birch; piano polish finish; height, 84 inches; width, 60 inches; tile opening, 42x39 inches; first quality French bevel plate mirror, 18x36 inches.

Mantel only, without trimmings_____$46.00   Mantel, with outfit "A"_____$76.00
Mantel, with outfit "B"_____ 88.50   Mantel, with outfit "C"_____ 83.00
Mantel, with outfit "D"_____$101.50

For full description of outfits, see pages 279 and 280. In ordering, please specify which outfit is wanted with mantel. If mantel is wanted with outfit different from those priced above, write for price on same.

PRICES SUBJECT TO DISCOUNT.

HARDWOOD MANTELS.

1712

A Very Pretty, Inexpensive Column Mantel.

Neat carved work, useful shelves, French beveled mirror.   Has a phenomenal sale.

Made of finest selected quarter-sawed oak or red birch; finish, piano polish; height, 84 inches; width, 60 inches; tile opening, 42x39 inches; column, 3½ inches.

Mantel only, without trimmings_____$41.50   Mantel, with outfit "A"_____$71.50
Mantel, with outfit "B" _____ 82.50   Mantel, with outfit "C"_____ 78.50
Mantel, with outfit "D"_____$96.50

For full description of outfits, see pages 279 and 280. In ordering, please specify which outfit is wanted with mantel. If mantel is wanted with outfit different from those priced above, write for price on same.

PRICES SUBJECT TO DISCOUNT.

HARDWOOD MANTELS.

1692

A Massive Design for Hall, Library or Dining Room.

Very heavy, yet graceful in its proportions. Beautifully hand-carved panels, Ionic capitals and brackets under the shelf. Observe the fine detail work on this mantel; nothing finer has ever been made.

Made of finest selected quarter-sawed oak or birch; piano polish finish; height, 83 inches; width, 60 inches; tile opening, 42x48 inches; veneered columns, 4½ inches.

Mantel only, without trimmings____$103.50   Mantel, with outfit "A"_____$132.50
Mantel, with outfit "B"_____ 143.50   Mantel, with outfit "C"_____ 139.50
Mantel, with outfit "D"_____$157.50

For full description of outfits, see pages 279 and 280. In ordering please specify which outfit is wanted with mantel. If mantel is wanted with outfit different from those priced above, write for price on same.

PRICES SUBJECT TO DISCOUNT.

HARDWOOD MANTELS.

1639

A Fine Hall, Library or Dining Room Mantel.

We claim this Mantel absolutely WITHOUT AN EQUAL at the price, in point of design, finish, construction and selection of lumber.

Made of beautiful, selected quarter-sawed oak or birch; finish, piano polish; height, 6 feet, 3 inches; width, 60 inches; tile opening, 42x48 inches.

Mantel only, without trimmings____$ 63.50   Mantel, with outfit "A"_____$ 94.00
Mantel, with outfit "B"_____ 105.00   Mantel, with outfit "C"_____ 101.50
Mantel, with outfit "D"_____$119.50

For full description of outfits, see pages 279 and 280. In ordering please specify which outfit is wanted with mantel. If mantel is wanted with outfit different from those priced above, write for price on same.

PRICES SUBJECT TO DISCOUNT.

HARDWOOD MANTELS.

1700

For Hall, Library or Bed Room.

A new colonial design. The beautiful wood, large field of tile above grate, combined with excellent proportions throughout, makes this a very handsome setting. Carefully consider the great amount of fine workmanship necessary to produce this design, and you will be surprised at the low price we quote.

Made of choicest grade quarter-sawed oak or red birch, selected for finest figure; finish, piano polish; height, 74 inches; width, 60 inches; tile opening, 42x48 inches; veneered columns 3½ inches.

Mantel only, without trimmings____ $43.50   Mantel, with outfit "A"_____ $73.50
Mantel, with outfit "B"_____ 84.50   Mantel, with outfit "C"_____ 80.50
Mantel, with outfit "D"_____ $98.50

For full description of outfits, see pages 279 and 280. In ordering please specify which outfit is wanted with mantel. If mantel is wanted with outfit different from those priced above, write for price on same.

PRICES SUBJECT TO DISCOUNT.

HARDWOOD MANTELS.

1737

A Handsome Mantel for Hall, Dining Room or Bed Room.

Not overdone with carving, but each figure appropriate and in its proper place. Has beautifully veneered columns, with swelled shelf.

Made of finest selected quarter-sawed oak or red birch; finish, piano polish; height, 72 inches; width, 60 inches; tile opening, 42x48 inches.

Mantel only, without trimmings	$36.00	Mantel, with outfit "A"	$66.00
Mantel, with outfit "B"	77.00	Mantel, with outfit "C"	73.00
	Mantel, with outfit "D"	$91.00	

For full description of outfits, see pages 279 and 290. In ordering please specify which outfit is wanted with mantel. If mantel is wanted with outfit different from those priced above, write for price on same.

PRICES SUBJECT TO DISCOUNT.

HARDWOOD MANTELS.

1874

For Hall, Bed Room or any Room.

A high-class design in a low priced mantel.   Inexpensive, but not cheap looking.

Made of choice selected quarter-sawed oak or red birch; finish, piano polish; height, 4 feet, 10 inches; width, 5 feet; tile opening, 36x36 inches, veneered columns, 3¼ inches.

Mantel only, without trimmings____ $25.50	Mantel, with outfit "A"_____ $55.50
Mantel, with outfit "B"_____ 66.50	Mantel, with outfit "C"_____ 62.50
Mantel, with outfit "D"_____ $80.50	

For full description of outfits, see pages 279 and 280.   In ordering please specify which outfit is wanted with mantel.   If mantel is wanted with outfit different from those priced above, write for price on same.

PRICES SUBJECT TO DISCOUNT.

HARDWOOD MANTELS.

1061

An Inexpensive but Fine Mantel.

Appropriate mantel for any apartment. A graceful and neat design; useful shelves; elegant proportions throughout.

Made of selected stock throughout. Can be had in oak or birch; well finished; height, 81 inches; width, 60 inches; tile opening, 36x36 inches; French beveled mirror, 16x28 inches.

Mantel only, without trimmings____ $28.50   Mantel, with outfit "A"_____ $58.50
Mantel, with outfit "B"_____ 69.50   Mantel, with outfit "C"_____ 65.50
Mantel, with outfit "D"_____ $83.50

For full description of outfits, see pages 279 and 280. In ordering please specify which outfit is wanted with mantel. If mantel is wanted with outfit different from those priced above, write for price on same.

PRICES SUBJECT TO DISCOUNT.

HARDWOOD MANTELS.

1059

A Special Bargain Mantel.

Graceful columns; good proportions throughout; well finished; mirror surmounted by beautiful hand carvings.

Made of selected oak; well finished; height, 81 inches; width, 60 inches; tile opening, 36x36 inches; French beveled mirror, 16x28 inches; columns, 3¼ inches.

Mantel only, without trimmings____ $32.50   Mantel, with outfit "A"_____ $62.50
Mantel, with outfit "B"_____ 73.50   Mantel, with outfit "C"_____ 69.50
Mantel, with outfit "D"_____ $87.50

For full description of outfits, see pages 279 and 280. In ordering please specify which outfit is wanted with mantel. If mantel is wanted with outfit different from those priced above, write for price on same.

PRICES SUBJECT TO DISCOUNT.

HARDWOOD MANTELS.

1057

Special Bargain Mantel.

Made of selected materials and well finished. Can be had in oak or birch; height, 48 inches; width, 60 inches; tile opening, 36x36 inches.

Mantel only, without trimmings____ $31.00   Mantel, with outfit "A"_____ $61.00
Mantel, with outfit "B"_____ 72.00   Mantel, with outfit "C"_____ 68.00
Mantel, with outfit "D"_____ $86.00

For full description of outfits, see pages 279 and 280. In ordering please specify which outfit is wanted with mantel. If mantel is wanted with outfit different from those priced above, write for price on same.

PRICES SUBJECT TO DISCOUNT.

HARDWOOD CONSOL.

1026

Selected quarter-sawed oak or birch. Veneered columns, 3½ inches; height, 8 feet 1 inch; width, 5 feet. Best quality French beveled mirror, 40x60 inches; piano polish; all hand carving.

List price_____ _____$130.00

PRICES SUBJECT TO MANTEL DISCOUNT.

HARDWOOD CONSOL.

1301

Consol, for Hall, Parlor or Dressing Room.

Made of selected quarter-sawed oak or birch; finish, piano polish; height, 8 feet, ½ inch; width,
5 feet; best quality French bevel plate mirror, 38x58 inches.

List price_____$122.50

ABOVE PRICE SUBJECT TO MANTEL DISCOUNT.

HARDWOOD CONSOL.

1300

Consol, for Hall, Parlor or Dressing Room.

Made of selected quarter-sawed oak or birch; finish, piano polish; height, 7 feet, 10 inches; width, 5 feet; best quality French bevel plate mirror, 38x58 inches.

List price_____$112.50

ABOVE PRICE SUBJECT TO MANTEL DISCOUNT.

A NEW IDEA.

MOUNTING TILE IN SLABS.

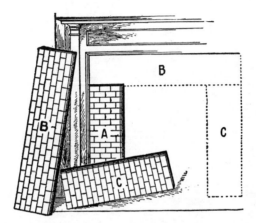

The fact that you cannot procure the services of a skilled mason to set the tiles need not deter you from buying a tiled mantel   Our method of mounting tile on slate provides for this contingency and obviates the need of a mason, makes the setting up of a tiled mantel almost as easy as the erection of a bedstead.   This is not an experiment.   Its practicability is attested by hundreds who have purchased these mantles.

The most flattering testimonial is that some dealers have copied above idea, even going so far as to copy the description verbatim.   When wanting the BEST, consult the EXPERTS AND ORIGINATORS, not the imitators and followers.

The accompanying illustration shows our tiling mounted on slabs of slate, as we send it out for erecting.   "A" represents a section in position; "B" and "C" similar sections, to occupy the blank spaces so marked.

Any tile work sent out by us failing to give satisfaction may be returned at our expense.

When furnished mounted in this manner tiling can be easily set in position by an ordinary mechanic, and at the same time it gives a job so thoroughly excellent and durable as to constitute its additional cost an eminently wise investment.

Price for Mounting Tile Facings _____$6.00 list extra.

OUTFITS.

1309

Open Superior Grate.

Regarding outfits—The following outfits can be furnished with mantels mentioned in this book. In ordering please specify which outfit is wanted.

OUTFIT "A."

Consists of: fireplace—No. 1309, Open Superior Grate, with plated frame; 24½ inches wide, 30¼ inches high; 20-inch Berlin black basket and ash screen.

Facing—Best quality plain enameled tile.

Hearth—60x21 inches. Best quality plain enameled tile.

Extra charge if double draft damper is wanted with this outfit, $2.00.

FIRE BRICK.

Regarding Fire Brick—Outfit "A" does not include the fire brick, as same can usually be bought in your town for less than the freight would amount to, but in cases where you cannot purchase fire brick in your town, we will furnish same at $2.00 per mantel extra.

The Superior Grate, which we show herewith, is one of the most serviceable grates made. The basket is made of heavy iron, and the fire brick should be built to fit snugly up to basket. The basket is so made that it is very easy to poke out the ashes. For burning soft coal or wood these grates cannot be excelled.

1035

Buckeye Grate.

24½ inches wide, 30¼ inches high; 20-inch basket, 12 inches deep.

Side view, showing damper arrangement.

OUTFIT "B."

Consists of: fireplace—No. 1035, Plated Buckeye Grate; 24½ inches wide, 30¼ inches high, with 20-inch basket and plated summer front.

Facing—Best quality plain enameled tile.

Hearth—60x21 inches. Best quality plain enameled tiling.

The Buckeye Grate which we show above, is without doubt one of the most beautiful grates of its kind ever produced. It has all of the desirable features of the Monarch Grate, having the same damper arrangement, and also a shaking bottom. The fire pot is lined in the back with fire clay lining, while the sides are of very heavy iron. These grates being made all in one piece, like the Monarch, they do not require any labor or expense in setting. While they are not quite as heavy as the Monarch, still they will prove to be excellent heaters, and will warrant them to give perfect satisfaction.

OUTFITS.

924

30½x30¼ and 24½x30¼; five row steel burner; deep or shallow back.

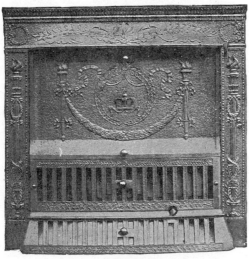

1116

Monarch Grate.

30½ inches wide, 30¼ inches high; 24-inch basket, 12 inches deep.

OUTFIT "C."

Consists of: fireplace—No. 924, complete mounted Gas Grate and Summer Front, copper-plated; 24½ inches wide, 30¼ inches high. This grate has copper reflecting sides and base; made with five row steel burner; double hood; damper full width of back, operated by handle on top of grate. Has double ventilating back, which takes cold and foul air from the floor and passes through opening in back of chimney.

Facing—Best quality plain enameled tile.

Hearth—60x21 inches. Best quality plain enameled tile.

In ordering this outfit state whether natural or artificial gas will be used.

OUTFIT "D."

Consists of: fireplace—No. 1116, Plated Monarch Grate; 30½ inches wide, 30¼ inches high, with 24-inch basket and plated summer front.

Facing—Best quality plain enameled tile.

Hearth—60x21 inches. Best quality plain enameled tile.

Side view, showing damper arrangement.

We recommend Monarch Mounted Grates to those who desire the comforts of a furnace and the cheer of an open fireplace. They are made like a stove, complete, all in one piece, and do not require the services of a skilled mason to set them, as all that is necessary is to push them into the fireplace and they are ready for use. The fire pot in the Monarch Grate is lined with heavy fire clay lining that will not burn out and also has latest improved shaking bottom. These grates are supplied with double dampers, which are operated from the front with knobs (see illustration). The lower damper is immediately over the fire, and in opening same you heat the flue, forming a current that carries off the dense smoke.

SPARK AND NURSERY GUARDS.

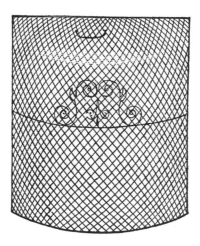

1. Coppered, fine wire lining, 24 inches wide by 30 inches high, each _____ $3.50
2. Coppered, fine wire lining, 30 inches wide by 30 inches high, each _____ 4.50

ASH PIT COVER.

ASH PIT DOOR.

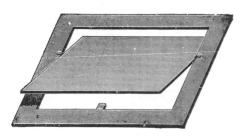

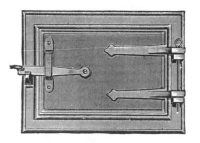

10 inches long, 7 inches wide; works automatically.

Price, each _____ $1.50

20 inches long, 16 inches wide.

Price, each _____ $3.50

PRICES SUBJECT TO MANTEL DISCOUNT.

BRASS AND IRON ANDIRONS.

541

18 inches high.

Price, per pair------$12.00

593

18 inches high.

Price, per pair--------$6.00

535

19 inches high.

Price, per pair-------$6.00

POLISHED BRASS FIRE SETS.

890

Price, per set---------$13.20

892

Price, per set---------$17.00

895

Price, per set---------$17.00

POLISHED BRASS FENDER.

608

With fancy rail, 36 or 42 inches long--$15.00

PRICES SUBJECT TO MANTEL DISCOUNT.

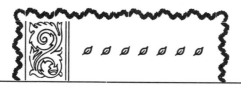

Composition Capitals

Illustrated
and
described
on
following
pages.

COMPOSITION CAPITALS and BRACKETS.

The increasing demand for Capitals, both Column and Pilaster in composition instead of wood warrants us, we believe, in making this class of work a feature of our new catalogue. We show on the following pages a number of designs in different styles of architecture suitable for either inside or outside use. And we also include a large and varied list of the sizes in which they can be furnished. We recommend them as follows :

In beauty they easily surpass wood carvings, the detail in execution being brought to a fineness impossible in wood.

In durability they are the equal of wood, and for outside use they are specially prepared and guaranteed to stand any conditions of climate.

In cost they are very much cheaper than wood.

Write us for prices or any desired information.

EXPLANATION and INSTRUCTIONS.

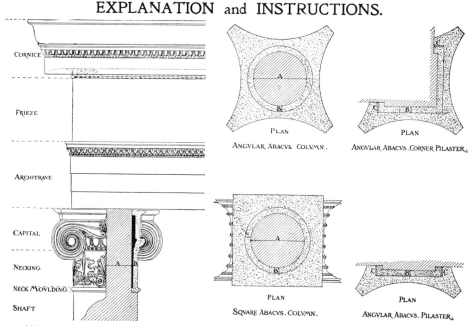

The above plate illustrates one of our modern Ionic Capitals with necking (Empire), as applied to a column showing the wood shaft and core running through the Capital supporting the entablature above. The plans of the different abacus forms as given will serve as a further illustration of the relative position of shaft and our material.

"A" indicates the core or extended shaft running through Capital.

"B" shows thickness of our material.

"C" indicates the return of Pilaster Capital; which always must be mentioned in ordering Pilaster Capitals.

All our Capitals are furnished as shown in the Catalogue, each Capital having a complete finish to connect with shaft. The diameter given in Catalogue represents the top of Column. The width represents the top of Pilaster. The height given is the exact height of Capital. Always allow a trifle more height for your core so the weight will rest on shaft and not on Capital, ⅛ of an inch up to a 10-inch diameter; ¼ of an inch above that size will be sufficient to insure a safe application.

The thickness of our material is one inch up to a 10-inch diameter Capital, making the core of a 10-inch diameter Capital 8 inches, of an 8-inch Capital 6 inches. Above 10 inches allow ⅛ of an inch more for the thickness of material for every two inches of increased size, making core for a 14-inch diameter Capital 11½ inches, a 16-inch Capital 13¼ inches, etc.

In ordering Capital, give name, number and size of diameter or width; also state material wanted, viz: whether Exterior Composition, warranted to stand in any climate, or Interior Composition, made with grain to match any wood; (Interior Composition having a solid wood body requires no core on Column. Always state the kind of wood and finish.)

The sizes of our brackets given are:

1st   The entire width across abacus moulding.

2d   Width of face on body.

3d   Drop or length.

4th   Projection.

GREEK IONIC (Erechtheum).

COLUMN CAPITAL

EXTERIOR.

Number.	Diameter, Inches.	Height. Inches.	Prices, Each.
1	4	3⅝	$ 2.25
2	5	4½	2.50
3	6	5½	3.00
4	7	6⅜	4.00
5	8	7	5.00
6	9	8¼	6.00
7	10	9⅛	7.00
8	11	10	8.00
9	12	11	9.00
10	14	12¾	12.00
11	16	14⅝	16.00
12	17	16¼	18.00
13	18	16½	20.00

INTERIOR.

Number.	Diameter, Inches.	Height, Inches.	Prices, Each.
25	3	2¾	$ 2.50
26	3½	3⅛	3.00
27	4	3⅝	3.50
28	4½	4	4.00
29	5	4½	4.50
30	5½	5	5.00
31	6	5½	5.50
32	6½	5⅞	6.00
33	7	6⅜	7.00
34	8	7	8.00

PILASTER CAPITAL.

EXTERIOR.

Number.	Width, Inches.	Height, Inches.	Prices, Each.
51	5	4⅜	$ 1.50
52	5½	4¼	2.00
53	6	5⅛	2.25
54	7	4½	2.50
55	8	8	3.00
56	9¾	9½	3.50
57	10	8	4.00
58	11	7⅛	4.50
59	12	7¾	5.00
60	14	9	5.50
61	16	10⅜	6.50
62	18	11⅝	8.00

INTERIOR.

Number.	Width, Inches.	Height. Inches.	Prices, Each.
76	3	2	$ 1.50
77	3½	2¼	1.50
78	4	2½	2.00
79	4½	3	2.00
80	5	3¼	2.50
81	5½	3⅝	2.50
82	6	4	3.00
83	6½	4¼	3.00
84	7	4½	3.50
85	8	5	4.00

GREEK IONIC (Erechtheum).

COLUMN CAPITAL.

COPY'Y 1899.   DECORATORS SUP'Y CO.

PILASTER CAPITAL.

COPY'D 1899   DECORATORS SUP'Y CO.

ROMAN CORINTHIAN (Pantheon).

COLUMN CAPITAL.

EXTERIOR.

Number.	Diameter, Inches.	Height, Inches.	Prices, Each.
301	5	7	$ 4.00
302	6	9	5.00
303	7	10½	6.00
304	8	12	6.50
305	9	12½	7 00
306	10	14⅝	8.00
307	11	15⅜	9.00
308	12	16¾	10.00
309	13	18	11.00
310	14	19½	12.00
311	15	21	14.00
312	16	22⅜	16.00
313	18	25	20.00
314	20	28	25 00
315	24	33½	40.00

INTERIOR.

Number.	Diameter, Inches.	Height, Inches.	Prices, Each.
326	1	1⅜	$ 1.25
327	1½	2	1.50
328	2	2⅝	1.75
329	2½	3⅜	2.25
330	3	4	3.00
331	3½	4¾	3.50
332	4	5½	4.00
333	4½	6¼	4.50
334	5	7	5.00
335	5½	7¾	6.00
336	6	9	7.00
337	8	12	10.00

PILASTER CAPITAL.

EXTERIOR.

Number.	Width, Inches.	Height, Inches.	Prices, Each.
351	5	7	$ 2.50
352	6	9	3.00
353	7	10½	3 50
354	8	12	3.75
355	9	12½	4 00
356	10	14⅝	4.50
357	11	15⅜	5.00
358	12	16¾	6.00
359	13	18	7.00
360	14	19½	8.00
361	15	21	8 50
362	16	22⅜	9.00
363	18	25	11.00
364	20	28	15.00
365	24	33½	25.00

INTERIOR.

Number.	Width, Inches.	Height, Inches.	Prices, Each.
376	1	1⅜	$0.80
377	1½	2	1.00
378	2	2⅝	1.25
379	2½	3⅜	1.50
380	3	4	1.75
381	3½	4¾	2.25
382	4	5½	2.50
383	4½	6¼	3.00
384	5	7	4.00
385	5½	7¾	4.50
386	6	9	5.25
387	8	12	6.50

ROMAN CORINTHIAN (Pantheon).
COLUMN CAPITAL.

COPY'D 1899.   DECORATORS SUP'Y CO.

PILASTER CAPITAL.

COPY'D 1899.   DECORATORS SUP'Y C O.

MODERN IONIC with NECKING (Empire).

COLUMN CAPITAL.

EXTERIOR.

Number.	Diameter, Inches.	Height, Inches.	Prices, Each.
1051	4	5	$2.50
1052	5	6¼	3.00
1053	6	7½	3 25
1054	6½	7¾	3.75
1055	7	8⅞	4.00
1056	7½	9⅜	4.50
1057	8	10¼	5.00
1058	8½	10½	5.50
1059	9	11½	6.00
1060	9½	11⅞	6.50
1061	10	12½	7.50
1062	11	13¾	8.00
1063	12	15	8.50
1064	14	17½	9.50
1065	15	18¾	10.50
1066	16	20	13.00
1067	17	21¼	14.50
1068	18	22½	17.00
1069	21	26¼	22.00

INTERIOR.

Number.	Diameter, Inches.	Height, Inches.	Prices, Each.
1101	1	1¼	$0.70
1102	1½	1⅞	.85
1103	2	2½	1.00
1104	2½	3⅛	1.20
1105	3	3¾	1.50
1106	3½	4⅜	1.75
1107	4	5	2.00
1108	4½	5⅝	2.30
1109	5	6¼	2.70
1110	5½	6⅞	3.00
1111	6	7½	4.00
1112	7	8⅞	5.00
1113	8	10¼	7.00
1114	9	11½	9.00
1115	10	12½	11.00
1116	11	13¾	13.50
1117	12	15	15.00
1118	14	17½	20.00
1119	15	18¾	25.00
1120	16	20	30.00
1121	17	21¼	38.00
1122	18	22½	45.00

PILASTER CAPITAL.

EXTERIOR.

Number.	Width, Inches.	Height, Inches.	Prices, Each.
1151	4	5	$1.50
1152	5	6¼	1.75
1153	6	7½	2.00
1154	6½	7¾	2.25
1155	7	8⅞	2.50
1156	7½	9⅜	2.75
1157	8	10¼	3.00
1158	8½	10½	3.25
1159	9	11½	3.50
1160	9½	11⅞	3.75
1161	10	12½	4.00
1162	11	13¾	4.50
1163	12	15	5.00
1164	14	17½	5.50
1165	15	18¾	6.25
1166	16	20	7.50
1167	17	21¼	8.75
1168	18	22½	9.50
1169	21	26¼	12.50

INTERIOR.

Number	Width, Inches.	Height, Inches.	Prices, Each.
1201	1	1¼	$0.50
1202	1½	1⅞	.60
1203	2	2½	.70
1204	2½	3⅛	.80
1205	3	3¾	.90
1206	3½	4⅜	1.00
1207	4	5	1.25
1208	4½	5⅝	1.50
1209	5	6¼	1.75
1210	5½	6⅞	2.00
1211	6	7½	2.50
1212	7	8⅞	3 00
1213	8	10¼	4.00
1214	9	11½	5.00
1215	10	12½	6.00
1216	11	13¾	7.25
1217	12	15	8.50
1218	14	17½	11.00
1219	15	18¾	14.00
1220	16	20	16.50
1221	17	21¼	20.00
1222	18	22½	25.00

MODERN IONIC with NECKING (Empire).
COLUMN CAPITAL.

COPY'D 1899.   DECORATORS SUP'Y CO.

PILASTER CAPITAL.

COPY'D 1899.   DECORATORS SUP'Y CO.

ITALIAN RENAISSANCE CORINTHIAN (Sansovino).

COLUMN CAPITAL.

EXTERIOR.

Number.	Diameter, Inches.	Height, Inches.	Prices, Each.
1626	5	7	$ 2.50
1627	6	8⅜	3.50
1628	7	9⅝	4.50
1629	8	11	5.50
1630	9	12½	6.50
1631	10	13⅞	7.50
1632	12	16¾	9.00
1633	14	19½	11.00
1634	16	22¼	14.00
1635	18	25	17.00

INTERIOR.

Number.	Diameter, Inches.	Height, Inches.	Prices, Each.
1676	1	1⅜	$ 0.70
1677	1½	2	.80
1678	2	2¾	1.00
1679	2½	3½	1.20
1680	3	4⅛	1.50
1681	3½	4¾	1.80
1682	4	5½	2.20
1683	4½	6¼	2.60
1684	5	7	3 00
1685	5½	7¾	3.50
1686	6	8⅜	4.50
1687	6½	9	5.00
1688	7	9⅝	6.00

PILASTER CAPITAL.

EXTERIOR.

Number.	Width. Inches.	Height, Inches.	Prices, Each.
1726	5	7	$ 1.50
1727	6	8⅜	2.00
1728	7	9⅝	2.50
1729	8	11	3.00
1730	9	12½	3.50
1731	10	13⅞	4.00
1732	12	16¾	5.00
1733	14	19½	6.00
1734	16	22¼	7.50
1735	18	25	9.00

INTERIOR.

Number.	Width, Inches.	Height Inches.	Prices, Each.
1776	1	1⅜	$0.50
1777	1½	2	.60
1778	2	2¾	.70
1779	2½	3½	.90
1780	3	4⅛	1.10
1781	3½	4¾	1.25
1782	4	5½	1.50
1783	4½	6¼	1.75
1784	5	7	2.00
1785	5½	7¾	2.25
1786	6	8⅜	2.50
1787	6½	9	3.00
1788	7	9⅝	3 50

ITALIAN RENAISSANCE CORINTHIAN (Sansovino).

COLUMN CAPITAL.

COPY'D 1899. DECORATORS SUP'Y CO.

PILASTER CAPITAL.

COPY'D 1899. DECORATORS SUP'Y CO.

GREEK ANGULAR IONIC   (Minerva Polías).

COLUMN CAPITAL.

EXTERIOR.

Number.	Diameter, Inches.	Height, Inches.	Prices, Each,
201	5	3⅛	$ 2.50
202	6	3⅜	3.00
203	6½	4	3.25
204	7	4⅛	3.50
205	7½	4¼	3.75
206	8	5	4.50
207	8½	5¼	4.75
208	9	5⅝	5.00
209	9½	6	5.50
210	10	6¼	6.00
211	11	6⅞	6.75
212	12	7½	7.50
213	14	8¾	9.00
214	15	9⅜	10.00
215	18	11¼	14.00
216	21	13⅛	18.00
217	25	14⅜	30.00

INTERIOR.

Number.	Diameter, Inches.	Height, Inches.	Prices. Each.
226	1½	$\frac{15}{16}$	$1.00
227	2	¼	1.10
228	2½	1 $\frac{9}{16}$	1.20
229	3	1⅞	1.30
230	3½	2 $\frac{3}{16}$	1.40
231	4	2½	1.60
232	4½	2 $\frac{13}{16}$	1.80
233	5	3⅛	2.00
234	5½	3 $\frac{7}{16}$	2.50
235	6	3¾	3.00
236	7	4⅛	4.00
237	7½	4¼	5.00

PILASTER CAPITAL.

EXTERIOR.

Number.	Width, Inches.	Height, Inches.	Prices, Each.
251	5	3⅛	$ 1.75
252	6	3⅜	2.00
253	6½	4	2.10
254	7	4⅛	2.25
255	7½	4¼	2.50
256	8	5	2.75
257	8½	5¼	3.00
258	9	5⅝	3.25
259	9½	6	3.50
260	10	6¼	3.75
261	11	6⅞	4.00
262	12	7½	4.25
263	14	8¾	5.00
264	15	9⅜	5.50
265	18	11¼	8.00
266	21	13⅛	10.00
267	25	14⅜	18.00

INTERIOR.

Number.	Width, Inches.	Height, Inches.	Prices, Each.
276	1½	$\frac{15}{16}$	$ .70
277	2	1¼	.80
278	2½	1 $\frac{9}{16}$	.90
279	3	1⅞	1 00
280	3½	2 $\frac{3}{16}$	1.10
281	4	2½	1.20
282	4½	2 $\frac{13}{16}$	1.30
283	5	3⅛	1.50
284	5½	3 $\frac{7}{16}$	1.80
285	6	3¾	2.00
286	7	4⅛	2 50
287	7½	4¼	3.00

GREEK ANGULAR IONIC (Minerva Polias).

COLUMN CAPITAL

COPY'D 1899. DECORATORS SUP'Y CO.

PILASTER CAPITAL.

COPY'D 1899. DECORATORS SUP'Y CO.

ITALIAN RENAISSANCE IONIC (Scamozzi).

COLUMN CAPITAL.

EXTERIOR.

Number.	Diameter, Inches.	Height. Inches.	Prices, Each.
1426	4	2¼	$ 2.00
1427	5	2⅞	2.50
1428	5½	3⅛	2.75
1429	6	3⅜	3.00
1430	6½	3⅝	3.25
1431	7	3¾	3.50
1432	7½	4¼	3.75
1433	8	4⅝	4.00
1434	8½	4¾	4.25
1435	9	5⅛	4.50
1436	9½	5⅜	4.75
1437	10	5¾	5.00
1438	10½	5⅞	5.50
1439	11	6¼	6.00
1440	12	6¾	7.00
1441	13	7½	8.00
1442	14	7⅞	9.50
1443	15	8⅜	10.50
1444	16	9	12.00
1445	17	9¾	13.00
1446	18	10⅛	14.00
1447	20	11⅜	18 00
1448	22	12½	22.00
1449	24	13½	25.00
1450	28	16	35.00
1451	31	17¾	45.00

INTERIOR.

Number.	Diameter, Inches.	Height, Inches.	Prices, Each.
1476	1	9/16	$ 0.60
1477	1½	⅞	.70
1478	2	1⅛	.80
1479	2½	1⅜	.90
1480	3	1¾	1.00
1481	3½	2	1.20
1482	4	2¼	1.40
1483	4½	2½	1.60
1484	5	2⅞	1 80
1485	5½	3⅛	2.00
1486	6	3⅜	2.25
1487	6½	3⅝	2 50
1488	7	3¾	3 00
1489	7½	4¼	3.50
1490	8	4⅝	4.50
1491	9	5⅛	6.00
1492	10	5¾	7.50
1493	11	6¼	9.00
1494	12	6¾	11.00
1495	14	7⅞	15.00

PILASTER CAPITAL.

EXTERIOR.

Number.	Width, Inches.	Height, Inches.	Prices, Each.
1526	4	2¼	$ 1.25
1527	5	2⅞	1.50
1528	5½	3⅛	1.50
1529	6	3⅜	1.75
1530	6½	3⅝	1.75
1531	7	3¾	2 00
1532	7½	4¼	2.00
1533	8	4⅝	2.25
1534	8½	4¾	2.25
1535	9	5⅛	2.50
1536	9½	5⅜	2.50
1537	10	5¾	2.75
1538	10½	5⅞	2.75
1539	11	6¼	3.00
1540	12	6¾	3.75
1541	13	7½	4.25
1542	14	7⅞	5.00
1543	15	8⅜	6.00
1544	16	9	7.00
1545	17	9¾	8.00
1546	18	10⅛	9.00
1547	20	11⅜	10.00
1548	22	12½	11.50
1549	24	13½	13.00
1550	28	16	18.00
1551	31	17¾	25.00

INTERIOR.

Number.	Width, Inches.	Height, Inches.	Prices, Each.
1576	1	9/16	$ 0.40
1577	1½	⅞	.50
1578	2	1⅛	.60
1579	2½	1⅜	.70
1580	3	1¾	.80
1581	3½	2	.90
1582	4	2¼	1.00
1583	4½	2½	1.25
1584	5	2⅞	1.30
1585	5½	3⅛	1.45
1586	6	3⅜	1.60
1587	6½	3⅝	1 80
1588	7	3¾	2.10
1589	7½	4¼	2.50
1590	8	4⅝	3.00
1591	9	5⅛	3.75
1592	10	5¾	4.50
1593	11	6¼	5 00
1594	12	6¾	6.00
1595	14	7⅞	8.00

ITALIAN RENAISSANCE IONIC (Scamozzi).

COLUMN CAPITAL.

COPY'D 1899.   DECORATORS SUP'Y CO.

PILASTER CAPITAL.

COPY'D 1899.   DECORATORS SUP'Y CO

BRACKETS.

ROMAN PANTHEON.

EXTERIOR.

Number.	Abacus Width, Inches.	Face Width, Inches.	Projection, Inches.	Drop, Inches.	Prices, Each.
2351	4	3	6¾	3½	$1.50
2352	5½	4	9	4¾	2.00
2353	6¾	5	11¼	5¾	2.50
2354	8	6	13½	7	3.00
2355	11	8	18	9½	4.00
2356	13	10	22½	11¼	5.00

INTERIOR.

Number.	Abacus Width, Inches.	Face Width, Inches.	Projection, Inches.	Drop, Inches.	Prices, Each.
2376	4	3	6¾	3½	$3.00
2377	5½	4	9	4¾	4.00
2378	6¾	5	11¼	5¾	5.00

MODERN RENAISSANCE (Empire).

EXTERIOR.

Number.	Abacus Width, Inches.	Face Width, Inches.	Projection, Inches.	Drop, Inches.	Prices, Each.
2400	1¼	1	3	1¼	$0.50
2401	1½	1¼	3¾	1½	.60
2402	1⅞	1½	4½	1⅞	.70
2403	2⅛	1¾	5¼	2⅛	.80
2404	2½	2	6	2½	.90
2405	2¾	2¼	6¾	2¾	1.00
2406	3	2½	7½	3	1.15
2407	3⅜	2¾	8¼	3⅜	1.30
2408	3⅝	3	9	3⅝	1.50
2409	4¼	3½	10½	4¼	1.70
2410	5	4	12	5	1.90
2411	5½	4½	13½	5½	2.10
2412	6	5	15	6	2.30
2413	6¾	5½	16½	6¾	2.50
2414	7¼	6	18	7¼	2.80

INTERIOR.

Number.	Abacus Width, Inches.	Face Width, Inches.	Projection, Inches.	Drop, Inches.	Prices, Each.
2426	1¼	1	3	1¼	$0.50
2427	1½	1¼	3¾	1½	.60
2428	1⅞	1½	4½	1⅞	.70
2429	2⅛	1¾	5¼	2⅛	.80
2430	2½	2	6	2½	.90
2431	2¾	2¼	6¾	2¾	1.00
2432	3	2½	7½	3	1.30
2433	3⅜	2¾	8¼	3⅜	1.50
2434	3⅝	3	9	3⅝	1.75
2435	4¼	3½	10½	4¼	2.00
2436	5	4	12	5	2.50

ROMAN VATICAN.

EXTERIOR.

Number.	Abacus Width, Inches.	Face Width, Inches.	Projection, Inches.	Drop, Inches.	Prices, Each.
2651	1⅜	1	1¾	⅞	$0.50
2652	1⅝	1¼	2⅛	1	.60
2653	2	1½	2⅝	1¼	.70
2654	2¼	1¾	3	1½	.80
2655	2⅝	2	3½	1¾	.90
2656	3	2¼	3⅞	2	1.00
2657	3¼	2½	4⅜	2¼	1.15
2658	3⅝	2¾	4¾	2⅜	1.30
2659	4	3	5¼	2⅝	1.50
2660	4½	3½	6	3	1.65
2661	5¼	4	6⅞	3⅜	1.80
2662	6	4⅝	8	4	1.90
2663	6½	5	8⅝	4¼	2.10
2664	7¼	5½	9½	4¾	2.30
2665	8	6	10⅜	5¼	2.50

INTERIOR.

Number.	Abacus Width, Inches.	Face Width, Inches.	Projection, Inches.	Drop, Inches.	Prices, Each.
2701	1⅜	1	1¾	⅞	$0.50
2702	1⅝	1¼	2⅛	1	.60
2703	2	1½	2⅝	1¼	.70
2704	2¼	1¾	3	1½	.80
2705	2⅝	2	3½	1¾	.90
2706	3	2¼	3⅞	2	1.00
2707	3¼	2½	4⅜	2¼	1.25
2708	3⅝	2¾	4¾	2⅜	1.50
2709	4	3	5¼	2⅝	1.75
2710	4½	3½	6	3	2.00
2711	5¼	4	6⅞	3⅜	2.20
2712	6	4⅝	8	4	2.50
2713	6½	5	8⅝	4¼	3.00

BRACKETS.
ROMAN PANTHEON.

COPY'D 1899.
DECORATORS SUP'Y CO.

MODERN RENAISSANCE (Empire).

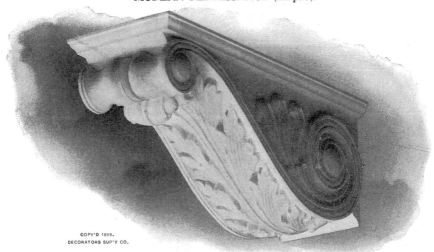

COPY'D 1899.
DECORATORS SUP'Y CO.

ROMAN VATICAN.

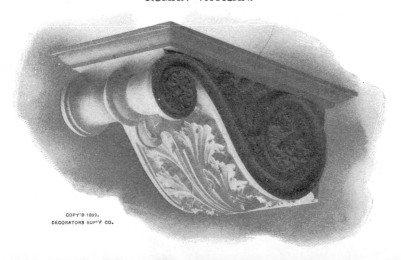

COPY'D 1899.
DECORATORS SUP'Y CO.

LADDERS.

COMMON LONG LADDERS.

Made of Norway Pine, clear and select. Hickory rungs, strong, light and durable. We carry in stock lengths from 10 to 20 feet.

Price, 18c per foot.

EXTENSION LADDER.

Strong, light and durable. Made of Norway Pine, clear and select. Hickory rungs. This ladder is far superior to any in the market, as it has a new patent hook which enables the ladder to be used as a trestle. This hook is made in such a manner that when the ladder is being raised a spring throws hook on rungs, making it light and easy to raise. Made in two sections. 20 to 40 feet long.

Price, 28c per foot.

STEP LADDERS.

Made of Clear Norway Pine, well braced, light and strong.

Price, 20c per foot.

CAST IRON DOOR SILLS.

Cast Iron Door Sill for 2x6 Doors, each_____$1.20
Cast Iron Door Sill for 2x8 Doors, each_____ 1.30

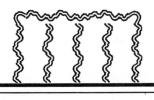

We handle and constantly carry in stock all the ordinary sizes of Window Glass, and can furnish promptly all sizes of Plate Glass and the various designs of Fancy Glass shown herein. · . · . We can also supply you with any of the varieties of Glass in ordinary use, such as Ground, Chipped, Enamel, Figured, Wire Glass, for skylights, and the different kinds of Colored Glass, viz: Cathedral, Ondoyant, Venetian, etc.

Write us for any desired information and we will be pleased to be of service to you. ✿ ✿

PATTERNS ENAMEL GLASS.

5016

5017

5018

5019

If semi-obscure D. S. Glass_____24 cents per square foot
If full obscure D. S. Glass_____30 cents per square foot

COLORED and FANCY GLASS.

Chipped. Single Process.
22 cents per square foot.

Chipped. Double Process.
24 cents per square foot.

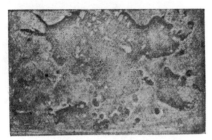

Rolled Cathedral.
24 cents per square foot.

Radiant.
30 cents per square foot.

Florentine.
22 cents per square foot.

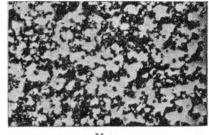

Moss.
30 cents per square foot.

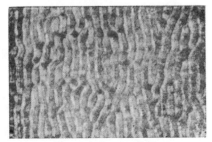

Riffled.
20 cents per square foot.

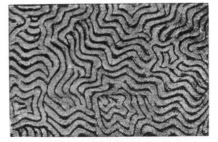

Irridescent.
24 cents per square foot.

Can furnish above in Clear or Assorted Colors.

GEOMETRIC CHIPPED and GROUND GLASS.

1400
90 cents per square foot.

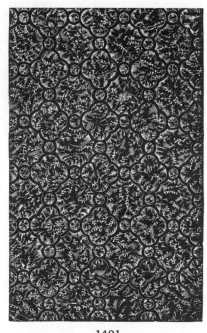

1401
90 cents per square foot.

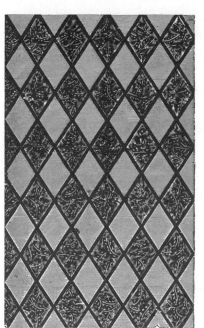

1403
95 cents per square foot.

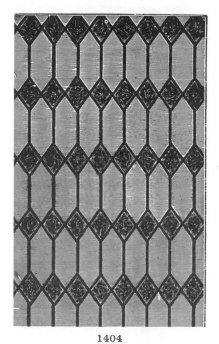

1404
95 cents per square foot.

ART SAND BLAST GLASS.

1423

$1.00 per square foot.

1424

$1.00 per square foot.

1446

$1.00 per square foot.

1447

$1.00 per square foot.

ART SAND BLAST GLASS.

1425

$1.00 per square foot.

1426

$1.00 per square foot.

1427

$1.00 per square foot.

1428

$1.00 per square foot.

ART SAND BLAST GLASS.

1415.
$1.25 per square foot.

1416.
$1.25 per square foot.

1417.
$1.25 per square foot.

1418.
$1.25 per square foot.

ART SAND BLAST GLASS.

5012

$1.00 per square foot.

5013

$1.00 per square foot.

5014

$1.00 per square foot.

5015

$1.00 per square foot.

ART SAND BLAST GLASS.

5000

$1.00 per square foot.

5001

$1.00 per square foot.

5002

$1.00 per square foot.

5003

$1.00 per square foot.

ART SAND BLAST GLASS.

5004
$1.00 per square foot.

5005
$1.00 per square foot.

5006
$1.00 per square foot.

5007
$1.00 per square foot.

ART SAND BLAST GLASS.

5008
$1.00 per square foot.

5009
$1.00 per square foot.

5010
$1.00 per square foot.

5011
$1.00 per square foot.

SPECIAL GLASS DESIGNS.

5016
$1.00 per square foot.

5017
$1.00 per square foot.

5018
$1.00 per square foot.

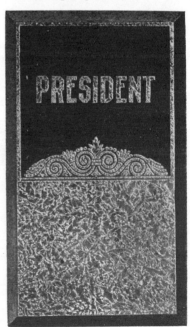

5019
$1.00 per square foot.

Letters 15c each, net extra.

4052. $3.00 per square foot

4048. $1.25 per square foot.

4051. $2.50 per square foot.

LEADED ART GLASS.

4046. $3.00 per square foot.

4047. $2.00 per square foot.

4050. $1.75 per square foot.

4049. $1.25 per square foot.

4057. $1.80 per sq. ft.

4060. $2.75 per square foot.

4054. $1.60 per square foot.

4056. $1.75 per square foot.

4059. $1.50 per sq. ft.

4053. $1.60 per square foot.

4055. $3.00 per square foot.

4058. $1.60 per square foot.

LEADED COLORED ART GLASS.

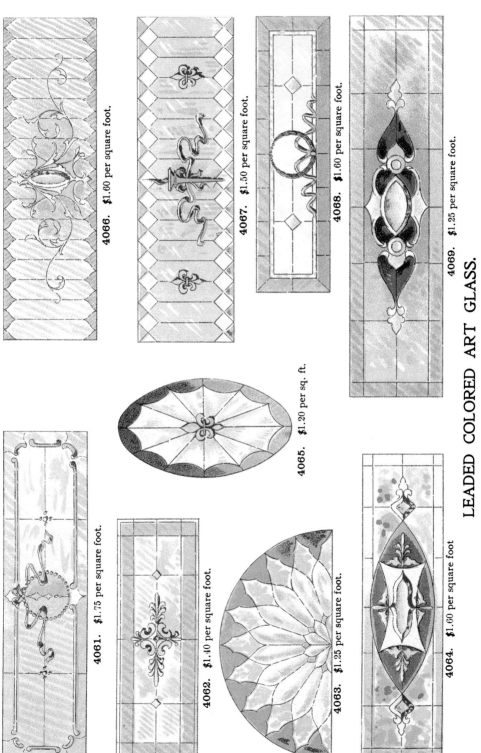

4066. $1.60 per square foot.

4067. $1.50 per square foot.

4068. $1.60 per square foot.

4069. $1.25 per square foot.

4065. $1.20 per sq. ft.

4061. $1.75 per square foot.

4062. $1.40 per square foot.

4063. $1.25 per square foot.

4064. $1.60 per square foot

LEADED COLORED ART GLASS.

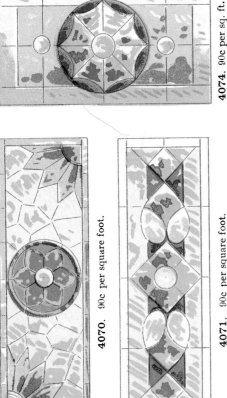

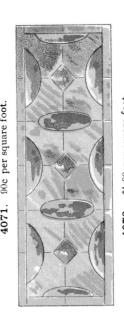

4076.   90c per square foot.

4077. $1.00 per square foot.

4078.   90c per square foot.

4079.   90c per square foot.

4074.   90c per sq. ft.

4075. $1.20 per sq. ft.

4070.   90c per square foot.

4071.   90c per square foot.

4072. $1.00 per square foot.

4073. $1.00 per square foot.

LEADED COLORED ART GLASS.

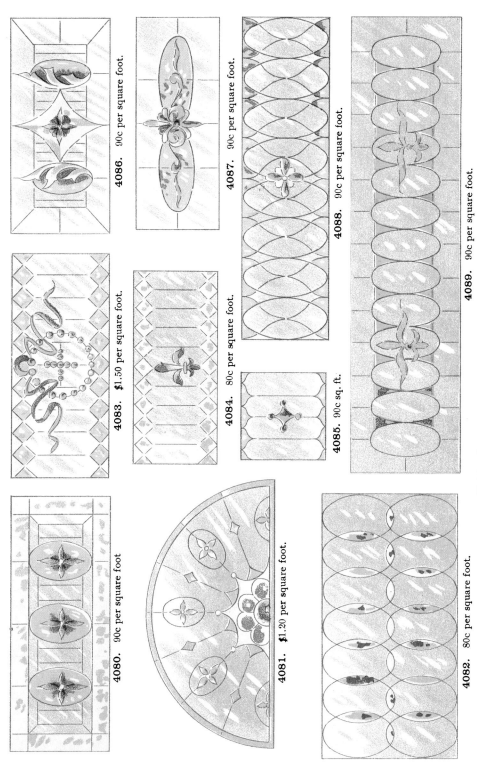

4086.   90c per square foot.

4087.   90c per square foot.

4088.   90c per square foot.

4089.   90c per square foot.

4083. $1.50 per square foot.

4084.   80c per square foot.

4085.   90c sq. ft.

4080.   90c per square foot

4081. $1.20 per square foot.

4082.   80c per square foot.

LEADED COLORED ART GLASS.

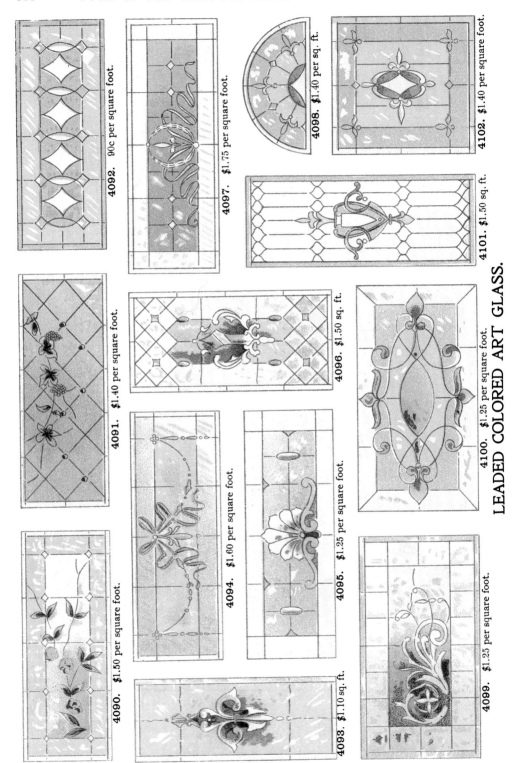

4092.   90c per square foot.

4097. $1.75 per square foot.

4098. $1.40 per sq. ft.

4102. $1.40 per square foot.

4101. $1.50 sq. ft.

4091. $1.40 per square foot.

4096. $1.50 sq. ft.

4100. $1.25 per square foot.

LEADED COLORED ART GLASS.

4090. $1.50 per square foot.

4094. $1.60 per square foot.

4095. $1.25 per square foot.

4099. $1.25 per square foot.

4093. $1.10 sq. ft.

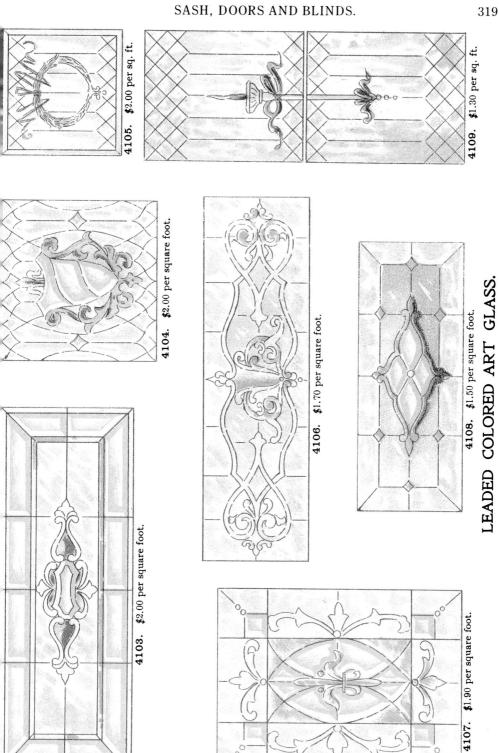

4105. $2.00 per sq. ft.

4109. $1.30 per sq. ft.

4104. $2.00 per square foot.

4106. $1.70 per square foot.

4108. $1.50 per square foot.

4103. $2.00 per square foot.

4107. $1.90 per square foot.

LEADED COLORED ART GLASS.

4116. $2.10 per square foot.

4114. 80c sq. ft.

4115. 80c sq. ft.

4111. $1.40 per square foot.

4113. $2.50 per square foot.

4110. $1.60 per square foot.

4112. $1.00 per sq. ft.

4118. $2.50 per square foot

LEADED COLORED ART GLASS.

4117. $2.00 per square foot.

4120. $1.80 per square foot.

4122. $1.80 per square foot.

4125. $1.50 per square foot.

4127. $2.00 per square foot.

4124. $2.20 per sq. ft.

4119. $1.60 per square foot.

4121. $1.80 per square foot.

4123. $1.80 per square foot.

4126. $2.75 per square foot.

LEADED COLORED ART GLASS.

4130. $2.60 per square foot.

4133. $2.20 per square foot.

4129. $2.00 per square foot.

4131. $2.60 per square foot.

4128. $2.50 per square foot.

4132. $1.80 per square foot.

LEADED COLORED ART GLASS.

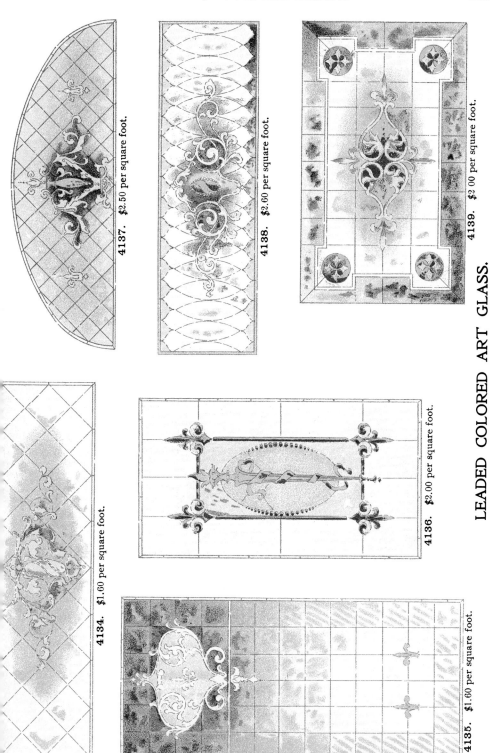

4187. $2.50 per square foot.

4138. $2.60 per square foot.

4139. $2.00 per square foot.

4134. $1.60 per square foot.

4136. $2.00 per square foot.

4135. $1.60 per square foot.

LEADED COLORED ART GLASS.

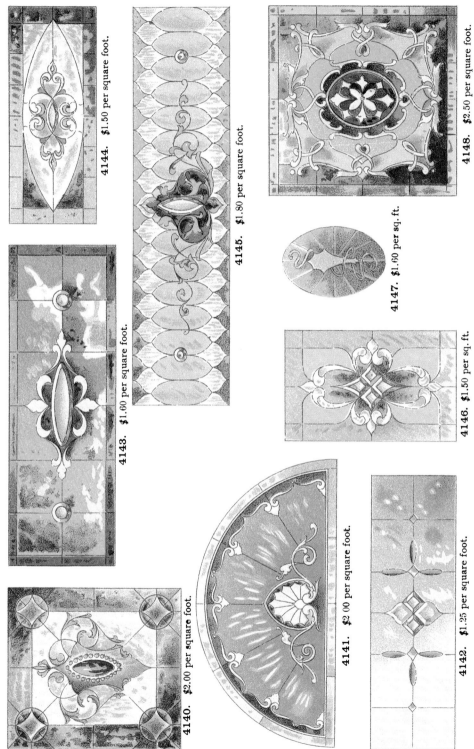

4144. $1.50 per square foot.

4145. $1.80 per square foot.

4148. $2.50 per square foot.

4143. $1.60 per square foot.

4147. $1.60 per sq. ft.

4146. $1.50 per sq. ft.

4140. $2.00 per square foot.

4141. $2.00 per square foot.

4142. $1.25 per square foot.

LEADED COLORED ART GLASS.

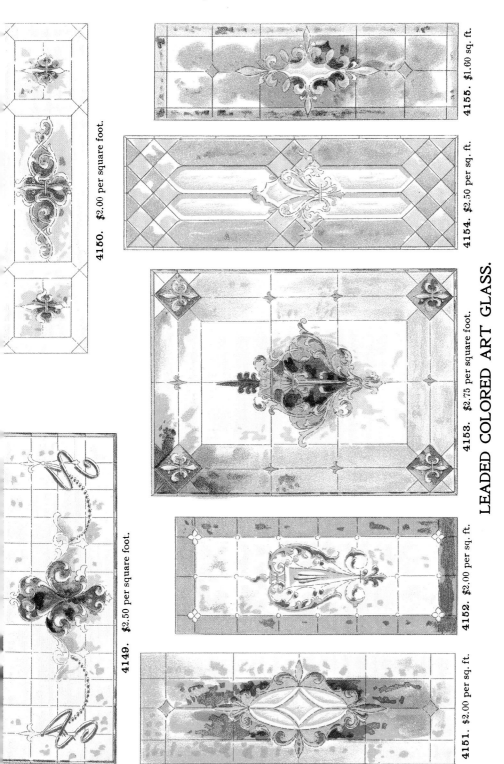

4150. $2.00 per square foot.

4155. $1.60 sq. ft.

4154. $2.50 per sq. ft.

4153. $2.75 per square foot.

LEADED COLORED ART GLASS.

4149. $2.50 per square foot.

4152. $2.00 per sq. ft.

4151. $2.00 per sq. ft.

4158. $2.00 per square foot.

4161. $1.80 per square foot.

4157. $1.60 per sq. ft.

4159. $2.00 per square foot

4160. $1.50 per square foot.

4156. $1.60 per square foot.

LEADED COLORED BEVELED GLASS

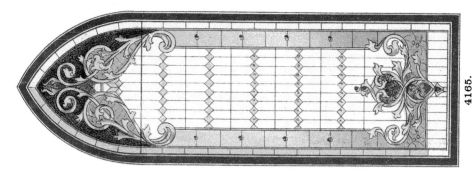

4165.

4164.

4163.

4162.

Price will depend on size and number of lights required.

Special prices furnished on application.

LEADED COLORED ART GLASS for CHURCH WINDOWS.

4171. $4.00 per square foot.

4174. $3.50 per sq. ft.

4168. $2.50 per square foot.

4169. $3.00 per square foot.

4170. $3.00 per square foot.

4173. $2.50 per square foot. Door lights should be set in metal.

4167. $3.75 per sq. ft.

4166. $3.50 per sq. ft.

4172. $4.00 per square foot.
If above are set in metal instead of lead, add 60c per square foot.

LEADED BEVEL PLATE

4177. $2.10 per sq. ft.

4182. $2.20 per sq. ft.

4176. $1.40 per sq. ft.

4181. $1.60 per sq. ft.

4180. $2.50 per sq. ft.

4175. $2.20 per sq. ft.

4179. $1.60 per sq. ft.

4178. $2.50 per sq. ft.

MITRED BEVEL PLATE.

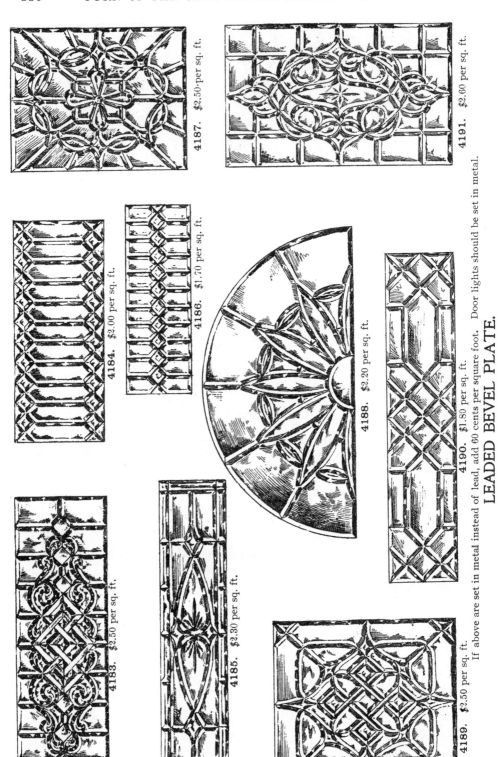

4187. $2.50-per sq. ft.

4191. $2.60 per sq. ft.

4184. $2.00 per sq. ft.

4186. $1.70 per sq. ft.

4188. $2.20 per sq. ft.

4190. $1.80 per sq. ft.

4183. $2.50 per sq. ft.

4185. $2.30 per sq. ft.

4189. $2.50 per sq. ft.

If above are set in metal instead of lead, add 60 cents per square foot.   Door lights should be set in metal.

LEADED BEVEL PLATE.

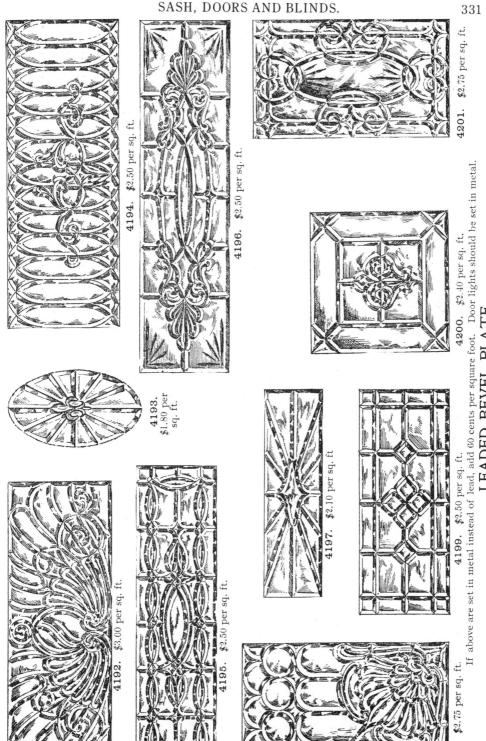

4194. $2.50 per sq. ft.

4196. $2.50 per sq. ft.

4201. $2.75 per sq. ft.

4200. $2.40 per sq. ft. Door lights should be set in metal.

4193. $1.80 per sq. ft.

4192. $3.00 per sq. ft.

4195. $2.50 per sq. ft.

4197. $2.10 per sq. ft.

4199. $2.50 per sq. ft. If above are set in metal instead of lead, add 60 cents per square foot.

4198. $2.75 per sq. ft.

LEADED BEVEL PLATE.

4207. $2.75 per sq. ft.

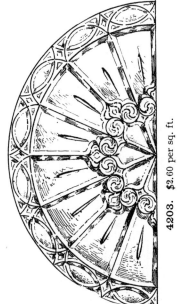

4203. $2.60 per sq. ft.

4206. $3.00 per sq. ft.   Door lights should be set in metal.

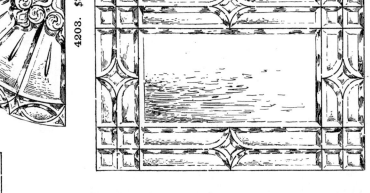

4205. $2.20 per sq. ft.

If above are set in metal instead of lead, add 60 cents per square foot.

LEADED BEVEL PLATE.

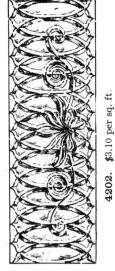

4202. $3.10 per sq. ft.

4204. $3.20 per sq. ft.

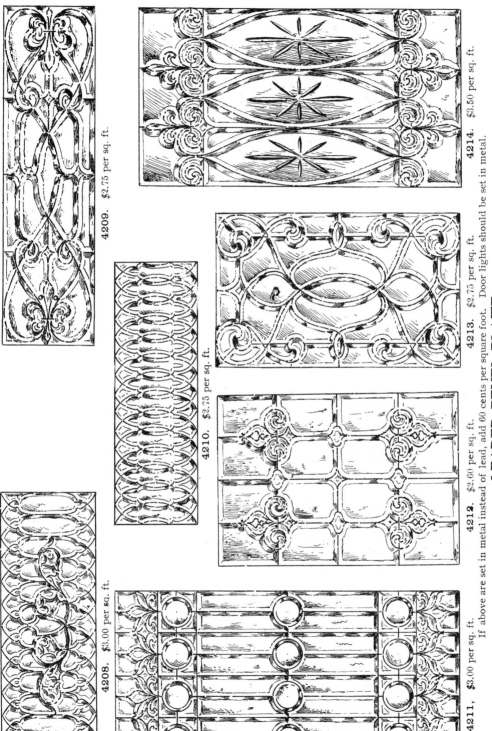

4209. $2.75 per sq. ft.

4214. $3.50 per sq. ft.

4210. $2.75 per sq. ft.

4213. $2.75 per sq. ft.

4212. $2.60 per sq. ft.

4208. $3.00 per sq. ft.

4211, $3.00 per sq. ft.

If above are set in metal instead of lead, add 60 cents per square foot. Door lights should be set in metal.

LEADED BEVEL PLATE.

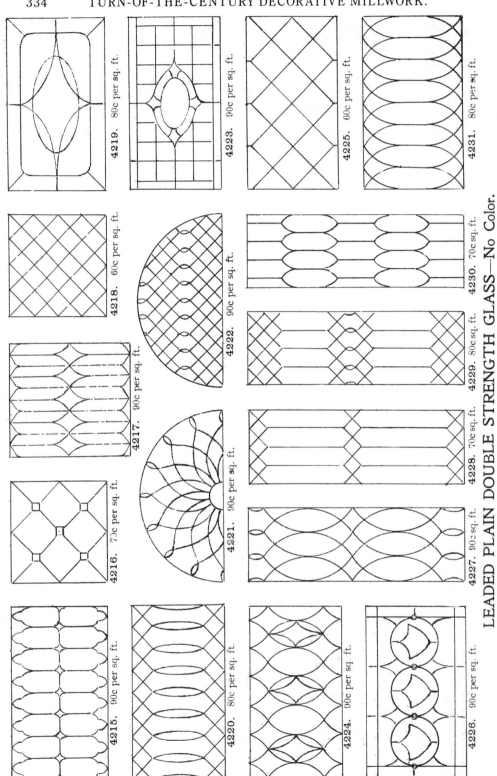

4219. 80c per sq. ft.

4223. 90c per sq. ft.

4225. 60c per sq. ft.

4231. 80c per sq. ft.

4218. 60c per sq. ft.

4222. 90c per sq. ft.

4230. 70c sq. ft.

4217. 90c per sq. ft.

4229. 80c sq. ft.

4221. 90c per sq. ft.

4228. 70c sq. ft.

4216. 70c per sq. ft.

4227. 90c sq. ft.

4215. 90c per sq. ft.

4220. 80c per sq. ft.

4224. 90c per sq. ft.

4226. 90c per sq. ft.

LEADED PLAIN DOUBLE STRENGTH GLASS—No Color.

GLASS MEASUREMENT.

A table giving the number of square feet in glass of given dimensions.

Length	WIDTH of GLASS														
	6	7	8	9	10	12	14	16	18	20	22	24	26	28	30
20	0 5/6	1	1 1/12	1 1/4	1 5/12	1 2/3	1 11/12	2 1/4	2 1/2	2 3/4	----	----	----	----	----
22	0 11/12	1 1/12	1 1/4	1 5/12	1 1/2	1 5/6	2 1/6	2 5/12	2 3/4	3 1/12	3 1/3	----	----	----	----
24	1	1 1/6	1 1/3	1 1/2	1 2/3	2	2 1/3	2 2/3	3	3 1/3	3 2/3	4	----	----	----
26	1 1/12	1 1/4	1 5/12	1 2/3	1 5/6	2 1/6	2 1/2	2 11/12	3 1/4	3 7/12	4	4 1/3	4 2/3	----	----
28	1 1/6	1 1/3	1 7/12	1 3/4	1 11/12	2 1/3	2 3/4	3 1/12	3 1/2	3 11/12	4 1/4	4 2/3	5 1/12	5 5/12	----
30	1 1/4	1 1/2	1 2/3	1 11/12	2 1/12	2 1/2	2 11/12	3 1/3	3 3/4	4 1/6	4 7/12	5	5 5/12	5 5/6	6 1/4
32	1 1/3	1 7/12	1 3/4	2	2 1/4	2 2/3	3 1/12	3 7/12	4	4 5/12	4 11/12	5 1/3	5 3/4	6 1/4	6 2/3
34	1 5/12	1 2/3	1 11/12	2 1/6	2 1/3	2 5/6	3 1/3	3 3/4	4 1/4	4 3/4	5 1/6	5 2/3	6 1/6	6 7/12	7 1/12
36	1 1/2	1 3/4	2	2 1/4	2 1/2	3	3 1/2	4	4 1/2	5	5 1/2	6	6 1/2	7	7 1/2
38	1 7/12	1 5/6	2 1/12	2 5/12	2 2/3	3 1/6	3 2/3	4 1/4	4 3/4	5 1/4	5 5/6	6 1/3	6 5/6	7 5/12	7 11/12
40	1 2/3	1 11/12	2 1/4	2 1/2	2 3/4	3 1/3	3 11/12	4 5/12	5	5 7/12	6 1/12	6 2/3	7 1/4	7 3/4	8 1/3
42	1 3/4	2 1/12	2 1/3	2 2/3	2 11/12	3 1/2	4 1/12	4 2/3	5 1/4	5 5/6	6 5/12	7	7 7/12	8 1/6	8 3/4
44	1 5/6	2 1/6	2 5/12	2 3/4	3 1/12	3 2/3	4 1/4	4 11/12	5 1/2	6 1/12	6 3/4	7 1/3	7 11/12	8 7/12	9 1/6
46	1 11/12	2 1/4	2 7/12	2 11/12	3 1/6	3 5/6	4 1/2	5 1/12	5 3/4	6 5/12	7	7 2/3	8 1/3	8 11/12	9 7/12
48	2	2 1/3	2 2/3	3	3 1/3	4	4 2/3	5 1/3	6	6 2/3	7 1/3	8	8 2/3	9 1/3	10
50	2 1/12	2 5/12	2 3/4	3 1/6	3 1/2	4 1/6	4 5/6	5 7/12	6 1/4	6 11/12	7 2/3	8 1/3	9	9 3/4	10 5/12
52	2 1/6	2 1/2	2 11/12	3 1/4	3 7/12	4 1/3	5 1/12	5 3/4	6 1/2	7 1/4	7 11/12	8 2/3	9 5/12	10 1/12	10 5/6
54	2 1/4	2 2/3	3	3 5/12	3 3/4	4 1/2	5 1/4	6	6 3/4	7 1/2	8 1/4	9	9 3/4	10 1/2	11 1/4
56	2 1/3	2 3/4	3 1/12	3 1/2	3 11/12	4 2/3	5 5/12	6 1/4	7	7 3/4	8 7/12	9 1/3	10 1/12	10 11/12	11 2/3
58	2 5/12	2 5/6	3 1/4	3 2/3	4	4 5/6	5 2/3	6 5/12	7 1/4	8 1/12	8 5/6	9 2/3	10 1/2	11 1/4	12 1/12
60	2 1/2	2 11/12	3 1/3	3 3/4	4 1/6	5	5 5/6	6 2/3	7 1/2	8 1/3	9 1/6	10	10 5/6	11 2/3	12 1/2
62	2 7/12	3	3 5/12	3 11/12	4 1/3	5 1/6	6	6 11/12	7 3/4	8 7/12	9 1/2	10 1/3	11 1/6	12 1/12	12 11/12
64	2 2/3	3 1/12	3 7/12	4	4 5/12	5 1/3	6 1/4	7 1/12	8	8 11/12	9 3/4	10 2/3	11 7/12	12 5/12	13 1/3
66	2 3/4	3 1/4	3 2/3	4 1/6	4 7/12	5 1/2	6 5/12	7 1/3	8 1/4	9 1/6	10 1/12	11	11 11/12	12 5/6	13 3/4
68	2 5/6	3 1/3	3 3/4	4 1/4	4 3/4	5 2/3	6 7/12	7 7/12	8 1/2	9 5/12	10 5/12	11 1/3	12 1/4	13 1/4	14 1/6
70	2 11/12	3 5/12	3 11/12	4 5/12	4 5/6	5 5/6	6 5/6	7 3/4	8 3/4	9 3/4	10 2/3	11 2/3	12 2/3	13 7/12	14 7/12
72	3	3 1/2	4	4 1/2	5	6	7	8	9	10	11	12	13	14	15

OFFICIAL BENDING LIST.

(Adopted March 1st, 1900.)

PLATE AND WINDOW GLASS, NOT EXCEEDING QUARTER CIRCLE.

PLATE GLASS.

Plates where length and width added are less than 76 in. say 34x40 ... $0.60
Plate of 76 in. or more, but less than 90 united in.. .75
  " 90 " " " " 100 " .. 1.00
  " 100 " " " " 110 " .. 1.50
  " 110 " " " " 120 " .. 2.00
  " 120 " " " " 140 " .. 2.50

Plates of 140 in. or more, but less than 160 united in.. $3.00
  " 160 " " " " 180 " .. 3.50
  " 180 " " " " 200 " .. 4.00
  " 200 " " " " 210 " .. 4.50
  " 210 " " " " 220 " .. 5.00
  " 220 " " " " 230 " .. 5.50
  " 230 " " " " 240 " .. 6.00

Minimum charge for bending plate is $1.00, irrespective of size.

WINDOW GLASS.

Lights of less than 60 united in.... $0.25
  " 60 in. or more, but less than 70 united in.. .30
  " 70 " " " " 80 " .. .40

Lights of 80 in. or more, but less than 90 united in. $0.50
  " 90 " " " " 100 " .. .60
  " 100 " " " " 110 " .. .90

Minimum charge for bending light is 50c, irrespective of size.
Beveled glass, 25 per cent additional and at owner's risk.
Bending on the length where it exceeds the width by more than 6 in., 25 per cent additional.
Odd or fractional parts of inches charged as even inches of next larger size. Sizes containing less than one square foot will be charged as a full foot, and in narrow widths no size will be figured as less than 12 inches wide.
Above prices are for bending only. Boxing extra.

Wire Glass made by the new and improved process makes the very best skylights known, and is strongly recommended for the following reasons:

That having a fine wire imbedded midway between its surfaces, the glass will not drop out when, by any accident, it becomes cracked.

Wire Glass requires no netting as protection from falling fragments. It may crack but cannot fall down, and need not necessarily be replaced.

It is also practically Fire Proof, Burglar Proof and Stone Proof, and withal is easier cleaned than when netting is used.

Wire Glass is either Ribbed or Rough Rolled Glass, having wire netting imbedded in its centre during the process of manufacture.

Skylight Glass wired in this manner possesses the combined strength of the wire netting and the glass plate, and the wire being imbedded in the glass is protected from rust or corrosion.

WRITE FOR PRICES.

AMERICAN WINDOW GLASS.

Official List Prices, January 21st, 1901.

United Inches.	BRACKET. SIZES.	SINGLE. AA.	A.	B.	C.	DOUBLE. AA.	A.	B.
25	6x 8 to 10x15	$32.00	$26.75	$25.50	$24.00	$42.75	$37.50	$35.50
34	11x14) 12x13 } to 14x20	33.50	28.00	26.75	25.50	46.75	41.50	38.75
40	10x26 to 16x24	36.00	30.00	28.00	26.50	52.00	45.50	41.50
50	18x22) 20x20 } to 20x30	37.50	31.75	29.50	------	56.00	49.50	46.00
54	15x36 to 24x30	38.75	32.75	30.00	------	57.50	50.75	46.75
60	26x28 to 24x36	40.00	34.75	31.00	------	58.75	52.00	47.50
70	26x34) 28x32 } to 30x40 30x30)	42.75	38.50	33.75	------	62.75	56.00	50.75
80	32x38) 34x36 } to 30x50	48.75	44.50	38.50	------	68.00	61.50	55.50
84	30x52 to 30x54	52.00	47.50	41.75	------	69.50	62.75	56.75
90	-------------------	------	------	------	------	73.50	66.75	61.50
94	-------------------	------	------	------	------	74.75	68.00	62.75
100	-------------------	------	------	------	------	88.00	80.00	74.75
105	-------------------	------	------	------	------	94.75	86.75	80.00
110	-------------------	------	------	------	------	105.50	97.50	90.75
115	-------------------	------	------	------	------	118.75	108.00	101.50
120	-------------------	------	------	------	------	140.00	126.75	120.00
125	-------------------	------	------	------	------	153.50	140.25	133.50
130	-------------------	------	------	------	------	167.00	153.75	147.00

An additional 10 per cent. will be charged for all Glass more than 40 inches wide.   All sizes over 52 inches in length and not making more than 81 united inches, will be charged in the 84 united inches bracket.   All glass 54 inches wide or wider, not making more than 116 united inches, will be charged in the 120 united inches bracket.

AMERICAN WINDOW GLASS.

Official Price List, January 21, 1901.

PRICE PER BOX OF FIFTY FEET.						SIZES.	PRICE PER SINGLE LIGHT.						No. Lights per Box
SINGLE.			DOUBLE.				SINGLE.			DOUBLE.			
AA	A	B	AA	A	B		AA	A	B	AA	A	B	
32.00	26.75	25.50	42.75	37.50	35.50	6x 8	.25	.21	.20	.33	.29	.28	150
"	"	"	"	"	"	7x 9	.32	.27	.26	.43	.38	.36	115
"	"	"	"	"	"	8x10	.41	.35	.33	.55	.48	.46	90
"	"	"	"	"	"	12	.50	.42	.40	.66	.58	.55	75
"	"	"	"	"	"	13	.54	.45	.43	.72	.63	.60	69
"	"	"	"	"	"	14	.58	.49	.46	.77	.68	.64	64
"	"	"	"	"	"	15	.62	.52	.49	.82	.72	.69	60
"	"	"	"	"	"	16	.66	.55	.53	.88	.78	.73	56
33.50	28.00	26.75	46.75	41.50	38.75	18	.78	.65	.62	1.08	.96	.90	50
"	"	"	"	"	"	20	.86	.72	.69	1.20	1.07	1.00	45
32.00	26.75	25.50	42.75	37.50	35.50	9x11	.51	.43	.41	.68	.60	.56	73
"	"	"	"	"	"	12	.55	.46	.44	.74	.65	.61	67
"	"	"	"	"	"	13	.59	.50	.48	.80	.70	.66	62
"	"	"	"	"	"	14	.65	.54	.52	.87	.76	.72	57
"	"	"	"	"	"	15	.70	.59	.56	.93	.82	.78	53
"	"	"	"	"	"	16	.74	.62	.59	.99	.87	.82	50
33.50	28.00	26.75	46.75	41.50	38.75	18	.86	.72	.69	1.20	1.07	1.00	45
"	"	"	"	"	"	20	.97	.81	.77	1.35	1.20	1.12	40
"	"	"	"	"	"	22	1.07	.90	.86	1.50	1.33	1.24	36
32.00	26.75	25.50	42.75	37.50	35.50	10x12	.62	.52	.49	.82	.72	.69	60
"	"	"	"	"	"	13	.67	.56	.54	.90	.79	.75	55
"	"	"	"	"	"	14	.71	.59	.57	.95	.83	.79	52
"	"	"	"	"	"	15	.77	.65	.62	1.03	.90	.86	48
33.50	28.00	26.75	46.75	41.50	38.75	16	.87	.72	.69	1.20	1.07	1.00	45
"	"	"	"	"	"	18	.97	.81	.77	1.35	1.20	1.12	40
"	"	"	"	"	"	19	1.02	.85	.81	1.42	1.26	1.18	38
"	"	"	"	"	"	20	1.07	.90	.86	1.50	1.33	1.24	36
"	"	"	"	"	"	22	1.17	.97	.94	1.63	1.45	1.36	33
"	"	"	"	"	"	24	1.29	1.07	1.03	1.80	1.60	1.49	30
36.00	30.00	28.00	52.00	45.50	41.50	26	1.48	1.24	1.15	2.14	1.87	1.71	28
"	"	"	"	"	"	28	1.60	1.33	1.24	2.30	2.02	1.84	26
"	"	"	"	"	"	30	1.74	1.44	1.35	2.50	2.19	1.99	24
37.50	31.75	29.50	56.00	49.50	46.00	32	1.88	1.59	1.48	2.80	2.48	2.30	23
"	"	"	"	"	"	34	2.06	1.74	1.62	3.07	2.72	2.52	21
"	"	"	"	"	"	36	2.16	1.83	1.70	3.22	2.85	2.65	20
"	"	"	"	"	"	38	2.27	1.93	1.79	3.39	3.00	2.79	19
"	"	"	"	"	"	40	2.40	2.03	1.89	3.58	3.17	2.94	18
38.75	32.75	30.00	57.50	50.75	46.75	42	2.63	2.22	2.03	3.89	3.44	3.17	17
"	"	"	"	"	"	44	2.79	2.36	2.16	4.14	3.65	3.37	16
40.00	34.75	31.00	58.75	52.00	47.50	46	2.88	2.50	2.23	4.23	3.74	3.42	16
"	"	"	"	"	"	48	3.07	2.67	2.38	4.51	3.99	3.65	15
"	"	"	"	"	"	50	3.29	2.86	2.55	4.83	4.28	3.91	14
32.00	26.75	25.50	42.75	37.50	35.50	11x12	.67	.56	.54	.90	.79	.75	55
33.50	28.00	26.75	46.75	41.50	38.75	14	.82	.69	.66	1.15	1.02	.95	47
"	"	"	"	"	"	15	.88	.74	.70	1.23	1.09	1.02	44
"	"	"	"	"	"	16	.94	.79	.76	1.32	1.15	1.09	41
"	"	"	"	"	"	18	1.05	.88	.84	1.46	1.29	1.21	37
"	"	"	"	"	"	19	1.14	.95	.91	1.59	1.41	1.32	34
"	"	"	"	"	"	20	1.17	.98	.94	1.63	1.45	1.36	33
"	"	"	"	"	"	22	1.29	1.08	1.03	1.80	1.60	1.49	30
36.00	30.00	28.00	52.00	45.50	41.50	24	1.54	1.28	1.20	2.22	1.94	1.77	27
"	"	"	"	"	"	26	1.66	1.38	1.29	2.40	2.10	1.91	25
"	"	"	"	"	"	28	1.80	1.50	1.40	2.60	2.28	2.08	23
37.50	31.75	29.50	56.00	49.50	46.00	30	1.90	1.66	1.55	2.93	2.59	2.41	22
"	"	"	"	"	"	32	2.16	1.83	1.70	3.22	2.85	2.65	20
"	"	"	"	"	"	34	2.27	1.93	1.79	3.39	3.00	2.79	19
"	"	"	"	"	"	36	2.40	2.03	1.89	3.58	3.17	2.94	18
"	"	"	"	"	"	38	2.54	2.15	2.00	3.79	3.35	3.12	17
38.75	32.75	30.00	57.50	50.75	46.75	40	2.79	2.36	2.16	4.14	3.65	3.37	16
						42							16
40.00	34.75	31.00	58.75	52.00	47.50	44	3.07	2.67	2.39	4.51	3.99	3.65	15
"	"	"	"	"	"	46	3.29	2.86	2.55	4.83	4.28	3.91	14
						48							14
42.75	38.50	33.75	62.75	56.00	50.75	50	3.79	3.41	2.99	5.56	4.96	4.49	13
32.00	26.75	25.50	42.75	37.50	35.50	12x12	.74	.62	.59	.99	.87	.82	50
33.50	28.00	26.75	46.75	41.50	38.75	13	.84	.70	.67	1.17	1.04	.98	46
"	"	"	"	"	"	14	.90	.75	.72	1.26	1.11	1.04	43
"	"	"	"	"	"	15	.97	.81	.77	1.35	1.20	1.12	40
"	"	"	"	"	"	16	1.01	.85	.81	1.42	1.26	1.18	38
"	"	"	"	"	"	18	1.14	.95	.91	1.59	1.41	1.32	34
"	"	"	"	"	"	19	1.21	1.01	.97	1.69	1.50	1.40	32
"	"	"	"	"	"	20	1.29	1.08	1.03	1.80	1.60	1.49	30
"	"	"	"	"	"	22	1.43	1.20	1.14	2.00	1.77	1.66	27
36.00	30.00	28.00	52.00	45.50	41.50	24	1.66	1.38	1.29	2.40	2.10	1.91	25
"	"	"	"	"	"	26	1.80	1.50	1.40	2.60	2.28	2.08	23
"	"	"	"	"	"	28	1.89	1.57	1.47	2.72	2.38	2.17	22
37.50	31.75	29.50	56.00	49.50	46.00	30	2.16	1.83	1.70	3.22	2.85	2.65	20
"	"	"	"	"	"	32	2.27	1.93	1.79	3.39	3.00	2.79	19
"	"	"	"	"	"	34	2.40	2.03	1.89	3.58	3.17	2.94	18
"	"	"	"	"	"	36	2.54	2.15	2.00	3.79	3.35	3.12	17
"	"	"	"	"	"	38	2.70	2.29	2.13	4.03	3.56	3.31	16
38.75	32.75	30.00	57.50	50.75	46.75	40	2.97	2.52	2.30	4.41	3.90	3.59	15
						42	3.19	2.69	2.47	4.73	4.17	3.85	14

AMERICAN WINDOW GLASS.

Official Price List, January 21, 1901.

PRICE PER BOX OF FIFTY FEET.						SIZES.	PRICE PER SINGLE LIGHT.						No. Lights per Box
SINGLE.			DOUBLE.				SINGLE.			DOUBLE.			
AA	A	B	AA	A	B		AA	A	B	AA	A	B	
40.00	34.75	31.00	58.75	52.00	47.50	12x44	3.29	2.86	2.55	4.83	4.28	3.91	14
"	"	"	"	"	"	46	3.54	3.08	2.75	5.20	4.60	4.21	13
"	"	"	"	"	"	48							13
42.75	38.50	33.75	62.75	56.00	50.75	50	4.10	3.69	3.24	6.02	5.37	4.87	12
"	"	"	"	"	"	52							12
52.00	47.50	41.75	69.50	62.75	56.75	54	5.44	4.97	4.36	7.27	6.57	5.94	11
"	"	"	"	"	"	56							11
"	"	"	"	"	"	58	5.98	5.47	4.80	8.00	7.22	6.53	10
"	"	"	"	"	"	60							10
33.50	28.00	26.75	46.75	41.50	38.75	13x15	1.05	.88	.84	1.46	1.29	1.21	37
"	"	"	"	"	"	16	1.11	.92	.88	1.54	1.37	1.28	35
"	"	"	"	"	"	18	1.25	1.04	1.00	1.74	1.54	1.44	31
"	"	"	"	"	"	20	1.38	1.15	1.10	1.93	1.71	1.60	28
36.00	30.00	28.00	52.00	45.50	41.50	22	1.66	1.38	1.29	2.40	2.10	1.91	25
"	"	"	"	"	"	24	1.80	1.50	1.40	2.60	2.28	2.08	23
"	"	"	"	"	"	26	1.98	1.64	1.54	2.85	2.50	2.28	21
37.50	31.75	29.50	56.00	49.50	46.00	28	2.16	1.83	1.70	3.22	2.85	2.65	20
"	"	"	"	"	"	30	2.27	1.93	1.79	3.39	3.00	2.79	19
"	"	"	"	"	"	32	2.54	2.15	2.00	3.79	3.35	3.12	17
"	"	"	"	"	"	34	2.70	2.29	2.12	4.03	3.56	3.31	16
"	"	"	"	"	"	36	2.88	2.44	2.27	4.30	3.80	3.53	15
38.75	32.75	30.00	57.50	50.75	46.75	38	2.97	2.51	2.30	4.41	3.90	3.59	15
40.00	34.75	31.00	58.75	52.00	47.50	40	3.19	2.69	2.47	4.73	4.17	3.85	14
"	"	"	"	"	"	42	3.54	3.08	2.75	5.20	4.60	4.21	13
"	"	"	"	"	"	44							13
42.75	38.50	33.75	62.75	56.00	50.75	46	3.84	3.33	2.98	5.64	4.99	4.56	12
"	"	"	"	"	"	48	4.10	3.69	3.23	6.02	5.37	4.87	12
"	"	"	"	"	"	50	4.47	4.03	3.53	6.57	5.86	5.31	11
33.50	28.00	26.75	46.75	41.50	38.75	14x14	1.05	.88	.84	1.46	1.29	1.21	37
"	"	"	"	"	"	16	1.21	1.01	.97	1.69	1.50	1.40	32
"	"	"	"	"	"	18	1.33	1.12	1.07	1.86	1.65	1.54	29
"	"	"	"	"	"	20	1.49	1.24	1.19	2.07	1.84	1.72	26
36.00	30.00	28.00	52.00	45.50	41.50	22	1.73	1.44	1.35	2.50	2.19	1.99	24
"	"	"	"	"	"	24	1.88	1.57	1.47	2.72	2.38	2.17	22
"	"	"	"	"	"	26	2.07	1.73	1.61	2.99	2.62	2.39	20
37.50	31.75	29.50	56.00	49.50	46.00	28	2.27	1.93	1.79	3.39	3.00	2.79	19
"	"	"	"	"	"	30	2.54	2.15	2.00	3.79	3.35	3.12	17
"	"	"	"	"	"	32	2.70	2.29	2.13	4.03	3.56	3.31	16
"	"	"	"	"	"	34	2.88	2.44	2.27	4.30	3.80	3.53	15
"	"	"	"	"	"	36	3.09	2.61	2.43	4.60	4.07	3.78	14
38.75	32.75	30.00	57.50	50.75	46.75	38	3.19	2.69	2.47	4.73	4.17	3.85	14
40.00	34.75	31.00	58.75	52.00	47.50	40	3.43	2.90	2.66	5.09	4.49	4.14	13
"	"	"	"	"	"	42	3.84	3.33	2.98	5.64	4.99	4.56	12
"	"	"	"	"	"	44							12
42.75	38.50	33.75	62.75	56.00	50.75	46	4.19	3.64	3.25	6.15	5.44	4.97	11
"	"	"	"	"	"	48	4.47	4.03	3.53	6.57	5.86	5.31	11
"	"	"	"	"	"	50	4.92	4.43	3.88	7.22	6.44	5.84	10
"	"	"	"	"	"	52							10
52.00	47.50	41.75	69.50	62.75	56.75	54	5.98	5.47	4.81	8.00	7.22	6.53	10
"	"	"	"	"	"	56	6.65	6.07	5.34	8.89	8.02	7.26	9
"	"	"	"	"	"	58							9
"	"	"	"	"	"	60							9
33.50	28.00	26.75	46.75	41.50	38.75	15x15	1.21	1.01	.97	1.69	1.50	1.40	32
"	"	"	"	"	"	16	1.29	1.08	1.03	1.80	1.60	1.49	30
"	"	"	"	"	"	18	1.43	1.20	1.14	2.00	1.77	1.66	27
36.00	30.00	28.00	52.00	45.50	41.50	20	1.73	1.44	1.35	2.50	2.19	1.99	24
"	"	"	"	"	"	22	1.89	1.57	1.47	2.72	2.38	2.17	22
"	"	"	"	"	"	24	2.07	1.73	1.61	2.99	2.62	2.39	20
37.50	31.75	29.50	56.00	49.50	46.00	26	2.27	1.93	1.79	3.39	3.00	2.79	19
"	"	"	"	"	"	28	2.54	2.15	2.00	3.79	3.35	3.12	17
"	"	"	"	"	"	30	2.70	2.29	2.13	4.03	3.56	3.31	16
"	"	"	"	"	"	32	2.88	2.44	2.27	4.30	3.80	3.53	15
"	"	"	"	"	"	34	3.09	2.61	2.43	4.60	4.07	3.78	14
38.75	32.75	30.00	57.50	50.75	46.75	36	3.43	2.90	2.66	5.09	4.49	4.14	13
"	"	"	"	"	"	38							13
40.00	34.75	31.00	58.75	52.00	47.50	40	3.84	3.33	2.98	5.64	4.99	4.56	12
"	"	"	"	"	"	42	4.19	3.64	3.25	6.15	5.44	4.97	11
"	"	"	"	"	"	44							11
42.75	38.50	33.75	62.75	56.00	50.75	46	4.92	4.43	3.88	7.22	6.44	5.84	10
"	"	"	"	"	"	48							10
"	"	"	"	"	"	50							10
33.50	28.00	26.75	46.75	41.50	38.75	16x16	1.38	1.15	1.10	1.93	1.71	1.60	28
"	"	"	"	"	"	18	1.55	1.29	1.24	2.16	1.91	1.79	25
36.00	30.00	28.00	52.00	45.50	41.50	20	1.80	1.50	1.40	2.60	2.28	2.08	23
"	"	"	"	"	"	22	1.98	1.65	1.54	2.85	2.50	2.28	21
"	"	"	"	"	"	24	2.18	1.82	1.70	3.15	2.76	2.52	19
37.50	31.75	29.50	56.00	49.50	46.00	26	2.54	2.15	2.00	3.79	3.35	3.12	17
"	"	"	"	"	"	28	2.70	2.29	2.13	4.03	3.56	3.31	16
"	"	"	"	"	"	30	2.88	2.44	2.27	4.30	3.80	3.53	15
"	"	"	"	"	"	32	3.09	2.61	2.43	4.60	4.07	3.78	14
"	"	"	"	"	"	34	3.32	2.81	2.61	4.96	4.38	4.07	13
38.75	32.75	30.00	57.50	50.75	46.75	36	3.43	2.90	2.66	5.09	4.49	4.14	13
"	"	"	"	"	"	38	3.72	3.14	2.88	5.52	4.87	4.49	12
40.00	34.75	31.00	58.75	52.00	47.50	40	4.19	3.64	3.25	6.15	5.44	4.97	11
"	"	"	"	"	"	42							11

AMERICAN WINDOW GLASS.

Official Price List, January 21, 1901.

PRICE PER BOX OF FIFTY FEET.						SIZES.	PRICE PER SINGLE LIGHT.						No. Lights per Box
SINGLE.			DOUBLE.				SINGLE.			DOUBLE.			
AA	A	B	AA	A	B		AA	A	B	AA	A	B	
40.00	34.75	31.00	58.75	52.00	47.50	16x44	4.60	4.00	3.57	6.76	5.98	5.47	10
42.75	38.50	33.75	62.75	56.00	50.75	46	4.92	4.43	3.88	7.22	6.44	5.84	10
"	"	"	"	"	"	48	5.47	4.92	4.31	8.02	7.16	6.49	9
"	"	"	"	"	"	50	"	"	"	"	"	"	9
						52							9
......	......	......	69.50	62.75	56.75	54	......	......	......	10.00	9.03	8.16	8
......	......	......	"	"	"	56	......			"	"	"	8
......	......	......	"	"	"	58				"	"	"	8
......	......	......	"	"	"	60				"	"	"	8
......	......	......	"	"	"	62				11.42	10.31	9.33	7
......	......	......	"	"	"	64				"	"	"	7
......	......	......	"	"	"	66				"	"	"	7
......	......	......	"	"	"	68				"	"	"	7
......	......	......	73.50	66.75	61.50	70				14.09	12.80	11.79	6
......	......	......	"	"	"	72				"	"	"	6
......	......	......	"	"	"	74				"	"	"	6
......	......	......	74.75	68.00	62.75	76				14.33	13.04	12.03	6
36.00	30.00	28.00	52.00	45.50	41.50	18x18	1.89	1.57	1.47	2.72	2.38	2.17	22
"	"	"	"	"	"	20	2.07	1.73	1.61	2.99	2.62	2.39	20
37.50	31.75	29.50	56.00	49.50	46.00	22	2.40	2.03	1.89	3.58	3.17	2.94	18
"	"	"	"	"	"	24	2.54	2.15	2.00	3.79	3.35	3.12	17
"	"	"	"	"	"	26	2.70	2.29	2.13	4.03	3.56	3.31	16
"	"	"	"	"	"	28	3.09	2.61	2.43	4.60	4.07	3.78	14
"	"	"	"	"	"	30							14
"	"	"	"	"	"	32	3.32	2.81	2.61	4.96	4.38	4.07	13
38.75	32.75	30.00	57.50	50.75	46.75	34	3.72	3.14	2.88	5.52	4.87	4.49	12
"	"	"	"	"	"	36	4.06	3.43	3.14	6.02	5.31	4.89	11
40.00	34.75	31.00	58.75	52.00	47.50	38	4.19	3.64	3.25	6.15	5.44	4.97	11
"	"	"	"	"	"	40	4.60	4.00	3.57	6.76	5.98	5.47	10
						42							10
42.75	38.50	33.75	62.75	56.00	50.75	44	5.47	4.92	4.32	8.02	7.16	6.49	9
"	"	"	"	"	"	46							9
"	"	"	"	"	"	48	6.15	5.54	4.86	9.03	8.05	7.30	8
"	"	"	"	"	"	50	"	"	"	"	"	"	8
"	"	"	"	"	"	52							8
......	......	......	69.50	62.75	56.75	54	......	......	......	11.42	10.31	9.33	7
......	......	......	"	"	"	56	......	......	......	"	"	"	7
......	......	......	"	"	"	58	......	......	......	"	"	"	7
......	......	......	"	"	"	60	......	......	......	"	"	"	6
......	......	......	"	"	"	62	......	......	......	13.33	12.03	10.88	6
......	......	......	"	"	"	64	......	......	......	"	"	"	6
......	......	......	"	"	"	66	......	......	......	"	"	"	6
......	......	......	73.50	66.75	61.50	68	......	......	......	14.09	12.80	11.79	6
......	......	......	"	"	"	70	......	......	......	"	"	"	6
......	......	......	"	"	"	72	......	......	......	"	"	"	6
......	......	......	74.75	68.00	62.75	74	......	......	......	17.20	15.64	14.44	5
......	......	......	"	"	"	76	......	......	......				5
37.50	31.75	29.50	56.00	49.50	46.00	20x20	2.40	2.03	1.89	3.58	3.16	2.94	18
"	"	"	"	"	"	22	2.70	2.29	2.13	4.03	3.56	3.31	16
"	"	"	"	"	"	24	2.88	2.44	2.27	4.30	3.80	3.53	15
"	"	"	"	"	"	26	3.09	2.61	2.43	4.60	4.07	3.78	14
"	"	"	"	"	"	28	3.32	2.81	2.61	4.96	4.38	4.07	13
"	"	"	"	"	"	30	3.60	3.05	2.83	5.37	4.75	4.41	12
38.75	32.75	30.00	57.50	50.75	46.75	32	4.06	3.43	3.14	6.02	5.31	4.89	11
"	"	"	"	"	"	34							11
40.00	34.75	31.00	58.75	52.00	47.50	36	4.60	4.00	3.57	6.76	5.98	5.47	10
"	"	"	"	"	"	38							10
"	"	"	"	"	"	40	5.12	4.43	3.97	7.51	6.65	6.07	9
42.75	38.50	33.75	62.75	56.00	50.75	42	5.47	4.92	4.31	8.02	7.16	6.49	9
"	"	"	"	"	"	44	6.15	5.54	4.86	9.03	8.05	7.30	8
"	"	"	"	"	"	46	"	"	"	"	"	"	8
"	"	"	"	"	"	48							8
						50	7.03	6.33	5.55	10.31	9.20	8.34	7
48.75	44.50	38.50	68.00	61.50	55.50	52	8.01	7.32	6.33	11.18	10.11	9.13	7
......	......	......	69.50	62.75	56.75	54	......	......	......	11.42	10.31	9.33	7
......	......	......	"	"	"	56	......	......	......	13.33	12.03	10.88	6
......	......	......	"	"	"	58	......	......	......	"	"	"	6
......	......	......	"	"	"	60	......	......	......	"	"	"	6
......	......	......	"	"	"	62	......	......	......	"	"	"	6
......	......	......	"	"	"	64	......	......	......	"	"	"	6
......	......	......	73.50	66.75	61.50	66	......	......	......	16.91	15.36	14.15	5
......	......	......	"	"	"	68	......	......	......	"	"	"	5
......	......	......	"	"	"	70	......	......	......	"	"	"	5
......	......	......	74.75	68.00	62.75	72	......	......	......	17.20	15.64	14.44	5
......	......	......	"	"	"	74	......	......	......	"	"	"	5
......	......	......	88.00	80.00	74.75	76	......	......	......	20.24	18.40	17.20	5
......	......	......	"	"	"	78	......	......	......	25.30	23.00	21.50	4
......	......	......				80	......	......	......				4
......	......	......	94.75	86.75	80.00	82	......	......	......	27.25	24.95	23.00	4
......	......	......	"	"	"	84	......	......	......	"	"	"	4
......	......	......	105.50	97.50	90.75	86	......	......	......	30.34	28.04	26.10	4
......	......	......	"	"	"	88	......	......	......	"	"	"	4
......	......	......				90	......	......	......				4
37.50	31.75	29.50	56.00	49.50	46.00	22x22	2.88	2.44	2.27	4.30	3.80	3.53	15
"	"	"	"	"	"	24	3.09	2.61	2.43	4.60	4.07	3.78	14
						26	3.32	2.81	2.61	4.96	4.38	4.07	13

AMERICAN WINDOW GLASS.

Official Price List, January 21, 1901.

PRICE PER BOX OF FIFTY FEET.						SIZES.	PRICE PER SINGLE LIGHT.						No. Lights per Box
SINGLE.			DOUBLE.				SINGLE.			DOUBLE.			
AA	A	B	AA	A	B		AA	A	B	AA	A	B	
37.50	31.75	29.50	56.00	49.50	46.00	**22x28**	3.60	3.05	2.83	5.37	4.75	4.41	12
38.75	32.75	30.00	57.50	50.75	46.75	30	4.06	3.43	3.14	6.02	5.31	4.89	11
"	"	"				32	4.46	3.77	3.45	6.62	5.84	5.38	10
40.00	34.75	31.00	58.75	52.00	47.50	34	4.60	4.00	3.57	6.76	5.98	5.47	10
"	"	"				36	5.12	4.44	3.97	7.51	6.65	6.07	9
"	"	"				38							9
42.75	38.50	33.75	62.75	56.00	50.75	40	6.15	5.54	4.85	9.03	8.05	7.30	8
"	"	"	"	"	"	42							8
"	"	"	"	"	"	44	7.03	6.33	5.55	10.31	9.20	8.34	7
"	"	"	"	"	"	46							7
"	"	"	"	"	"	48							7
48.75	44.50	38.50	68.00	61.50	55.50	50	8.01	7.32	6.33	11.18	10.11	9.13	7
"	"	"				52	9.34	8.53	7.38	13.04	11.79	10.64	6
------	------	------	69.50	62.75	56.75	54	------	------	------	13.33	12.03	10.88	6
------	------	------	"	"	"	56							6
------			"	"	"	58							6
------			"	"	"	60				15.99	14.44	13.06	5
------			"	"	"	62							5
------			73.50	66.75	61.50	64				16.91	15.36	14.15	5
------			"	"	"	66							5
------			"	"	"	68							5
------			74.75	68.00	62.75	70				17.20	15.64	14.44	5
------			"	"	"	72							4
------			88.00	80.00	74.75	74				25.30	23.00	21.50	4
------			"	"	"	76							4
------			"	"	"	78							4
------			94.75	86.75	80.00	80				27.25	24.95	23.00	4
------			"	"	"	82							4
------			105.50	97.50	90.75	84				30.34	28.04	26.10	4
------			"	"	"	86							4
------			"	"	"	88							4
------			118.75	108.00	101.50	90				34.15	31.05	29.19	4
37.50	31.75	29.50	56.00	49.50	46.00	**24x24**	3.60	3.05	2.83	5.37	4.75	4.41	12
						26							12
38.75	32.75	30.00	57.50	50.75	46.75	28	4.06	3.43	3.14	6.02	5.31	4.89	11
						30	4.46	3.77	3.45	6.62	5.84	5.38	10
40.00	34.75	31.00	58.75	52.00	47.50	32	4.60	4.00	3.57	6.76	5.98	5.47	10
"	"	"	"	"	"	34	5.12	4.44	3.97	7.51	6.65	6.07	9
"	"	"	"	"	"	36							8
42.75	38.50	33.75	62.75	56.00	50.75	38	6.15	5.54	4.85	9.03	8.05	7.30	8
"	"	"	"	"	"	40							7
"	"	"	"	"	"	42	7.03	6.33	5.55	10.31	9.20	8.34	7
"	"	"	"	"	"	44							7
"	"	"	"	"	"	46							7
48.75	44.50	38.50	68.00	61.50	55.50	48	9.34	8.53	7.38	13.04	11.79	10.64	6
"	"	"	"	"	"	50							6
52.00	47.50	41.75	69.50	62.75	56.75	52							6
"	"	"	"	"	"	54	9.97	9.11	8.00	13.33	12.03	10.88	6
"	"	"	"	"	"	56	11.96	10.93	9.61	15.99	14.44	13.06	5
------	------	------	"	"	"	58							5
------	------	------	"	"	"	60							5
------	------	------	73.50	66.75	61.50	62				16.91	15.36	14.15	5
------			"	"	"	64							5
------			"	"	"	66							5
------		------	74.75	68.00	62.75	68				21.50	19.55	18.05	4
------		------	"	"	"	70							4
------		------	88.00	80.00	74.75	72				25.30	23.00	21.50	4
------		------	"	"	"	74							4
------			"	"	"	76							4
------			94.75	86.75	80.00	78				27.25	24.95	23.00	4
------			"	"	"	80							4
------			105.50	97.50	90.75	82				30.34	28.04	26.10	4
------			"	"	"	84							4
------			"	"	"	86				40.45	37.38	34.79	3
------			118.75	108.00	101.50	88				45.53	41.40	38.91	3
------			"			90							3
38.75	32.75	30.00	57.50	50.75	46.75	**26x26**	4.06	3.43	3.14	6.02	5.31	4.89	11
40.00	34.75	31.00	58.75	52.00	47.50	28	4.60	4.00	3.57	6.76	5.98	5.47	10
"	"	"	"	"	"	30	5.12	4.44	3.97	7.51	6.65	6.07	9
"	"	"	"	"	"	32							9
42.75	38.50	33.75	62.75	56.00	50.75	34	6.15	5.54	4.85	9.03	8.05	7.30	8
"	"	"	"	"	"	36							8
"	"	"	"	"	"	38	7.03	6.33	5.55	10.31	9.20	8.34	7
"	"	"	"	"	"	40							7
"	"	"	"	"	"	42							7
"	"	"	"	"	"	44	8.19	7.38	6.47	12.03	10.74	9.73	6
48.75	44.50	38.50	68.00	61.50	55.50	46	9.34	8.53	7.38	13.04	11.79	10.64	6
"	"	"	"	"	"	48							6
"	"	"	"	"	"	50							6
------	------	------	69.50	62.75	56.75	52	11.21	10.24	8.86	15.64	14.15	12.77	5
------	------	------	"	"	"	54				15.99	14.44	13.06	5
------	------	------	"	"	"	56							5
------			"	"	"	58							5
------			73.50	66.75	61.50	60				16.91	15.36	14.15	5
------			"	"	"	62				21.14	19.20	17.69	5
------			"	"	"	64							4
------			74.75	68.00	62.75	66				21.50	19.55	18.05	4

AMERICAN WINDOW GLASS.

Official Price List, January 21, 1901.

PRICE PER BOX OF FIFTY FEET.						SIZES.	PRICE PER SINGLE LIGHT.						No. Lights per Box
SINGLE.			DOUBLE.				SINGLE.			DOUBLE.			
AA	A	B	AA	A	B		AA	A	B	AA	A	B	
......	......	......	74.75	68.00	62.75	**26x68**	......	......	......	21.50	19.55	18.05	4
			88.00	80.00	74.75	70				25.30	23.00	21.50	4
			"	"	"	72							4
			"	"	"	74							4
			94.75	86.75	80.00	76				27.25	24.95	23.00	4
						78							4
			105.50	97.50	90.75	80				40.45	37.38	34.79	3
			"	"	"	82							3
			"	"	"	84							3
			118.75	108.00	101.50	86				45.53	41.40	38.91	3
			"	"	"	88							3
			140.00	126.75	120.00	90				53.67	48.59	46.00	3
40.00	34.75	31.00	58.75	52.00	47.50	**28x28**	5.12	4.44	3.97	7.51	6.65	6.07	9
"	"	"	"	"	"	30				"	"	"	9
42.75	38.50	33.75	62.75	56.00	50.75	32	6.15	5.54	4.85	9.03	8.05	7.30	8
"	"	"	"	"	"	34				"	"	"	8
"	"	"	"	"	"	36	7.03	6.33	5.55	10.31	9.20	8.34	7
"	"	"	"	"	"	38	"	"	"	"	"	"	7
"	"	"	"	"	"	40	"	"	"	"	"	"	7
"	"	"	"	"	"	42	8.20	7.38	6.47	12.03	10.74	9.73	6
48.75	44.50	38.50	68.00	61.50	55.50	44	9.34	8.53	7.38	13.04	11.79	10.64	6
"	"	"	"	"	"	46	"	"	"	"	"	"	6
"	"	"	"	"	"	48	11.21	10.24	8.86	15.64	14.15	12.77	5
"	"	"	"	"	"	50	"	"	"	"	"	"	5
"	"	"	"	"	"	52							5
52.00	47.50	41.75	69.50	62.75	56.75	54	11.96	10.93	9.61	15.99	14.44	13.06	5
						56							5
			73.50	66.75	61.50	58				21.14	19.20	17.69	4
						60							4
			"	"	"	62							4
			74.75	68.00	62.75	64				21.50	19.55	18.05	4
						66							4
			88.00	80.00	74.75	68				25.30	23.00	21.50	4
						70							4
						72							4
			94.75	86.75	80.00	74				36.33	33.26	30.67	3
						76							3
			105.50	97.50	90.75	78				40.45	37.38	34.79	3
						80							3
			"	"	"	82							3
			118.75	108.00	101.50	84				45.53	41.40	38.91	3
						86							3
			140.00	126.75	120.00	88				53.67	48.59	46.00	3
			"	"	"	90							3
42.75	38.50	33.75	62.75	56.00	50.75	**30x30**	6.15	5.54	4.85	9.03	8.05	7.30	8
"	"	"	"	"	"	32	7.03	6.33	5.55	10.31	9.20	8.34	7
"	"	"	"	"	"	34	"	"	"	"	"	"	7
"	"	"	"	"	"	36	"	"	"	"	"	"	7
"	"	"	"	"	"	38	"	"	"	"	"	"	7
"	"	"	"	"	"	40	8.20	7.38	6.47	12.03	10.74	9.73	6
48.75	44.50	38.50	68.00	61.50	55.50	42	9.34	8.53	7.38	13.04	11.79	10.64	6
"	"	"	"	"	"	44							6
"	"	"	"	"	"	46	11.21	10.24	8.86	15.64	14.15	12.77	5
"	"	"	"	"	"	48	"	"	"	"	"	"	5
"	"	"	"	"	"	50							5
52.00	47.50	41.75	69.50	62.75	56.75	52	11.96	10.93	9.61	15.99	14.44	13.06	5
"	"	"	"	"	"	54	14.95	13.66	12.00	19.99	18.05	16.32	4
			73.50	66.75	61.50	56				21.14	19.20	17.69	4
						58							4
						60							4
			74.75	68.00	62.75	62				21.50	19.55	18.05	4
						64							4
			88.00	80.00	74.75	66				25.30	23.00	21.50	4
						68							4
						70					33.74	30.67	28.66	3
			94.75	86.75	80.00	72				36.33	33.26	30.67	3
						74							3
			105.50	97.50	90.75	76				40.45	37.38	34.79	3
						78							3
			"	"	"	80							3
			118.75	108.00	101.50	82				45.53	41.40	38.91	3
						84							3
			140.00	126.75	120.00	86				53.67	48.59	46.00	3
			"	"	"	88							3
						90							3
42.75	38.50	33.75	62.75	56.00	50.75	**32x32**	7.03	6.33	5.55	10.31	9.20	8.34	7
"	"	"	"	"	"	34							7
						36	8.20	7.38	6.47	12.03	10.74	9.73	6
48.75	44.50	38.50	68.00	61.50	55.50	38	9.35	8.53	7.38	13.04	11.79	10.64	6
"	"	"	"	"	"	40							6
"	"	"	"	"	"	42							6
"	"	"	"	"	"	44	11.21	10.24	8.86	15.64	14.15	12.77	5
"	"	"	"	"	"	46							5
"	"	"	"	"	"	48	"	"	"	"	"	"	5
52.00	47.50	41.75	69.50	62.75	56.75	50	11.96	10.93	9.61	15.99	14.44	13.06	5
						52	14.95	13.66	12.00	19.99	18.05	16.32	4

AMERICAN WINDOW GLASS.

Official Price List, January 21, 1901.

| PRICE PER BOX OF FIFTY FEET. | | | | | | SIZES. | PRICE PER SINGLE LIGHT. | | | | | | No. Lights per Box |
| SINGLE | | | DOUBLE | | | | SINGLE | | | DOUBLE | | | |
AA	A	B	AA	A	B		AA	A	B	AA	A	B	
------	------	------	73.50	66.75	61.50	**32x54**	------	------	------	21.14	19.20	17.69	4
------	------	------	"	"	"	56	------	------	------	"	"	"	4
------	------	------	74.75	68.00	62.75	58	------	------	------	21.50	19.55	18.05	4
------	------	------	"	"	"	60	------	------	------	"	"	"	4
------	------	------	88.00	80.00	74.75	62	------	------	------	25.30	23.00	21.50	4
------	------	------				64	------	------	------	33.74	30.67	28.66	3
------	------	------	"	"	"	66	------	------	------				3
------	------	------				68	------	------	------				3
------		------	94.75	86.75	80.00	70	------	------	------	36.33	33.26	30.67	3
------	------	------				72	------	------	------				3
------	------	------	105.50	97.50	90.75	74	------	------	------	40.45	37.38	34.79	3
------	------	------	"	"	"	76	------	------	------				3
------	------	------				78	------	------	------				3
------	------	------	118.75	108.00	101.50	80	------	------	------	45.53	41.40	38.91	3
------	------	------				82	------	------	------				3
------	------	------	140.00	126.75	120.00	84	------	------	------	53.67	48.59	46.00	3
------	------	------				86	------	------	------				3
42.75	38.50	33.75	62.75	56.00	50.75	**34x34**	8.20	7.38	6.47	12.03	10.74	9.73	6
48.75	44.50	38.50	68.00	61.50	55.50	36	9.35	8.53	7.38	13.04	11.79	10.64	6
"	"	"	"	"	"	38	"	"	"	"	"	"	6
"	"	"	"	"	"	40	"	"	"	"	"	"	6
"	"	"	"	"	"	42	11.21	10.24	8.86	15.64	14.15	12.77	5
"	"	"	"	"	"	44	"	"	"	"	"	"	5
"	"	"	"	"	"	46	"	"	"	"	"	"	5
52.00	47.50	41.75	69.50	62.75	56.75	48	11.96	10.93	9.61	15.99	14.44	13.06	5
"	"	"	73.50	66.75	61.50	50	14.95	13.66	12.00	19.99	18.05	16.32	4
------	------	------	"	"	"	52	------	------	------	21.14	19.20	17.69	4
------	------	------				54	------	------	------				4
------	------	------				56	------	------	------				4
------	------	------	74.75	68.00	62.75	58	------	------	------	21.50	19.55	18.05	4
------	------	------				60	------	------	------				4
------	------	------	88.00	80.00	74.75	62	------	------	------	33.74	30.67	28.66	3
------	------	------				64	------	------	------				3
------	------	------	"	"	"	66	------	------	------				3
------	------	------	94.75	86.75	80.00	68	------	------	------	36.33	33.26	30.67	3
------	------	------				70	------	------	------				3
------	------	------	105.50	97.50	90.75	72	------	------	------	40.45	37.38	34.79	3
------	------	------	"	"	"	74	------	------	------				3
------	------	------				76	------	------	------				3
------	------	------	118.75	108.00	101.50	78	------	------	------	45.53	41.40	38.91	3
------	------	------				80	------	------	------				3
------	------	------	140.00	126.75	120.00	82	------	------	------	53.67	48.59	46.00	3
------	------	------				84	------	------	------				3
------	------	------				86	------	------	------				3
48.75	44.50	38.50	68.00	61.50	55.50	**36x36**	9.35	8.53	7.38	13.04	11.79	10.64	6
"	"	"	"	"	"	38	11.21	10.24	8.86	15.64	14.15	12.77	5
"	"	"	"	"	"	40	"	"	"	"	"	"	5
"	"	"	"	"	"	42	"	"	"	"	"	"	5
"	"	"	"	"	"	44	"	"	"	"	"	"	5
52.00	47.50	41.75	69.50	62.75	56.75	46	14.95	13.66	12.00	19.99	18.05	16.32	4
"	"	"	"	"	"	48							4
------	------	------	73.50	66.75	61.50	50	------	------	------	21.14	19.20	17.69	4
------	------	------	"	"	"	52	------	------	------				4
------	------	------				54	------	------	------				4
------	------	------	74.75	68.00	62.75	56	------	------	------	21.50	19.55	18.05	4
------	------	------				58	------	------	------	28.66	26.07	24.06	3
------	------	------	88.00	80.00	74.75	60	------	------	------	33.74	30.67	28.66	3
------	------	------				62	------	------	------				3
------	------	------	"	"	"	64	------	------	------				3
------	------	------	94.75	86.75	80.00	66	------	------	------	36.33	33.26	30.67	3
------	------	------				68	------	------	------				3
------	------	------	105.50	97.50	90.75	70	------	------	------	40.45	37.38	34.79	3
------	------	------				72	------	------	------				3
------	------	------				74	------	------	------				3
------	------	------	118.75	108.00	101.50	76	------	------	------	45.53	41.40	38.91	3
------	------	------				78	------	------	------				3
------	------	------	140.00	126.75	120.00	80	------	------	------	53.67	48.59	46.00	3
------	------	------	"	"	"	82	------	------	------				3
------	------	------				84	------	------	------				3
------	------	------	153.50	140.25	133.50	86	------	------	------	58.85	53.77	51.18	3
------	------	------	68.00	61.50	55.50	**38x38**	------	------	------	15.64	14.15	12.77	5
------	------	------	"	"	"	40	------	------	------	"	"	"	5
------	------	------				42	------	------	------				5
------	------	------	69.50	62.75	56.75	44	------	------	------	19.99	18.05	16.32	4
------	------	------				46	------	------	------				4
------	------	------	73.50	66.75	61.50	48	------	------	------	21.14	19.20	17.69	4
------	------	------	"	"	"	50	------	------	------				4
------	------	------				52	------	------	------				4
------	------	------	74.75	68.00	62.75	54	------	------	------	21.50	19.55	18.05	4
------	------	------				56	------	------	------	28.66	26.07	24.06	3
------	------	------	88.00	80.00	74.75	58	------	------	------	33.74	30.67	28.66	3
------	------	------				60	------	------	------				3
------	------	------	"	"	"	62	------	------	------				3
------	------	------	94.75	86.75	80.00	64	------	------	------	36.33	33.26	30.67	3
------	------	------				66	------	------	------				3
------	------	------	105.50	97.50	90.75	68	------	------	------	40.45	37.38	34.79	3

AMERICAN WINDOW GLASS.

Official Price List, January 21, 1901.

PRICE PER BOX OF FIFTY FEET.						SIZES.	PRICE PER SINGLE LIGHT.						No. Lights per Box
SINGLE AA	SINGLE A	SINGLE B	DOUBLE AA	DOUBLE A	DOUBLE B		SINGLE AA	SINGLE A	SINGLE B	DOUBLE AA	DOUBLE A	DOUBLE B	
-----	-----	-----	105.50	97.50	90.75	38x70	-----	-----	-----	40.45	37.38	34.79	3
-----	-----	-----	"	"	"	72	-----	-----	-----	"	"	"	3
-----	-----	-----	118.75	108.00	101.50	74	-----	-----	-----	45.53	41.40	38.91	3
-----	-----	-----	-----	-----	-----	76	-----	-----	-----	-----	-----	-----	3
-----	-----	-----	140.00	126.75	120.00	78	-----	-----	-----	53.67	48.59	46.00	3
-----	-----	-----	"	"	"	80	-----	-----	-----	"	"	"	3
-----	-----	-----	"	"	"	82	-----	-----	-----	"	"	"	3
-----	-----	-----	153.50	140.25	133.50	84	-----	-----	-----	58.85	53.77	51.18	3
-----	-----	-----	-----	-----	-----	86	-----	-----	-----	-----	-----	-----	3
-----	-----	-----	68.00	61.50	55.50	40x40	-----	-----	-----	15.64	14.15	12.77	5
-----	-----	-----	69.50	62.75	56.75	42	-----	-----	-----	19.99	18.05	16.32	4
-----	-----	-----	-----	-----	-----	44	-----	-----	-----	-----	-----	-----	4
-----	-----	-----	73.50	66.75	61.50	46	-----	-----	-----	21.14	19.20	17.69	4
-----	-----	-----	-----	-----	-----	48	-----	-----	-----	-----	-----	-----	4
-----	-----	-----	"	"	"	50	-----	-----	-----	"	"	"	4
-----	-----	-----	74.75	68.00	62.75	52	-----	-----	-----	28.66	26.07	24.06	3
-----	-----	-----	-----	-----	-----	54	-----	-----	-----	-----	-----	-----	3
-----	-----	-----	88.00	80.00	74.75	56	-----	-----	-----	33.74	30.67	28.66	3
-----	-----	-----	-----	-----	-----	58	-----	-----	-----	-----	-----	-----	3
-----	-----	-----	"	"	"	60	-----	-----	-----	"	"	"	3
-----	-----	-----	94.75	86.75	80.00	62	-----	-----	-----	36.33	33.26	30.67	3
-----	-----	-----	-----	-----	-----	64	-----	-----	-----	-----	-----	-----	3
-----	-----	-----	105.50	97.50	90.75	66	-----	-----	-----	40.45	37.38	34.79	3
-----	-----	-----	-----	-----	-----	68	-----	-----	-----	-----	-----	-----	3
-----	-----	-----	"	"	"	70	-----	-----	-----	"	"	"	3
-----	-----	-----	118.75	108.00	101.50	72	-----	-----	-----	45.53	41.40	38.91	3
-----	-----	-----	-----	-----	-----	74	-----	-----	-----	-----	-----	-----	3
-----	-----	-----	140.00	126.75	120.00	76	-----	-----	-----	53.67	48.59	46.00	3
-----	-----	-----	-----	-----	-----	78	-----	-----	-----	-----	-----	-----	3
-----	-----	-----	"	"	"	80	-----	-----	-----	"	"	"	3
-----	-----	-----	153.50	140.25	133.50	82	-----	-----	-----	58.85	53.77	51.18	3
-----	-----	-----	-----	-----	-----	84	-----	-----	-----	-----	-----	-----	3
-----	-----	-----	76.45	69.03	62.43	42x42	-----	-----	-----	21.99	19.85	17.95	4
-----	-----	-----	80.85	73.63	67.65	44	-----	-----	-----	23.25	21.12	19.46	4
-----	-----	-----	-----	-----	-----	46	-----	-----	-----	-----	-----	-----	4
-----	-----	-----	"	"	"	48	-----	-----	-----	"	"	"	4
-----	-----	-----	82.23	74.80	69.03	50	-----	-----	-----	31.53	28.68	26.47	3
-----	-----	-----	-----	-----	-----	52	-----	-----	-----	-----	-----	-----	3
-----	-----	-----	96.80	88.00	82.23	54	-----	-----	-----	37.11	33.74	31.53	3
-----	-----	-----	-----	-----	-----	56	-----	-----	-----	-----	-----	-----	3
-----	-----	-----	"	"	"	58	-----	-----	-----	"	"	"	3
-----	-----	-----	104.23	95.43	88.00	60	-----	-----	-----	39.96	36.59	33.74	3
-----	-----	-----	-----	-----	-----	62	-----	-----	-----	-----	-----	-----	3
-----	-----	-----	116.05	107.25	99.83	64	-----	-----	-----	44.49	41.12	38.27	3
-----	-----	-----	-----	-----	-----	66	-----	-----	-----	-----	-----	-----	3
-----	-----	-----	"	"	"	68	-----	-----	-----	"	"	"	3
-----	-----	-----	130.63	118.80	111.65	70	-----	-----	-----	50.08	45.54	42.81	3
-----	-----	-----	-----	-----	-----	72	-----	-----	-----	-----	-----	-----	3
-----	-----	-----	154.00	139.43	132.00	74	-----	-----	-----	59.04	53.45	50.60	3
-----	-----	-----	-----	-----	-----	76	-----	-----	-----	-----	-----	-----	3
-----	-----	-----	"	"	"	78	-----	-----	-----	"	"	"	3
-----	-----	-----	168.85	154.28	146.85	80	-----	-----	-----	64.73	59.15	56.30	3
-----	-----	-----	80.85	73.63	67.65	44x44	-----	-----	-----	23.25	21.12	19.46	4
-----	-----	-----	-----	-----	-----	46	-----	-----	-----	-----	-----	-----	4
-----	-----	-----	82.23	74.80	69.03	48	-----	-----	-----	31.53	28.68	26.47	3
-----	-----	-----	-----	-----	-----	50	-----	-----	-----	-----	-----	-----	3
-----	-----	-----	96.80	88.00	82.23	52	-----	-----	-----	37.11	33.74	31.53	3
-----	-----	-----	-----	-----	-----	54	-----	-----	-----	-----	-----	-----	3
-----	-----	-----	"	"	"	56	-----	-----	-----	"	"	"	3
-----	-----	-----	104.23	95.43	88.00	58	-----	-----	-----	39.96	36.59	33.74	3
-----	-----	-----	-----	-----	-----	60	-----	-----	-----	-----	-----	-----	3
-----	-----	-----	116.05	107.25	99.83	62	-----	-----	-----	44.49	41.12	38.27	3
-----	-----	-----	-----	-----	-----	64	-----	-----	-----	-----	-----	-----	3
-----	-----	-----	"	"	"	66	-----	-----	-----	"	"	"	3
-----	-----	-----	130.63	118.80	111.65	68	-----	-----	-----	50.08	45.54	42.81	3
-----	-----	-----	-----	-----	-----	70	-----	-----	-----	-----	-----	-----	3
-----	-----	-----	154.00	139.43	132.00	72	-----	-----	-----	59.04	53.45	50.60	3
-----	-----	-----	-----	-----	-----	74	-----	-----	-----	-----	-----	-----	3
-----	-----	-----	"	"	"	78	-----	-----	-----	"	"	"	3
-----	-----	-----	168.85	154.28	146.85	78	-----	-----	-----	64.73	59.15	56.30	3
-----	-----	-----	-----	-----	-----	80	-----	-----	-----	-----	-----	-----	3
-----	-----	-----	82.23	74.80	69.03	46x46	-----	-----	-----	31.53	28.68	26.47	3
-----	-----	-----	-----	-----	-----	48	-----	-----	-----	-----	-----	-----	3
-----	-----	-----	96.80	88.00	82.23	50	-----	-----	-----	37.11	33.74	31.53	3
-----	-----	-----	-----	-----	-----	52	-----	-----	-----	-----	-----	-----	3
-----	-----	-----	"	"	"	54	-----	-----	-----	"	"	"	3
-----	-----	-----	104.23	95.43	88.00	56	-----	-----	-----	39.96	36.59	33.74	3
-----	-----	-----	-----	-----	-----	58	-----	-----	-----	-----	-----	-----	3
-----	-----	-----	116.05	107.25	99.83	60	-----	-----	-----	44.49	41.12	38.27	3
-----	-----	-----	-----	-----	-----	62	-----	-----	-----	-----	-----	-----	3
-----	-----	-----	"	"	"	64	-----	-----	-----	"	"	"	3
-----	-----	-----	130.63	118.80	111.65	66	-----	-----	-----	50.08	45.54	42.81	3
-----	-----	-----	-----	-----	-----	68	-----	-----	-----	-----	-----	-----	3
-----	-----	-----	154.00	139.43	132.00	70	-----	-----	-----	59.04	53.45	50.60	3
-----	-----	-----	-----	-----	-----	72	-----	-----	-----	-----	-----	-----	3

AMERICAN WINDOW GLASS.

Official Price List, January 21, 1901.

PRICE PER BOX OF FIFTY FEET.						SIZES.	PRICE PER SINGLE LIGHT.						No. Lights per Box
SINGLE.			DOUBLE.				SINGLE.			DOUBLE.			
AA	A	B	AA	A	B		AA	A	B	AA	A	B	
------	------	------	154.00	139.43	132.00	46x74	------	------	------	59.04	53.45	50.60	3
------	------	------	168.85	154.28	146.85	76	------	------	------	64.73	59.15	56.30	3
------	------	------				78	------	------	------				3
------	------	------	183.70	169.13	161.70	80	------	------	------	70.42	64.84	61.99	3
------	------	------	96.80	88.00	82.23	48x48	------	------	------	37.11	33.74	31.53	3
------	------	------	"	"	"	50	------	------	------	"	"	"	3
------	------	------				52	------	------	------				3
------	------	------	104.23	95.43	88.00	54	------	------	------	39.96	36.59	33.74	3
------	------	------	"	"	"	56	------	------	------				3
------	------	------	116.05	107.25	99.83	58	------	------	------	44.49	41.12	38.27	3
------	------	------	"	"	"	60	------	------	------	"	"	"	3
------	------	------	"	"	"	62	------	------	------				3
------	------	------	130.63	118.80	111.65	64	------	------	------	50.08	45.54	42.81	3
------	------	------	"	"	"	66	------	------	------				3
------	------	------	154.00	139.43	132.00	68	------	------	------	59.04	53.45	50.60	3
------	------	------	"	"	"	70	------	------	------	"	"	"	3
------	------	------	"	"	"	72	------	------	------				3
------	------	------	168.85	154.23	146.85	74	------	------	------	64.73	59.15	56.30	3
------	------	------	"	"	"	76	------	------	------				3
------	------	------	183.70	169.13	161.70	78	------	------	------	70.42	64.84	61.99	3
------	------	------				80	------	------	------				3
------	------	------	96.80	88.00	82.23	50x50	------	------	------	37.11	33.74	31.53	3
------	------	------	104.23	95.43	88.00	52	------	------	------	39.96	36.59	33.74	3
------	------	------	"	"	"	54	------	------	------				3
------	------	------	116.05	107.25	99.83	56	------	------	------	44.49	41.12	38.27	3
------	------	------				58	------	------	------				3
------	------	------	"	"	"	60	------	------	------	"	"	"	3
------	------	------	130.63	118.80	111.65	62	------	------	------	50.08	45.54	42.81	3
------	------	------				64	------	------	------				3
------	------	------	154.00	139.43	132.00	66	------	------	------	59.04	53.45	50.60	3
------	------	------	"	"	"	68	------	------	------	"	"	"	3
------	------	------	"	"	"	70	------	------	------	"	"	"	3
------	------	------	168.85	154.28	146.85	72	------	------	------	64.73	59.15	56.30	3
------	------	------	"	"	"	74	------	------	------	"	"	"	3
------	------	------	104.23	95.43	88.00	52x52	------	------	------	39.96	36.59	33.74	3
------	------	------	116.05	107.25	99.83	54	------	------	------	44.49	41.12	38.27	3
------	------	------	"	"	"	56	------	------	------				3
------	------	------	"	"	"	58	------	------	------				3
------	------	------	130.63	118.80	111.65	60	------	------	------	50.08	45.54	42.81	3
------	------	------	"	"	"	62	------	------	------				3
------	------	------	154.00	139.43	132.00	64	------	------	------	59.04	53.45	50.60	3
------	------	------	"	"	"	66	------	------	------				3
------	------	------	"	"	"	68	------	------	------	"	"	"	3
------	------	------	168.85	154.28	146.85	70	------	------	------	64.73	59.15	56.30	3
------	------	------	"	"	"	72	------	------	------	"	"	"	3
------	------	------	154.00	139.43	132.00	54x54	------	------	------	59.04	53.45	50.60	3
------	------	------	"	"	"	56	------	------	------	"	"	"	3
------	------	------	"	"	"	58	------	------	------	"	"	"	3
------	------	------	"	"	"	60	------	------	------	"	"	"	3
------	------	------	"	"	"	62	------	------	------	"	"	"	3
------	------	------	"	"	"	64	------	------	------	"	"	"	3
------	------	------	"	"	"	66	------	------	------	"	"	"	3
------	------	------	168.85	154.28	146.85	68	------	------	------	64.73	59.15	56.30	3
------	------	------	"	"	"	70	------	------	------				3
------	------	------	183.70	169.13	161.70	72	------	------	------	70.42	64.84	61.99	3
------	------	------	154.00	139.43	132.00	56x56	------	------	------	59.04	53.45	50.60	3
------	------	------	"	"	"	58	------	------	------	"	"	"	3
------	------	------	"	"	"	60	------	------	------	"	"	"	3
------	------	------	"	"	"	62	------	------	------	"	"	"	3
------	------	------	"	"	"	64	------	------	------	"	"	"	3
------	------	------	168.85	154.28	146.85	66	------	------	------	64.73	59.15	56.30	3
------	------	------	"	"	"	68	------	------	------				3
------	------	------	183.70	169.13	161.70	70	------	------	------	70.42	64.84	61.99	3
------	------	------	"	"	"	72	------	------	------				3
------	------	------	154.00	139.43	132.00	58x58	------	------	------	59.04	53.45	50.60	3
------	------	------	"	"	"	60	------	------	------	"	"	"	3
------	------	------	"	"	"	62	------	------	------				3
------	------	------	168.85	154.28	146.85	64	------	------	------	64.73	59.15	56.30	3
------	------	------	"	"	"	66	------	------	------				3
------	------	------	183.70	169.13	161.70	68	------	------	------	70.42	64.84	61.99	3
------	------	------	"	"	"	70	------	------	------	"	"	"	3
------	------	------				72	------	------	------				3
------	------	------	154.00	139.43	132.00	60x60	------	------	------	59.04	53.45	50.60	3
------	------	------	168.85	154.28	146.85	62	------	------	------	64.73	59.15	56.30	3
------	------	------				64	------	------	------				3
------	------	------	183.70	169.13	161.70	66	------	------	------	70.42	64.84	61.99	3
------	------	------	"	"	"	68	------	------	------	"	"	"	3
------	------	------				70	------	------	------				3

POLISHED PLATE GLASS

ODD and fractional parts of inches are charged at the price of the next highest even number. Irregular shaped glass, or glass cut to pattern, will be charged as it squares. No special thickness guaranteed; but when heavy plate is required, and so ordered, care will be exercised in selecting the heaviest in stock at the time.

Discounts apply to "glazing quality" only, and to glass of ordinary thickness. Selected glass and special thickness charged at special prices.

Glass exceeding the sizes comprised in the tables will be furnished at special prices.

On all orders amounting to less than $100 net, or for less than three plates of whatever value, boxing will be charged at the rate of 8 cents per square foot, lid measurement. Said measurement to be six inches larger each way than the widest and longest plates in the case.

To Approximate Weight of Polished Plate Glass Boxed.

Extend the glass at $3\frac{1}{2}$ lbs. per square foot. Weight of box equals the contents of a plate of greatest width and length of those packed therein multiplied by 10.

Thus :

$$
\left.
\begin{array}{l}
\text{1 plate } 36'' \text{ x } 96'' \\
\text{1 plate } 60'' \text{ x } 84''
\end{array}
\right\} = 59 \text{ ft. x } 3\frac{1}{2} \text{--------} 206\frac{1}{2} \text{ lbs.}
$$

Size of box 60" x 96"=40 ft. x 10 _____ 400   "

606½   "

POLISHED PLATE GLASS.

Official List, July, 1895.

Length	6	7	8	9	10
			WIDTH.		
6	$0.30	------	------	------	------
8	.40	$0.50	$0.5?	$0.65	------
10	.50	.60	.70	.80	$0.85
12	.60	.75	.85	.95	1.05
14	.70	.85	1.00	1.10	1.20
16	.80	1.00	1.15	1.25	1.40
18	.95	1.10	1.25	1.40	1.55
20	1.05	1.20	1.40	1.55	1.75
22	1.15	1.35	1.50	1.70	1.95
24	1.25	1.45	1.65	1.90	2.10
26	1.35	1.60	1.80	2.05	2.25
28	1.45	1.70	1.95	2.20	2.45
30	1.55	1.85	2.10	2.35	2.60
32	1.65	1.95	2.25	2.50	2.75
34	1.80	2.10	2.40	2.65	2.95
36	1.90	2.20	2.50	2.80	3.15
38	2.00	2.30	2.60	3.00	3.30
40	2.10	2.45	2.75	3.15	4.15
42	2.20	2.55	2.90	3.30	4.35
44	2.30	2.65	3.05	4.15	4.60
46	2.40	2.80	3.20	4.30	4.80
48	2.50	2.90	3.35	4.50	5.00
50	2.60	3.05	4.20	4.70	5.20
52	2.70	3.20	4.35	4.90	5.40
54	2.80	3.30	4.50	5.10	5.60
56	2.90	4.10	4.65	5.25	5.85
58	3.00	4.25	4.80	5.45	6.05
60	3.15	4.40	5.00	5.65	6.25
62	6.20	7.25	8.25	9.30	10.35
64	6.40	7.45	8.55	9.60	10.65
66	6.60	7.70	8.80	9.90	11.00
68	6.80	7.95	9.05	10 20	11.35
70	7.00	8.15	9.35	10.50	11.65
72	7.20	8.40	9.60	10.80	12.00
74	7.40	8.65	9.85	11.10	16.70
76	7.60	8.85	10.15	11.40	17.15
78	7.80	9.10	10.40	11.70	17.60
80	8.00	9.35	10.65	12.00	18.05
82	8.20	9.55	10.95	16.65	18.50
84	8.40	9.80	11.20	17.05	18.95
86	8.60	10.05	11.45	17.45	19.40
88	8.80	10.25	11.75	17.90	19.85
90	9.00	10.50	12.00	18.30	20 30
92	9.20	10.75	16.60	18.70	20.75
94	9.40	10.95	16.95	19.10	21.20
96	9.60	11.20	17.35	19.50	21.70
98	9.80	11.45	17.70	19.90	22.15
100	10.00	11.65	18.05	20.30	22.60
102	10.20	11.90	18.45	20.70	23.05
104	10.40	16.45	18.80	21.10	23.50
106	10.60	16.75	19.15	21.55	23.95
108	10.80	17.05	19.50	21.95	24.40
110	11.00	17.35	19.85	22.35	24.85
112	11.20	17.70	20.25	22.75	25.30
114	11.40	18.00	20.60	23.15	25.75

WIDTH.—*Continued.*

Length	6	7	8	9	10
116	$11.60	$18.35	$20.95	$23.55	$26.20
118	11.80	18.65	21.30	23.95	26.65
120	12.00	19.00	21.70	24.40	27.10

Length	12	14	16	18
		WIDTH.		
12	$1.25	------	------	------
14	1.45	$1.70	------	------
16	1.65	1.95	$2.20	------
18	1.90	2.20	2.50	$2.80
20	2.10	2.45	2.75	3.15
22	2.30	2.65	3.05	4.15
24	2.50	2.90	3.35	4.50
26	2.70	3.15	4.35	4.90
28	2.90	4.10	4.65	5.25
30	3.15	4.40	5.00	5.65
32	3.35	4.65	5.35	6.00
34	4.25	4.95	5.65	6.40
36	4.50	5.25	6.00	6.75
38	4.75	5.55	6.35	7.15
40	5.00	5.85	6.65	7.50
42	5.25	6.15	7.00	12.60
44	5.50	6.40	7.35	13.20
46	5.75	6.70	12.30	13.80
48	6.00	7.00	12.80	14.40
50	6.25	7.30	13.30	15.00
52	6.50	12.10	13.90	15.60
54	6.75	12.60	14.40	16.20
56	7.00	13.10	14.90	16.80
58	7.25	13.50	15.50	17.40
60	7.50	14.00	16.00	18.00
62	12.40	14.50	16.50	18.60
64	12.80	14.90	17.10	19.20
66	13.20	15.40	17.60	19.80
68	13.60	15.90	18.10	20.40
70	14.00	16.30	18.70	21.00
72	14.40	16.80	19.20	21.60
74	14.80	17.30	19.70	22.20
76	15.20	17.70	20.30	22.80
78	15.60	18.20	20.80	23.40
80	16.00	18.70	21.30	24.00
82	16.40	19.10	21.90	33.30
84	16.80	19.60	22.40	34.10
86	17.20	20.10	22.90	34.90
88	17.60	20.50	23.50	35.80
90	18.00	21.00	24.00	36.60
92	18.40	21.50	33.20	37.40
94	18.80	21.90	33.90	38.20
96	19.20	22.40	34.70	39.00
98	19.60	22.90	35.40	39.80
100	20.00	23.30	36.10	40.60
102	20.40	23.80	36.90	41.40
104	20.80	32.90	37.60	42.20
106	21.20	33.50	38.30	43.10
108	21.60	34.10	39.00	43.90

POLISHED PLATE GLASS.

Official List, July, 1895.

Length.	WIDTH.—Continued.				Length.	WIDTH.—Continued.				
	12	14	16	18		20	22	24	26	28
110	$22.00	$34.70	$39.70	$44.70	62	$20.70	$22.70	$33.60	$36.40	$39.20
112	22.40	35.40	40.50	45.50	64	21.30	23.50	34.70	37.60	40.50
114	22.80	36.00	41.20	46.30	66	22.00	32.80	35.80	38.70	41.70
116	23.20	36.70	41.90	47.10	68	22.70	33.70	36.90	39.90	43.00
118	23.60	37.30	42.60	47.90	70	23.30	34.70	38.00	41.00	44.30
120	24.00	38.00	43.40	48.80	72	24.00	35.70	39.00	42.20	45.50
122	33.00	38.60	44.10	49.60	74	33.40	36.70	40.10	43.40	46.80
124	33.60	39.20	44.80	50.40	76	34.30	37.70	41.20	44.60	48.10
126	34.10	39.80	45.50	51.20	78	35.20	38.70	42.30	45.80	49.30
128	34.70	40.50	46.20	52.00	80	36.10	39.70	43.40	47.00	50.60
130	35.20	41.10	47.00	52.80	82	37.00	40.70	44.50	48.20	51.90
132	35.80	41.70	47.70	53.60	84	37.90	41.70	45.50	49.30	53.10
134	36.30	42.30	48.50	54.40	86	38.80	42.70	46.60	50.50	54.40
136	36.90	43.00	49.20	55.30	88	39.70	43.70	47.70	51.70	55.70
138	37.40	43.70	49.90	56.10	90	40.60	44.70	48.80	52.80	56.90
140	38.00	44.30	50.60	56.90	92	41.50	45.70	49.90	54.00	58.20
142	38.50	44.90	51.30	57.70	94	42.40	46.70	51.00	55.20	59.50
144	39.00	45.50	52.00	58.50	96	43.40	47.70	52.00	56.40	60.70
146	39.60	46.10	52.70	59.30	98	44.30	48.70	53.10	57.60	62.00
148	40.10	46.80	53.40	60.10	100	45.20	49.70	54.20	58.70	63.30
150	40.60	47.40	54.20	60.90	102	46.10	50.70	55.30	59.90	64.50
152	41.20	48.00	54.90	61.80	104	47.00	51.70	56.40	61.00	68.70
154	41.70	48.70	55.60	62.60	106	47.90	52.60	57.50	62.20	70.10
156	42.20	49.30	56.40	63.40	108	48.80	53.60	58.50	63.40	71.40
158	42.80	50.00	57.10	64.20	110	49.70	54.60	59.60	64.60	72.70
160	43.40	50.60	57.80	65.00	112	50.60	55.60	60.70	68.70	74.10
162	43.90	51.20	58.50	68.80	114	51.50	56.60	61.80	70.00	75.40
164	44.50	51.80	59.20	69.70	116	52.40	57.60	62.90	71.20	76.70
166	45.00	52.50	60.00	70.60	118	53.30	58.60	64.00	72.40	78.00
168	45.50	53.10	60.70	71.40	120	54.20	59.60	65.00	73.70	79.30
170	46.00	53.70	61.40	72.30	122	55.10	60.60	69.10	74.90	80.70
					124	56.00	61.60	70.30	76.10	82.00
					126	56.90	62.60	71.40	77.40	83.30
					128	57.80	63.60	72.50	78.60	84.70
					130	58.70	64.60	73.70	79.80	86.00
					132	59.60	68.60	74.80	81.10	87.30
					134	60.50	69.60	76.00	82.30	88.60
					136	61.40	70.70	77.10	83.50	89.90
					138	62.30	71.70	78.20	84.80	91.30
					140	63.20	72.70	79.30	86.00	92.60
					142	64.10	73.80	80.50	87.20	93.90
					144	65.00	74.80	81.60	88.40	95.20
					146	68.90	75.90	82.70	89.60	96.50
					148	69.90	76.90	83.90	90.90	97.80
					150	70.90	77.90	85.00	92.10	99.20
					152	71.80	79.00	86.10	93.30	101.00
					154	72.70	80.00	87.30	94.60	102.00
					156	73.70	81.10	88.40	95.80	103.00
					158	74.60	82.10	89.50	97.00	104.00
					160	75.60	83.10	90.70	98.30	106.00
					162	76.50	84.20	91.80	99.50	107.00
					164	77.50	85.20	92.90	101.00	108.00
					166	78.40	86.20	94.10	102.00	110.00
					168	79.30	87.30	95.20	103.00	111.00
					170	80.30	88.30	96.30	104.00	112.00

Length.	WIDTH.				
	20	22	24	26	28
20	$4.15	------	------	------	------
22	4.60	$5.05	------	------	------
24	5.00	5.50	$6.00	------	------
26	5.40	5.95	6.50	$7.05	------
28	5.85	6.40	7.10	12.10	$13.10
30	6.25	6.90	7.50	13.00	14.00
32	6.65	7.35	12.80	13.90	14.90
34	7.10	12.50	13.60	14.70	15.90
36	7.50	13.20	14.40	15.60	16.80
38	12.70	13.90	15.20	16.50	17.70
40	13.30	14.70	16.00	17.30	18.70
42	14.00	15.40	16.80	18.20	19.60
44	14.70	16.10	17.60	19.10	20 50
46	15.30	16.90	18.40	19.90	21.50
48	16.00	17.60	19.20	20.80	22.40
50	16.70	18.30	20.00	21.70	23.30
52	17.30	19.10	20.80	22.50	32.90
54	18.00	19.80	21.60	23.40	34.10
56	18.70	20.50	22.40	32.90	35.40
58	19.30	21.30	23.20	34.00	36.70
60	20.00	22.00	24.00	35.20	37.90

POLISHED PLATE GLASS.

Official List, July, 1895.

Length	\$15.00 width 30	32	34	36	38
30	$15.00				
32	16.00	$17.10			
34	17.00	18.10	$19.30		
36	18.00	19.20	20.40	$21.60	
38	19.00	20.30	21.50	22.80	$32.60
40	20.00	21.30	22.70	24.00	34.30
42	21.00	22.40	23.80	34.10	36.00
44	22.00	23.50	33.70	35.80	37.80
46	23.00	33.20	35.30	37.40	39.50
48	24.00	34.70	36.90	39.00	41.20
50	33.80	36.10	38.40	40.60	42.90
52	35.20	37.60	39.90	42.20	44.60
54	36.60	39.00	41.40	43.90	46.30
56	38.00	40.50	43.00	45.50	48.00
58	39.30	41.90	44.50	47.10	49.80
60	40.60	43.40	46.00	48.80	51.50
62	42.00	44.80	47.60	50.40	53.20
64	43.40	46.20	49.20	52.00	54.90
66	44.70	47.70	50.70	53.60	56.60
68	46.00	49.20	52.20	55.30	58.30
70	47.40	50.60	53.70	56.90	60.00
72	48.80	52.00	55.30	58.50	61.80
74	50.10	53.40	56.80	60.10	63.50
76	51.50	54.90	58.30	61.80	68.20
78	52.80	56.40	59.90	63.40	70.00
80	54.20	57.80	61.40	65.00	71.80
82	55.50	59.20	63.00	69.70	73.60
84	56.90	60.70	64.50	71.40	75.40
86	58.20	62.10	69.00	73.10	77.20
88	59.60	63.60	70.70	74.80	79.00
90	60.90	65.00	72.30	76.50	80.80
92	62.30	69.50	73.90	78.20	82.60
94	63.70	71.00	75.50	79.90	84.40
96	65.00	72.50	77.10	81.60	86.20
98	69.40	74.10	78.70	83.30	88.00
100	70.90	75.60	80.30	85.00	89.80
102	72.30	77.10	81.90	86.70	91.60
104	73.70	78.60	83.50	88.40	93.40
106	75.10	80.10	85.10	90.10	95.20
108	76.50	81.60	86.70	91.80	97.00
110	77.90	83.10	88.30	93.50	98.70
112	79.30	84.60	89.90	95.20	101.00
114	80.80	86.10	91.50	96.90	102.00
116	82.20	87.60	93.10	98.60	104.00
118	83.60	89.10	94.70	100.00	106.00
120	85.00	90.70	96.30	102.00	108.00
122	86.40	92.20	98.00	104.00	109.00
124	87.90	93.70	99.50	105.00	111.00
126	89.30	95.20	101.00	107.00	113.00
128	90.70	96.70	103.00	109.00	115.00
130	92.10	98.20	104.00	110.00	117.00
132	93.50	99.70	106.00	112.00	118.00
134	95.00	101.00	108.00	114.00	120.00
136	96.40	103.00	109.00	116.00	122.00
138	97.80	104.00	111.00	118.00	124.00
140	99.20	106.00	112.00	119.00	126.00
142	101.00	107.00	114.00	120.00	127.00
144	102.00	109.00	116.00	122.00	129.00
146	103.00	110.00	117.00	124.00	131.00
148	105.00	112.00	119.00	126.00	133.00
150	106.00	113.00	120.00	127.00	135.00
152	108.00	115.00	122.00	129.00	136.00
154	109.00	116.00	124.00	131.00	138.00
156	110.00	118.00	125.00	133.00	140.00
158	111.00	119.00	127.00	135.00	142.00
160	113.00	121.00	128.00	136.00	144.00
162	115.00	122.00	130.00	137.00	145.00
164	116.00	124.00	132.00	139.00	147.00
166	118.00	126.00	133.00	141.00	149.00
168	119.00	127.00	135.00	143.00	151.00
170	120.00	128.00	136.00	144.00	152.00

WIDTH.

Length	40	42	44	46	48
40	$36.10				
42	37.90	$39.80			
44	39.70	41.70	$43.80		
46	41.50	43.60	45.70	$47.80	
48	43.40	45.50	47.70	49.90	$52.00
50	45.20	47.40	49.70	51.90	54.20
52	47.00	49.30	51.70	54.00	56.40
54	48.80	51.20	53.60	56.10	58.50
56	50.60	53.10	55.60	58.10	60.70
58	52.40	55.00	57.60	60.20	62.90
60	54.20	56.90	59.60	62.30	65.00
62	56.00	58.80	61.60	64.40	70.30
64	57.80	60.70	63.60	69.50	72.50
66	59.60	62.60	68.60	71.70	74.80
68	61.40	64.50	70.70	73.90	77.10
70	63.20	69.40	72.70	76.10	79.30
72	65.00	71.40	74.80	78.20	81.60
74	69.90	73.40	76.90	80.40	83.90
76	71.80	75.40	79.00	82.60	86.10
78	73.70	77.40	81.10	84.80	88.40
80	75.60	79.40	83.10	86.90	90.70
82	77.50	81.40	85.20	89.10	92.90
84	79.40	83.30	87.30	91.30	95.20
86	81.30	85.30	89.40	93.40	97.50
88	83.10	87.30	91.50	95.60	99.70
90	85.00	89.30	93.50	97.80	102.00
92	86.90	91.30	95.60	100.00	104.00
94	88.80	93.20	97.70	102.00	107.00
96	90.70	95.20	99.70	104.00	109.00
98	92.60	97.20	102.00	106.00	111.00
100	94.50	99.20	104.00	109.00	113.00
102	96.40	101.00	106.00	111.00	116.00
104	98.30	103.00	108.00	113.00	118.00
106	100.00	105.00	110.00	115.00	120.00
108	102.00	107.00	112.00	117.00	122.00

POLISHED PLATE GLASS.

Official List, July, 1895.

Length	WIDTH.—Continued.					Length	WIDTH.				
	40	42	44	46	48		50	52	54	56	58
110	104.00	109.00	114.00	120.00	125.00	50	56.50	------	------	------	------
112	106.00	111.00	116.00	122.00	127.00	52	58.70	61.00	------	------	------
114	108.00	113.00	118.00	124.00	129.00	54	60.90	63.40	68.80	------	------
116	110.00	115.00	121.00	126.00	131.00	56	63.20	68.70	71.40	74.10	------
118	112.00	117.00	123.00	128.00	134.00	58	68.50	71.20	74.00	76.70	79.40
120	114.00	119.00	125.00	130.00	136.00	60	70.90	73.70	76.50	79.30	82.20
122	115.00	121.00	127.00	132.00	138.00	62	73.20	76.10	79.00	82.00	84.90
124	117.00	123.00	129.00	135.00	141.00	64	75.60	78.60	81.60	84.70	87.70
126	119.00	125.00	131.00	137.00	143.00	66	77.90	81.10	84.20	87.30	90.40
128	121.00	127.00	133.00	139.00	145.00	68	80.30	83.50	86.70	89.90	93.10
130	123.00	129.00	135.00	141.00	147.00	70	82.60	85.90	89.30	92.50	95.80
132	125.00	131.00	137.00	143.00	150.00	72	85.00	88.40	91.80	95.20	98.60
134	126.00	133.00	139.00	146.00	152.00	74	87.40	90.90	94.40	97.90	101.00
136	128.00	135.00	141.00	148.00	163.00	76	89.70	93.30	96.90	101.00	104.00
138	130.00	137.00	143.00	150.00	166.00	78	92.10	95.70	99.40	103.00	107.00
140	132.00	139.00	145.00	152 00	168.00	80	94.50	98.30	102.00	106.00	110.00
142	134.00	141.00	147.00	163.00	170.00	82	96.80	101.00	105.00	108.00	112.00
144	136.00	143.00	150.00	166.00	173.00	84	99.20	103.00	107.00	111.00	115.00
146	138.00	145.00	152.00	168.00	175.00	86	102.00	106.00	110.00	113.00	118.00
148	140.00	147.00	163.00	170.00	178.00	88	104.00	108.00	112.00	116.00	121.00
150	142.00	149.00	165.00	172.00	180.00	90	106.00	110.00	115.00	119.00	123.00
152	144.00	151.00	167.00	175.00	182.00	92	109.00	113.00	117.00	122.00	126.00
154	145.00	153.00	169.00	177.00	185.00	94	111.00	115.00	120.00	124.00	129.00
156	147.00	164.00	172.00	179.00	187.00	96	113.00	118.00	123.00	127.00	131.00
158	149.00	166.00	174.00	182.00	190.00	98	116.00	120.00	125.00	130.00	134.00
160	151.00	168.00	176.00	184.00	192.00	100	118.00	123.00	127.00	132.00	137.00
162	153.00	170.00	178.00	186.00	194.00	102	120.00	125.00	130.00	135.00	140.00
164	164.00	172.00	180.00	189.00	197.00	104	123.00	128.00	133.00	138.00	142.00
166	166.00	174.00	183.00	191.00	199.00	106	125.00	130.00	135.00	140.00	145.00
168	168.00	177.00	185.00	193.00	202.00	108	127.00	133.00	138.00	143.00	148.00
170	170.00	179.00	187.00	195.00	204.00	110	130.00	135.00	140.00	145.00	151.00
172	172.00	181.00	189.00	198.00	206.00	112	132.00	137.00	143.00	148.00	162.00
174	174.00	183.00	191.00	200.00	209.00	114	135.00	140 00	145.00	151.00	165.00
176	176.00	185.00	194.00	202.00	211.00	116	137.00	142.00	148.00	162.00	168.00
178	178.00	187.00	196.00	205.00	214.00	118	139.00	145.00	150.00	165.00	171.00
180	180.00	189.00	198.00	207.00	216.00	120	142.00	147.00	153.00	168.00	174.00
182	202.00	212.00	222.00	232.00	243.00	122	144.00	150.00	165.00	171.00	177.00
184	204.00	215.00	225.00	235.00	246.00	124	146.00	152.00	167.00	174.00	180.00
186	207.00	217.00	227.00	237.00	248.00	126	149.00	164.00	170.00	176.00	183.00
188	209.00	220.00	230.00	240.00	251.00	128	151.00	166.00	173.00	179.00	186.00
190	211.00	222.00	232.00	243.00	253.00	130	162.00	169.00	175.00	182.00	188.00
192	293.00	308.00	323.00	337.00	352.00	132	165.00	172.00	178.00	185.00	191.00
194	297.00	311.00	326.00	340.00	356.00	134	167.00	174.00	181.00	188.00	194.00
196	300.00	315.00	330.00	344.00	360.00	136	170.00	177.00	184.00	190.00	197.00
198	303.00	318.00	333.00	348.00	363.00	138	172.00	179.00	186.00	193.00	200.00
200	306.00	321.00	336.00	352.00	367.00	140	175.00	182.00	189.00	196.00	203.00
202	309.00	325.00	340.00	355.00	370.00	142	177.00	185.00	192.00	199.00	206.00
204	312.00	328.00	343.00	359.00	374.00	144	180.00	187.00	194.00	202.00	209.00
206	315.00	331.00	346.00	362.00	378.00	146	182.00	190.00	197.00	204.00	212.00
208	318.00	334.00	350.00	366.00	381.00	148	185.00	192.00	200.00	207.00	215.00
210	321.00	337.00	353.00	369.00	385.00	150	187.00	195.00	202.00	210.00	218.00
212	324.00	340.00	356.00	373.00	389.00	152	190.00	198.00	205.00	213.00	220.00
214	327.00	343.00	360.00	376.00	393.00	154	192.00	200.00	208.00	216.00	223.00
216	330.00	346.00	363.00	379.00	396.00	156	195.00	203.00	210.00	218.00	226.00
218	333.00	350.00	366.00	383.00	400.00	158	197.00	205.00	213.00	221.00	229.00

POLISHED PLATE GLASS.

Official List, July, 1895.

Length.	WIDTH.—Continued.					Length.	WIDTH.—Continued.				
	50	52	54	56	58		60	62	64	66	68
160	200.00	208.00	216.00	224.00	232.00	104	147.00	152.00	166.00	172.00	177.00
162	202.00	210.00	219.00	227.00	235.00	106	150.00	164.00	170.00	175.00	180.00
164	205.00	213.00	221.00	230.00	238.00	108	153.00	167.00	173.00	178.00	184.00
166	207.00	216.00	224.00	232.00	241.00	110	165.00	170.00	176.00	181.00	187.00
168	210.00	218.00	227.00	235.00	244.00	112	168.00	174.00	179.00	185.00	190.00
170	212.00	221.00	229.00	238.00	246.00	114	171.00	177.00	182.00	188.00	194.00
172	215.00	224.00	232.00	241.00	249.00	116	174.00	180.00	185.00	191.00	197.00
174	217.00	226.00	235.00	244.00	252.00	118	177.00	183.00	189.00	195.00	201.00
176	220.00	229.00	238.00	246.00	255.00	120	180.00	186.00	192.00	198.00	204.00
178	222.00	231.00	240.00	249.00	258.00	122	183.00	189.00	195.00	201.00	207.00
180	225.00	234.00	243.00	252.00	261.00	124	186.00	192.00	198.00	205.00	211.00
182	253.00	263.00	273.00	283.00	293.00	126	189.00	195.00	202.00	208.00	214.00
184	256.00	266.00	276.00	286.00	297.00	128	192.00	198.00	205.00	211.00	218.00
186	258.00	269.00	279.00	290.00	300.00	130	195.00	201.00	208.00	214.00	221.00
188	261.00	271.00	282.00	293.00	303.00	132	198.00	205.00	211.00	218.00	224.00
190	264.00	274.00	285.00	296.00	306.00	134	201.00	208.00	214.00	221.00	228.00
192	367.00	381.00	396.00	411.00	425.00	136	204.00	211.00	218.00	224.00	231.00
194	370.00	385.00	400.00	415.00	430.00	138	207.00	214.00	221.00	228.00	234.00
196	374.00	389.00	404.00	419.00	434.00	140	210.00	217.00	224.00	231.00	238.00
198	378.00	393.00	408.00	424.00	439.00	142	213.00	220.00	227.00	234.00	241.00
200	382.00	397.00	412.00	428.00	443.00	144	216.00	223.00	230.00	238.00	245.00
202	386.00	401.00	417.00	432.00	447.00	146	219.00	226.00	234.00	241.00	248.00
204	389.00	405.00	421.00	437.00	452.00	148	222.00	229.00	237.00	244.00	252.00
206	393.00	409.00	425.00	441.00	456.00	150	225.00	232.00	240.00	247.00	255.00
208	397.00	413.00	429.00	445.00	460.00	152	228.00	236.00	243.00	251.00	258.00
210	400.00	417.00	433.00	449.00	465.00	154	231.00	239.00	246.00	254.00	262.00
212	404.00	421.00	437.00	454.00	470.00	156	234.00	242.00	250.00	257.00	265.00
214	408.00	425.00	441.00	458.00	474.00	158	237.00	245.00	253.00	261.00	269.00
216	413.00	429.00	445.00	462.00	478.00	160	240.00	248.00	256.00	264.00	272.00
218	417.00	434.00	450.00	467.00	483.00	162	243.00	251.00	259.00	267.00	275.00

Length.	WIDTH.					Length.	WIDTH.—Continued.				
	60	62	64	66	68		60	62	64	66	68
						164	246.00	254.00	262.00	271.00	279.00
						166	249.00	257.00	266.00	274.00	282.00
						168	252.00	260.00	269.00	277.00	286.00
60	85.00	------	------	------	------	170	255.00	263.00	272.00	280.00	289.00
62	88.00	91.00	------	------	------	172	258.00	267.00	275.00	284.00	292.00
64	91.00	94.00	97.00	------	------	174	261.00	270.00	278.00	287.00	296.00
66	94.00	97.00	100.00	103.00	------	176	264.00	273.00	282.00	290.00	299.00
68	96.00	100.00	103.00	106.00	109.00	178	267.00	276.00	285.00	294.00	303.00
70	99.00	102.00	106.00	109.00	112.00	180	270.00	279.00	288.00	297.00	306.00
72	102.00	105.00	109.00	112.00	116.00	182	303.00	314.00	324.00	334.00	344.00
74	105.00	108.00	112.00	115.00	119.00	184	307.00	317.00	327.00	337.00	347.00
76	108.00	111.00	115.00	118.00	122.00	186	310.00	320.00	331.00	341.00	351.00
78	110.00	114.00	118.00	121.00	125.00	188	314.00	324.00	334.00	345.00	355.00
80	113.00	117.00	121.00	125.00	128.00	190	317.00	327.00	338.00	348.00	359.00
82	116.00	120.00	124.00	128.00	132.00	192	440.00	455.00	469.00	484.00	499.00
84	119.00	123.00	127.00	131.00	135.00	194	445.00	459.00	474.00	489.00	504.00
86	122.00	126.00	130.00	134.00	138.00	196	449.00	464.00	479.00	494.00	509.00
88	125.00	129.00	133.00	137.00	141.00	198	454.00	469.00	484.00	499.00	514.00
90	127.00	132.00	136.00	140.00	144.00	200	458.00	473.00	489.00	504.00	520.00
92	130.00	135.00	139.00	143.00	148.00	202	463.00	478.00	494.00	509.00	525.00
94	133.00	138.00	142.00	146.00	151.00	204	468.00	483.00	499.00	514.00	530.00
96	136.00	141.00	145.00	150.00	163.00	206	472.00	488.00	504.00	519.00	535.00
98	139.00	143.00	148.00	153.00	167.00	208	477.00	492.00	508.00	524.00	540.00
100	142.00	146.00	151.00	165.00	170.00	210	481.00	497.00	513.00	529.00	545.00
102	144.00	149.00	163.00	168.00	173.00	212	486.00	501.00	518.00	534.00	601.00

POLISHED PLATE GLASS.

Official List, July, 1895.

Length.	\- WIDTH.—Continued.					Length.	WIDTH.—Continued.				
	60	62	64	66	68		70	72	74	76	78
214	490.00	506.00	523.00	539.00	606.00	168	294.00	302.00	311.00	319.00	328.00
216	495.00	512.00	528.00	545.00	612.00	170	297.00	306.00	314.00	323.00	331.00
218	500.00	517.00	533.00	550.00	618.00	172	301.00	310.00	318.00	327.00	335.00

Length.	WIDTH.				
	70	72	74	76	78
70	116.00	------	------	------	------
72	119.00	122.00	------	------	------
74	122.00	126.00	129.00	------	------
76	126.00	129.00	133.00	136.00	------
78	129.00	133.00	136.00	140.00	144.00
80	132.00	136.00	139.00	144.00	147.00
82	136.00	139.00	143.00	147.00	151.00
84	139.00	143.00	147.00	151.00	164.00
86	142.00	146.00	150.00	163.00	168.00
88	145.00	150.00	163.00	167.00	172.00
90	149.00	153.00	166.00	171.00	175.00
92	152.00	166.00	170.00	175.00	179.00
94	165.00	169.00	174.00	179.00	183.00
96	168.00	173.00	178.00	182.00	187.00
98	171.00	176.00	181.00	186.00	191.00
100	175.00	180.00	185.00	190.00	195.00
102	178.00	184.00	189.00	194.00	199.00
104	182.00	187.00	192.00	198.00	203.00
106	185.00	191.00	196.00	201.00	207.00
108	189.00	194.00	200.00	205.00	210.00
110	192.00	198.00	203.00	209.00	214.00
112	196.00	202.00	207.00	213.00	218.00
114	199.00	206.00	211.00	217.00	222.00
116	203.00	209.00	215.00	220.00	226.00
118	206.00	212.00	218.00	224.00	230.00
120	210.00	216.00	222.00	228.00	234.00
122	213.00	220.00	226.00	232.00	238.00
124	217.00	223.00	230.00	236.00	242.00
126	220.00	227.00	233.00	239.00	246.00
128	224.00	230.00	237.00	243.00	250.00
130	227.00	234.00	240.00	247.00	253.00
132	231.00	238.00	244.00	251.00	257.00
134	234.00	241.00	248.00	255.00	261.00
136	238.00	245.00	251.00	258.00	265.00
138	241.00	248.00	255.00	262.00	269.00
140	245.00	252.00	259.00	266.00	273.00
142	248.00	256.00	263.00	270.00	277.00
144	252.00	259.00	266.00	274.00	281.00
146	255.00	263.00	270.00	277.00	285.00
148	259.00	266.00	274.00	281.00	289.00
150	262.00	270.00	277.00	285.00	292.00
152	266.00	274.00	281.00	289.00	296.00
154	269.00	277.00	285.00	293.00	300.00
156	273.00	281.00	288.00	296.00	304.00
158	276.00	284.00	292.00	300.00	308.00
160	280.00	288.00	296.00	304.00	312.00
162	283.00	292.00	300.00	308.00	316.00
164	287.00	295.00	303.00	312.00	320.00
166	290.00	299.00	307.00	315.00	324.00

Right-hand continuation:

Length.	WIDTH.—Continued.				
	70	72	74	76	78
174	304.00	313.00	322.00	331.00	339.00
176	308.00	317.00	325.00	334.00	343.00
178	311.00	320.00	329.00	338.00	347.00
180	315.00	324.00	333.00	342.00	351.00
182	354.00	364.00	374.00	384.00	394.00
184	358.00	368.00	378.00	388.00	399.00
186	362.00	372.00	382.00	393.00	443.00
188	366.00	376.00	386.00	397.00	448.00
190	370.00	380.00	391.00	441.00	453.00
192	513.00	528.00	543.00	608.00	624.00
194	518.00	534.00	548.00	615.00	631.00
196	524.00	539.00	604.00	621.00	637.00
198	529.00	545.00	610.00	627.00	643.00
200	534.00	550.00	617.00	633.00	650.00
202	540.00	606.00	623.00	640.00	656.00
204	545.00	612.00	630.00	646.00	663·00
206	601.00	618.00	636.00	652.00	669.00
208	607.00	624.00	642.00	659.00	676.00
210	612.00	630.00	648.00	665.00	682.00
212	618.00	636.00	654.00	672.00	689.00
214	624.00	642.00	660.00	678.00	696.00
216	630.00	648.00	666.00	684.00	702.00
218	636.00	654.00	672.00	690.00	708.00

Length.	WIDTH.				
	80	82	84	86	88
80	151.00	------	------	------	------
82	164.00	168.00	------	------	------
84	168.00	172.00	176.00	------	------
86	172.00	176.00	181.00	185.00	------
88	176.00	180.00	185.00	189.00	194.00
90	180.00	184.00	189.00	193.00	198.00
92	184.00	189.00	193.00	198.00	202.00
94	188.00	193.00	197.00	202.00	207.00
96	192.00	197.00	202.00	206.00	211.00
98	196.00	201.00	206.00	211.00	216.00
100	200.00	205.00	210.00	215.00	220.00
102	204.00	209.00	214.00	219.00	224.00
104	208.00	213.00	218.00	224.00	229.00
106	212.00	217.00	223.00	228.00	233.00
108	216.00	221.00	227.00	232.00	237.00
110	220.00	225.00	231.00	237.00	242.00
112	224.00	230.00	235.00	241.00	246.00
114	228.00	234.00	239.00	245.00	251.00
116	232.00	238.00	244.00	250.00	255.00
118	236.00	242.00	248.00	254.00	260.00
120	240.00	246.00	252.00	258.00	264.00
122	244.00	250.00	256.00	262.00	268.00
124	248.00	254.00	260.00	267.00	273.00
126	252.00	258.00	265.00	271.00	277.00
128	256.00	262.00	269.00	275.00	282.00
130	260.00	266.00	273.00	279.00	286.00

POLISHED PLATE GLASS.

Official List, July, 1895.

Length	WIDTH.—Continued.					Length	WIDTH.—Continued.			
	80	82	84	86	88		90	92	94	96
132	264.00	271.00	277.00	284.00	290.00	104	234.00	239.00	244.00	250.00
134	268.00	275.00	281.00	288.00	295.00	106	238.00	244.00	249.00	254.00
136	272.00	279.00	286.00	292.00	299.00	108	243.00	248.00	254.00	259.00
138	276.00	283.00	290.00	297.00	304.00	110	247.00	253.00	258.00	264.00
140	280.00	287.00	294.00	301.00	308.00	112	252.00	258.00	263.00	269.00
142	284.00	291.00	298.00	305.00	312.00	114	256.00	262.00	268.00	274.00
144	288.00	295.00	302.00	310.00	317.00	116	261.00	267.00	273.00	278.00
146	292.00	299.00	307.00	314.00	321.00	118	265.00	272.00	277.00	283.00
148	296.00	303.00	311.00	318.00	326.00	120	270.00	276.00	282.00	288.00
150	300.00	307.00	315.00	322.00	330.00	122	274.00	281.00	287.00	293.00
152	304.00	312.00	319.00	327.00	334.00	124	279.00	285.00	291.00	298.00
154	308.00	316.00	323.00	331.00	339.00	126	283.00	290.00	296.00	302.00
156	312.00	320.00	328.00	335.00	343.00	128	288.00	294.00	301.00	307.00
158	316.00	324.00	332.00	340.00	348.00	130	292.00	299.00	305.00	312.00
160	320.00	328.00	336.00	344.00	352.00	132	297.00	304.00	310.00	317.00
162	324.00	332.00	340.00	348.00	356.00	134	301.00	308.00	315.00	322.00
164	328.00	336.00	344.00	353.00	401.00	136	306.00	313.00	320.00	326.00
166	332.00	340.00	349.00	357.00	406.00	138	310.00	317.00	324.00	331.00
168	336.00	344.00	353.00	401.00	411.00	140	315.00	322.00	329.00	336.00
170	340.00	348.00	357.00	406.00	416.00	142	319.00	327.00	334.00	341.00
172	344.00	353.00	401.00	411.00	420.00	144	324.00	331.00	339.00	346.00
174	348.00	357.00	406.00	416.00	425.00	146	328.00	336.00	343.00	350.00
176	352.00	401.00	411.00	420.00	430.00	148	333.00	340.00	348.00	355.00
178	356.00	405.00	415.00	425.00	435.00	150	337.00	345.00	352.00	360.00
180	360.00	410.00	420.00	430.00	440.00	152	342.00	350.00	357.00	405.00
182	445.00	456.00	467.00	478.00	489.00	154	346.00	354.00	402.00	411.00
184	450.00	461.00	472.00	483.00	495.00	156	351.00	359.00	407.00	416.00
186	455.00	466.00	477.00	489.00	500.00	158	355.00	404.00	413.00	421.00
188	460.00	471.00	482.00	494.00	506.00	160	360.00	409.00	418.00	427.00
190	464.00	476.00	488.00	500.00	511.00	162	405.00	414.00	423.00	432.00
192	640.00	656.00	672.00	688.00	704.00	164	410.00	419.00	428.00	437.00
194	647.00	663.00	679.00	695.00	711.00	166	415.00	424.00	433.00	443.00
196	653.00	670.00	686.00	703.00	719.00	168	420.00	429.00	439.00	448.00
198	660.00	676.00	693.00	710.00	907.00	170	425.00	434.00	444.00	453.00
200	666.00	683.00	700.00	717.00	917.00	172	430.00	440.00	449.00	459.00
202	673.00	690.00	707.00	905.00	926.00	174	435.00	445.00	454.00	464.00
204	679.00	697.00	714.00	914.00	935.00	176	440.00	450.00	460.00	469.00
206	686.00	704.00	901.00	923.00	944.00	178	445.00	455.00	465.00	475.00
208	693.00	711.00	910.00	932.00	953.00	180	450.00	460.00	470.00	480.00
210	700.00	718.00	918.00	941.00	962.00	182	500.00	511.00	523.00	758.00
212	706.00	905.00	927.00	950.00	972.00	184	506.00	517.00	751.00	767.00
214	713.00	914.00	936.00	959.00	981.00	186	511.00	523.00	759.00	775.00
216	720.00	923.00	944.00	967.00	990.00	188	517.00	751.00	767.00	783.00
218	908.00	931.00	953.00	976.00	999.00	190	522.00	759.00	775.00	792.00

Length	WIDTH.				Length	90	92	94	96
	90	92	94	96	192	720.00	920.00	940.00	960.00
					194	909.00	930.00	950.00	970.00
					196	919.00	939.00	960.00	980.00
					198	928.00	949.00	970.00	990.00
90	202.00	------	------	------	200	937.00	958.00	979.00	1000.00
92	207.00	212.00	------	------	202	947.00	968.00	989.00	1010.00
94	211.00	216.00	221.00	------	204	956.00	977.00	999.00	1020.00
96	216.00	221.00	226.00	230.00	206	965.00	987.00	1009.00	1030.00
98	220.00	225.00	230.00	235.00	208	975.00	997.00	1018.00	1040.00
100	225.00	230.00	235.00	240.00	210	984.00	1006.00	1028.00	1050.00
102	229.00	235.00	240.00	245.00	212	994.00	1016.00	1038.00	1060.00

POLISHED PLATE GLASS.
Official List, July, 1895.

Length	WIDTH.—Continued.			
	90	92	94	96
214	1003.00	1025.00	1048.00	1070.00
216	1012.00	1035.00	1057.00	1080.00
218	1022.00	1045.00	1067.00	1090.00

Length	WIDTH.			
	98	100	102	104
98	240.00	------	------	------
100	245.00	250.00	------	------
102	250.00	255.00	260.00	------
104	255.00	260.00	265.00	270.00
106	260.00	265.00	270.00	276.00
108	265.00	270.00	275.00	281.00
110	269.00	275.00	280.00	286.00
112	274.00	280.00	285.00	291.00
114	279.00	285.00	290.00	296.00
116	284.00	290.00	296.00	302.00
118	289.00	295.00	301.00	307.00
120	294.00	300.00	306.00	312.00
122	299.00	305.00	311.00	317.00
124	304.00	310.00	316.00	322.00
126	309.00	315.00	321.00	328.00
128	314.00	320.00	326.00	333.00
130	318.00	325.00	331.00	338.00
132	323.00	330.00	337.00	343.00
134	328.00	335.00	342.00	348.00
136	333.00	340.00	347.00	354.00
138	338.00	345.00	352.00	359.00
140	343.00	350.00	357.00	404·00
142	348.00	355.00	402.00	410.00
144	353.00	360.00	408.00	416.00
146	358.00	406.00	414.00	422.00
148	403.00	411.00	419.00	428.00
150	408.00	417.00	425.00	433.00
152	414.00	422.00	431.00	439.00
154	419.00	428.00	436.00	445.00
156	425.00	433.00	442.00	451.00
158	430.00	439.00	448.00	456.00
160	436.00	444.00	453.00	462.00
162	441.00	450.00	459.00	468.00
164	446.00	456.00	465.00	474.00
166	452.00	461.00	470.00	480.00
168	457.00	467.00	476.00	758.00
170	463.00	472.00	753.00	767.00
172	468.00	478.00	761.00	776.00
174	474.00	755.00	770.00	785.00
176	479.00	764.00	779.00	794.00
178	757.00	773.00	788.00	803.00
180	766.00	781.00	797.00	812.00
182	774.00	790.00	806.00	986.00
184	783.00	799.00	977.00	997.00
186	791·00	807.00	988.00	1007·00
188	800.00	979.00	999.00	1018.00
190	808.00	990.00	1009.00	1029.00
192	980.00	1000.00	1020.00	1040.00
194	990.00	1010.00	1031.00	1051.00

Length	WIDTH.—Continued.			
	98	100	102	104
196	1000.00	1021.00	1041.00	1062.00
198	1011.00	1031.00	1052.00	1072.00
200	1021.00	1042.00	1062.00	1083.00
202	1031.00	1052.00	1073.00	1094.00
204	1041.00	1062.00	1084.00	1105.00
206	1051.00	1073.00	1094.00	1116.00
208	1062.00	1083.00	1105.00	1314.00
210	1072.00	1094.00	1116.00	1327.00
212	1082.00	1104.00	1314.00	1340.00
214	1092.00	1115.00	1326.00	1352.00
216	1102.00	1125.00	1339.00	1365.00
218	1113.00	1325.00	1351.00	1378.00

Length	WIDTH.			
	106	108	110	112
106	281.00	------	------	------
108	286.00	292.00	------	------
110	291.00	297.00	302.00	------
112	297.00	302.00	308.00	348.00
114	302.00	308.00	314.00	355.00
116	307.00	313.00	319.00	361.00
118	313.00	319.00	324.00	367.00
120	318.00	324.00	330.00	373.00
122	323.00	329.00	335.00	380.00
124	329.00	335.00	341.00	386.00
126	334.00	340.00	346.00	392.00
128	339.00	346.00	352.00	398.00
130	345.00	351.00	357.00	404.00
132	350.00	356.00	403.00	411.00
134	355.00	402.00	409.00	417.00
136	400.00	408.00	415.00	423.00
138	406.00	414.00	422.00	429.00
140	412.00	420.00	428.00	436.00
142	418.00	426.00	434.00	442.00
144	424.00	432.00	440.00	448.00
146	430.00	438.00	446.00	454.00
148	436.00	444.00	452.00	460.00
150	442.00	450.00	458.00	467.00
152	448.00	456.00	464.00	473.00
154	453.00	462.00	471.00	479.00
156	459.00	468.00	477.00	758.00
158	465.00	474.00	754.00	768.00
160	471.00	480.00	764.00	778.00
162	477.00	759.00	773.00	787.00
164	755.00	769.00	783.00	797.00
166	764.00	778.00	793.00	807.00
168	773.00	787.00	802.00	980.00
170	782.00	797.00	812.00	992.00
172	791.00	806.00	985.00	1003.00
174	801.00	979.00	997.00	1015.00
176	810.00	990.00	1008.00	1027.00
178	983.00	1001.00	1020.00	1038.00
180	994.00	1012.00	1031.00	1050.00
182	1005.00	1024.00	1043.00	1062.00
184	1016.00	1035.00	1054.00	1073.00

POLISHED PLATE GLASS.

Official List, July, 1895.

Length	WIDTH.—Continued. 106	108	110	112
186	1027.00	1046.00	1066.00	1085.00
188	1038.00	1057.00	1077.00	1097.00
190	1049.00	1069.00	1089.00	1108.00
192	1060.00	1080.00	1100.00	1120.00
194	1071.00	1091.00	1111.00	1320.00
196	1082.00	1102.00	1123.00	1334.00
198	1093.00	1114.00	1323.00	1347.00
200	1104.00	1125.00	1337.00	1361.00
202	1115.00	1326.00	1350.00	1375.00
204	1314.00	1339.00	1364.00	1388.00
206	1327.00	1352.00	1377.00	1402.00
208	1340.00	1365.00	1390.00	1416.00
210	1353.00	1378.00	1404.00	1429.00
212	1365.00	1391.00	1417.00	1443.00
214	1378.00	1404.00	1430.00	1456.00
216	1391.00	1417.00	1444.00	1470.00
218	1404.00	1431.00	1457.00	1484.00

Length	WIDTH.—Continued. 114	116	118	120
182	1081.00	1100.00	1119.00	1327.00
184	1092.00	1112.00	1319.00	1342.00
186	1104.00	1124.00	1334.00	1356.00
188	1116.00	1325.00	1348.00	1371.00
190	1316.00	1339.00	1362.00	1385.00
192	1330.00	1353.00	1376.00	1400.00
194	1344.00	1367.00	1391.00	1415.00
196	1358.00	1382.00	1405.00	1429.00
198	1372.00	1396.00	1419.00	1444.00
200	1385.00	1410.00	1434.00	1458.00
202	1399.00	1424.00	1448.00	1473.00
204	1413.00	1438.00	1463.00	1487.00
206	1427.00	1452.00	1477.00	1502.00
208	1441.00	1466.00	1491.00	1517.00
210	1455.00	1480.00	1506.00	1531.00
212	1469.00	1494.00	1520.00	2208.00
214	1482.00	1508.00	2192.00	2229.00
216	1496.00	1522.00	2212.00	2250.00
218	1510.00	2195.00	2233.00	2271.00

Length	WIDTH. 114	116	118	120
114	361.00	------	------	------
116	367.00	374.00	------	------
118	374.00	380.00	387.00	------
120	380.00	387.00	393.00	400.00
122	386.00	393.00	400.00	407.00
124	393.00	400.00	406.00	413.00
126	399.00	406.00	413.00	420.00
128	405.00	412.00	420.00	427.00
130	412.00	419.00	426.00	433.00
132	418.00	425.00	433.00	440.00
134	424.00	432.00	439.00	447.00
136	431.00	438.00	446.00	453.00
138	437.00	445.00	452.00	460.00
140	443.00	451.00	459.00	467.00
142	450.00	457.00	465.00	473.00
144	456.00	464.00	472.00	480.00
146	462.00	470.00	479.00	760.00
148	469.00	477.00	758.00	771.00
150	475.00	755.00	768.00	781.00
152	752.00	765.00	778.00	792.00
154	762.00	775.00	789.00	802.00
156	772.00	785.00	799.00	812.00
158	782.00	795.00	809.00	987.00
160	792.00	805.00	983.00	1000.00
162	802.00	979.00	996.00	1012.00
164	812.00	991.00	1008.00	1025.00
166	986.00	1003.00	1020.00	1037.00
168	997.00	1015.00	1032.00	1050.00
170	1009.00	1027.00	1045.00	1062.00
172	1021.00	1039.00	1057.00	1075.00
174	1033.00	1051.00	1069.00	1087.00
176	1045.00	1063.00	1082.00	1100.00
178	1057.00	1075.00	1094.00	1112.00
180	1069.00	1087.00	1106.00	1125.00

Length	WIDTH. 122	124	126	128
122	455.00	------	------	------
124	462.00	470.00	------	------
126	470.00	477.00	485.00	------
128	478.00	485.00	493.00	501.00
130	485.00	493.00	501.00	509.00
132	493.00	501.00	508.00	516.00
134	500.00	509.00	516.00	524.00
136	507.00	516.00	524.00	756.00
138	515.00	523.00	755.00	767.00
140	522.00	753.00	766.00	778.00
142	752.00	764.00	777.00	789.00
144	762.00	775.00	787.00	800.00
146	773.00	786.00	798.00	811.00
148	784.00	796.00	809.00	987.00
150	794.00	807.00	984.00	1000.00
152	805.00	982.00	997.00	1013.00
154	979.00	995.00	1011.00	1027.00
156	991.00	1007.00	1024.00	1040.00
158	1004.00	1020.00	1037.00	1053.00
160	1017.00	1033.00	1050.00	1067.00
162	1029.00	1046.00	1063.00	1080.00
164	1042.00	1059.00	1076.00	1093.00
166	1055.00	1072.00	1089.00	1107.00
168	1067.00	1085.00	1102.00	1120.00
170	1080.00	1098.00	1116.00	1322.00
172	1093.00	1111.00	1317.00	1338.00
174	1106 00	1124.00	1332.00	1353.00
176	1118.00	1326.00	1347.00	1369.00
178	1320.00	1341.00	1363.00	1384.00
180	1334.00	1356.00	1378.00	1400.00
182	1349.00	1371.00	1393.00	1416.00
184	1364.00	1386.00	1409.00	1431.00
186	1379.00	1401.00	1424.00	1447.00

POLISHED PLATE GLASS.

Official List, July, 1895.

Length	WIDTH.—Continued.				Length	WIDTH.—Continued.			
	122	124	126	128		130	132	134	136
188	1394.00	1417.00	1439.00	1462.00	194	2189.00	2223.00	2257.00	2290 00
190	1408.00	1432.00	1455.00	1478.00	196	2212.00	2246.00	2280.00	2314.00
192	1423.00	1447.00	1470.00	1493.00	198	2234.00	2269.00	2303.00	2337.00
194	1438.00	1462.00	1485.00	1509.00	200	2257.00	2292.00	2326.00	2361.00
196	1453.00	1477.00	1501.00	1524.00	202	2280.00	2315.00	2350.00	2385.00
198	1468.00	1492.00	1516.00	2200.00	204	2302.00	2337.00	2373.00	2408.00
200	1483.00	1507.00	1531.00	2222.00	206	2325.00	2360.00	2396.00	2432.00
202	1497.00	1522.00	2209.00	2244.00	208	2347.00	2383.00	2419.00	2456.00
204	1512.00	2196.00	2231.00	2267.00	210	2370.00	2406.00	2443.00	2479.00
206	1527.00	2217.00	2253.00	2289.00	212	2392.00	2429.00	2466.00	------
208	2203.00	2239.00	2275.00	2311.00	214	2415.00	2452.00	2489.00	------
210	2224.00	2260.00	2297.00	2333.00	216	2437.00	2475.00	------	------
212	2245.00	2282.00	2319.00	2356.00	218	2460.00	2498.00	------	------
214	2266.00	2303.00	2341.00	2378.00					
216	2287.00	2325.00	2362.00	2400.00					
218	2309.00	2347.00	2384.00	2422.00					

Length	WIDTH.			
	138	140	142	144
138	992.00	------	------	------
140	1006.00	1021.00	------	------
142	1021.00	1035.00	1400.00	------
144	1035.00	1050.00	1420.00	1440.00
146	1049.00	1065.00	1440.00	1460.00
148	1064.00	1079.00	1460.00	1480.00
150	1078.00	1094.00	1480 00	1500.00
152	1092.00	1108.00	1500.00	1520.00
154	1107.00	1123.00	1519.00	1540.00
156	1121.00	1327.00	1538.00	1560.00
158	1325.00	1344.00	1558.00	1580.00
160	1342.00	1361.00	1578.00	1600.00
162	1358.00	1378.00	1598.00	1620.00
164	1375.00	1395.00	1617.00	1640.00
166	1392.00	1412.00	1637.00	1660.00
168	1409.00	1429.00	1657.00	1680.00
170	1426.00	1446.00	1676.00	1700.00
172	1442.00	1463.00	1696.00	1720.00
174	1459.00	1480.00	1716.00	1740.00
176	1476.00	1497.00	1736.00	2200.00
178	1493.00	1514.00	2194.00	2225.00
180	1509.00	1531.00	2219.00	2250.00
182	1526.00	2212.00	2243.00	2275.00
184	2204.00	2236.00	2268.00	2300.00
186	2228.00	2260.00	2293.00	2325.00
188	2252.00	2285.00	2317.00	2350.00
190	2276.00	2309.00	2342.00	2375.00
192	2300.00	2333.00	2367.00	2400.00
194	2324.00	2358.00	2391.00	2425.00
196	2348.00	2382.00	2416.00	2450.00
198	2372.00	2406.00	2441.00	2475.00
200	2396.00	2431.00	2465.00	2500.00
202	2420.00	2455.00	2490.00	------
204	2444.00	2479.00	------	------
206	2468.00	------	------	------
208	2492.00	------	------	------

Length	WIDTH.			
	130	132	134	136
130	516.00	------	------	------
132	525.00	847.00	------	------
134	756.00	860.00	873.00	------
136	767.00	873.00	886.00	899.00
138	779.00	886.00	899.00	977.00
140	790.00	898.00	977.00	992.00
142	801.00	976.00	991.00	1006.00
144	812.00	990.00	1005.00	1020.00
146	989.00	1004.00	1019.00	1034.00
148	1002.00	1017.00	1033.00	1048.00
150	1016.00	1031.00	1047.00	1062.00
152	1029.00	1045.00	1061.00	1077.00
154	1043.00	1059.00	1075.00	1091.00
156	1056.00	1072.00	1089.00	1105.00
158	1070.00	1086.00	1103.00	1119.00
160	1083.00	1100.00	1117.00	1329.00
162	1097.00	1114.00	1319.00	1339.00
164	1110.00	1315.00	1335.00	1355.00
166	1124.00	1331.00	1352.00	1372.00
168	1327.00	1347.00	1368.00	1388.00
170	1343.00	1364.00	1384.00	1405.00
172	1359.00	1380.00	1400.00	1421.00
174	1374.00	1396.00	1417.00	1438.00
176	1390.00	1412.00	1433.00	1454.00
178	1406.00	1428.00	1449.00	1471.00
180	1422.00	1444.00	1466.00	1487.00
182	1438.00	1460.00	1482.00	1504.00
184	1453.00	1476.00	1498.00	1521.00
186	1469.00	1492.00	1514.00	2196.00
188	1485.00	1508.00	1531.00	2219.00
190	1501.00	1524.00	2210.00	2243.00
192	1517.00	2200.00	2233.00	2267.00

OFFICIAL

MOULDING BOOK

(ILLUSTRATED)

SHOWING FULL FINISHED SIZE OF

MOULDINGS

WITH EXACT SIZE AND LIST PRICE PER ONE HUNDRED
LINEAL FEET MARKED ON EACH.

ADOPTED MARCH 1, 1897.

REVISED MAY 2, 1901.

PUBLISHED BY

THE CHICAGO MILLWORK AND MOULDING COMPANY,

CANALPORT AVE. AND SANGAMON ST.

CHICAGO.

CROWN MOULDINGS.

List Prices as given are per 100 lineal feet.

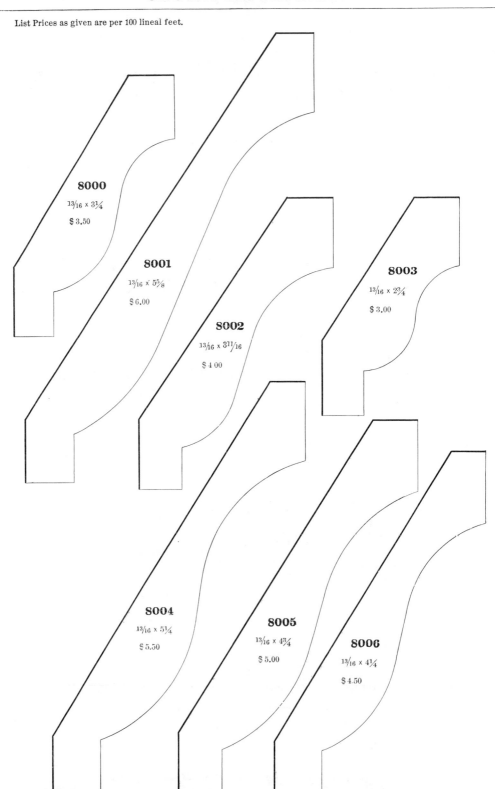

8000

$13/16 \times 3\frac{1}{4}$

$ 3.50

8001

$13/16 \times 5\frac{5}{8}$

$ 6.00

8002

$13/16 \times 3\frac{11}{16}$

$ 4 00

8003

$13/16 \times 2\frac{3}{4}$

$ 3.00

8004

$13/16 \times 5\frac{1}{4}$

$ 5.50

8005

$13/16 \times 4\frac{3}{4}$

$ 5.00

8006

$13/16 \times 4\frac{1}{4}$

$ 4.50

List Prices as given are per 100 lineal feet.

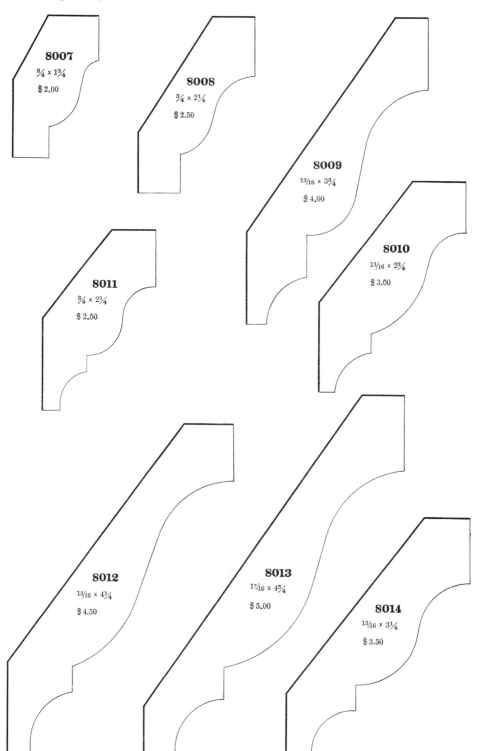

8007
¾ x 1¾
$ 2.00

8008
¾ x 2¼
$ 2.50

8009
13/16 x 3¾
$ 4.00

8011
¾ x 2¼
$ 2.50

8010
13/16 x 2¾
$ 3.00

8012
13/16 x 4¼
$ 4.50

8013
1 3/16 x 4¾
$ 5.00

8014
13/16 x 3¼
$ 3.50

List Prices as given are per 100 lineal feet.

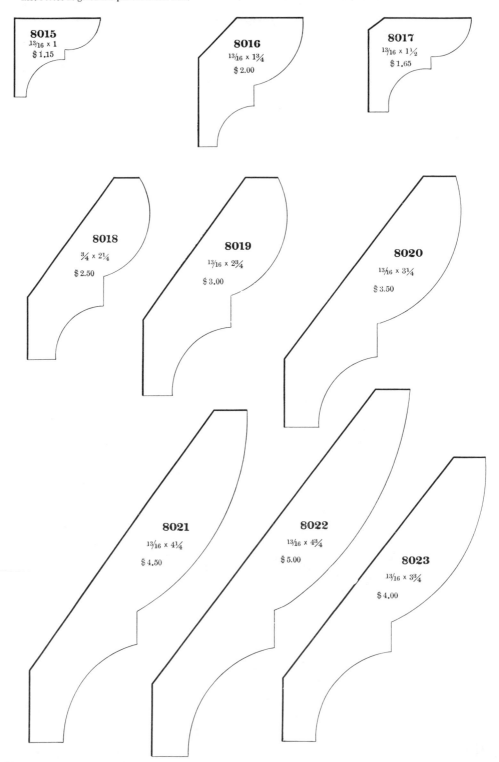

8015
13/16 x 1
$ 1.15

8016
13/16 x 1¾
$ 2.00

8017
13/16 x 1½
$ 1.65

8018
¾ x 2¼
$ 2.50

8019
13/16 x 2¾
$ 3.00

8020
13/16 x 3¼
$ 3.50

8021
13/16 x 4¼
$ 4.50

8022
13/16 x 4¾
$ 5.00

8023
13/16 x 3¾
$ 4.00

List Prices as given are per 100 lineal feet.

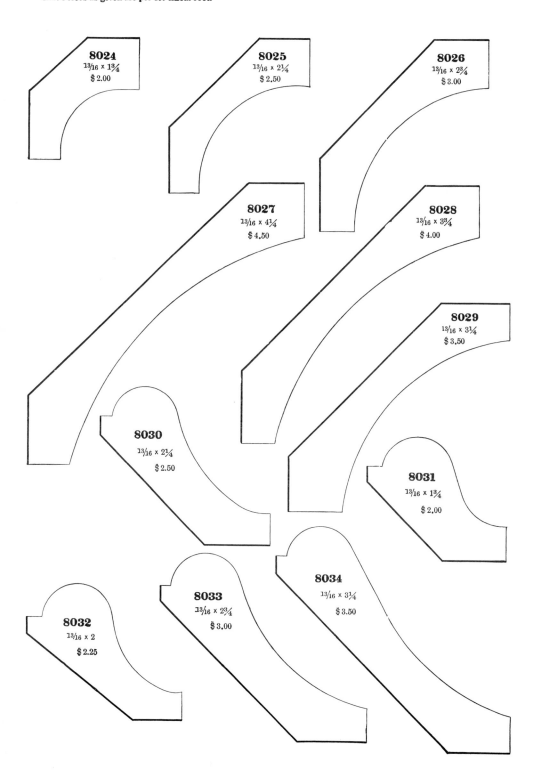

8024
13/16 x 13/4
$ 2.00

8025
13/16 x 21/4
$ 2.50

8026
13/16 x 23/4
$ 3.00

8027
13/16 x 41/4
$ 4.50

8028
13/16 x 33/4
$ 4.00

8029
13/16 x 31/4
$ 3.50

8030
13/16 x 21/4
$ 2.50

8031
13/16 x 13/4
$ 2.00

8032
13/16 x 2
$ 2.25

8033
13/16 x 23/4
$ 3.00

8034
13/16 x 31/4
$ 3.50

List Prices as given are per 100 lineal feet.

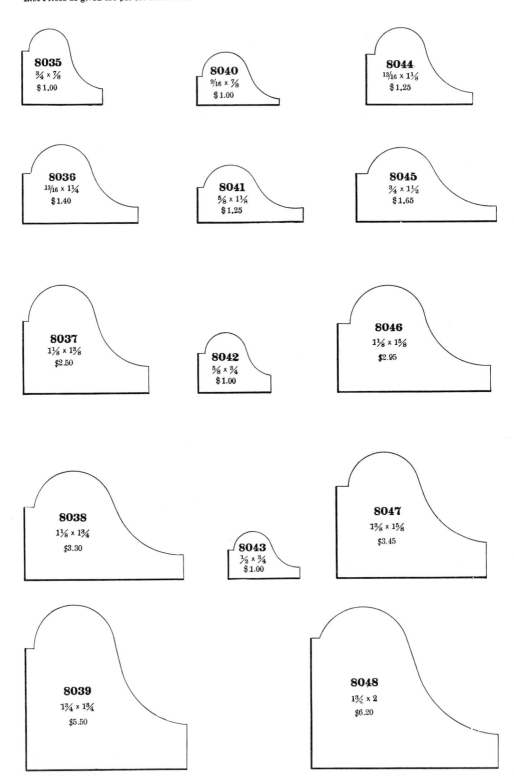

8035
¾ × ⅞
$1.00

8040
9/16 × ⅞
$1.00

8044
13/16 × 1⅛
$1.25

8036
13/16 × 1¼
$1.40

8041
⅝ × 1⅛
$1.25

8045
¾ × 1½
$1.65

8037
1⅛ × 1⅜
$2.50

8042
⅝ × ¾
$1.00

8046
1⅛ × 1⅝
$2.95

8038
1⅛ × 1¾
$3.30

8043
½ × ¾
$1.00

8047
1⅜ × 1⅝
$3.45

8039
1¾ × 1¾
$5.50

8048
1¾ × 2
$6.20

List Prices as given are per 100 lineal feet.

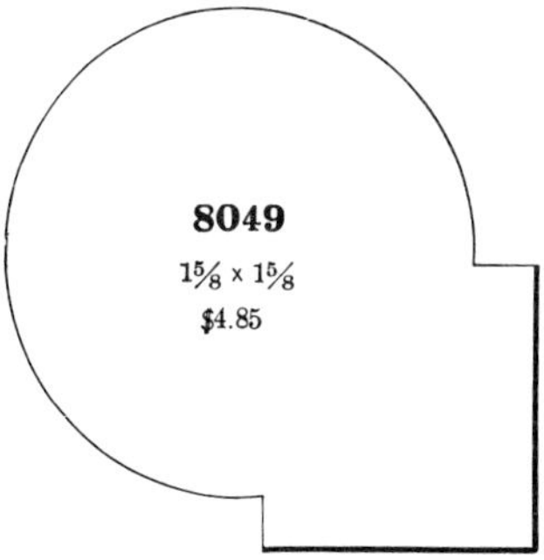
8049
1⅝ x 1⅝
$4.85

8054
13/16 x 1
$1.15

8058
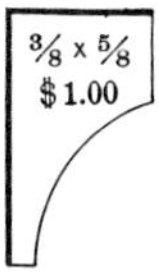
⅜ x ⅝
$1.00

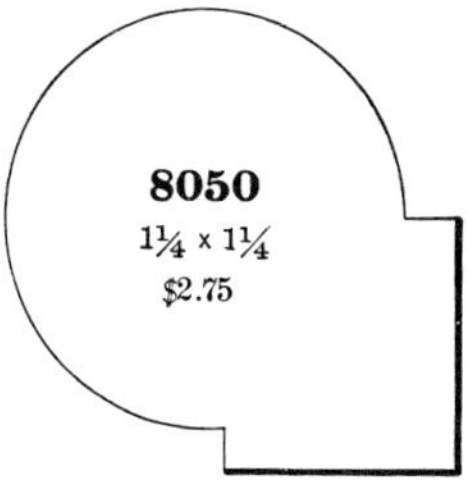
8050
1¼ x 1¼
$2.75

8055
1⅜
$3.30

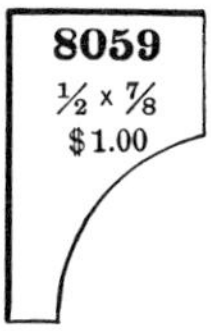
8059
½ x ⅞
$1.00

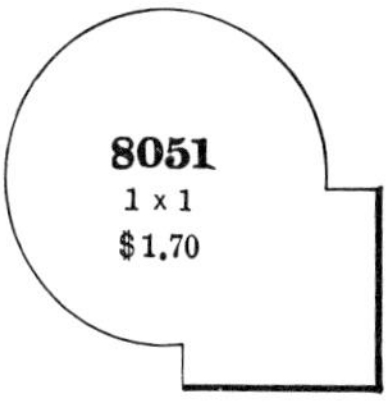
8051
1 x 1
$1.70

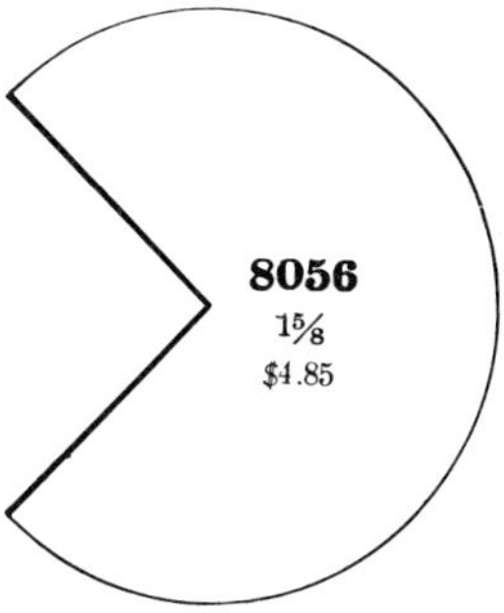
8056
1⅝
$4.85

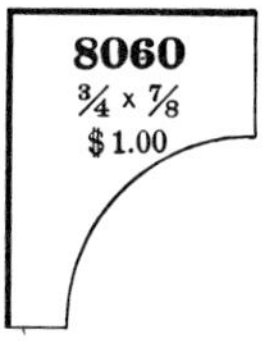
8060
¾ x ⅞
$1.00

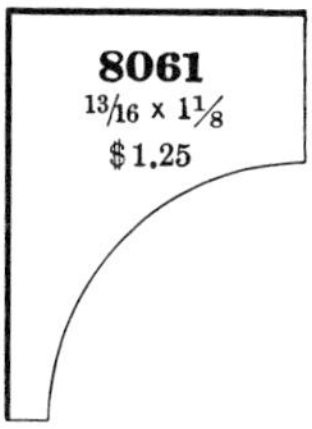
8061
13/16 x 1⅛
$1.25

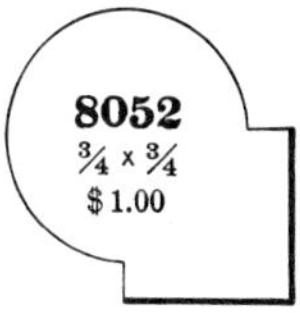
8052
¾ x ¾
$1.00

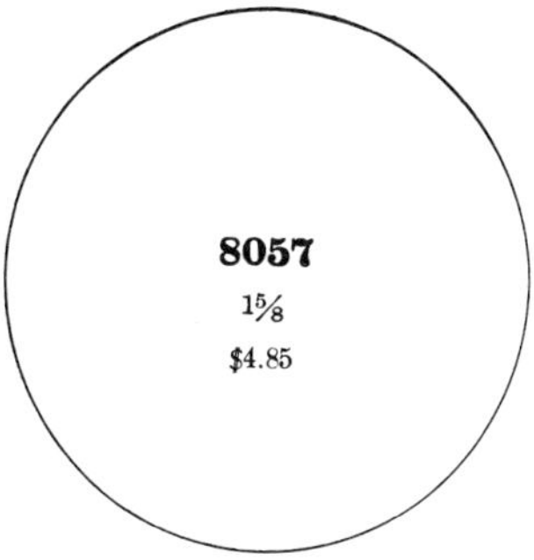
8057
1⅝
$4.85

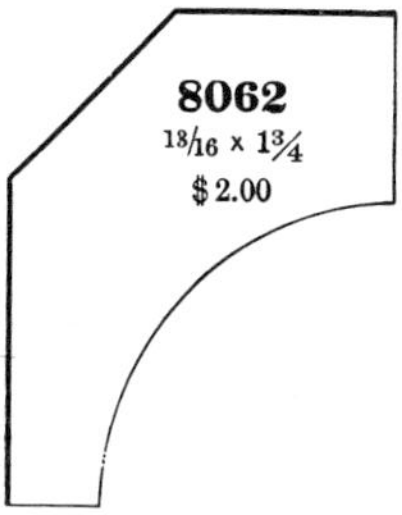
8062
13/16 x 1¾
$2.00

8053
⅝ x ⅝
$1.00

List Prices as given are per 100 lineal feet.

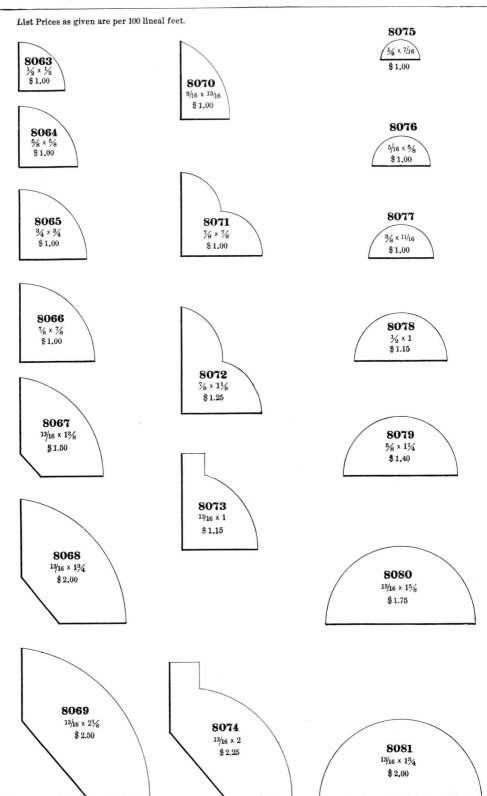

8075
¼ x ⁷⁄₁₆
$ 1.00

8063
½ x ½
$ 1.00

8070
⁹⁄₁₆ x ¹³⁄₁₆
$ 1.00

8064
⅝ x ⅝
$ 1.00

8076
⁵⁄₁₆ x ⅝
$ 1.00

8065
¾ x ¾
$ 1.00

8071
⅞ x ⅞
$ 1.00

8077
⅜ x ¹¹⁄₁₆
$ 1.00

8066
⅞ x ⅞
$ 1.00

8078
½ x 1
$ 1.15

8072
⅞ x 1⅛
$ 1.25

8067
¹³⁄₁₆ x 1⅜
$ 1.50

8079
⅝ x 1¼
$ 1.40

8073
¹³⁄₁₆ x 1
$ 1.15

8068
¹³⁄₁₆ x 1¾
$ 2.00

8080
¹³⁄₁₆ x 1⅝
$ 1.75

8069
¹³⁄₁₆ x 2⅛
$ 2.50

8074
¹³⁄₁₆ x 2
$ 2.25

8081
¹³⁄₁₆ x 1¾
$ 2.00

List Prices as given are per 100 lineal feet.

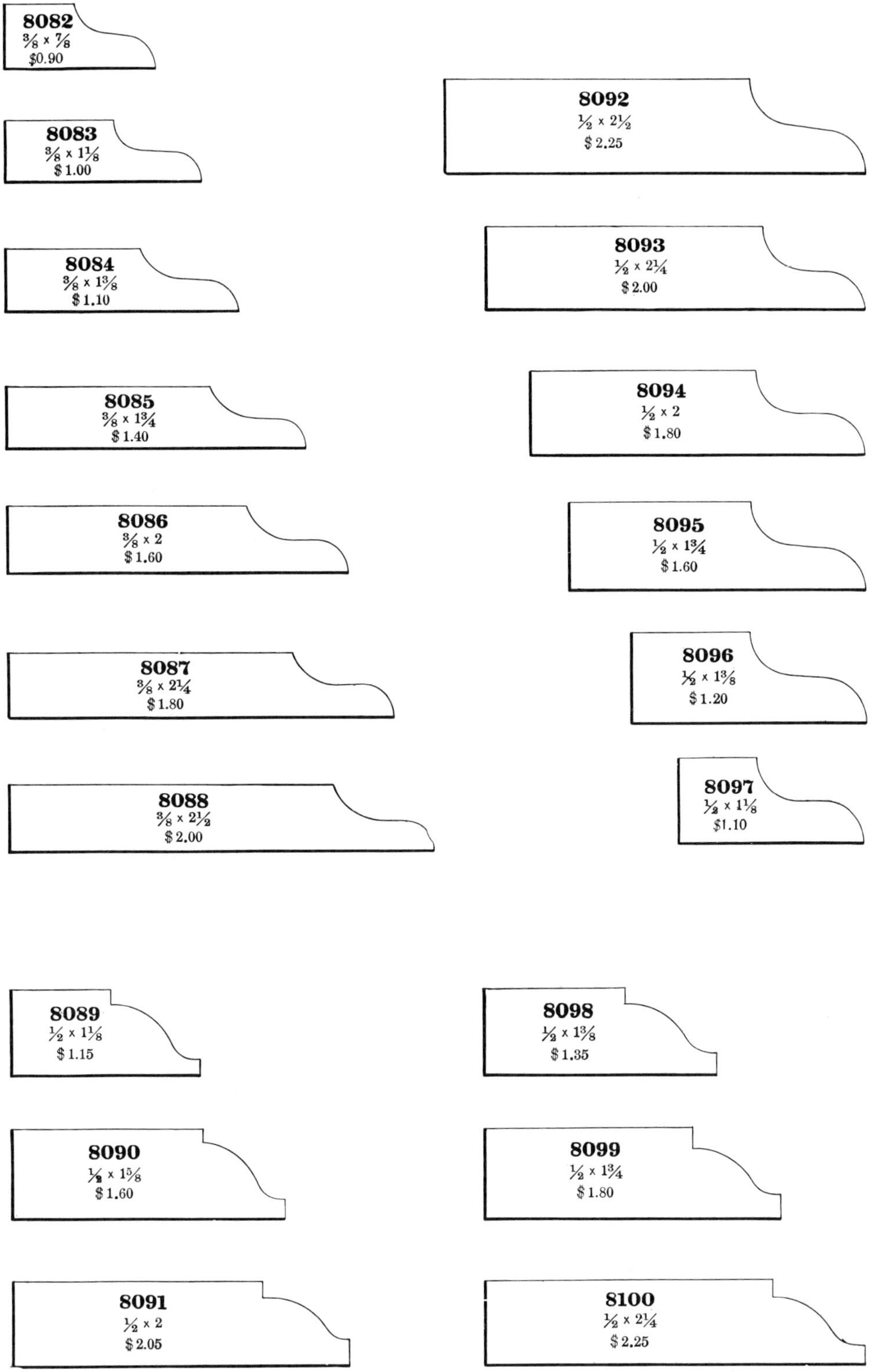

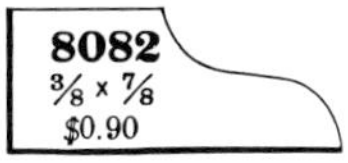

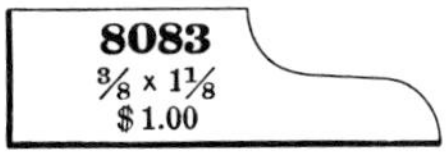

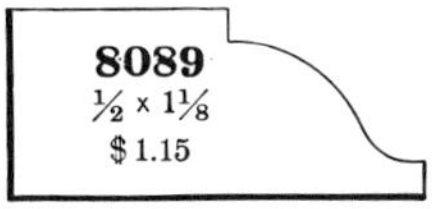

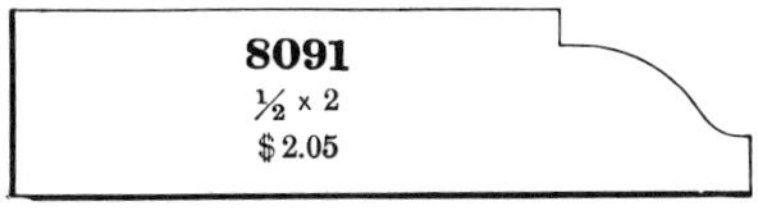

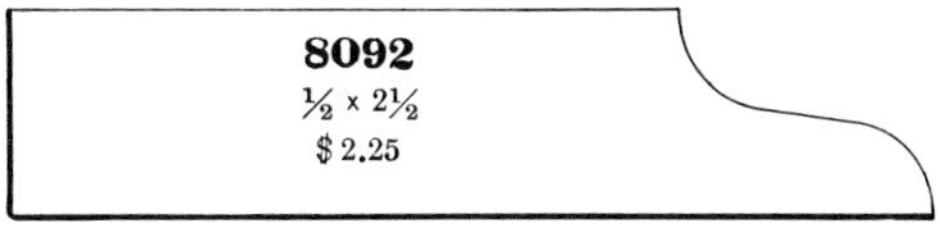

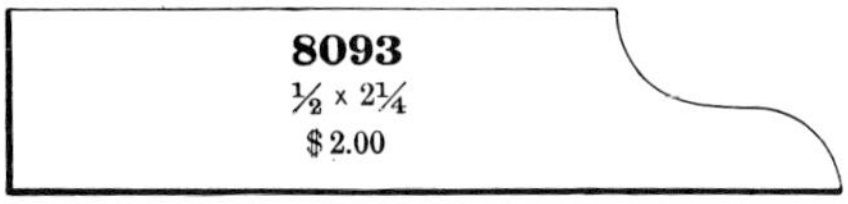

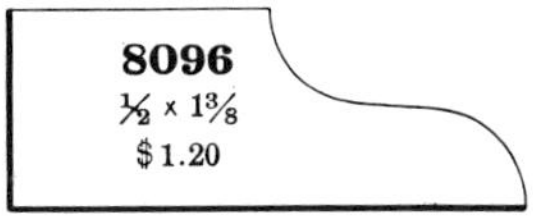

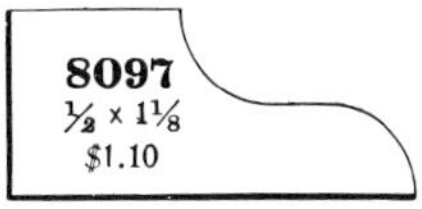

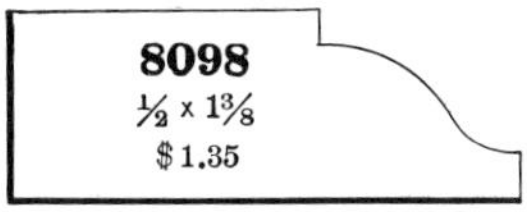

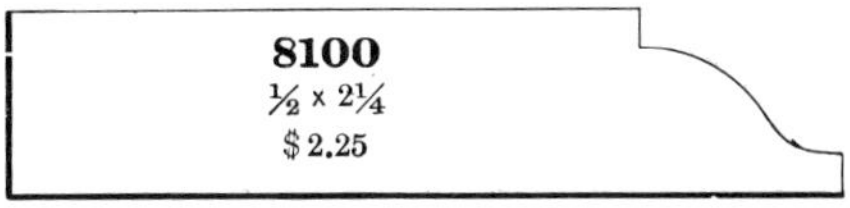

8082
⅜ × ⅞
$0.90

8083
⅜ × 1⅛
$1.00

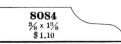

8084
⅜ × 1⅜
$1.10

8085
⅜ × 1¾
$1.40

8086
⅜ × 2
$1.60

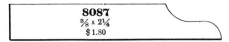

8087
⅜ × 2¼
$1.80

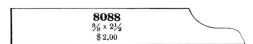

8088
⅜ × 2½
$2.00

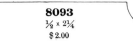

8092
½ × 2½
$2.25

8093
½ × 2¼
$2.00

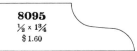

8094
½ × 2
$1.80

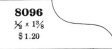

8095
½ × 1¾
$1.60

8096
½ × 1⅜
$1.20

8097
½ × 1⅛
$1.10

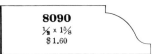

8089
½ × 1⅛
$1.15

8090
½ × 1⅝
$1.60

8091
½ × 2
$2.05

8098
½ × 1⅜
$1.35

8099
½ × 1¾
$1.80

8100
½ × 2¼
$2.25

P. G. AND BEAD STOPS.

List Prices as given are per 100 lineal feet.

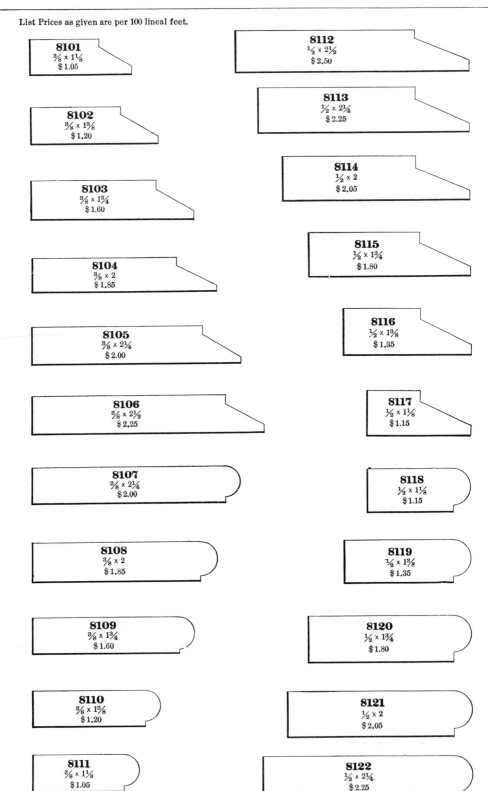

8101 — 3/8 x 1 1/8 — $1.05

8102 — 3/8 x 1 3/8 — $1.20

8103 — 3/8 x 1 3/4 — $1.60

8104 — 3/8 x 2 — $1.85

8105 — 3/8 x 2 1/4 — $2.00

8106 — 3/8 x 2 1/2 — $2.25

8107 — 3/8 x 2 1/4 — $2.00

8108 — 3/8 x 2 — $1.85

8109 — 3/8 x 1 3/4 — $1.60

8110 — 3/8 x 1 3/8 — $1.20

8111 — 3/8 x 1 1/8 — $1.05

8112 — 1/2 x 2 1/2 — $2.50

8113 — 1/2 x 2 1/4 — $2.25

8114 — 1/2 x 2 — $2.05

8115 — 1/2 x 1 3/4 — $1.80

8116 — 1/2 x 1 3/8 — $1.35

8117 — 1/2 x 1 1/8 — $1.15

8118 — 1/2 x 1 1/8 — $1.15

8119 — 1/2 x 1 3/8 — $1.35

8120 — 1/2 x 1 3/4 — $1.80

8121 — 1/2 x 2 — $2.05

8122 — 1/2 x 2 1/4 — $2.25

List Prices as given are per 100 lineal feet.

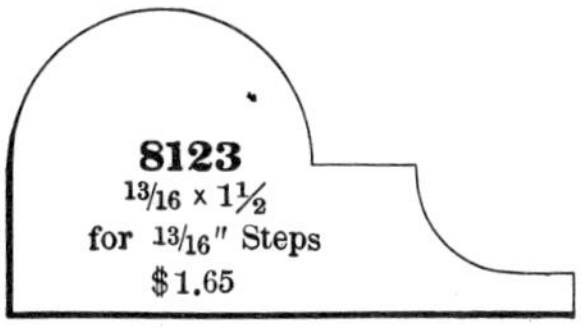

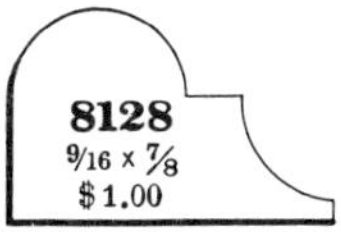

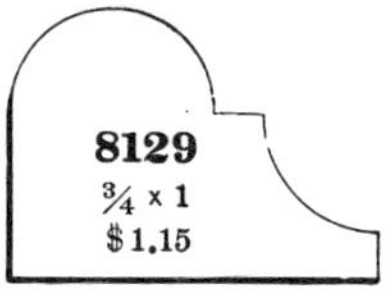

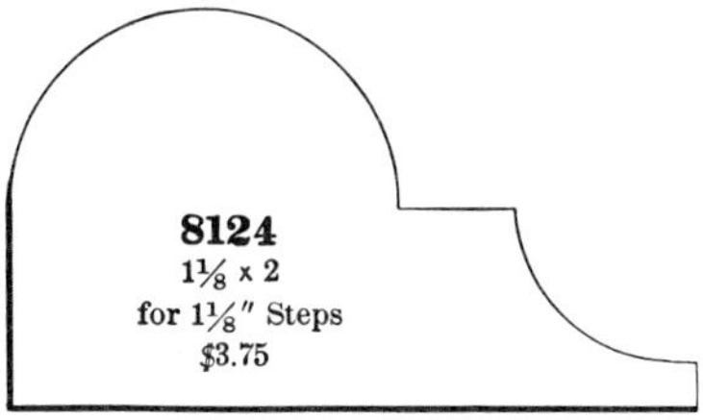

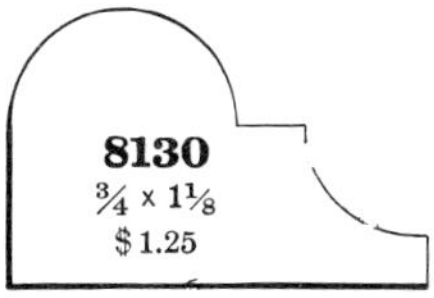

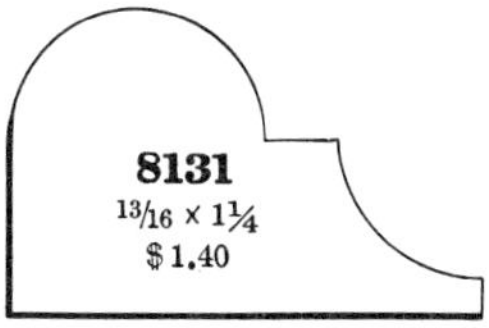

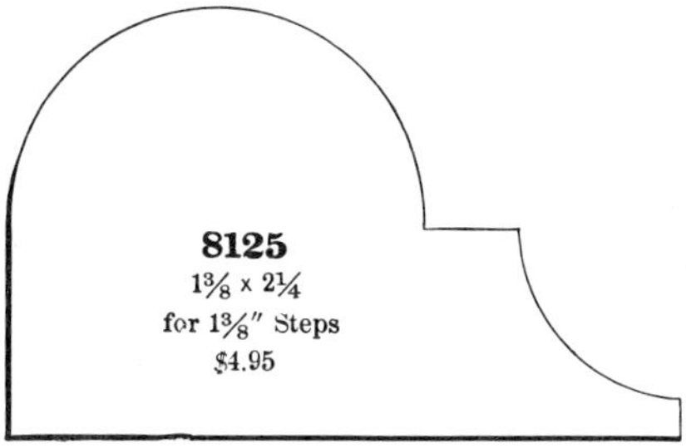

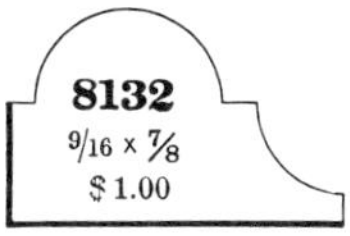

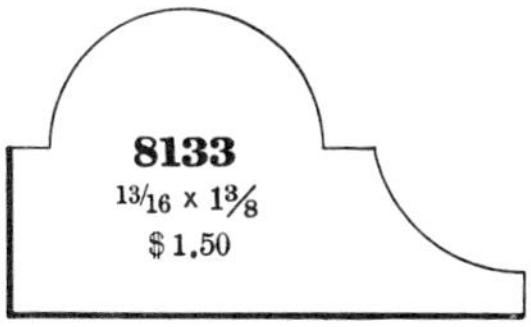

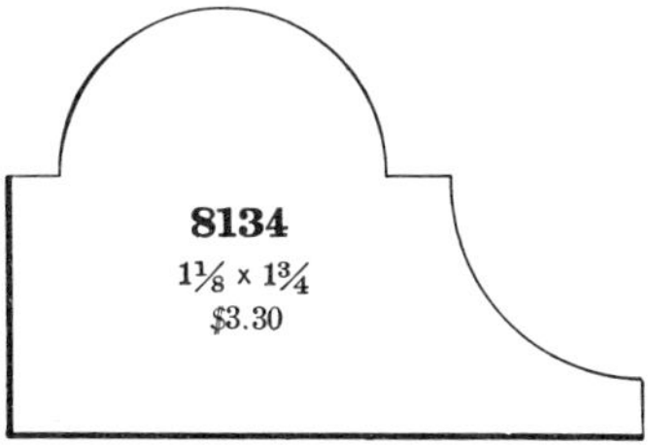

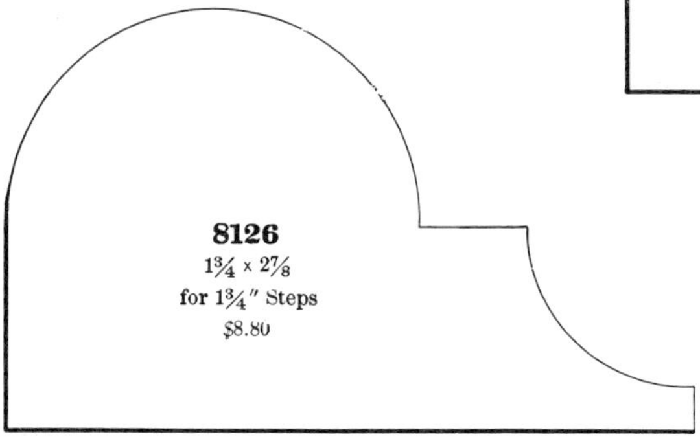

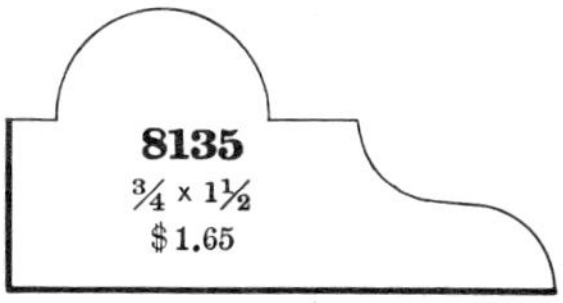

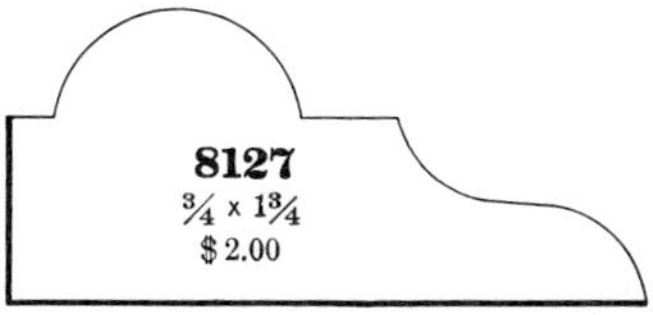

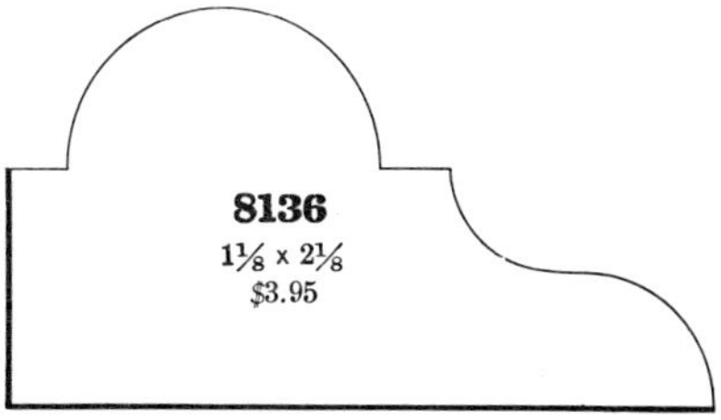

8123
13/16 × 1½
for 13/16″ Steps
$1.65

8128
9/16 × 7/8
$1.00

8129
¾ × 1
$1.15

8124
1⅛ × 2
for 1⅛″ Steps
$3.75

8130
¾ × 1⅛
$1.25

8131
13/16 × 1¼
$1.40

8125
1⅜ × 2¼
for 1⅜″ Steps
$4.95

8132
9/16 × 7/8
$1.00

8133
13/16 × 1⅜
$1.50

8134
1⅛ × 1¾
$3.30

8126
1¾ × 2⅞
for 1¾″ Steps
$8.80

8135
¾ × 1½
$1.65

8127
¾ × 1¾
$2.00

8136
1⅛ × 2⅛
$3.95

List Prices as given are per 100 lineal feet.

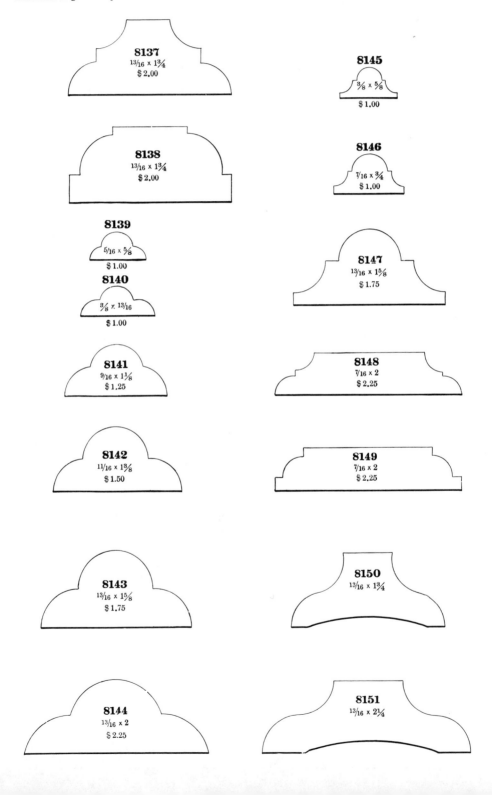

8137
13/16 x 1¾
$2.00

8145
⅜ x ⅝
$1.00

8138
13/16 x 1¾
$2.00

8146
7/16 x ¾
$1.00

8139
5/16 x ⅝
$1.00

8140
⅜ x 13/16
$1.00

8147
13/16 x 1⅝
$1.75

8141
9/16 x 1⅛
$1.25

8148
7/16 x 2
$2.25

8142
11/16 x 1⅜
$1.50

8149
7/16 x 2
$2.25

8143
13/16 x 1⅝
$1.75

8150
13/16 x 1¾

8144
13/16 x 2
$2.25

8151
13/16 x 2¼

List Prices as given are per 100 lineal feet.

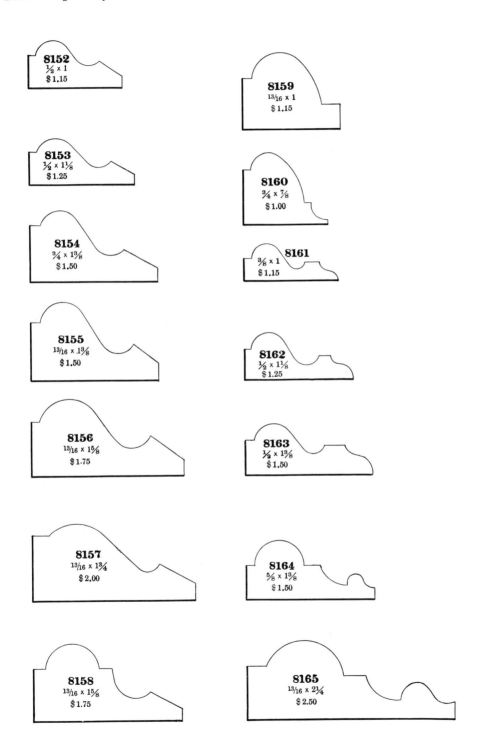

8152
½ x 1
$1.15

8153
½ x 1⅛
$1.25

8154
¾ x 1⅜
$1.50

8155
13/16 x 1⅜
$1.50

8156
13/16 x 1⅝
$1.75

8157
13/16 x 1¾
$2.00

8158
13/16 x 1⅝
$1.75

8159
13/16 x 1
$1.15

8160
¾ x ⅞
$1.00

8161
⅜ x 1
$1.15

8162
½ x 1⅛
$1.25

8163
½ x 1⅜
$1.50

8164
⅝ x 1⅜
$1.50

8165
13/16 x 2¼
$2.50

List Prices as given are per 100 lineal feet.

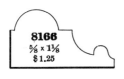

8166
⅝ x 1⅛
$1.25

8172
⁹⁄₁₆ x 1¾
$2.00

8167
⅝ x 1¼
$1.40

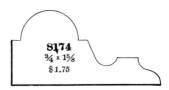

8173
¹³⁄₁₆ x 1¾
$2.00

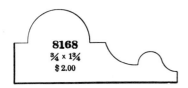

8168
¾ x 1¾
$2.00

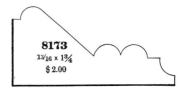

8174
¾ x 1⅝
$1.75

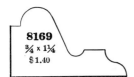

8169
¾ x 1¼
$1.40

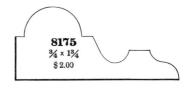

8175
¾ x 1¾
$2.00

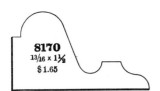

8170
¹³⁄₁₆ x 1⅛
$1.65

8176
¹³⁄₁₆ x 1¾
$2.00

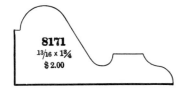

8171
¹³⁄₁₆ x 1¾
$2.00

8177
¹³⁄₁₆ x 2
$2.25

List Prices as given are per 100 lineal feet.

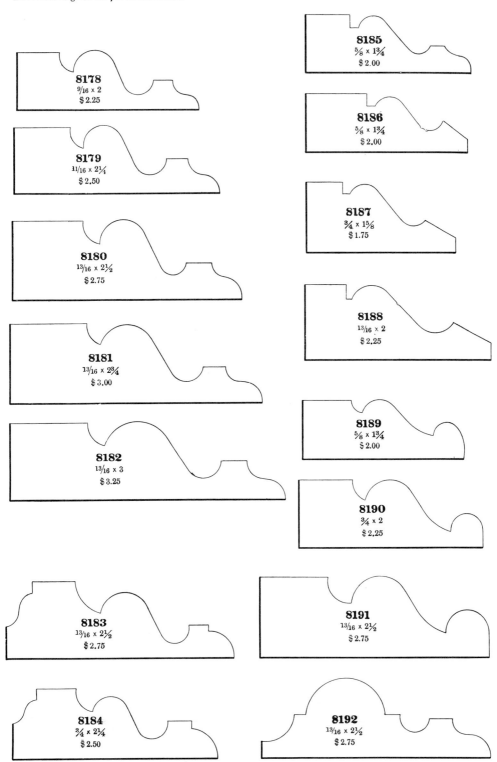

8178
9/16 x 2
$ 2.25

8179
11/16 x 2¼
$ 2.50

8180
13/16 x 2½
$ 2.75

8181
13/16 x 2¾
$ 3.00

8182
13/16 x 3
$ 3.25

8183
13/16 x 2½
$ 2.75

8184
¾ x 2¼
$ 2.50

8185
⅝ x 1¾
$ 2.00

8186
⅝ x 1¾
$ 2.00

8187
¾ x 1⅝
$ 1.75

8188
13/16 x 2
$ 2.25

8189
⅝ x 1¾
$ 2.00

8190
¾ x 2
$ 2.25

8191
13/16 x 2½
$ 2.75

8192
13/16 x 2½
$ 2.75

List Prices as given are per 100 lineal feet.

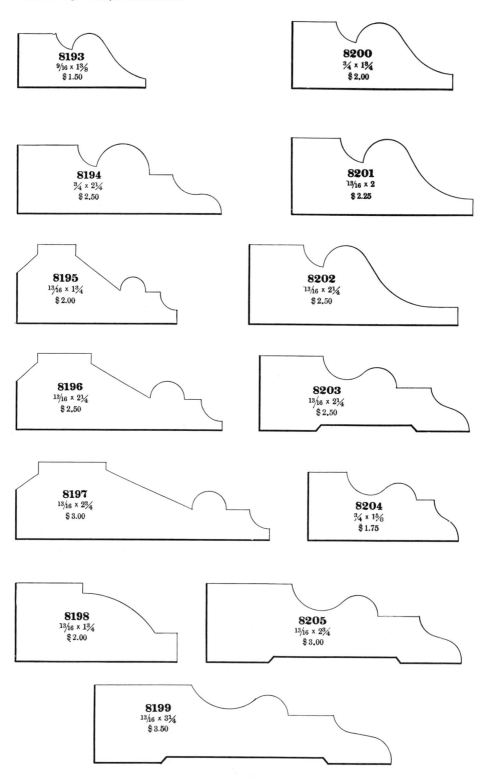

8193
9/16 x 1⅜
$ 1.50

8200
¾ x 1¾
$ 2.00

8194
¾ x 2¼
$ 2.50

8201
13/16 x 2
$ 2.25

8195
13/16 x 1¾
$ 2.00

8202
13/16 x 2¼
$ 2.50

8196
13/16 x 2¼
$ 2.50

8203
13/16 x 2¼
$ 2.50

8197
13/16 x 2¾
$ 3.00

8204
¾ x 1⅝
$ 1.75

8198
13/16 x 1¾
$ 2.00

8205
13/16 x 2¾
$ 3.00

8199
13/16 x 3¼
$ 3.50

List Prices as given are per 100 lineal feet.

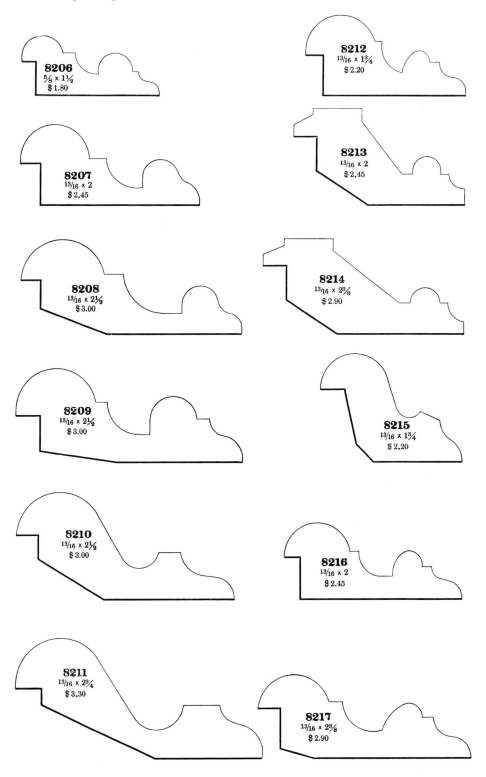

8206
5/8 x 1½
$1.80

8207
13/16 x 2
$2.45

8208
13/16 x 2½
$3.00

8209
13/16 x 2½
$3.00

8210
13/16 x 2½
$3.00

8211
13/16 x 2¾
$3.30

8212
13/16 x 1¾
$2.20

8213
13/16 x 2
$2.45

8214
13/16 x 2⅜
$2.90

8215
13/16 x 1¾
$2.20

8216
13/16 x 2
$2.45

8217
13/16 x 2⅜
$2.90

List Prices as given are per 100 lineal feet.

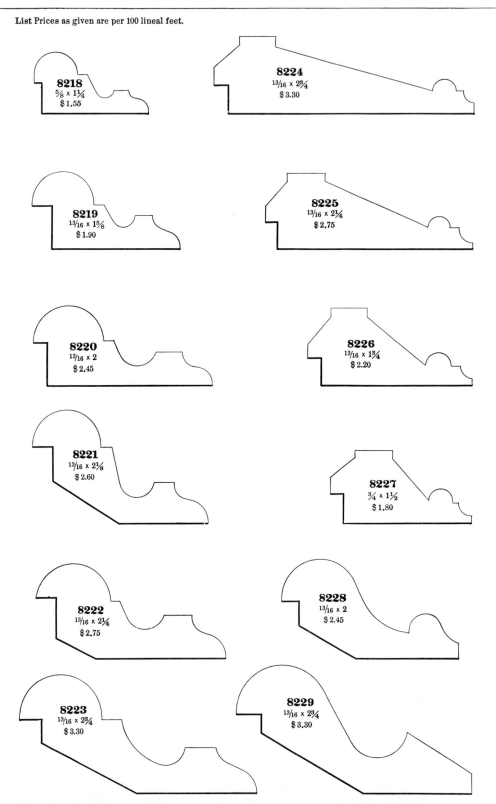

8218
$\frac{5}{8}$ x 1$\frac{1}{4}$
$ 1.55

8224
$\frac{13}{16}$ x 2$\frac{3}{4}$
$ 3.30

8219
$\frac{13}{16}$ x 1$\frac{5}{8}$
$ 1.90

8225
$\frac{13}{16}$ x 2$\frac{1}{4}$
$ 2.75

8220
$\frac{13}{16}$ x 2
$ 2.45

8226
$\frac{13}{16}$ x 1$\frac{3}{4}$
$ 2.20

8221
$\frac{13}{16}$ x 2$\frac{1}{8}$
$ 2.60

8227
$\frac{3}{4}$ x 1$\frac{1}{2}$
$ 1.80

8222
$\frac{13}{16}$ x 2$\frac{1}{4}$
$ 2.75

8228
$\frac{13}{16}$ x 2
$ 2.45

8223
$\frac{13}{16}$ x 2$\frac{3}{4}$
$ 3.30

8229
$\frac{13}{16}$ x 2$\frac{3}{4}$
$ 3.30

List Prices as given are per 100 lineal feet.

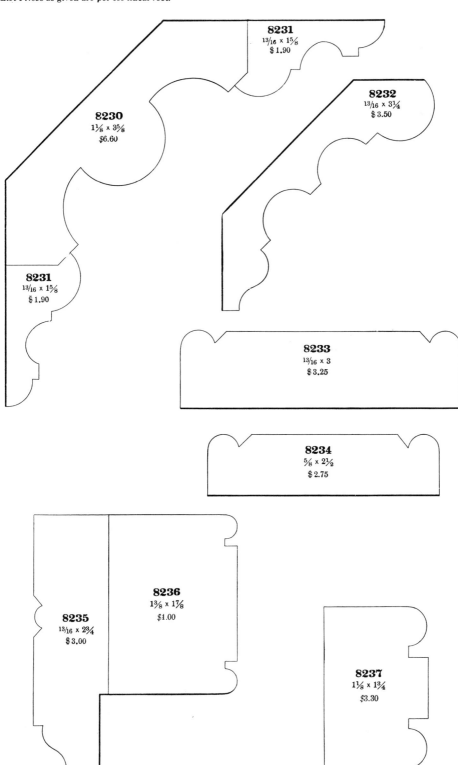

8231
13/16 x 1⅝
$1.90

8232
13/16 x 3¼
$3.50

8230
1⅛ x 3⅝
$6.60

8231
13/16 x 1⅝
$1.90

8233
13/16 x 3
$3.25

8234
⅝ x 2½
$2.75

8236
1⅜ x 1⅞
$1.00

8235
13/16 x 2¾
$3.00

8237
1⅛ x 1¾
$3.30

List Prices as given are per 100 lineal feet.

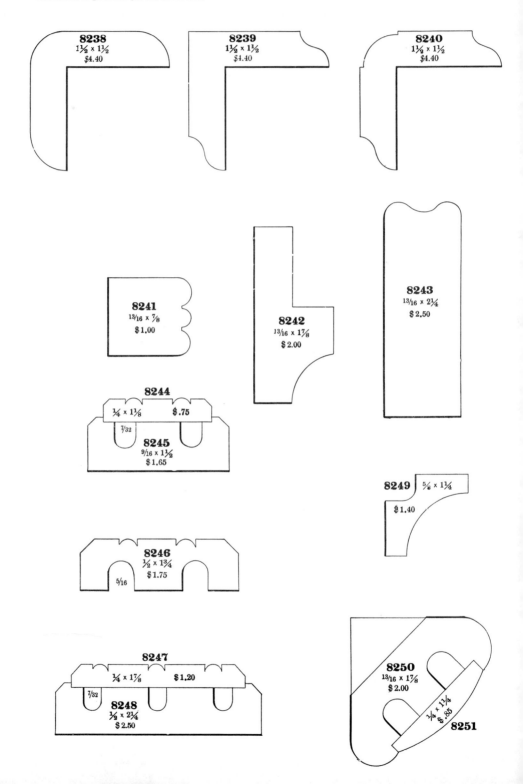

8238
1½ × 1½
$4.40

8239
1½ × 1½
$4.40

8240
1½ × 1½
$4.40

8241
13/16 × ⅞
$1.00

8242
13/16 × 1⅞
$2.00

8243
13/16 × 2¼
$2.50

8244
¼ × 1⅛ $.75
7/32

8245
9/16 × 1½
$1.65

8249   ⅝ × 1¼
$1.40

8246
½ × 1¾
$1.75
5/16

8247
¼ × 1⅞ $1.20
7/32

8248
½ × 2¼
$2.50

8250
13/16 × 1⅞
$2.00

¼ × 1¼
$.85
8251

List Prices as given are per 100 lineal feet.

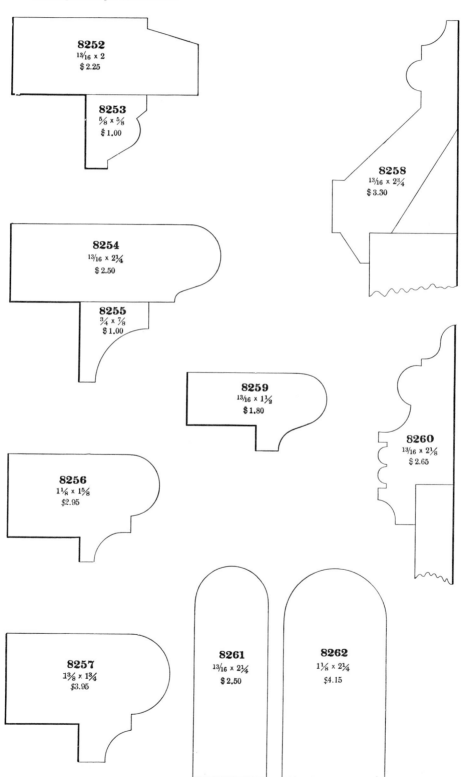

8252
$13/16 \times 2$
$ 2.25

8253
$5/8 \times 5/8$
$ 1.00

8258
$13/16 \times 2\frac{3}{4}$
$ 3.30

8254
$13/16 \times 2\frac{1}{4}$
$ 2.50

8255
$3/4 \times 7/8$
$ 1.00

8259
$13/16 \times 1\frac{1}{2}$
$ 1.80

8260
$13/16 \times 2\frac{1}{8}$
$ 2.65

8256
$1\frac{1}{4} \times 1\frac{5}{8}$
$2.95

8257
$1\frac{3}{8} \times 1\frac{3}{4}$
$3.95

8261
$13/16 \times 2\frac{1}{4}$
$ 2.50

8262
$1\frac{1}{8} \times 2\frac{1}{4}$
$4.15

List Prices as given are per 100 lineal feet.

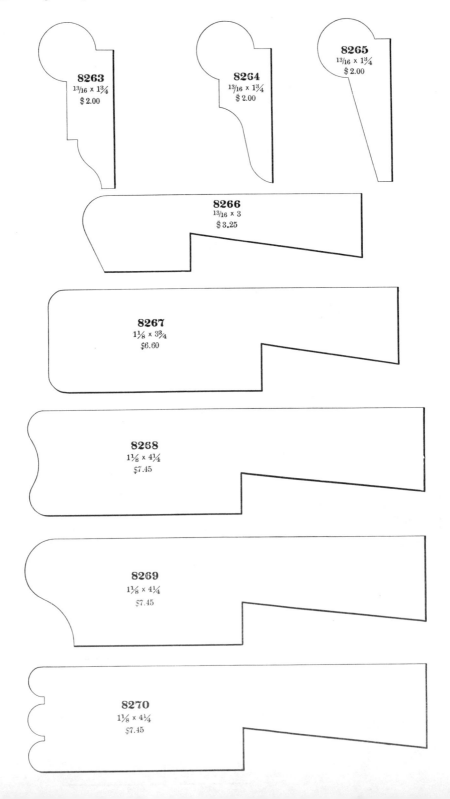

8263
13/16 x 13/4
$ 2.00

8264
13/16 x 13/4
$ 2.00

8265
13/16 x 13/4
$ 2.00

8266
13/16 x 3
$ 3.25

8267
1⅛ x 3¾
$6.60

8268
1⅛ x 4¼
$7.45

8269
1⅛ x 4¼
$7.45

8270
1⅛ x 4¼
$7.45

List Prices as given are per 100 lineal feet.

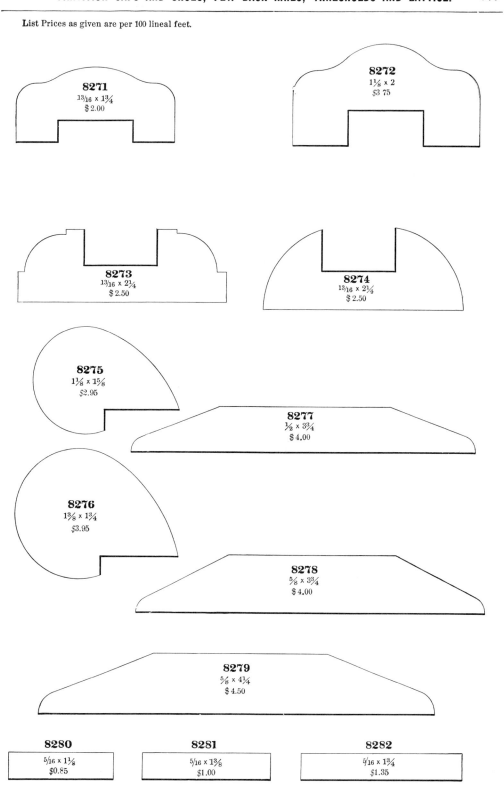

8271
$^{13}/_{16}$ x $1\frac{3}{4}$
$ 2.00

8272
$1\frac{1}{8}$ x 2
$3 75

8273
$^{13}/_{16}$ x $2\frac{1}{4}$
$ 2.50

8274
$^{13}/_{16}$ x $2\frac{1}{4}$
$ 2.50

8275
$1\frac{1}{8}$ x $1\frac{5}{8}$
$2.95

8277
$\frac{1}{2}$ x $3\frac{3}{4}$
$ 4.00

8276
$1\frac{3}{8}$ x $1\frac{3}{4}$
$3.95

8278
$\frac{5}{8}$ x $3\frac{3}{4}$
$ 4.00

8279
$\frac{5}{8}$ x $4\frac{1}{4}$
$ 4.50

8280
$^{5}/_{16}$ x $1\frac{1}{8}$
$0.85

8281
$^{5}/_{16}$ x $1\frac{3}{8}$
$1.00

8282
$^{5}/_{16}$ x $1\frac{3}{4}$
$1.35

List Prices as given are per 100 lineal feet.

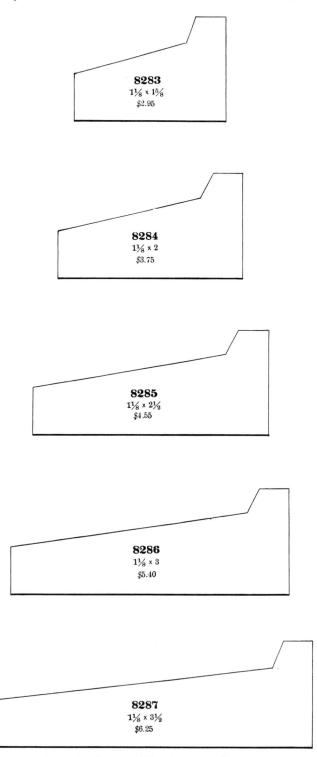

8283
1⅛ x 1⅝
$2.95

8284
1⅛ x 2
$3.75

8285
1⅛ x 2½
$4.55

8286
1⅛ x 3
$5.40

8287
1⅛ x 3½
$6.25

List Prices as given are per 100 lineal feet.

8288
$13/16 \times 3\frac{3}{4}$
$4.20

8289
$13/16 \times 4\frac{1}{4}$
$4.75

8290
$13/16 \times 4\frac{3}{4}$
$5.25

8291
$13/16 \times 5\frac{1}{4}$
$5.75

8292
$13/16 \times 3\frac{3}{4}$
$4 20

8293
$13/16 \times 4\frac{1}{4}$
$4 75

8294
$13/16 \times 4\frac{3}{4}$
$5.25

8295
$13/16 \times 5\frac{1}{4}$
$5.75

CASINGS.

List Prices as given are per 100 lineal feet.

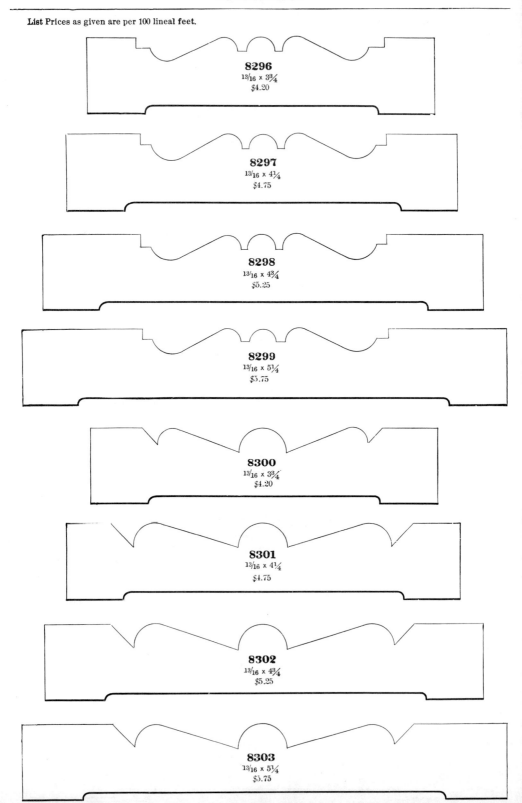

8296
13/16 x 3¾
$4.20

8297
13/16 x 4¼
$4.75

8298
13/16 x 4¾
$5.25

8299
13/16 x 5¼
$5.75

8300
13/16 x 3¾
$4.20

8301
13/16 x 4¼
$4.75

8302
13/16 x 4¾
$5.25

8303
13/16 x 5¼
$5.75

List Prices as given are per 100 lineal feet.

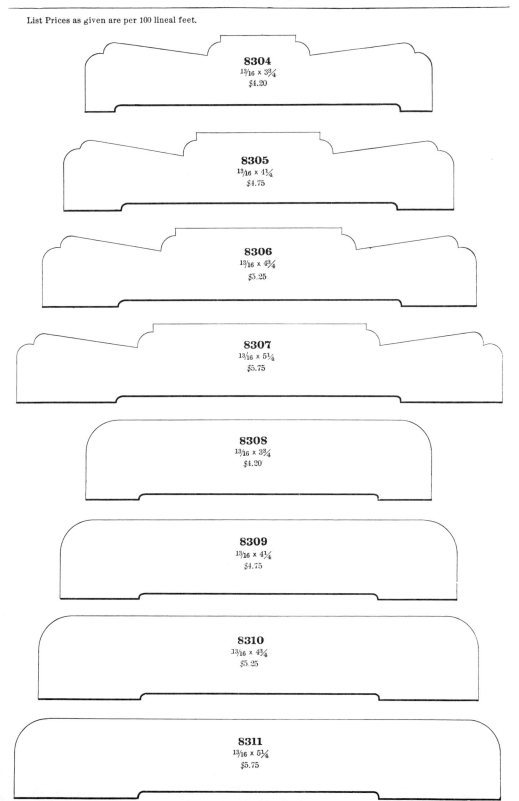

8304
13/16 x 3¾
$4.20

8305
13/16 x 4¼
$4.75

8306
13/16 x 4¾
$5.25

8307
13/16 x 5¼
$5.75

8308
13/16 x 3¾
$4.20

8309
13/16 x 4¼
$4.75

8310
13/16 x 4¾
$5.25

8311
13/16 x 5¼
$5.75

List Prices as given are per 100 lineal feet.

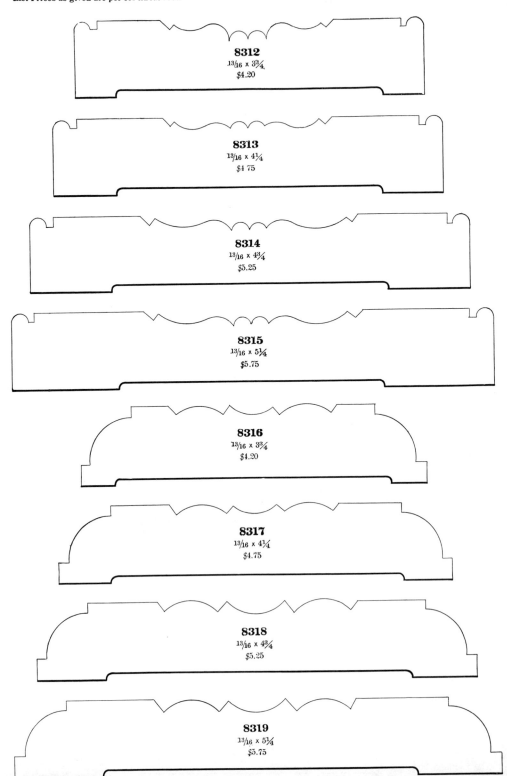

8312
13/16 x 3¾
$4.20

8313
13/16 x 4¼
$4 75

8314
13/16 x 4¾
$5.25

8315
13/16 x 5¼
$5.75

8316
13/16 x 3¾
$4.20

8317
13/16 x 4¼
$4.75

8318
13/16 x 4¾
$5.25

8319
13/16 x 5¼
$5.75

List Prices as given are per 100 lineal feet.

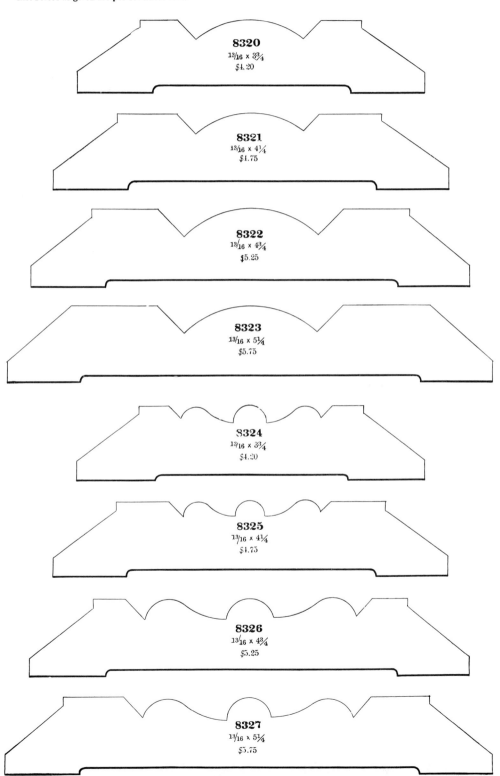

8320
$^{13}\!/_{16}$ x $3\frac{3}{4}$
$4.20

8321
$^{13}\!/_{16}$ x $4\frac{1}{4}$
$4.75

8322
$^{13}\!/_{16}$ x $4\frac{3}{4}$
$5.25

8323
$^{13}\!/_{16}$ x $5\frac{1}{4}$
$5.75

8324
$^{13}\!/_{16}$ x $3\frac{3}{4}$
$4.20

8325
$^{13}\!/_{16}$ x $4\frac{1}{4}$
$4.75

8326
$^{13}\!/_{16}$ x $4\frac{3}{4}$
$5.25

8327
$^{13}\!/_{16}$ x $5\frac{1}{4}$
$5.75

List Prices as given are per 100 lineal feet.

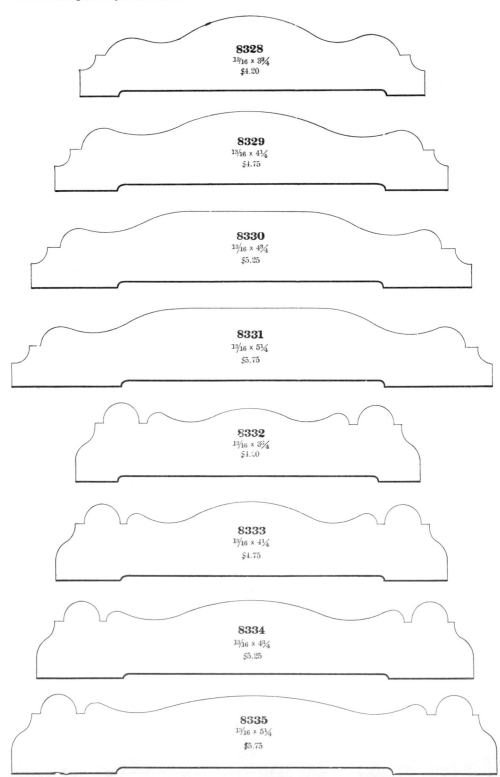

8328
1³/₁₆ x 3¾
$4.20

8329
1³/₁₆ x 4¼
$4.75

8330
1³/₁₆ x 4¾
$5.25

8331
1³/₁₆ x 5¼
$5.75

8332
1³/₁₆ x 3¾
$4.20

8333
1³/₁₆ x 4¼
$4.75

8334
1³/₁₆ x 4¾
$5.25

8335
1³/₁₆ x 5¼
$5.75

List Prices as given are per 100 lineal feet.

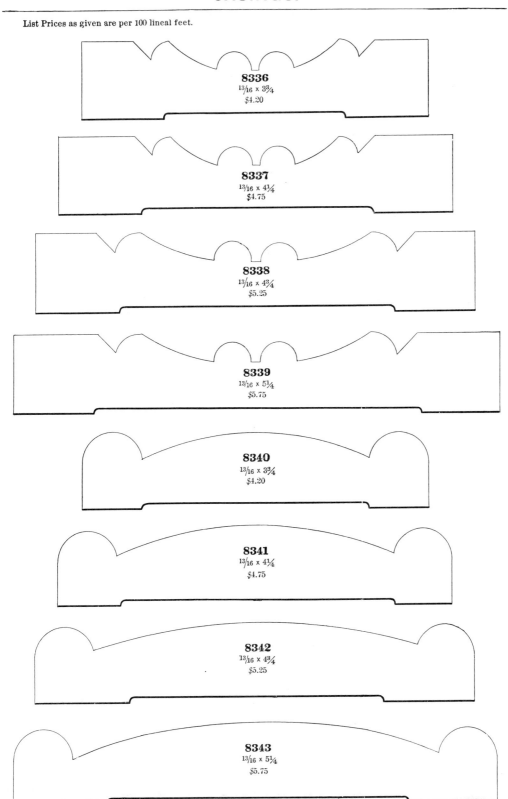

8336
13/16 x 3¾
$4.20

8337
13/16 x 4¼
$4.75

8338
13/16 x 4¾
$5.25

8339
13/16 x 5¼
$5.75

8340
13/16 x 3¾
$4.20

8341
13/16 x 4¼
$4.75

8342
13/16 x 4¾
$5.25

8343
13/16 x 5¼
$5.75

List Prices as given are per 100 lineal feet.

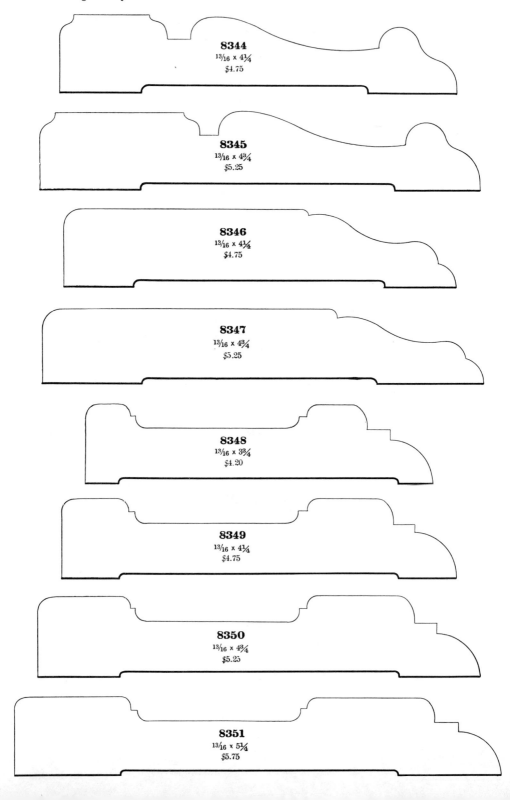

8344
$^{13}/_{16}$ x 4$^1/_4$
$4.75

8345
$^{13}/_{16}$ x 4$^3/_4$
$5.25

8346
$^{13}/_{16}$ x 4$^1/_4$
$4.75

8347
$^{13}/_{16}$ x 4$^3/_4$
$5.25

8348
$^{13}/_{16}$ x 3$^3/_4$
$4.20

8349
$^{13}/_{16}$ x 4$^1/_4$
$4.75

8350
$^{13}/_{16}$ x 4$^3/_4$
$5.25

8351
$^{13}/_{16}$ x 5$^1/_4$
$5.75

List Prices as given are per 100 lineal feet.

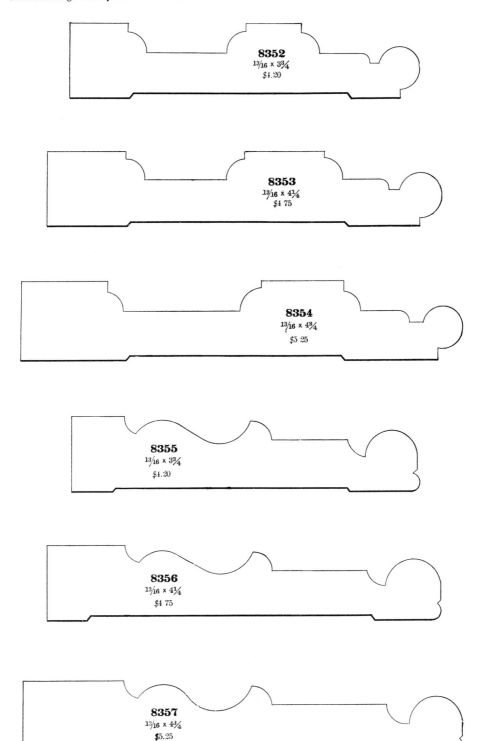

8352
13/16 x 33/4
$4.20

8353
13/16 x 41/4
$4 75

8354
13/16 x 43/4
$5 25

8355
13/16 x 33/4
$4.20

8356
13/16 x 41/4
$4 75

8357
13/16 x 43/4
$5.25

List Prices as given are per 100 lineal feet.

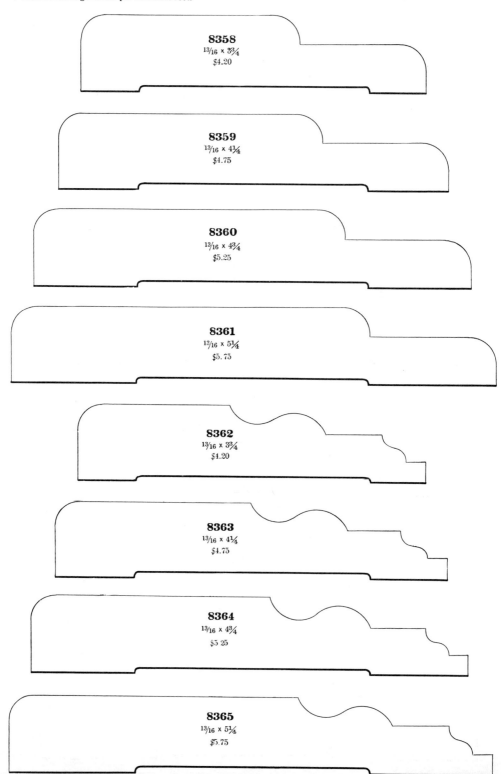

8358
13/16 x 3¾
$4.20

8359
13/16 x 4¼
$4.75

8360
13/16 x 4¾
$5.25

8361
13/16 x 5¼
$5.75

8362
13/16 x 3¾
$4.20

8363
13/16 x 4¼
$4.75

8364
13/16 x 4¾
$5 25

8365
13/16 x 5¼
$5.75

List Prices as given are per 100 lineal feet.

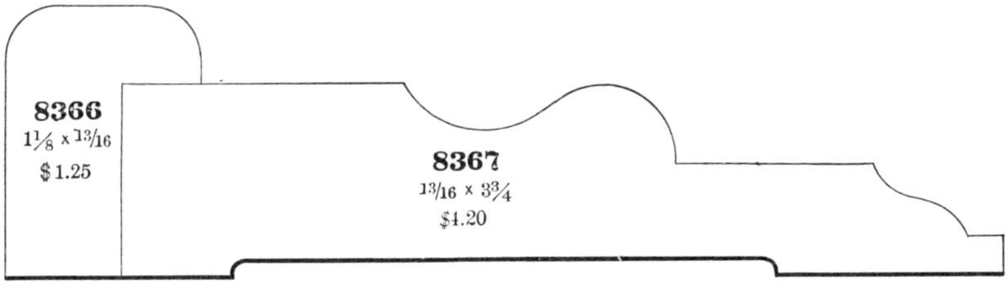
8366
1 1/8 x 13/16
$1.25
8367
13/16 x 3 3/4
$4.20

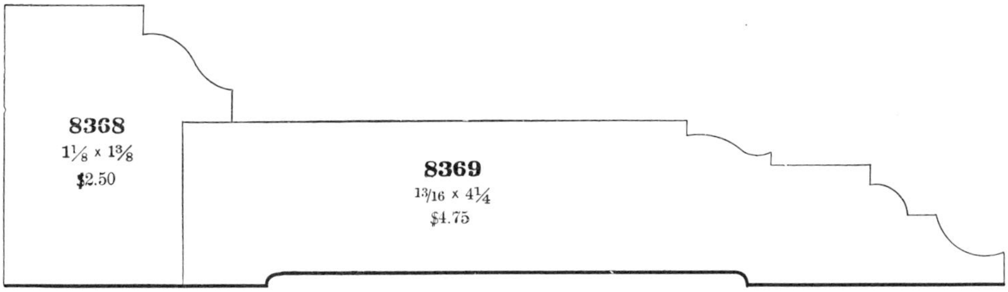
8368
1 1/8 x 1 3/8
$2.50
8369
13/16 x 4 1/4
$4.75

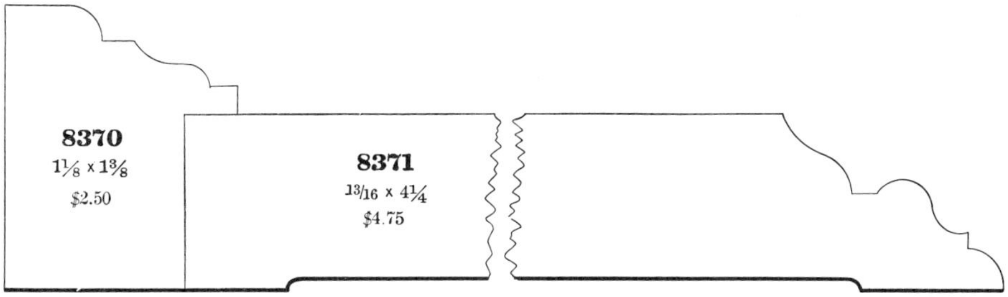
8370
1 1/8 x 1 3/8
$2.50
8371
13/16 x 4 1/4
$4.75

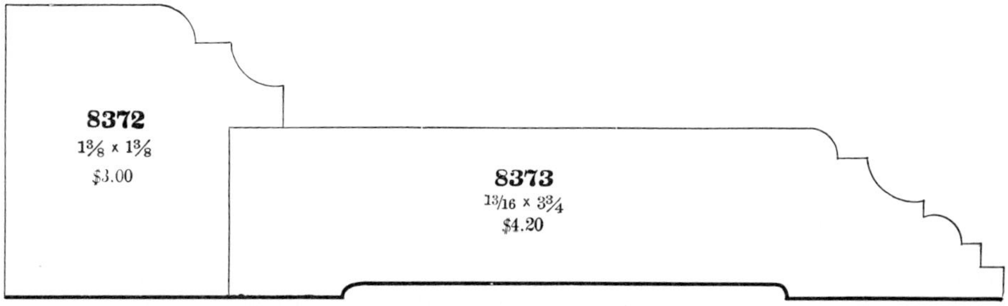
8372
1 3/8 x 1 3/8
$3.00
8373
13/16 x 3 3/4
$4.20

CASINGS AND BACK BANDS.

List Prices as given are per 100 lineal feet.

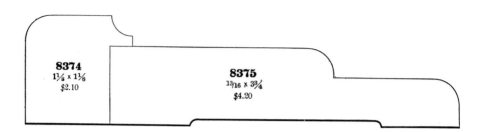

8374
1⅛ x 1⅛
$2.10

8375
13⁄16 x 3¾
$4.20

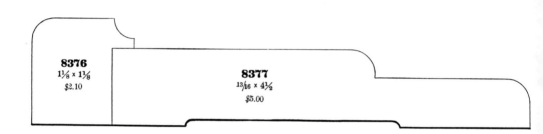

8376
1⅛ x 1⅛
$2.10

8377
13⁄16 x 4½
$5.00

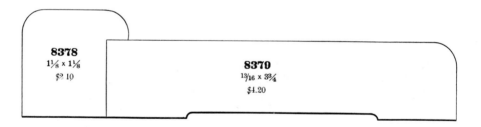

8378
1⅛ x 1⅛
$2.10

8370
13⁄16 x 3¾
$4.20

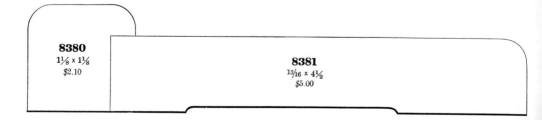

8380
1⅛ x 1⅛
$2.10

8381
13⁄16 x 4½
$5.00

List Prices as given are per 100 lineal feet.

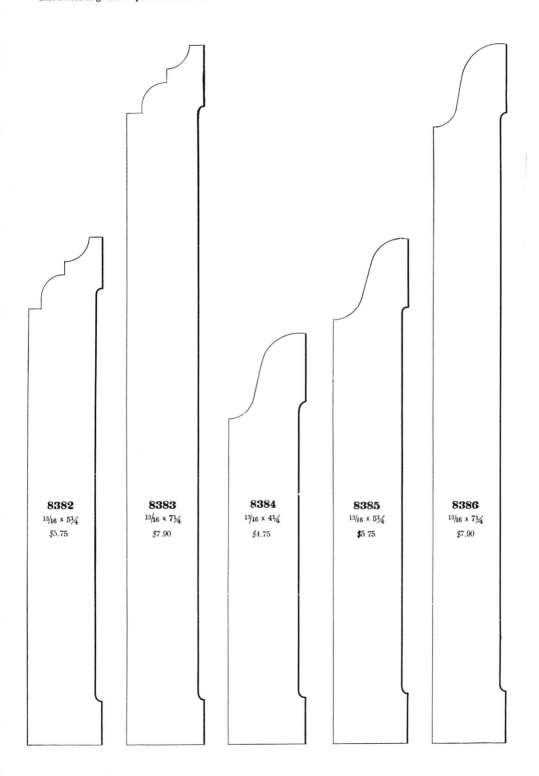

8382	8383	8384	8385	8386
$13/16 \times 5\frac{1}{4}$	$13/16 \times 7\frac{1}{4}$	$13/16 \times 4\frac{1}{4}$	$13/16 \times 5\frac{1}{4}$	$13/16 \times 7\frac{1}{4}$
$5.75	$7.90	$4.75	$5.75	$7.90

List Prices as given are per 100 lineal feet.

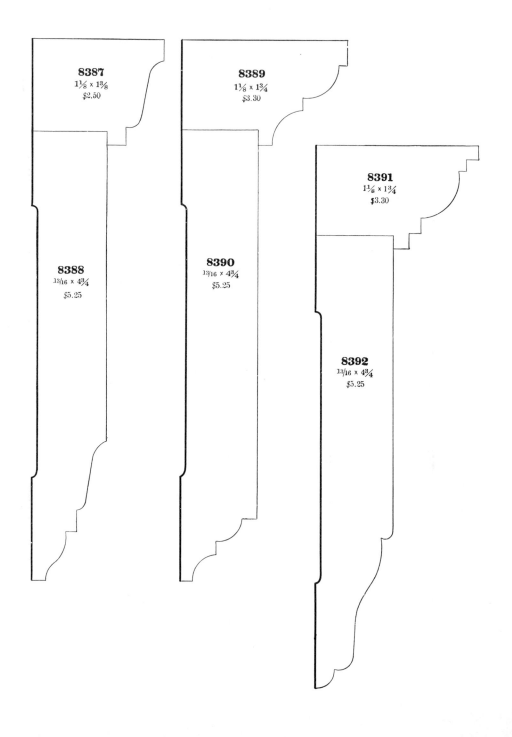

8387
1⅛ × 1⅜
$2.50

8389
1⅛ × 1¾
$3.30

8391
1⅛ × 1¾
$3.30

8388
13/16 × 4¾
$5.25

8390
13/16 × 4¾
$5.25

8392
13/16 × 4¾
$5.25

List Prices as given are per 100 lineal feet.

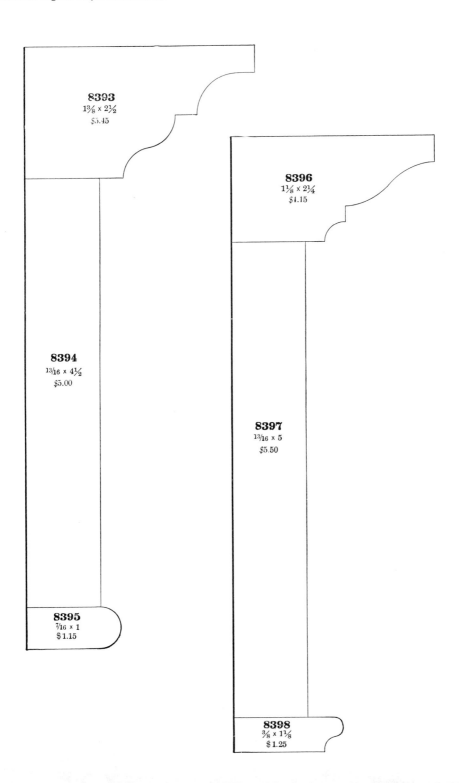

8393
1⅜ × 2½
$5.45

8396
1⅛ × 2¼
$4.15

8394
13⁄16 × 4½
$5.00

8397
13⁄16 × 5
$5.50

8395
7⁄16 × 1
$1.15

8398
⅜ × 1⅛
$1.25

Cap Mouldings, Head Casing, Fillet and Quarter-Round Turned Bead Moulding for Door and Window Trim.

List Prices as given are per 100 lineal feet.

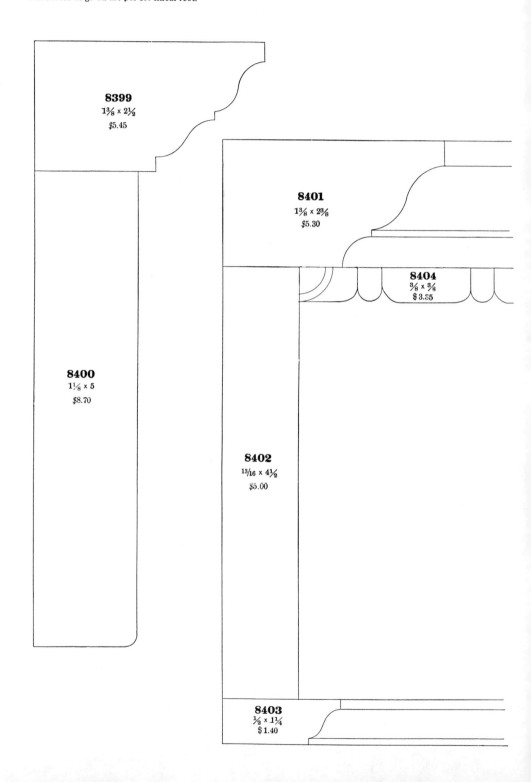

8399
1⅜ x 2½
$5.45

8401
1⅜ x 2⅜
$5.30

8404
⅜ x ⅜
$3.85

8400
1⅛ x 5
$8.70

8402
13/16 x 4½
$5.00

8403
½ x 1¼
$1.40

List Prices as given are per 100 lineal feet.

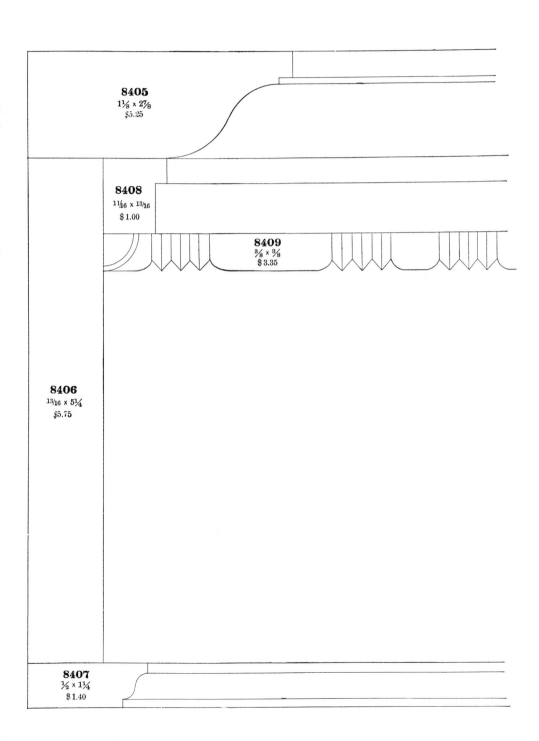

8405
1⅛ x 2⅞
$5.25

8408
1¹⁄₁₆ x 1³⁄₁₆
$1.00

8409
⅜ x ⅜
$3.35

8406
¹³⁄₁₆ x 5¼
$5.75

8407
½ x 1¼
$1.40

List Prices as given are per 100 lineal feet.

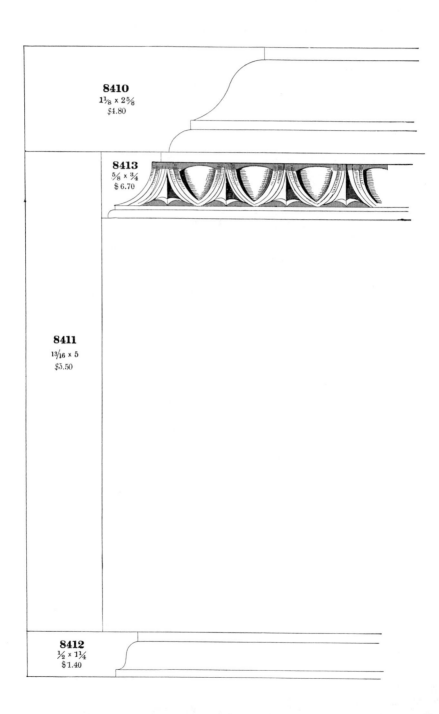

8410
$1\frac{1}{8}$ x $2\frac{5}{8}$
$4.80

8413
$\frac{5}{8}$ x $\frac{3}{4}$
$ 6.70

8411
$1\frac{3}{16}$ x 5
$5.50

8412
$\frac{1}{2}$ x $1\frac{1}{4}$
$ 1.40

List Prices as given are per 100 lineal feet.

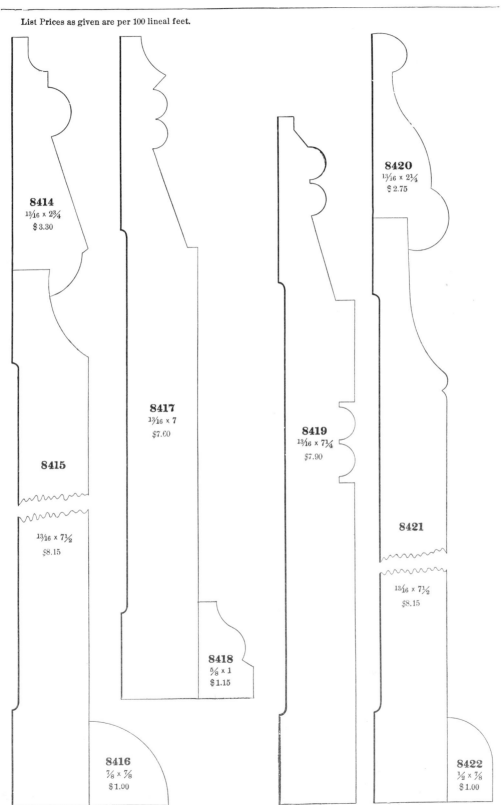

8414
13⁄16 x 2¾
$ 3.30

8415

13⁄16 x 7½
$8.15

8416
⅞ x ⅞
$1.00

8417
13⁄16 x 7
$7.60

8418
⅝ x 1
$1.15

8419
13⁄16 x 7¼
$7.90

8420
13⁄16 x 2¼
$ 2.75

8421

13⁄16 x 7½
$8.15

8422
½ x ⅞
$1.00

List Prices as given are per 100 lineal feet.

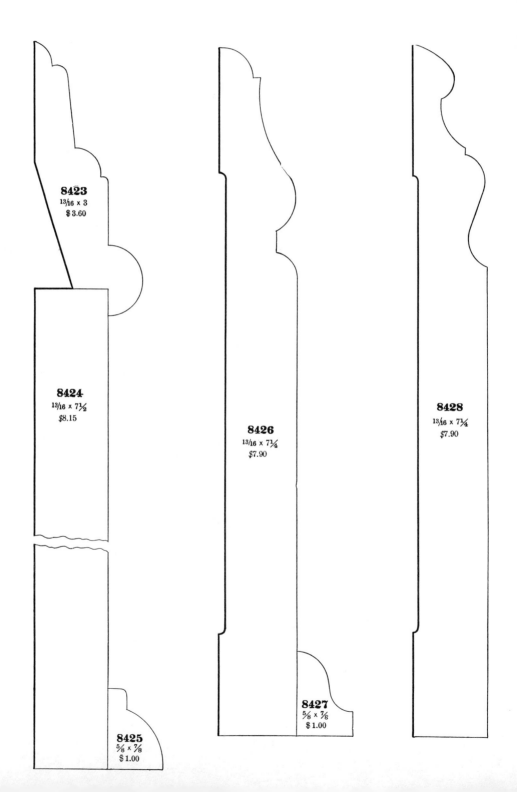

8423
13/16 x 3
$ 3.60

8424
13/16 x 7½
$8.15

8425
⅝ x ⅞
$ 1.00

8426
13/16 x 7¼
$7.90

8427
⅝ x ⅞
$ 1.00

8428
13/16 x 7¼
$7.90

List Prices as given are per 100 lineal feet.

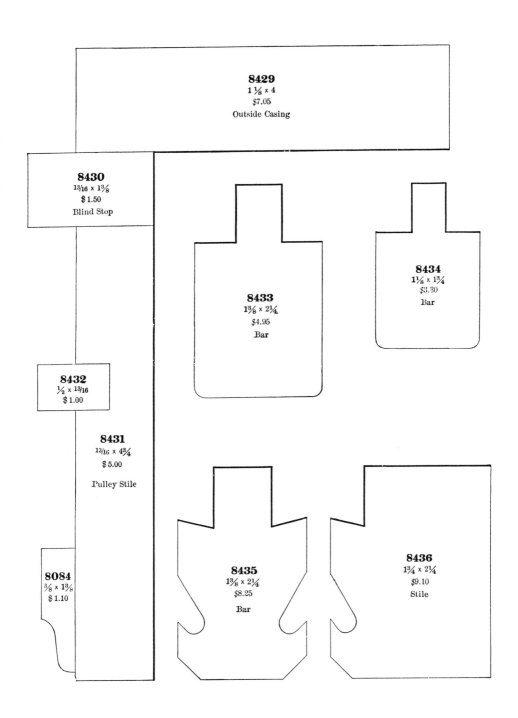

8429
1 ⅛ x 4
$7.05
Outside Casing

8430
13/16 x 1⅜
$ 1.50
Blind Stop

8434
1⅛ x 1¾
$3.30
Bar

8433
1⅜ x 2¼
$4.95
Bar

8432
½ x 13/16
$ 1.00

8431
13/16 x 4¾
$ 5.00

Pulley Stile

8436
1¾ x 2¼
$9.10
Stile

8435
1⅜ x 2¼
$8.25
Bar

8084
⅜ x 1⅜
$ 1.10

List Prices as given are per 100 lineal feet.

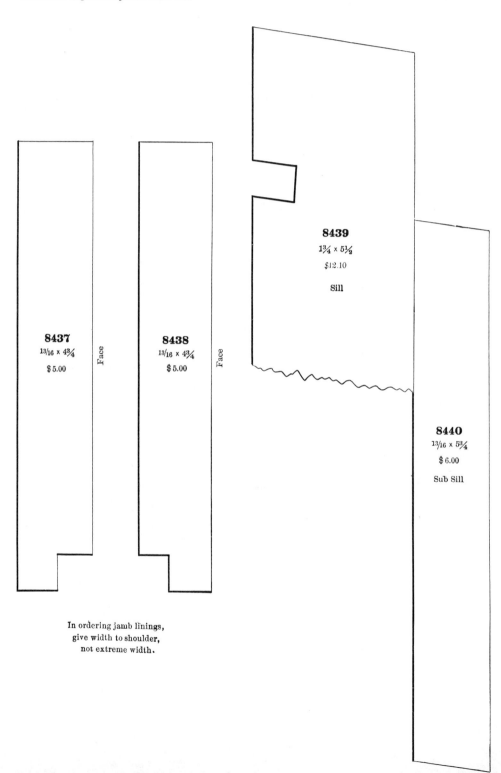

8439

1¾ x 5½

$12.10

Sill

8437

13⁄16 x 4¾

$5.00

Face

8438

13⁄16 x 4¾

$5.00

Face

8440

13⁄16 x 5¾

$6.00

Sub Sill

In ordering jamb linings,
give width to shoulder,
not extreme width.

List Prices as given are per 100 lineal feet.

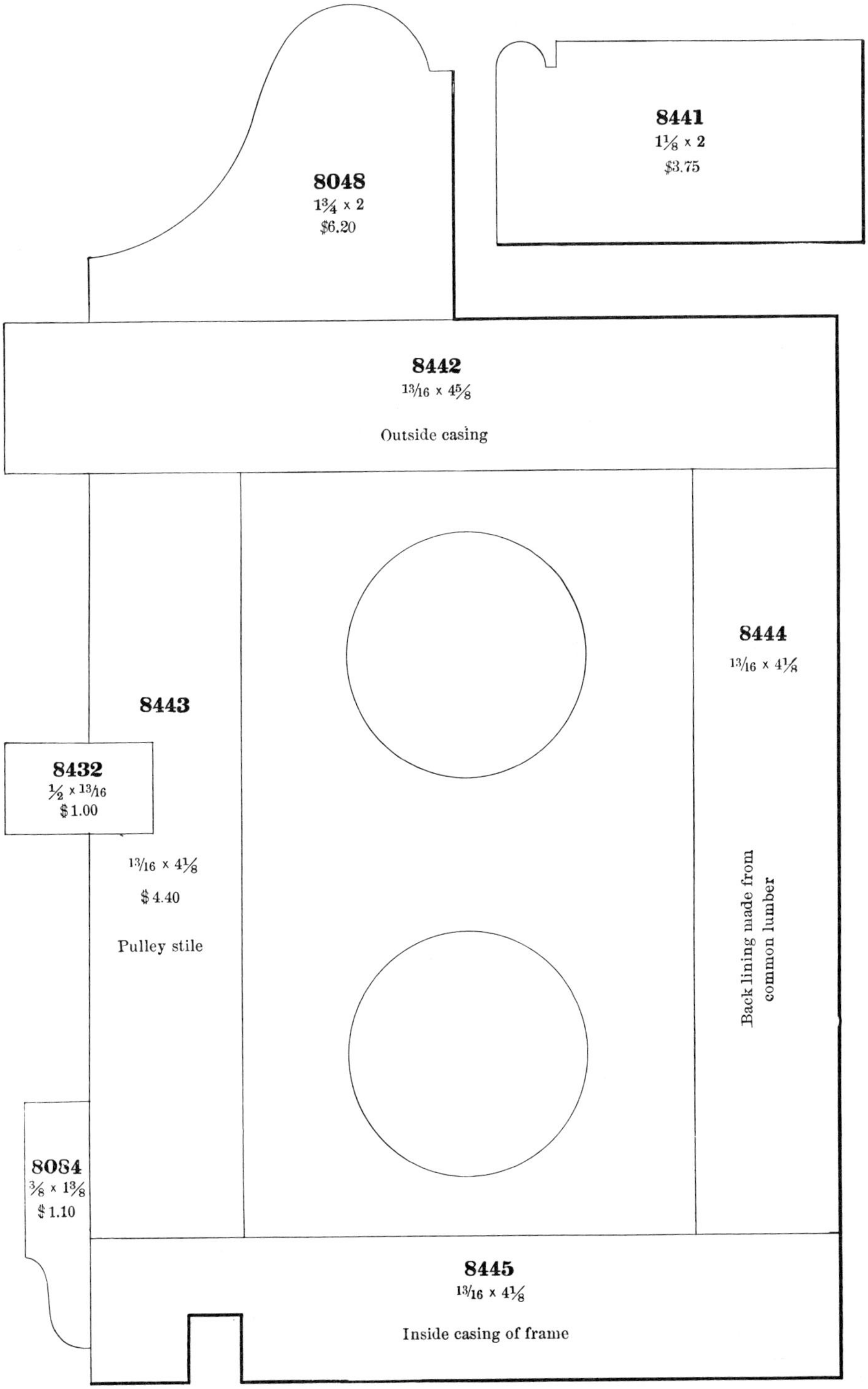
8048
1¾ x 2
$6.20
8441
1⅛ x 2
$3.75
8442
13/16 x 4⅝
Outside casing
8444
13/16 x 4⅛
Back lining made from common lumber
8443
13/16 x 4⅛
$4.40
Pulley stile
8432
½ x 13/16
$1.00
8084
⅜ x 1⅜
$1.10
8445
13/16 x 4⅛
Inside casing of frame

ASTRAGALS FOR SLIDING AND FOLDING DOORS.

List Prices as given are per 100 lineal feet.

8446

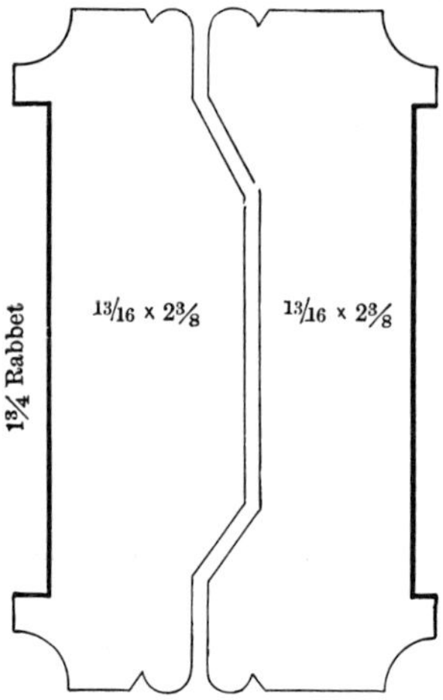
1¾ Rabbet
13/16 x 2⅜
13/16 x 2⅜

50 Cents per pair Net.

8447

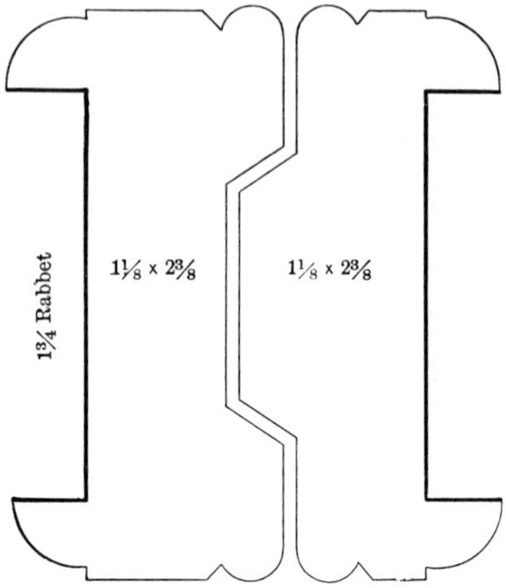
1¾ Rabbet
1⅛ x 2⅜
1⅛ x 2⅜

50 Cents per pair Net.

8448

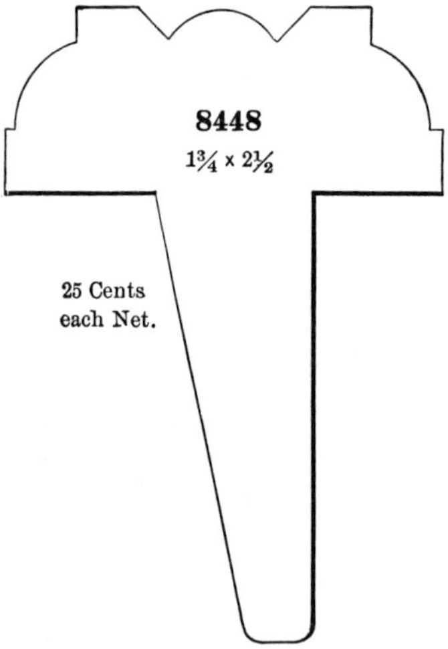
1¾ x 2½

25 Cents each Net.

8449

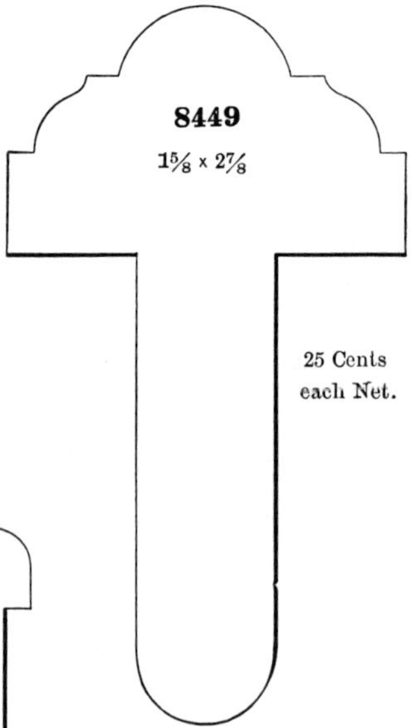
1⅝ x 2⅞

25 Cents each Net.

8450

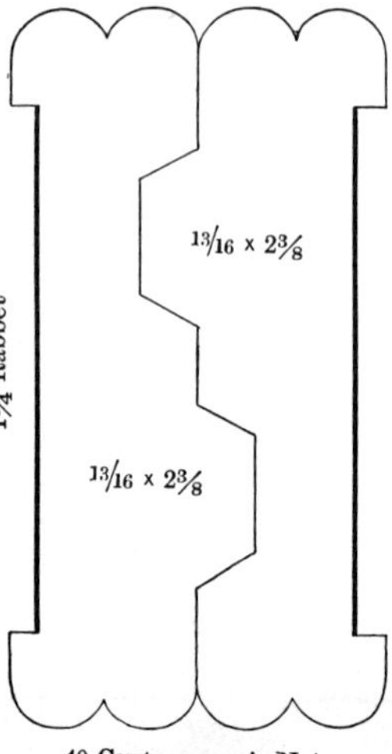
13/16 x 2⅜
1¾ Rabbet
13/16 x 2⅜

40 Cents per pair Net.

List Prices as given are per 100 lineal feet.

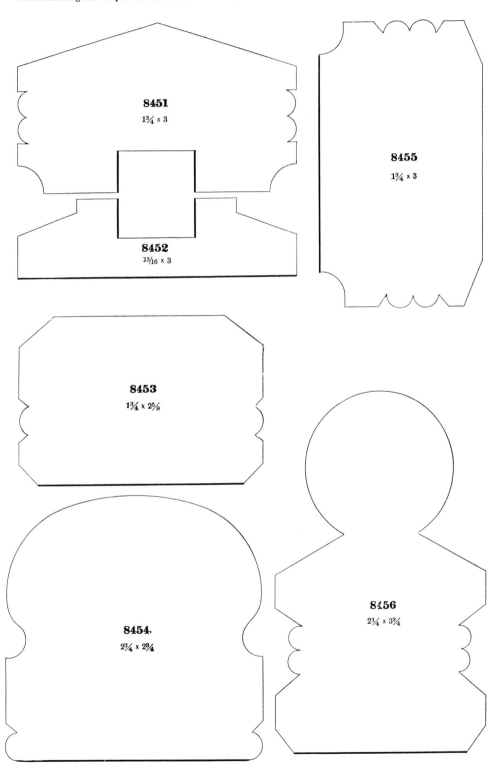

8451
1¾ x 3

8452
1³⁄₁₆ x 3

8455
1¾ x 3

8453
1¾ x 2⅝

8454.
2¾ x 2¾

8456
2¼ x 3¾

List Prices as given are per 100 lineal feet.

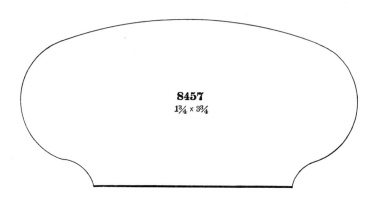

8457
1¾ × 3¾

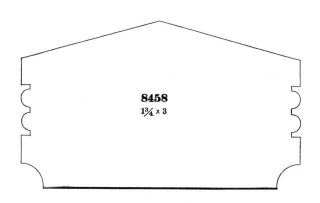

8458
1¾ × 3

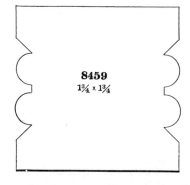

8459
1¾ × 1¾

8460
1⅜ × 1⅜

LIST PRICE OF MOULDINGS.

PRICES GIVEN ARE PER 100 LINEAL FEET.

No.	Price	No.	Price	No.	Price	No.	Price	No.	Price
8000	$3.50	8055	$3.30	8110	$1.20	8165	$2.50	8220	$2.45
8001	6.00	8056	4.85	8111	1.05	8166	1.25	8221	2.60
8002	4.00	8057	4.85	8112	2.50	8167	1.40	8222	2.75
8003	3.00	8058	1 00	8113	2.25	8168	2.00	3223	3.30
8004	5.50	8059	1.00	8114	2.05	8169	1.40	8224	3 30
8005	5.00	8060	1.00	8115	1.80	8170	1.65	8225	2 75
8006	4.50	8061	1.25	8116	1.35	8171	2.00	8226	2.20
8007	2.00	8062	2.00	8117	1.15	8172	2.00	8227	1 80
8008	2.50	8063	1.00	8118	1.15	8173	2.00	8228	2.45
8009	4.00	8064	1.00	8119	1.35	8174	1.75	8229	3 30
8010	3.00	8065	1.00	8120	1.80	8175	2 00	8230	6.60
8011	2.50	8066	1.00	8121	2 05	8176	2.00	8231	1.90
8012	4.50	8067	1.50	8122	2.25	8177	2 25	8232	3.50
8013	5.00	8068	2.00	8123	1.65	8178	2.25	8233	3.25
8014	3.50	8069	2.50	8124	3.75	8179	2.50	8234	2.75
8015	1.15	8070	1.00	8125	4.95	8180	2.75	8235	3.00
8016	2.00	8071	1.00	8126	8.80	8181	3.00	8236	4.00
8017	1.65	8072	1.25	8127	2 00	8182	3.25	8237	3.30
8018	2.50	8073	1.15	8128	1.00	8183	2.75	8238	4.40
8019	3.00	8074	2.25	8129	1.15	8184	2.50	8239	4 40
8020	3.50	8075	1.00	8130	1.25	8185	2.00	8240	4.40
8021	4.50	8076	1.00	8131	1.40	8186	2.00	8241	1.00
8022	5.00	8077	1.00	8132	1.00	8187	1.75	8242	2.00
8023	4.00	8078	1 15	8133	1.50	8188	2.25	8243	2.50
8024	2.00	8079	1.40	8134	3.30	8189	2.00	8244	.75
8025	2.50	8080	1.75	8135	1.65	8190	2.25	8245	1.65
8026	3.00	8081	2.00	8136	3.95	8191	2 75	8246	1.75
8027	4.50	8082	.90	8137	2.00	8192	2.75	8247	1.20
8028	4.00	8083	1.00	8138	2.00	8193	1.50	8248	2.50
8029	3.50	8084	1.10	8139	1.00	8194	2.50	8249	1.40
8030	2.50	8085	1.40	8140	1.00	8195	2.00	8250	2.00
8031	2.00	8086	1.60	8141	1.25	8196	2.50	8251	.85
8032	2.25	8087	1.80	8142	1.50	8197	3.00	8252	2.25
8033	3.00	8088	2.00	8143	1.75	8198	2.00	8253	1.00
8034	3.50	8089	1.15	8144	2.25	8199	3.50	8254	2.50
8035	1.00	8090	1.60	8145	1.00	8200	2.00	8255	1.00
8036	1.40	8091	2.05	8146	1.00	8201	2.25	8256	2.95
8037	2.50	8092	2.25	8147	1.75	8202	2.50	8257	3 95
8038	3.30	8093	2.00	8148	2.25	8203	2.50	8258	3.30
8039	5.50	8094	1.80	8149	2.25	8204	1.75	8259	1.80
8040	1.00	8095	1.60	8150	....	8205	3.00	8260	2.65
8041	1.25	8096	1.20	8151	....	8206	1.80	8261	2.50
8042	1.00	8097	1.10	8152	1.15	8207	2.45	8262	4.15
8043	1.00	8098	1.35	8153	1.25	8208	3.00	8263	2.00
8044	1.25	8099	1.80	8154	1.50	8209	3.00	8264	2.00
8045	1.65	8100	2 25	8155	1.50	8210	3.00	8265	2.00
8046	2.95	8101	1.05	8156	1.75	8211	3 30	8266	3.25
8047	3.45	8102	1.20	8157	2.00	8212	2.20	8267	6.60
8048	6.20	8103	1.60	8158	1.75	8213	2 45	8268	7.45
8049	4.85	8104	1.85	8159	1.15	8214	2.90	8269	7.45
8050	2.75	8105	2.00	8160	1.00	8215	2.20	8270	7.45
8051	1.70	8106	2.25	8161	1.15	8216	2.45	8271	2.00
8052	1.00	8107	2.00	8162	1.25	8217	2 90	8272	3.75
8053	1.00	8108	1.85	8163	1.50	8218	1.55	8273	2.50
8054	1.15	8109	1.60	8164	1.50	8219	1 90	8274	2.50

LIST PRICE OF MOULDINGS.

PRICES GIVEN ARE PER 100 LINEAL FEET.

No.	Price	No.	Price	No.	Price	No.	Price	No.	Price
8275	$2.95	8313	$4.75	8351	$5.75	8389	$3.30	8427	$1.00
8276	3.95	8314	5.25	8352	4.20	8390	5.25	8428	7.90
8277	4.00	8315	5.75	8353	4.75	8391	3.30	8429	7.05
8278	4.00	8316	4.20	8354	5.25	8392	5.25	8430	1.50
8279	4.50	8317	4.75	8355	4.20	8393	5.45	8431	5.00
8280	.85	8318	5.25	8356	4.75	8394	5.00	8432	1.00
8281	1.00	8319	5.75	8357	5.25	8395	1.15	8433	4.95
8282	1.35	8320	4.20	8358	4.20	8396	4.15	8434	3.30
8283	2.95	8321	4.75	8359	4.75	8397	5.50	8435	8 25
8284	3.75	8322	5.25	8360	5.25	8398	1.25	8436	9.10
8285	4.55	8323	5.75	8361	5.75	8399	5.45	8437	5.00
8286	5 40	8324	4.20	8362	4.20	8400	8.70	8438	5.00
8287	6.25	8325	4.75	8363	4.75	8401	5.30	8439	12.10
8288	4.20	8326	5.25	8364	5.25	8402	5.00	8440	6.00
8289	4 75	8327	5.75	8365	5.75	8403	1.40	8441	3.75
8290	5.25	8328	4.20	8366	1.25	8404	3.35	8442	....
8291	5.75	8329	4.75	8367	4.20	8405	5.25	8443	4.40
8292	4.20	8330	5.25	8368	2.50	8406	5.75	8444	....
8293	4.75	8331	5.75	8369	4.75	8407	1.40	8445	....
8294	5.25	8332	4.20	8370	2.50	8408	1.00	8446	....
8295	5.75	8333	4.75	8371	4.75	8409	3 35	8447	....
8296	4.20	8334	5.25	8372	3.00	8410	4.80	8448	....
8297	4.75	8335	5.75	8373	4.20	8411	5.50	8449	....
8298	5.25	8336	4.20	8374	2.10	8412	1.40	8450	....
8299	5.75	8337	4.75	8375	4.20	8413	6.70	8451	....
8300	4.20	8338	5.25	6376	2.10	8414	3.30	8452	....
8301	4.75	8339	5.75	8377	5.00	8415	8.15	8453	....
8302	5.25	8340	4.20	8378	2.10	8416	1.00	8454	....
8303	5.75	8341	4.75	8379	4.20	8417	7.60	8455	....
8304	4.20	8342	5.25	8380	2.10	8418	1.15	8456	....
8305	4.75	8343	5.75	8381	5.00	8419	7.90	8457	....
8306	5.25	8344	4.75	8382	5.75	8420	2.75	8458	....
8307	5.75	8345	5.25	8383	7.90	8421	8.15	8459	....
8308	4.20	8346	4.75	8384	4.75	8422	1.00	8460	....
8309	4.75	8347	5.25	8385	5.75	8423	3.60		
8310	5.25	8348	4.20	8386	7.90	8424	8 15		
8311	5.75	8349	4.75	8387	2.50	8425	1.00		
8312	4.20	8350	5.25	8388	5.25	8426	7.90		

IMPORTANT NOTICE.

When moulding is priced by the inch *it is in all cases understood* that the price is based on ripping width of lumber, that is: ¼ *of an inch wider than the finished size* of moulding. For example: A ⅞ inch thick panel moulding if made to finish 1¾ inches wide would be charged as 2 inches (being ripping size); to finish full 2 inches, would be charged as 2¼ inches, etc.

Approximate weight of Mouldings, 1x1 inch, per 100 lineal feet, 15 pounds.